GU00738174

English Solo Song

A guide for singers, teachers, librarians and the music trade of songs currently available

Michael Pilkington

Thames Publishing
London
Text © 1997 Michael Pilkington

Foreword

by Benjamin Luxon CBE

The English song-writing of the 20th century is without doubt one of this country's major musical achievements and legacies. The way was paved by the amazingly prolific and fertile outpourings of the Victorian composers of popular songs, ballads and music-hall material. The nation was singing; in the home, town and village halls, concert-halls, churches and chapels. Reputations and fortunes were being made by successful song-writers, lyricists and music publishers.

It is not surprising then that the serious composers of the 20th century turned to the song as an essential means of artistic expression. As in every great tradition of song-writing (e.g. the German Lied and French Chanson), composers looked not only to great poets and literary figures of the past but to the poetry of their contemporaries. Thus, in the most natural way, music and literature converged to create a unique artistic and sociological comment on the taste, fashion and attitudes of an era.

After World War II, and particularly since the 1970s, the interest in our song tradition has fallen away. This is not altogether surprising. With the incredible developments in sound recording, television and the pop-music industry, the populace in general has gradually and inexorably shifted from an active to a passive role as regards their music.

The market-place has become obsessed with being cost-effective, and printed music, recordings, even performances, do not survive for long if they do not generate a healthy market. In the world of vocal music, opera, with its combination of theatre and music, has become the darling of the vocal arts, and interest in song, particularly in live performance, has greatly diminished. All of this is nobody's fault, but the inevitable result of the commercialisation that has swept through all aspects of our late 20th-century life-style.

Unlike myself, who was brought up, so to speak, and trained in this song repertoire, many young singers to-day have, through no fault of their own, lost touch with so much of their native song repertoire. In the light of all these developments this volume incorporates the three requirements of success: it comes at the right time; in the right place; and it is compiled and published by the right people.

Michael Pilkington and Thames Publishing have produced a treasure house of practical information which will, without doubt, open the door to a largely neglected and forgotten tradition of song-writing. Would that it had existed some ten years or so ago, when I made a series of archival recordings with Chandos on some of the major English song-writers. At that time the problems of tracking down material that was no longer published became a small nightmare, and in retrospect I realise that I missed out on many marvellous songs.

However, this problem, with the aid of this volume, no longer exists for the enthusiast of English song, be he or she amateur or professional, young or old, teacher or performer. Using a very simple and easily decipherable system the song output of every serious British composer is laid out for us.

One heartening observation to do with the English song repertoire is the increasing number of anthologies and compilations being published. Wherever applicable, Michael Pilkington has also noted where songs appear in collections and volumes.

In short, I have been amazed at the amount of information available in this concise and clearly documented publication. Apart from having the music in front of you, I cannot conceive of a better method of conveying information about individual songs and the means of acquiring them.

My heartfelt congratulations go to Michael Pilkington for his research and industry in producing this mammoth volume, and to John Bishop of Thames Publishing for putting on to the market such an invaluable book of reference and inspiration.

Canterbury 1997.

Introduction

This repertoire guide is not concerned with value-judgments. It has one simple aim: to spread knowledge in a convenient form about the availability of English solo song — what can be bought over the counter or as an authorised photocopy. This information has not, it is thought, previously been collected in one place, and we hope singers, teachers, music librarians, retail shops, and others interested will be encouraged to explore as well as find answers to their queries quickly and accurately.

There has been a determined effort to make the book as comprehensive and up-to-date as possible — not always easy in today's publishing world. The aim is to revise and reissue it at regular intervals; computer technology helps to make this easier than it would have been in the past. Readers are invited to write to the publisher with corrections or additions that would make a future edition more complete.

The guide lists virtually all recital songs by British composers currently in print or available from publishers' archives. Songs such as Victorian and Edwardian ballads are only given if they are included in recent anthologies. Settings of foreign texts are given in Appendix 1; and accompaniments other than piano alone, from unaccompanied up to six players, are listed in Appendix 2.

Under 'Collections' are given volumes devoted solely to the particular composer's work, in chronological order of publication, which are then referred to with abbreviated titles after the songs listed. Note that the date of publication given is that of first publication, whereas the publisher's name is that of the current publisher, who may not have been the original publisher. Anthologies are given in italics, and listed in Appendix 1. Where applicable the key is given after the name of the poet; keys known not to be original are given in italics. The range of the song follows in most cases, (m) or (f) indicating the song is more suited to male or female voices respectively. In some cases it has not proved possible to acquire this amount of detail, but it has been decided to include whatever is known, rather than omit available material.

Publishers are then listed, any copies available in other keys coming after a semi-colon. Names given in brackets after the publisher indicate the editor. Publishers' names without volume names attached indicate a single copy of the song is available. Copies given between round brackets can be obtained from the publisher's archives, or on special order. Folk-song arrangements by composers listed here are given at the end of the sections devoted to their work.

I must record my thanks to the publishers here represented, all of whom have been helpful in providing catalogues and other information. Oxford University Press, Stainer & Bell, and Boosey & Hawkes kindly allowed me to inspect their archives, while Leslie East allowed me to work through the card indices listing the music held by Music Sales, including the collections of Novello, Chester, and Elkin. The British Music Information Centre kindly allowed me to work through the entire collection held at Stratford Place; and the Scottish and Welsh Music Information Centres sent me music and other material. Rhian Davies supplied details of the many Welsh songs in her own collection, for which I am most grateful. I also made considerable use of the

Introduction

library of The Guildhall School of Music and Drama. This book is the brain- child of John Bishop (Thames Publishing), who has provided support and assistance throughout the project ever since he suggested I take on the task of researching the immense amount of material available. Having studied this repertoire for some fifty years it is a pleasure to be able to provide the means for others to enjoy exploring this treasure house of English music.

Michael Pilkington.

Old Coulsdon 1997.

Publishers

Ashdown = Edwin Ashdown. Archive material held by William Elkin.

Banks = Banks Music Publications. The Old Forge, Sand Hutton, York YO4 1LB. Tel: 01904 468472 Fax: 01904 468679.

Bardic = Bardic Edition. 6 Fairfax crescent, Aylesbury, Bucks HP20 2ES. Tel: 01296 28609 Fax: 01296 28609.

Bayley & Ferguson = Bayley & Ferguson. 65 Berkeley Street, Glasgow, G3 7DZ. Tel: 0141 221 9444.

Bèrben = Bèrben Edizioni (Ancona) see Fentone.

BMIC = British Music Information Centre. 10 Stratford Place, London W1N 9AE. Tel: 0171 255 1444 Fax: 0171 499 4795. A large collection of 20th-century English music, printed, privately published and manuscript. All the material is available for study, and some of it may be photocopied.

B&H = Boosey & Hawkes Music Publishers Ltd. 295 Regent Street, London W1R 8JH. Tel. 0171 580 2060 fax: 0171 436 5815/3490/2850. Major publishers of English song, with a large archive collection, from which photocopies can be supplied. There is reasonably complete information on the songs in the archive, which can be visited by arrangement.

Bosworth = Bosworth & Co Ltd. 14-18 Heddon Street, Regent Street, London W1R 8DP. Tel: 0171 734 4961 Fax 0171 734 0475.

Braydeston = Braydeston Press see William Elkin, below.

Breitkopf = Breitkopf & Härtel. Castle House, Ivychurch, Romney Marsh, Kent TN29 0AL. Tel: 01797 344011 also Fax. Photocopies of archive material can be supplied from Germany.

Brunton = Brunton (Barry) Music Publisher. 52a Broad Street, Ely, Cambs C87 4AH. Tel: 01353 663252 Fax: 01353 663371.

Chappell = Warner Chappell Music Ltd. 129 Park Street, London W1Y 3FA. Tel: 0171 629 7600 Fax: 0171 514 5201.

Chester = Chester Music. Hire and Distribution, Newmarket Road, Bury St Edmunds, Suffolk IP33 3YB. Tel: 01284 702600 Fax: 01284 768301.

Cramer = Cramer Music. 23 Garrick Street, London WC2E 9AX. Tel: 0171 240 1612 Fax: 0171 240 2639. Publications currently in print are sold through Boosey & Hawkes. There is a catalogue of the large archive holding, giving composer and title.

Curwen = Curwen (J) & Sons Ltd. Some of the archive catalogue is held by Roberton, and some by William Elkin.

Elkin = The Elkin catalogue is now held by Novello. William Elkin are now distributors only.

Emerson = Emerson Edition Ltd. Windmill Farm, Ampleforth, Yorks YO6 4HF Tel: 01439 788324 Fax: 01439 788715.

Enoch = see Ashdown.

Faber = Faber Music Ltd. 3 Queen Square, London WC1N 3AU. Tel. 0171 278 7436; 0171 833 7906 (sales) Fax: 0171 278 3817. Faberprint is a service which enables customers to purchase copies of musical works not otherwise available for sale. Faberprint comprises high quality facsimile editions, reproduced in some cases from engraved originals and in other from autograph manuscript. Some works are only available on hire.

Faberprint = see Faber Music Ltd.

Fentone = Fentone Music Ltd. Fleming Road, Earlstrees, Corby, Northants NN17 2SN. Tel: 01536 260981 Fax: 01536 401075.

Forsyth = Forsyth Brothers Ltd.126-128 Deansgate, Manchester M3 2GR. Tel: 0161 834 3281 Fax: 0161 834 0630.

Publishers

Gwynn = Gwynn Publishing Co. Y Gerlan, Heol-y-Dwr, Penygroes, Caernafon, Gwynedd LL54 6LR.

International = International Music Publications. Woodford Trading Estate, Southend Road, Woodford Green, Essex IG8 8HN. Tel: 0181 551 6131 Fax: 0181 551 3919.

Keith Prowse = see EMI Music Publishing Ltd. 127 Charing Cross Road, London WC2H 0EA. Tel: 0171 434 2131 Fax: 0171 434 3531.

Lengnick = Alfred Lengnick & Co (division of Complete Music Ltd). 3rd Floor, 25-29 Fulham High Street, London SW6 3JH. Tel: 0171 731 8595 Fax: 0171 384 1854. Also at: Pigeon House Meadow, 27 Grove Road, Beaconsfield, Bucks HP9 1UR. Tel: 01494 681216 Fax: 01494 670443. Distributors William Elkin, see below.

Mayhew = Kevin Mayhew Ltd. Rattlesdon, Bury St Edmunds, Suffolk IP30 0SZ. Tel: 01449 737978 Fax: 01449 737834.

Novello = Novello & Co Ltd. Hire and Distribution, Newmarket Road, Bury St Edmunds, Suffolk IP33 3YB. Tel: 01284 702600 Fax: 01284 768301.

OUP = Oxford University Press Music Department. Walton Street, Oxford OX2 6DP. Tel: 01865 556767 Fax: 01865 267749. A large archive collection from which photo-copies can be supplied and which can be visited by arrangement.

Paterson = see Novello.

Paxton = see Novello.

Peters = Peters Edition Ltd. 19-21 Baches Street, London N1 6DN. Tel: 0171 253 1638 Fax: 0171 490 4921.

Roberton = Roberton Publications. The Windmill, Wendover, Aylesbury, Bucks HP22 6JJ. Tel: 01296 623107. Besides Roberton's own publications some Curwen archive material is available.

Schott = Schott & Co Ltd. Marketing and Sales Department, Brunswick Road, Ashford, Kent TN23 1DX. Tel: 01233 628987 Fax 01233 610232.

SMIC = Scottish Music Information Centre. 1 Bowmont Gardens, Glasgow G12 9LR. Tel: 0141 334 6393 Fax: 0141 337 1161.

Snell = Snell & Sons. 68 West Cross Lane, West Cross, Swansea SA3 5LU. Tel: 01792 405727. The catalogue lists a large collection of Welsh songs. The more important composers have been included here.

S&B = Stainer & Bell Ltd. PO Box 110, Victoria House, 23 Gruneisen Road, London N3 1DZ. Tel: 0181 343 3303 Fax: 0181 343 3024. A large archive collection, fully catalogued, from which photo-copies can be supplied. The collection can be visited by arrangement.

Thames = Thames Publishing. 14 Barlby Road, London W10 6AR. Tel: 0181 969 3579 fax: 0181 969 1465. Specialist in English music. Distributors William Elkin, see below.

Universal = Universal Edition (London) Ltd/Alfred Kalmus Ltd. 48 Great Marlborough Street, London W1V 2BN. Tel: 0171 437 5203 Fax: 0171 437 6115. Also at: 38 Eldon Way, Kent TN12 6BE. Tel: 01892 833422 Fax: 836038.

Weinberger = Weinberger (Josef) Ltd. 12-14 Mortimer Street, London W1N 7RD. Tel: 0171 580 2827 Fax: 0171 436 9616.

Welsh Music = Welsh Music Information Centre. c/o ASS Library, University of Wales, College of Cardiff, Corbett Road, Cardiff CF1 1XL. Tel: 01222 874000 ext 5126 Fax 01222 371921.

William Elkin Music Services, distributors. Station Road Industrial Estate, Salhouse, Norwich NR13 6NY. Tel: 01603 721302 Fax: 01603 721801.

Yorke = Yorke Edition, 31 Thornhill Square, London N1 1BQ. Tel: 0171 607 0849 Fax: 0171 700 4577.

Anthologies

6 Divine = Six Divine Hymns by Restoration Composers, Maurice Bevan, Thames 1989.

6 Restoration = Six Restoration Songs for Baritone/Bass and Keyboard, Maurice Bevan, Thames 1993.

8 Restoration = Eight Restoration Songs for Soprano and Keyboard, Maurice Bevan, Thames 1993.

(*12 18th Century* = Twelve Eighteenth Century Songs, arranged by Frederick Keel, B&H 1931.)

100 Best 1 = The 100 Best Short Songs, Book 1, Gerhardt, Henschel and Harford, Paterson 1930.

100 Best 2 = The 100 Best Short Songs, Book 2, Gerhardt, Henschel and Harford, Paterson 1930.

100 Best 3 = The 100 Best Short Songs, Book 3, Gerhardt, Henschel and Harford, Paterson 1930.

100 Best 4 = The 100 Best Short Songs, Book 4, Gerhardt, Henschel and Harford, Paterson 1930.

Ballad Operas = Songs from the Ballad Operas, Geoffrey Bush, Novello 1982.

Ballad Album 1 = Boosey Ballad Album (introduction Andrew Lamb), B&H 1990.

Ballad Album 2 = The 2nd Boosey Ballad Album (introduction Andrew Lamb), B&H 1991.

Banquet = Robert Dowland (compiler) A Musical Banquet, Peter Stroud, S&B 1986.

Cavalier = Cavalier Songs, Ian Spink, S&B 1976.

Celebrated 1 = The Chester Books of Celebrated Songs, Book 1, Shirley Leah, Chester 1981.

Celebrated 2 = The Chester Books of Celebrated Songs, Book 2, Shirley Leah, Chester 1981.

Celebrated 3 = The Chester Books of Celebrated Songs, Book 3, Shirley Leah, Chester 1981.

Century 1 = A Century of English Song, Volume 1, Ten Songs for Soprano and Piano, John Bishop, Gary Humphries, Michael Pilkington (Introduction Pilkington) Thames 1993.

Century 2 = A Century of English Song, Volume 2, Ten Songs for Baritone and Piano, John Bishop, Gary Humphries, Michael Pilkington (Introduction Pilkington) Thames 1994.

Century 3 = A Century of English Song, Volume 3, Ten Songs for Tenor and Piano, John Bishop, Gary Humphries, Michael Pilkington (Introduction Pilkington) Thames 1995.

Century 4 = A Century of English Song, Volume 4, Ten Songs for Mezzo Soprano/Contralto and Piano, John Bishop, Gary Humphries, Michael Pilkington (Introduction Pilkington) Thames 1996.

Christmas 1 = Christmas Song Album Volume 1, B&H 1987.

Christmas 2 = Christmas Song Album Volume 2, B&H 1987.

Countertenors 1 = Songs for Countertenors, Volume 1, Frederick Hodgson, Thames 1991.

Countertenors 2 = Songs for Countertenors, Volume 2, Frederick Hodgson, Thames 1991.

Cramer Folio 1 = The Cramer Song Folio, Volume 1, B&H 1986.

(*Dolmetsch 1* = Select English Songs and Dialogues of the 16th and 17th Centuries, Book 1, Arnold Dolmetsch, B&H 1898.)

(*Dolmetsch 2* = Select English Songs and Dialogues of the 16th and 17th Centuries, Book 2, Arnold Dolmetsch, B&H 1912.)

Drawing Room Songs = Drawing Room Songs, Robert Tear, B&H.

(*English Recital 1* = The English Recital Song, Volume 1, David Patrick, Chappell 1979.)

(*English Recital 2* = The English Recital Song, Volume 2, David Patrick, Chappell 1979.)

Gentlemen's Magazine = Songs from The Gentlemen's Magazine, Copley & Reitan, Thames 1982.

Georgian 1 = Early Georgian Songs, Bool 1, Medium Voice, Michael Pilkington, S&B 1978.

Georgian 2 = Early Georgian Songs, Book 2, High Voice, Michael Pilkington, S&B 1978.

Hardy Songbook = A Thomas Hardy Songbook, Gordon Pullin, Thames 1997.

Heritage 1 = A Heritage of 20th Century British Song, Volume 1, Winifred Radford, Lyndon Vanderpump, Michael Pilkington, B&H 1978.

Heritage 2 = A Heritage of 20th Century British Song, volume 2, Winifred Radford, Lyndon Vanderpump, Michael Pilkington, B&H 1978.

Anthologies

Heritage 3 = A Heritage of 20th Century British Song, volume 3, Winifred Radford, Lyndon Vander-pump, Michael Pilkington, B&H 1978.

Heritage 4 = A Heritage of 20th Century British Song, volume 4, Winifred Radford, Lyndon Vander-pump, Michael Pilkington, B&H 1978.

Holy Night = O Holy Night, Neil Jenkins, Kevin Mayhew 1994 (organ arrangements by Charles MacDonald).

Imperial 1 = New Imperial Edition, Soprano Songs, Sidney Northcote, B&H 1952.

Imperial 2 = New Imperial Edition, Mezzo-Soprano Songs, Sidney Northcote, B&H 1952.

Imperial 3 = New Imperial Edition, Contralto Songs, Sidney Northcote, B&H 1950.

Imperial 4 = New Imperial Edition, Tenor Songs, Sidney Northcote, B&H 1953.

Imperial 5 = New Imperial Edition, Baritone Songs, Sidney Northcote, B&H 1951.

Imperial 6 = New Imperial Edition, Bass Songs, Sidney Northcote, B&H 1950.

Love & Affection = Songs of Love and Affection, Sidney Northcote, B&H 1985.

Lovesongs 1 = Elizabethan Lovesongs, Book 1, Frederick Keel, B&H 1909, high & low keys.

Lovesongs 2 = Elizabethan Lovesongs, Book 2, Frederick Keel, B&H 1913, high & low keys.

Lute Songs 1 = English Lute Songs, Book 1, Michael Pilkington, S&B 1984.

Lute Songs 2 = English Lute Songs, Book 2, Michael Pilkington, S&B 1984

McCormack = John McCormack Song Album, B&H.

Manuscript 1 = Songs from Manuscript Sources: 1, David Greer, S&B 1979.

Manuscript 2 = Songs from Manuscript Sources: 2, David Greer, S&B 1979.

MB 33 = English Songs, 1625 - 1660, Ian Spink, S&B Musica Britannica XXXIII, 1971.

MB 43 = English Songs, 1800 - 1860, Geoffrey Bush and Nicholas Temperley, S&B Musica Britannica XLIII, 1979.

MB 56 = Songs, 1860 - 1900, Geoffrey Bush, S&B Musica Britannica LVI, 1989.

Old English = Old English Melodies, H Lane Wilson, B&H 1899.

Printed = Twenty Songs from Printed Sources, David Greer, S&B 1969.

Recitalist 1 = The Junior Recitalist, Book 1, Soprano, Noelle Barker, S&B 1988.

Recitalist 2 = The Junior Recitalist, Book 2, Mezzo Soprano/Contralto, Noelle Barker, S&B 1988.

Recitalist 3 = The Junior Recitalist, Book 3, Tenor, Noelle Barker, S&B 1988.

Recitalist 4 = The Junior Recitalist, Book 4, Baritone/Bass, Noelle Barker, S&B 1988.

Sacred Songs 1 = Sacred Songs for the Soloist, Medium High Voice, David Patrick, B&H 1996.

Sacred Songs 2 = Sacred Songs for the Soloist, Medium Low Voice, David Patrick, B&H 1996.

Shakespeare = The Boosey & Hawkes Shakespeare Song Album (introduction Guy Woolfenden), B&H 1996.

Singer's Collection 1 = The Singer's Collection, Book One: Alan Ridout, Kevin Mayhew 1992.

Singer's Collection 2 = The Singer's Collection, Book Two: Alan Ridout, Kevin Mayhew 1992.

Solo Baritone = Sing Solo Baritone, John Carol Case, OUP 1985.

Solo Christmas = Sing Solo Christmas, John Carol Case, OUP 1987, high and low keys.

Solo Contralto = Sing Solo Contralto, Constance Shacklock, OUP 1985.

Solo Soprano = Sing Solo Soprano, Jean Allister, OUP 1985.

Solo Tenor = Sing Solo Tenor, Robert Tear, OUP 1985.

Songs from Wales = Songs from Wales, Volume 1, The Guild for the Promotion of Welsh Music 1990.

Songs from Wales = Songs from Wales, Volume 2, The Guild for the Promotion of Welsh Music 1997.

Souvenirs = Among Your Souvenirs, Selected Victorian and Edwardian Ballads, B&H.

Three Spring Songs = Three Spring Songs, Gwynn.

Tuneful Voice = O Tuneful Voice, 25 Classical English Songs, Timothy Roberts. OUP 1992.

A

Stephen Adams. (Michael Maybrick). 1844 - 1913. 100 more songs, B&H archive.
  Nirvana, *Fred. E Weatherly*, D [f'#-g''](m), B&H *Ballad Album 1*; C, Cramer *Drawing Room Songs*; (B*b*, E*b*, B&H).
  The holy city, *Fred. E Weatherly*, C [e'-g''], B&H *Ballad Album 1*; (A*b*, B*b*, D*b*, B&H).
  The star of Bethlehem, *Fred. E Weatherly*, G [d'-g''], B&H *Ballad Album 2*; (E*b*, F, B&H).
  Thora, *Fred. E Weatherly*, G [d'-a''(g'')](m), B&H *Ballad Album 1*; (E*b*, F, B&H).

Thomas Adès. 1971 -
Collections: (*Five Eliot Landscapes*, Faberprint 1990) .
  (Cape Ann, *T S Eliot*, [b*b*-d'''](f), Faberprint 5 Eliot.)
  (Life Story, *Tennessee Williams*, [soprano], Faber hire)
  (New Hampshire, *T S Eliot*, [c'-c'''](f), Faberprint 5 Eliot.)
  (Rannoch by Glencoe, *T S Eliot*, [d'-c'''](f), Faberprint 5 Eliot.)
  (The Lover in Winter, *Anon*, [counter-tenor], Faber, hire)
  (Usk, *T S Eliot*, [d'-d'''*b*](f), Faberprint 5 Eliot.)
  (Virginia, *T S Eliot*, [b-b''](f), Faberprint 5 Eliot.)

Frances Allitsen. 1848 - 1912. 14 more songs, B&H archive; 7 more, Cramer archive.
  The Lord is my light, *Psalm 27*, E*b* [d-a''*b*(b''*b*)], B&H *Ballad Album 2*; (B*b*, C, B&H).

William Alwyn. 1905 - 1985. Collections: *Mirages*, Lengnick 1974; *A Leave-Taking*, Lengnick 1984; *Invocations*, Lengnick 1986.
  A Leave-Taking, *Lord de Tablay*, [c'-g''], Lengnick A Leave-Taking.
  Aquarium, *William Alwyn*, [e-f'](m), Lengnick Mirages.
  Daffodils, *Lord de Tablay*, [e'-b''(a')], Lengnick A Leave-Taking.
  Drought, *Michael Armstrong*, [e'*b*-b''*b*], Lengnick Invocations.
  Fortune's wheel, *Lord de Tablay*, [d'-f'#], Lengnick A Leave-Taking.
  Holding the night, *Michael Armstrong*, [f'#-b''*b*], Lengnick Invocations.
  Invocation to the Queen of Moonlight, *Michael Armstrong*, [e'-g''], Lengnick Invocations.
  Metronome, *William Alwyn*, [c-e'](m), Lengnick Mirages.
  Our magic horse, *Michael Armstrong*, [e'-b''], Lengnick Invocations.
  Paradise, *William Alwyn*, [f-f'#](m), Lengnick Mirages.
  Portrait in a mirror, *William Alwyn*, [d-f'](m), Lengnick Mirages.
  Separation, *Michael Armstrong*, [d'-c'''(b''*b*)], Lengnick Invocations.
  (Slum song, *Louis MacNeice*, [e'-e''], OUP.)
  Spring rain, *Michael Armstrong*, [d'-a''], Lengnick Invocations.
  Study of a spider, *Lord de Tablay*, [c'-a''], Lengnick A Leave-Taking.
  The honeysuckle, *William Alwyn*, [d#-g'#(f'#)](m), Lengnick Mirages.
  The ocean wood, *Lord de Tablay*, [d'-b''(g'')], Lengnick A Leave-Taking.
  The pilgrim cranes, *Lord de Tablay*, [c'-g''], Lengnick A Leave-Taking.
  The two old kings, *Lord de Tablay*, [e'-g''], Lengnick A Leave-Taking.
  Through the centuries, *Michael Armstrong*, [e'*b*-a''], Lengnick Invocations.
  Undine, *William Alwyn*, [c#-f'#](m), Lengnick Mirages.

W H Anderson.

Hospitality, *Kenneth Macleod*, Cm [c'e''*b*], Roberton; Dm, Roberton.

Old shepherd's prayer, *Helen Shackleton*, Dm [c'#-d''], Roberton.

Last year, *Duncan Campbell Scott*, F#m [c'#-c''#], Roberton.

To a girl on her birthday, *Blanche Pownall Garrett*, F [c'-d''], Roberton.

Arrangements: *Two Ukrainian Folksongs*, Em [b-e''], Roberton.

Alone

In the garden flowers are growing

H K Andrews. 1904 - 1965.

When cats run home, *Alfred Lord Tennyson*, [c'#-g''], Thames *Century 3*.

Anon.

As at noon Dulcina rested, *Anon*, E*b* [e'-g''], S&B (Greer) *Manuscript 2, Lute Songs 1*.

Danny boy (Londonderry Air), *Fred E Weatherly*, E*b* [c'-g''], B&H *Ballad Album 1*.

Go my flock, go get you hence, *Philip Sidney*, D [d'-d''](m), S&B (Stroud) *Banquet*.

Go now, my soul, to thy desired rest, *Anon*, Dm [c'-d''](m), S&B (Greer) *Manuscript 2*.

Go thy ways since thou wilt go, *Anon*, Gm [d'-f''], S&B (Spink) *MB 33*.

Have I caught my heav'nly jewel? *Anon*, B*b* [f'-g''](m), S&B (Greer) *Manuscript 1*.

Have you seen but a whyte lillie grow? *Ben Jonson*, F [e'-f''], (B&H *Dolmetsch 1*); G, Paterson (Diack) *100 Best 1*.

How now, shepherd, what means that? *Anon*, [e'-e''](m), S&B (Greer) *Manuscript 2*.

I prithee leave, love me no more, *Michael Drayton*, [g'-a''*b*](m), S&B (Greer) *Manuscript 2*.

If floods of tears, *Anon*, [g'-c''], S&B (Greer) *Manuscript 1*.

If I freely may discover, *Ben Jonson*, F [c'-c''](m), S&B (Greer) *Manuscript 2*.

If I seek t'enjoy the fruits, *Anon*, Gm [d'-d''](m), S&B (Greer) *Manuscript 2*.

If the deep sighs, *Michael Drayton*, [f'#-g''], S&B (Greer) *Manuscript 1*.

If, when I die, to hell's eternal shade, *William Fowler?*, Gm [d'-f'], S&B (Spink)*MB 33*.

(Lye still my deare, why dost thou rise? *John Donne?* Am [g'#-f''], B&H *Dolmetsch 2*.)

Most men do love the Spanish wine, *Anon*, [G-d'](m), S&B (Greer) *Manuscript 1*.

Music, thou soul of heav'n, *Robert Herrick*, Gm [d'-e''*b*], S&B (Greer) *Manuscript 2*.

Must your fair inflaming eye, *Anon*, Gm [g'-g''](m), S&B (Spink) *MB 33*.

My lytell prety one, *Anon*, B*b* [f'-g''](m), (B&H *Dolmetsch 1*); F, Paterson (Diack) *100 Best 4*.

My op'ning eyes are purg'd, *Anon*, Cm [c-f'], Thames (Bevan) *6 Restoration*.

(Now ye Springe is come, *Anon*, Em [d'-e''], B&H *Dolmetsch 2*.)

O dear life, when shall it be? *Philip Sidney*, Gm [d'-d''](m), S&B (Stroud) *Banquet*.

(O death, rock me asleep, *Anne Boleyn?*, [f'-d''](f), B&H *Dolmetsch 2*.)

O Lord, whose grace, *Mary Herbert*, C [c'-e''], S&B (Greer) *Manuscript 1*.

O Mary dear (Londonderry Air), *John McCormack*, E*b* [c'-g''](m), B&H *McCormack*.

Phyllis was a fair maid, *Anon*, G [f'#-g''], B&H (Keel) *Lovesongs 1*, E, *Lovesongs 1*.

Portsmouth, *Anon*, E*b*, [b*b*-g''](m), Banks (James Brown).

Salley in our alley, *Henry Carey*, C [e'-f''](m), Cramer *Drawing Room Songs*.

Shall I weep or shall I sing? *Anon*, [d'-d''](f), S&B (Greer) *Manuscript 2*.

Sing aloud harmonious spheres, *William Strode?*, G [d'-e''], S&B (Spink) *MB 33*.

Sleepe, sleepe, *Anon*, A [f'#-f''#], B&H (Keel) *Lovesongs 1*; F, *Lovesongs 1*.

Sweet muses, nurses of delights, *Anon*, C [c'-c''], S&B (Greer) *Manuscript 2*.

Sweet, stay awhile, *John Donne?* [f'#-g''], S&B (Greer) *Manuscript 2, Lute Songs 1.*
(The banks of roses, *Anon*, F [c'-f''](m), OUP (Jacob).)
The complaint, *Anon*, Em [e'-a''], Thames (Copley & Reitan) *Gentleman's Magazine.*
(The country girl's farewell, *Anon*, E [d'#-e''](f), OUP (Jacob).)
The invitation, *Anon*, A [d'#-f'#](m), Thames (Copley & Reitan) *Gentleman's Magazine.*
Why dost thou turn away? *Anon*, A [e'-f'#], B&H (Keel) *Lovesongs 1*; F, *Lovesongs 1.*
You meaner beauties of the night, *Henry Wotton*, Gm [d'-e''](m), S&B (Spink) *MB 33.*

Denis ApIvor. 1916 - (BMIC.)

Michael Arne. 1740 - 1786.
Collections: included in *Arne Selected Songs* (edited Barclay Wilson), Cramer 1975.
Homeward bound, *Anon*, F [g'-d''] (m), Cramer Selected.
The lass with the delicate air, *Anon*, G [d'-g''], Cramer Selected, Cramer.

Thomas Augustine Arne. 1710 - 1778.
Collections: *Arne Selected Songs* (edited Barclay Wilson), B&H 1975; *Twelve Songs for High Voice volumes 1 and 2* (edited Michael Pilkington), S&B 1978.
(A warning, *Anon*, G [c'-g''], OUP (Franklin).)
Bacchus, God of mirth and wine, *Anon*, Db [ab-e''b], B&H (Northcote) *Imperial 6.*
(Behold your faithful Ariel fly / Ere you can say, *Shakespeare*, A [e'-a''](f), Chappell (Young).)
Blow, blow, thou winter wind, *Shakespeare*, Ab [e'b-a''b], S&B *12 Songs 1*; F, B&H Selected, Paterson (Diack) *100 Best 3.*
(By dimpled brook and fountain trim, Cramer.)
(Come away, death, *Shakespeare*, Em [b(c')-g''](m), B&H (Keel) *12 18th Century.*)
Come, calm content, *James Thomson*, Dm [c'-e''b], Cramer Selected, Thames (Barclay Wilson) *Countertenors 2.*
(Come Mira, idol of the swains, *Anon*, F [d'-g''], B&H (Keel) *12 18th Century.*) (As 'The Invitation', Eb, S&B (Ivimey).)
Cymon and Iphigenia, *Anon*, C [c'-g''], S&B *12 Songs 1.*
(Go, lovely rose, *Edmund Waller*, G [b-g''](m), B&H (Keel) *12 18th Century.*)
(Hail, immortal Bacchus, *Isaac Bickerstaffe*, D [A(F#)-e''](m), Elkin (Bevan).)
(High Queen of State / Honor, riches, *Shakespeare*, G [d'-a''](f), Chappell (Young).)
How engaging, how endearing, *William Congreve*, F [d'-g''], Braydeston (Bevan).
Hymn of Eve, *Thomas Arne*, D [d'-e''](f), Cramer Selected.
(If those who live in shepherd's bower, *Thomson & Mallet*, Ab [c'-e''b], Curwen (Warrack).)
(Invitation to Ranelagh, *Anon*, G [d'-g''], S&B (Ivimey).)
Jenny, *Anon*, G [d'-a''](m), S&B *12 Songs 1.*
Love's a dream, *Anon*, E [b-c''](m), Cramer Selected.
Now Phoebus sinketh in the west, *John Milton*, Dm [d'-g''](m), Cramer Selected.
O come, O come my dearest, *Pritchard*, G [d'-g''], S&B *12 Songs 1.*
O how great is the vexation, *Thomas Arne*, Fm [d'-g''](f), S&B *12 Songs 2.*
(O peace, thou fairest child of heaven, *Thomson & Mallet*, Gm [d'-a''b], Curwen (Warrack).)
O ravishing delight, *William Congreve*, [c'#-a''], Novello (Cummings).
Pleasing tales in dear romances, *Thomas Arne*, A [e'-a''], Novello (Bush) *Ballad Operas.*
Rule Britannia, *James Thomson*, Bb [e'b-f''], Cramer Selected.
See liberty, virtue and honour appearing, *James Thomson*, A [e'-a''], Banks (Brown).

Should you ever find her complying, *George Colman*, D [A-d'](m), Novello (Bush) *Ballad Operas*.

Sleep, gentle cherub, *Isaac Bickerstaffe*, F [e'-a''](f), S&B 12 Songs 2, *Recitalist 1*.

(The complaint, *Anon*, G [c'#-g''](m), B&H (Keel) *12 18th Century*.)

The fond appeal, *Anon*, E [b-a''](f), S&B 12 Songs 2.

The invitation, *see* Come, Mira.

(The kind inconstant, *Anon*, G [d'-g''](m), B&H (Keel) *12 18th Century*.)

The plague of love, *see* The tout-ensemble.

The sycamore shade, *Anon*, D [d'-a''](f), S&B 12 Songs 2.

The timely admonition, *Anon*, E [e'-g''#](f), S&B 12 Songs 2.

The tout-ensemble, *Anon*, F [c'-a''], S&B 12 Songs 1; *E*, B&H Michael Head Songs of Romance; *Eb*,
  B&H (Lane Wilson) *Old English, Imperial 5*.

(To all the sex deceitful, *William Congreve*, Dm [c'#-g''](m), Elkin (Bevan).)

Under the greenwood tree, *Shakespeare*, F [d'-a''](m), S&B 12 Songs 2; *Eb*, B&H (Northcote) *Imperial 4*, Chester *Celebrated 1*.

When daisies pied, *Shakespeare*, G [d'-g''](f), S&B 12 Songs 2; *F*, Cramer Selected, B&H (Woolfenden) *Shakespeare*, (Northcote) *Imperial 2*, Paterson (Diack) 100 Best 2, S&B (Pilkington); (E*b*,
  Cramer).

Where the bee sucks, *Shakespeare*, G [d'-g''](f), B&H Selected, (Northcote) *Imperial 1*, S&B
  (Duncan); *F*, B&H (Woolfenden) *Shakespeare*, Paterson (Diack) *100 Best 2*.

Why so pale and wan, fond lover? *John Suckling*, Am [G-d'](m), Braydeston (Bevan).

(Ye fauns and ye dryads, *Anon*, Bb [bb-f''], Ashdown (Carmichael).)

Richard Arnell. 1917 - (BMIC.)

Malcolm Arnold. 1921 -
Collection: *Two Donne Songs*, Roberton.

The good-morrow, *John Donne*, F [f'-g''], Roberton 2 Donne Songs.

Woman's constancy, *John Donne*, G [g'-c''#], Roberton 2 Donne Songs.

Samuel Arnold. 1740 - 1802.

Elegy, *Anon*, G, [d'-g''], OUP (Roberts) *Tuneful Voice*.

The midsummer wish, *J Hawkesworth*, F [f'-g''], OUP (Roberts) *Tuneful Voice*.

John Atkins. ? - 1671.

I can love for an hour when I'm at leisure, *Anon*, C [c'-e''](m), S&B (Spink) *MB 33*.

This lady ripe and fair and fresh, *William Davenant*, F [e'-f''], S&B (Spink) *MB 33*.

Wert thou then fairer than thou art, *Walter Montague?* G [f'#-e''](m), S&B (Spink) *MB 33*.

When the chill Cherocco blows, *Thomas Bonham*, Am [e'-f''](m), S&B (Spink) *MB 33*.

René Atkinson. 1920 -
Ave Maria, tr. *René Atkinson*, [e'-g''], OUP *Solo Christmas*; [c'-e''*b*], *Solo Christmas*.

Arrangements: *Ma Bonny Lad*, Roberton .

Bobby Shaftoe, *Anon*, Roberton Bonny Lad.

Bonny at morn, *Anon*, Roberton Bonny Lad.

Elsie Marley, *Anon*, Roberton Bonny Lad.

Ma bonny lad, *Anon*, Roberton Bonny Lad.

The water of Tyne, *Anon*, Roberton Bonny Lad.

John Attey. *fl.*1622 - 1640.
Collection: (*The First Booke of Ayres* (edited Fellowes), S&B 1926). Only songs available in anthologies are listed individually here.
    On a time the amorous Silvy, *Anon*, G [d'-g''], S&B (Pilkington) *Lute 1*, B&H (Keel) *Lovesongs 1*; *E*, *Lovesongs 1*.
    Sweet was the song, *Anon*, Am [g'#-g''], B&H (Keel) *Lovesongs 2*; *Fm*, *Lovesongs 2*, (Patrick) *Sacred Songs 2*.

Thomas Attwood. 1765 - 1838.
    Coronach: He is gone on the mountain, *Walter Scott*, Dm [d'-f''], S&B (Bush & Temperley) *MB 43*.
    Go, lovely rose, *Edmund Waller*, F [c'-f''], S&B (Bush & Temperley) *MB 43*, *Recitalist 4*.
    In the grove, friend to love, *T Holcroft*, G [d-e'](m), Novello (Bush) *Ballad Operas*.
    The cold wave my love lies under, *Thomas Moore*, Eb [d'-g''], S&B (Bush & Temperley) *MB 43*.

Frederic Austin. 1872 - 1952.
Collections: (*Three Wessex Songs* (text Thomas Hardy), B&H 1927); (*All about me* (text John Drinkwater), B&H 1930)
    Orpheus with his lute, *Shakespeare*, Ab [d'-a''b], B&H *Shakespeare*.
    The fiddler, *Thomas Hardy*, Em [c'-e''b], Thames *Hardy Songbook* (B&H 3 Wessex).
Arrangement:
    The twelve days of Christmas, *Anon*, G [d'-f''#], Novello; (A, Novello).

B

Alfonso Bales. ? - 1635.
Chloris sigh'd, *Anon*, Cm [g'-g''], S&B (Spink) *MB 33*, (Diack Johnstone) *Recitalist 1*; (Bm, *Dolmetsch 2*).

Michael Balfe. 1808 - 1870. 10 more songs, Cramer archive.
Come into the garden, Maude, *Alfred Lord Tennyson*, D [f'#-g''](m), S&B (Bush & Temperley) *MB 43*.
The arrow and the song, *Longfellow*, G [b-c''], Thames *Countertenors 1*.
The sands of Dee, *Charles Kingsley*, G [d'-e''], S&B (Bush & Temperley) *MB 43*.
When other lips, *Alfred Bunn*, Bb [e'-f''], Banks.

Granville Bantock. 1868 - 1946.
Collections: (*Songs of Arabia, Songs of Japan*, Breitkopf & Härtel 1896); (*Songs of Egypt*, Breitkopf & Härtel 1897); (*Songs of Persia, Songs of India, Songs of China*; Breitkopf & Härtel 1898); (*Six Jester Songs, Five Ghazals of Hafiz, Lyrics from 'Ferishtah's Fancies'*, Breitkopf & Härtel 1905); (*Sappho*, Breitkopf & Härtel 1906); (*Songs of the Seraglio*, B&H 1913); (*Five Songs from the Chinese Poets*, Chester 1918); (*Five Songs from the Chinese Poets 2nd Series*, Chester 1919); (*Three Songs for Children*, S&B 1923); (*Three Celtic Songs, Book 2*, B&H 1925); (*Three Nocturnes*, Cramer 1925); (*Five Songs of Essex*, Weinberger 1929); (*Three Sheiling Songs*, Paterson 1935); (*Songs from the Chinese Poets*, Chappell 1935).
(A bean-stripe; &, Apple-eating, *Robert Browning*, [tenor], Breitkopf Ferishtah, Breitkopf.)
(A camel-driver, *Robert Browning*, [tenor], Breitkopf Ferishtah.)
A feast of lanterns, *Yüan Mei* tr. *L Cranmer-Byng*, D [f'#-a''], Thames *Century 3*; (Bb, Novello; C, Elkin).
(A lullaby, *Alexander Stewart*, F [c'-d''](f), Chappell.)
(A lullaby, *Helen Bantock*, Breitkopf China.)
(A pearl, a girl, *Robert Browning*, Db [e'b-a''b], Weinberger.)
(A Persian love song, *Helen Bantock*, B&H Seraglio.)
(A pillar at Sebzavah, *Robert Browning*, G [d'-g''], Breitkopf Ferishtah, Breitkopf.)
(A sheiling song, *Donald A Mackenzie*, Eb, Paterson 3 Sheiling.)
(A widow bird sate mourning, *P B Shelley*, Bm [e'-f''#], Weinberger).
(A woman's last word, *Robert Browning*, C [bb-f''#](f), Weinberger.)
(Admirals all, *Henry Newbolt*, Bb [d'-g''](m), S&B.)
Adrift, *Li Po* tr. *L Cranmer -Byng*, Gm [g'-a''b], Thames *Century 1*; (Cm, Bm, Elkin).
(Ala'ya! send the cup around, *Hafiz* tr. *Edwin Arnold*, [baritone], Breitkopf 5 Ghazals.)
(An Eastern love song, *Helen Bantock*, C, B&H; Eb, B&H.)
(And there are tears, *Wang Seng-Ju* tr. *Cranmer-Byng*, F#m [c'#-e''], Cramer.)
(As I ride through the Metijda, *Robert Browning*, Am, B&H.)
(At the rising of the moon, *Fiona Macleod*, Weinberger.)
(Babyland, *Graham Robertson*, Elkin.)
(Boat song of the isles, *Harold Boulton*, G [d'-e''], Elkin; Bb, Elkin.)
(Bridal song, *Helen Bantock*, Ab [bb-a''b], Breitkopf Egypt.)
(Bridal song, *Helen Bantock*, [contralto], Breitkopf Sappho.)

(Butterfly song, *Helen Bantock*, Breitkopf Japan.)
(By the fireside, *Robert Browning*, C [a-e''], Weinberger; E*b*, Weinberger.)
(By the Ganges, *Helen Bantock*, Breitkopf India.)
(By the rivers of Babylon, *Psalm 137*, [c'-g''], Cramer.)
Captain Harry Morgan, *J Marley*, Weinberger,
(Carrowmore, *AE (George W Russell)*, Dm [d'-f''], Weinberger,)
(Cherries, *Robert Browning*, [tenor], Breitkopf Ferishtah.)
(Cradle song, *Walter Scott*, D [c'#-f'#](f), Chappell.)
(Dancing, E*b*, *Alfred Hayes*, Cramer; D, Cramer.)
(Desolation, *Kao-Shih* tr. *Cranmer-Byng*, [c'-g''*b*], Chester 5 Chinese 2.)
(Dirge, *Helen Bantock*, Breitkopf India.)
(Doggie, *Alfred Hayes*, C [e'-f''], S&B 3 for Children.)
(Down the Hwai, *Po Chüi* tr. *L Cranmer Byng*, Cramer.)
(Dream merchandise, *Graham Robertson*, C, Elkin; E*b*, F, Elkin.)
(Drinking song, *Helen Bantock*, Breitkopf Persia.)
(Elfin lover, *Helen Bantock*, A*b* [e'*b*-g''], S&B; F, S&B.)
(Epilogue: Oh! love - no, love! *Robert Browning*, [tenor], Breitkopf Ferishtah.)
(Evening song, *Helen Bantock*, [contralto], Breitkopf Sappho, Breitkopf.)
(Fairyland, *Alfred Hayes*, F [d'-f''], S&B 3 for Children.)
(Faithful sailor boy, *L Cranmer-Byng*, G [d'-e''], Weinberger 5 Essex.)
(Fan song, *Helen Bantock*, Breitkopf Japan.)
(Festal song, *Helen Bantock*, B [f'#-b''(g''#)], Breitkopf Egypt.)
(Fireside fancies, *Alfred Hayes*, Cramer.)
(Flower song, *Helen Bantock*, Breitkopf Japan.)
(Forsaken, *Helen Bantock*, Breitkopf China.)
(Frolic, *A E*, E [e'-f'#], S&B 3 for Children.)
(From the tomb of an unknown woman, *Anon*, tr. *L Cranmer-Byng*, Gm, Elkin; Am, Elkin.)
(Great is the Lord, *Psalm 48*, C [c'-g''], Cramer.)
(Heap cassia, *Robert Browning*, Gm [c'-f''], B&H.)
Home thoughts, *Robert Browning*, B*b* [a-f'#], Weinberger.
(Home to Gower, *John Marley*, C [e'-g''](m), Weinberger.)
(Hymn of Pan, *P B Shelley*, [c'-a''](m), Weinberger.)
(Hymn of the Gebare, *Helen Bantock*, Breitkopf Persia.)
(Hymn to Aphrodite, *Helen Bantock*, [contralto], Breitkopf Sappho.)
(I go to prove my soul, *Robert Browning*, D*b* -d'*b*-f''], Weinberger.)
(I loved thee once, Atthis, long ago, *Helen Bantock*, [contralto], Breitkopf Sappho, Breitkopf.)
(If I were Lord of Tartary, *Walter de la Mare*, Em [a-d''], Chappell; Gm, Chappell.)
(If that angel of Shiraz, *Hafiz* tr. *J H McCarthy*, [baritone], B&H.)
(In the desert, *Helen Bantock*, C [e'-g''](m), Breitkopf Arabia.
(In a dream I spake, *Helen Bantock*, [contralto], Breitkopf Sappho.)
(In a year, *Robert Browning*, [b-f''](f), Weinberger.)
(In the garden, *Helen Bantock*, Em [c'-a''], Breitkopf Egypt.)
(In the harem, *Helen Bantock*, Breitkopf Persia.)
(In the hollows of quiet places, *Fiona Macleod*, C [c'-g''], Weinberger; D, Weinberger.)
(In the palace, *Anon* tr. *E Powys Mathers*, E*b*, Elkin; F, G, Elkin.)
(In the palace, *Helen Bantock*, Breitkopf China.)

(In the temple, *Helen Bantock*, Breitkopf Japan.)
(In the village, *Helen Bantock*, Breitkopf India.)
(In tyme of olde, *Helen Bantock*, A [c'#-e''], Breitkopf Jester.)
(Invocation to the Nile, *Helen Bantock*, E♭ [b♭-e''♭], Breitkopf Egypt, Breitkopf.)
(Isles of the sea, *Harold Boulton*, F, Elkin; G, Elkin.)
(Jack Frost, *L Cranmer-Byng*, B♭ [c'-g''(e''♭)], Weinberger 5 Essex.)
(King George the farmer, *L Cranmer-Byng*, E♭ [b♭-e''♭](m), Weinberger 5 Essex.)
(Lament, *Helen Bantock*, Gm [d'-f''♭], Breitkopf Arabia.)
(Lament of Isis, *Helen Bantock*, Cm [b-e''♭](f), Breitkopf Egypt, Breitkopf; [high], Breitkopf.)
(Lament of the Bedouin slave girl, *Helen Bantock*, B&H Seraglio.)
(Land of promise, *Harold Boulton*, C [c-g''], Elkin; C, Elkin.)
(Life in a love, *Robert Browning*, [c'b-g''], Weinberger.)
(Little Papoose Lake, *Porter B Coolidge*, B&H.)
(Longing, *Fiona Macleod*, Elkin.)
(Love's secret, *William Blake*, E [e'-g''](m), Novello.)
(Love song, *Helen Bantock*, Breitkopf China.)
(Lullabye, *Graham Robertson*, B♭, Elkin; D♭, Elkin.)
(Memories with the dusk return, *Li Po* tr. *L Cranmer-Byng*, Cramer.)
(Mihrab Shah, *Robert Browning*, [tenor], Breitkopf Ferishtah.)
(Molly Green of Maldon Town, *L Cranmer-Byng*, E♭ [d'-e''♭], Weinberger 5 Essex.)
(Morgan le Fay, *Sheila Kaye-Smith*, Cramer.)
(Muse of the golden throne, *Helen Bantock*, [contralto], Breitkopf Sappho.)
(My fairy lover, *Donald A Mackenzie*, G♭, B&H 3 Celtic, B&H.)
(My star, *Robert Browning*, C [e'-g''], Weinberger; A, Weinberger.)
(Never the time and the place, *Robert Browning*, [c'-a''♭](m), Weinberger.)
(Night in the mountains, *Ch'ang Ch'ien* tr. *L Cranmer-Byng*, Cramer.)
(Nocturne, *Raymond Bantock*, A [c'#-e''], Cramer 3 Nocturnes.)
(Nocturne, *Raymond Bantock*, F#m [c'-f''#], Cramer 3 Nocturnes.)
(Nocturne, *Raymond Bantock*, E [b♭-f''#], Cramer 3 Nocturnes.)
(Now, *Robert Browning*, A [a-e''], Weinberger; C, Weinberger.)
(Oh! glory of full-mooned fairness, *Hafiz* tr. *Edwin Arnold*, [baritone], Breitkopf 5 Ghazals.)
(Out of the depths, *Psalm 130*, [c'-f''], Cramer.)
(Ozymandias, *P B Shelley*, [c'-d''♭], Weinberger.)
(Peer of gods, *Helen Bantock*, [contralto], Breitkopf Sappho.)
(Pippa passes, *Robert Browning*, E♭ [f'-b''♭], Weinberger.)
(Plot-culture, *Robert Browning*, [tenor], Breitkopf Ferishtah.)
(Praise ye the Lord, *Psalm 150*, A♭ [c'-e''♭], Cramer; B♭, Cramer.)
(Prayer to Vishnu, *Helen Bantock*, Breitkopf India.)
(Robin redbreast, *Alfred Hayes*, G, Cramer.)
(Sáki! dye the cup's rim deeper, *Hafiz* tr. *Edwin Arnold*, [baritone], Breitkopf 5 Ghazals.)
(Salve Regina, Chester.)
(Serenade, *Helen Bantock*, D♭ [a♭-f''], Breitkopf Jester, Breitkopf; [high], Breitkopf.)
(Shah Abbas, *Robert Browning*, [tenor], Breitkopf Ferishtah.)
(Silent strings, *Helen Taylor*, D, B&H.)
(Song of the bells, *Helen Bantock*, Breitkopf China.)
(Song of the Genie, *Helen F Bantock*, Dm [d'-a''], Breitkopf.)

(Song of the peach-blossom fountain, *T'ao Ch'ien* tr. *Cranmer-Byng*, Ab [c'-e''], Chappell.)
(Song of the sword, *Helen Bantock*, Breitkopf Japan.)
Song to the seals, *Harold Boulton*, Eb [g-e''b], Thames *Century 4*; F, Cramer; (G, Cramer).
(Spring Song, *Alfred Hayes*, Ab, Cramer.)
(Stand face to face, friend, *Helen Bantock*, [contralto], Breitkopf Sappho, Breitkopf.)
(Súfi, hither gaze, *Hafiz* tr. *Edwin Arnold*, [baritone], Breitkopf 5 Ghazals.)
(Summum bonum, *Robert Browning*, [c'-a''b](m), Weinberger.)
(The bird of Arabia, *Helen Bantock*, Am [b-e''], S&B.)
(The bird of St Bride, *Harold Boulton*, [d'-f''], Cramer.)
(The blue men of the Minch, *Donald A Mackenzie*, Cm, B&H 3 Celtic, B&H.)
(The chieftain's battle song, *Helen Bantock*, Gm [e'-f''#](m), Breitkopf Arabia.)
(The court of dreams, *Sung Chih-Wên* tr. *L Cranmer-Byng*, Cramer.)
(The crippled faun, *Wilfrid Thorley*, [c'-a''](m), Weinberger.)
(The dead dryad, *Wilfrid Thorley*, [c'-g''#](m), Weinberger.)
(The demon of Mazinderan, *Helen Bantock*, B&H Seraglio.)
(The eagle, *Robert Browning*, [tenor], Breitkopf Ferishtah.)
(The emperor, *Anon* tr. *E Powys Mathers*, Elkin.)
(The enchanted wood, *Myrrha Bantock*, Fm [bb-e''b], S&B; Am, S&B.)
(The faun despondent, *Wilfrid Thorley*, [c'-a''](m), Weinberger.)
(The hind in ambush, *Wilfrid Thorley*, [c'-a''](m), Weinberger.)
(The fakir's song, *Helen Bantock*, Breitkopf India.)
(The family, *Robert Browning*, [tenor], Breitkopf Ferishta.)
(The festal hymn of Judith, *Bowker Andrews*, Bb [g'-g''], Weinberger.)
(The garden of bamboos, *Anon* tr. *E Powys Mathers*, Gm, Elkin; Am, Cm, Elkin.)
(The ghost road, *Tu Fu* tr. *Cranmer-Byng*, Am [c'#-e''], Chester 5 Chinese.)
(The golden Nenuphar, *Han Yü* tr. *L Cranmer-Byng*, Elkin.)
(The guardian angel, *Robert Browning*, Eb [d'-a''b], Weinberger; C, Weinberger.)
(The hedge of briar, *Helen Taylor*, Eb, B&H; Db, B&H.)
(The jester, *Helen Bantock*, Bb [g(c')-d''], Breitkopf Jester.)
(The last revel, *Ch'ên Tzû-ang* tr. *Cranmer-Byng*, D [c'#-e''], Chappell Chinese.)
(The Lord is my shepherd, *Psalm 23*, Bb [d'-f''], Chappell; Db, Chappell.)
(The Lord reigneth, *Psalm 93*, Ab [c'-g''], S&B.)
(The lost one, *Mêng Hao-Jan* tr. *Cranmer-Byng*, Db [c'-g''b], Cramer.)
(The meeting, *Helen Bantock*, Eb [d'-g''], Breitkopf Arabia.)
(The melon-seller, *Robert Browning*, [tenor], Breitkopf Ferishtah, Breitkopf.)
(The moon has set, *Helen Bantock*, [contralto], Breitkopf Sappho.)
(The moon maiden's song, *Ernest Dowson*, Bm [f'#-g''#](f), Weinberger.)
(The Musumë's song, *Helen Bantock*, Breitkopf Japan.)
(The Nautch girl, *Helen Bantock*, Breitkopf India.)
(The new moon's silver sickle, *Hafiz* tr. *Edwin Arnold*, [baritone], Breitkopf 5 Ghazals.)
(The nightingale's song, *Helen Bantock*, Bbm [d'b-g''](f), Breitkopf Arabia.)
(The odalisque, *Helen Bantock*, B&H Seraglio.)
(The parting, *Penuel Ross*, G, Elkin; Bb, Elkin.)
(The peach flower, *E Powys Mathers*, Gm [d'b-e''], Elkin; Am, Elkin.)
(The pearl and the rose, *Helen Bantock*, Breitkopf Persia.)
(The peewee, *Donald A Mackenzie*, Paterson 3 Sheiling.)

(The red lotus, *E Powys Mathers*, Am, Elkin; Bm, Dm, Elkin.)
(The reed player, *Fiona Macleod*, Weinberger.)
(The return, *Helen Bantock*, Breitkopf Arabia.)
(The seasons, *Alfred Hayes*, Cramer.)
(The Simurgh, *Helen Bantock*, Breitkopf Persia.)
(The singer in the woods, *Fiona Macleod*, Bm [c'-d''], Cramer.)
(The sun, *Robert Browning*, [tenor], Breitkopf Ferishta.)
(The twilight coast, *Donald A Mackenzie*, Paterson 3 Sheiling.)
(The two roses, *Myrrha Bantock*, Eb, Elkin; F, Elkin.)
(The unutterable, *Helen Bantock*, C [a-c''], Breitkopf Egypt.)
(The valley of silence, *Fiona Macleod*, F, Cramer.)
(The washer of the ford, *Fiona Macleod*, Am, Cramer.)
(The wee folk, *Donald A Mackenzie*, Eb, B&H 3 Celtic, B&H.)
(The wild Welsh coast, *John Marley*, C [d'-g''], Weinberger.)
(The youthful, charming Chloe, *Robert Burns*, Cramer.)
(There's a wee, wee glen, *Charles Murray*, Eb, Cramer.)
(Tra-la-la-lie! *Helen Bantock*, C [c'-e''], Breitkopf Jester.)
(Two camels, *Robert Browning*, [tenor], Breitkopf Ferishtah.)
(Under the rose, *Helen Bantock*, Dm [a-e''], Breitkopf Jester.)
(Waking song, *Harold Boulton*, Elkin.)
(Walden market, *L Cranmer-Byng*, Ab [c'-d''b](m), Weinberger 5 Essex.)
(Wanting is — what? *Robert Browning*, Bb [g'-f'], Weinberger.)
(War song, *Helen Bantock*, Breitkopf China.)
(When you sang to me, *Raymond Bantock*, Weinberger.)
(Whither away? *Myrrha Bantock*, Weinberger.)
(Will-o'-the-wisp, *Helen Bantock*, D [d'-d''], Breitkopf Jester.)
(Winter has gone, *May Chorley*, Bm [c'-g''], B&H.)
Yung Yang, *Po Chüi* tr. *L Cranmer Byng*, [medium voice], Novello; (Cm, Dm, Em, Elkin).
(Zál, *Helen Bantock*, Breitkopf Persia.)
Arrangement:
(Lord Rendal, *Anon*, D [c'#-d''], Cramer.)

John Barnett. 1802 - 1890.
' I arise from dreams of thee, *P B Shelley*, Bb [c'#-g''], S&B (Bush & Temperley) *MB 43*.
Ossian's glen, *William Wordsworth*, Ab [c'-f'], S&B (Bush & Temperley) *MB 43*.

Carol Barratt.
Collection: *Six 'Songs' for Singing*, B&H 1997.
(Love...a strange disease, Chester.)
Song (A widow bird sat mourning), *P B Shelley*, [G-d'](m), B&H 6 Songs.
Song (Pious Selinda goes to prayers), *William Congreve*, [d-e'](m), B&H 6 Songs.
Song (Time stands still), *Anon*, [A-d'], B&H 6 Songs.
Song without words, *no text*, [c-e'b](m), B&H 6 Songs.
Summer song (Strawberries swimming in the cream), *George Peele*, [c-e'b](m), B&H 6 Songs.
The bachelor's song (I thank you for that!), *Thomas Flatman*, [G-e'], B&H 6 Songs.

Bernard Barrell. 1919 - (BMIC.)

Joyce Barrell. 1917 - 1989. (BMIC.)

Richard Barrett. 1959 - (BMIC.)

Gerald Barry. 1952 -
Water parted, *Vincent Deane*, [f-g''] (C-Ten), OUP.

John Bartlet. *fl.*1606 - 1610.
Collection: (*A Booke of Ayres* (edited Fellowes), S&B 1925.) Only songs available in anthologies are listed individually here.
A pretty duck there was, *Anon*, G [g'-a''], S&B (Pilkington) *Lute 1*; F, B&H (Keel) *Lovesongs 2*; D, *Lovesongs 2*.
I heard of late, *Anon*, G [d'-g''], B&H (Keel) *Lovesongs 2*; Eb, *Lovesongs 2*.
If there be anyone, *Anon*, G [d'-d''], B&H (Keel) *Lovesongs 2*; Bb, *Lovesongs 2*.
O Lord, thy faithfulness, *Anon*, Dm [g'-g''], S&B (Pilkington) *Lute 1*.
What thing is love? *George Peele*, G [d'-e''], S&B (Pilkington) *Lute 1*; A, B&H (Keel) *Lovesongs 2*; F, *Lovesongs 2*.
When from my love, *Anon*, C [e'-g''](m), S&B (Pilkington) *Lute 1*, B&H (Keel) *Lovesongs 2*; A, *Lovesongs 2*.
Who doth behold my mistress' face, *Anon*, A, [a'-f''#](m), B&H (Keel) *Lovesongs 2*, F; *Lovesongs 2*.

Daniel Batchelor. *c.*1574 - after 1610.
To plead my faith, *Robert Devereux, Earl of Essex*, Cm [f-f''](m), S&B (Stroud) *Banquet*.

Alison Bauld. 1944 -
Collection: *Two Shakespeare Songs*, Novello.
Banquo's buried, *Shakespeare*, [bb-g''](f), Novello.
Cry, cock-a-doodle-doo, *Shakespeare*, [a-g''](f), Novello 2 Shakespeare.
The witches' song, (unaccompanied) *Shakespeare*, [f'-b''](f), Novello 2 Shakespeare.

Arnold Bax. 1883 - 1953.
Collections: *Seven Bax Songs*, Chester 1919; (*Three Enfantines*, Chester 1920); (*Five Irish Songs*, Chappell 1922); *Six Songs* (introduction Lewis Foreman), Thames 1994; *Twelve Songs* (introduction Lewis Foreman), Thames 1994.
(A celtic lullaby, *Fiona Macleod*, Eb [bb-a''b](f), Chester.)
A Christmas carol, *Anon*, F [d'-b-a''], Chester 7 Songs.
A lullaby, *Sheila MacCarthy (Arnold Bax)*, E [b-f''#](f), Thames 6 Songs.
A milking sian, *Fiona Macleod*, F [d'-g''](f), Chester 7 Songs.
(Across the door, *Padraic Colum*, Cm [c'-f''](f), Chappell 5 Irish.)
(As I came over the grey, grey hills, *Joseph Campbell*, Eb [bb-g''b], Chappell 5 Irish.)
(Beg-Innish, *JM Synge*, [c'-g''], Chappell 5 Irish.)
Carrey Clavel, *Thomas Hardy*, Fm [e'b-g''](m), Thames 12 Songs.
(Cradle song, *Padraic Colum*, Eb [d'b-g''b](m), Chappell *English Recital 2*, Chappell.)
Dermott Donn MacMorna, *Padraic Colum*, Dm [a-f''](f), Thames 6 Songs.
(Dream child, *Val Newton*, Eb [c'-e''], Chappell *English Recital 1*.)
Eternity, *Robert Herrick*, F [d'-a''], Thames 12 Songs.

Far in a western brookland, *A E Housman*, Dm [d'-f''], Thames 12 Songs.
(Golden Guendolen, *William Morris*, Chester.)
(I heard a piper piping, *Joseph Campbell*, [b-e''], Chappell 5 Irish.)
I heard a soldier, *Herbert Trench*, Gm [b♭-f''#], Thames 12 Songs.
In the morning, *A E Housman*, F [e'-f''], Thames 12 Songs, *Century 2*.
(Magnificat, (after a picture by D G Rossetti), *Luke 1*, Chester.)
On the bridge, *Thomas Hardy*, C [c'-f''](f), Thames 12 Songs.
Parting, *A E (George Russell)*, E, [d'#-g''], Thames 12 Songs.
Rann of exile, *Padraic Colum*, Am [d'-g''], Thames 12 Songs.
Rann of wandering, *Padraic Colum*, E♭ [b♭-f''], Thames 12 Songs.
Roundel, *Chaucer*, D [c'-f''#](m), Chester 7 Songs.
Shieling song, *Fiona Macleod*, F [c'#-a''](f), Chester 7 Songs.
Spring rain, *Friedrich Ruckert* tr. *Clifford Bax?*, G#m [d'#-g''#], Thames 6 Songs.
The enchanted fiddle, *Anon*, D [c'-a''](m), Chester 7 Songs.
(The fairies, *William Allingham*, Chester.)
The market girl, *Thomas Hardy*, F [d'-f''](m), Thames 12 Songs, *Hardy Songbook*.
(The pigeons, *Padraic Colum*, [b-d''](f), Chappell 5 Irish.)
The white peace, *Fiona Macleod*, A♭ [e'-b-g''♭], Chester 7 Songs.
The song in the twilight, *Freda Bax*, B♭m [b♭-g''♭], Thames 6 Songs.
To Eire, *J H Cousins*, F [c'-g''], Chester 7 Songs.
Watching the needleboats, *James Joyce*, Am [e'-g''], Thames 12 Songs.
When I was one-and-twenty, *A E Housman*, Em [d'-f''], Thames 12 Songs.
When we are lost, *Dermot O'Byrne (Arnold Bax)*, A♭ [d'-a''], Thames 6 Songs.
Youth, *Clifford Bax*, F [e'-b-f''](m), Thames 6 Songs.
Arrangements:
(Jack and Jone, *Thomas Campion*, Chester.)

Frank Bayford. 1941 - (BMIC).

David Bedford. 1937 -
An easy decision, *Kenneth Patchen*, [e'-c'''](f), Universal.
(Be music, Night, *Kenneth Patchen*, Universal.)
Some stars above magnitude 2.9, *Anon*, [d'-c'''#](f), Universal.

Arthur Benjamin. 1893 - 1960.
Collection: (*Three Greek Poems*, B&H 1934.)
(A heritage, *Arthur Lewis*, A, B&H.)
(A wine jug, *Anon* tr. *A C Benson*, Am, B&H 3 Greek.)
(Fire of your love, *F Eyton*, B&H.)
(Jamaicalypso, *Jamaican folk song*, F. B&H.)
(Jan, *Anon*, F [c'-d''♭(f')], B&H.)
(Linstead market, *Creole melody*, F, B&H.)
(On deck, *Anon* tr. *A C Benson*, A, B&H 3 Greek.)
Shepherd's holiday, *Elinor Wylie*, Gm [c'-f''](f), B&H *Heritage 4*; (Am, B&H).
(Song of the banana carriers, *Jamaican folk song*, F, B&H.)
(The flower girl, *Anon* tr. *A C Benson*, C, B&H 3 Greek.)
Wind's work, *Sturge Moore*, C [d'-f''], Thames *Century 1*.

Richard Rodney Bennett. 1936 - .

Collections: *Tenebrae*, Universal 1975; *A Garland for Marjorie Fleming*, Novello 1986; *Dream-songs*, Novello 1990; (*A History of the Thé Dansant*, Novello 1994).

A melancholy lay, *Marjorie Fleming*, Gm [b♭-f'](f), Novello Garland.

Adieu, farewell earth's bliss, *Thomas Nashe*, [A-g'](m), Universal Tenebrae.

Death, be not proud, *John Donne*, [A(c)-f'#](m), Universal Tenebrae.

Dream-song, *Walter de la Mare*, Gm [c'-e''b], Novello Dream-songs.

(Fox-trot, *M R Peacocke*, [c'-g''#](f), Novello History.)

Hey nonny no, *Anon*, [B♭-g'](m), Universal Tenebrae. ·

In Isas bed, *Marjorie Fleming*, F [d'-g''b](f), Novello Garland.

Like to the falling of a star, *Harry King*, [d#-f'#](m), Universal Tenebrae.

Music that Her Echo is (cycle), [tenor], Universal.

On Jessy Watsons elopement, *Marjorie Fleming*, [b-g''#](f), Novello Garland.

(Slow foxtrot, *M R Peacocke*, [c'#-g''b](f), Novello History.)

Sonnet on a monkey, *Marjorie Fleming*, G [e'-f''#](f), Novello Garland.

Sweet Isabell, *Marjorie Fleming*, F [d'-f''](f), Novello Garland.

(Tango, *M R Peacocke*, [b♭-g''](f), Novello History.)

The little ghost who died for love (cycle), *Edith Sitwell*, [soprano], Novello.

The song of the mad prince, *Walter de la Mare*, Fm [c'-e''], Novello Dream-songs.

The song of the wanderer, *Walter de la Mare*, [c'-f''], Novello Dream-songs.

The song of shadows, *Walter de la Mare*, [d'-e''], Novello Dream-songs.

This is the garden, *e e cummings*, [c'-a''], Novello.

(This Worldes Joie, *Anon*, [c'#-b''b], Novello hire.)

Written on the eve of execution, *Chidiock Tichbourne*, [A♭-g'](m), Universal Tenebrae.

Thomas Case Sterndale Bennett. ? - 1944. 24 more songs, B&H archive; 18 more, Cramer archive.

Leanin', *Hugh E Wright*, G [c'#-e''](m), B&H *Ballad Album 2*; F, B&H).

William Sterndale Bennett. 1816 - 1875.

(As lonesome through the woods, *Carl Klingemann* tr. *H F Johnston*, Gm [d'-e''b], B&H.)

(Dawn, gentle flower, *Barry Cornwall*, E [e'-e''], B&H.)

(Forget-me-not, *W Gerhard*, tr. *Letitia Elizabeth Landon*, E [c'#-e''](m), B&H.)

Gentle Zephyr, *Anon*, B♭ [f'-e''b](m), S&B (Bush & Temperley) *MB 43*.

Indian love, *Barry Cornwall*, Bm [f'#-e''](f), S&B (Bush & Temperley) *MB 43*.

(May-dew, *Uhland*, tr. *H W Pierson*, A♭ [e'-b-e''b], B&H.)

(Musing on the roaring ocean, *Robert Burns*, B♭ [e'-f''](f), B&H.)

The past, *Percy Bysshe Shelley*, E♭ [e'-b-e''b], S&B (Bush & Temperley) *MB 43*.

To Chloe in sickness, *Burns*, F#m [f'#-e''], S&B (Bush & Temperley) *MB 43*.

(Winter's gone, *John Clare*, E♭, [d'-f''](m), B&H.)

Lennox Berkeley. 1902 - 1989.

Collections: *Five Housman Songs Op. 14 No. 3*, Chester 1983; *Five Songs Op. 26*, Chester 1948; *Three Greek Songs Op. 38*, Chester 1953; *Five Poems Op. 53*, Chester 1960; *Autumn's Legacy Op. 58*, Chester 1963; *Five Chinese Songs Op. 78*, Chester 1975; *Another Spring Op. 93*, Chester 1978.

A memory, *Louis Labé* tr. *M D Calvocoressi*, [c'#-g''], OUP.

All night a wind of music, *Thomas Lovell Beddoes*, [f'-a''], Chester Op 58.

Another Spring, *Walter de la Mare*, F [b♭-g''], Chester Op 93.
Because I liked you better, *A E Housman*, D♭ [d'-b♭-g''](m), Chester Op 14/3.
Bells of Cordoba, *F G Lorca* tr. *Stanley Richardson*, [e'-b♭-g''], Chester.
Carry her over the water, *W H Auden*, [e'-g''], Chester Op 53.
(Counting the beats, *Robert Graves*, Fm [e♭-a''♭], Thames.)
Dreaming of a dead lady, *Shên-Yo* tr. *Waley*, [c'-g''], Chester Op 78.
Epitaph of Timas, *Sappho* tr. *Anon*, Fm [c'#-e''♭], Chester Op 38.
Eyes look into the well, *W H Auden*, [c'-e''♭], Chester Op 53.
He would not stay for me, *A E Housman*, [d'#-a''](m), Chester Op 14/3.
How love came in, *Robert Herrick*, F [e'-f''], B&H *Heritage 3*.
Hurrahing in harvest, *Gerard Manley Hopkins*, [e'-b♭-a''], Chester Op 58.
Late Spring, *Yang Knang* tr. *Kotewall & Smith*, [c'-f''#], Chester Op 78.
Lauds, *W H Auden*, E♭ [d'-f''#], Chester Op 53.
Lesbos, *Lawrence Durrell*, Fm [f'-g''], Chester Op 58.
Look not in my eyes, *A E Housman*, [d'-g''#](m), Chester Op 14/3.
Mistletoe, *Walter de la Mare*, F# [c'#-f''#], Chester Op 26.
Night covers up the rigid land, *W H Auden*, Cm [c'-g''♭], Thames *Century 3*.
O lurcher-loving collier, *W H Auden*, B♭ [d'-f''], Chester Op 53.
People hide their love, *Wu-Ti* tr. *Waley*, A♭ [d'-b♭-f''], Chester Op 78.
Poetry, *Walter de la Mare*, [c'-f''#], Chester Op 93.
Poor Henry, *Walter de la Mare*, A [c'-g''#], Chester Op 26.
Rich days, *W H Davies*, E♭ [e'-b♭-g''♭], Chester Op 58.
Silver, *Walter de la Mare*, E♭ [d'-g''], Chester Op 26.
(So sweet love seemed, *Robert Bridges*, Chester.)
Spring song, *Antipater* tr. *Anon*, G [c'#-f''], Chester Op 38.
The Autumn wind, *Wu-Ti* tr. *Waley*, [c'#-f''#], Chester Op 78.
The beacon barn, *Patrick O'Malley*, F [c'-f''], Chester.
The half-moon westers low, *A E Housman*, B [d'#-a''](m), Chester Op 14/3.
The horseman, *Walter de la Mare*, Gm [d'-f''#], Chester Op 26.
The mighty thoughts of an Old World, *Thomas Lovell Beddoes*, [c'-a''], Chester Op 58.
The riverside village, *Ssu-K'ung Shu* tr. *Kotewall & Smith*, D♭ [d'-b♭-f''], Chester Op 78.
The song of the soldiers, *Walter de la Mare*, Dm [c'-a''♭], Chester Op 26.
The street sounds to the soldiers' tread, *A E Housman*, [d'-a''♭](m), Chester Op 14/3.
The thresher, *Joachim du Bellay* tr. *M D Calvocoressi*, G [d'-g''], OUP.
To Aster, *Plato* tr. *Anon*, D♭ [d'-b♭-f''♭], Chester Op 38.
Tonight the winds begin to rise, *Alfred Lord Tennyson*, [e'-b''♭], Chester Op 58.
What's in your mind, my dove, my coney, *W H Auden*, [c'-f''#], Chester Op 53.
When we were idlers with the loitering rills, *Hartley Coleridge*, [e'-a''#], Chester Op 58.

Michael Berkeley. 1948 -
Collection: *Speaking Silence* OUP, (in preparation).
    And is it night? *Anon*, [baritone], OUP Speaking Silence.
    Blow, Northern Wind, *Anon*, [baritone], OUP Speaking Silence.
    Echo, *Christina Rossetti*, [baritone], OUP Speaking Silence.
    The ragged wood, *W B Yeats*, [baritone], OUP Speaking Silence.

Anthony Bernard. 1891 - 1963.
(Follow your saint, *Thomas Campion*, G, B&H; E*b*, B&H.)
(The cherry tree, *C A Claye*, A, B&H.)
When that I was and a little tiny boy, *Shakespeare*, Gm [d'-e''*b*](m), Chester.

Lord Berners. 1883 - 1950.
Collection: *The Collected Vocal Music*, Chester 1980.
A long time ago, *Traditional*, [c'-g''](m), Chester Collected.
Come on Algernon, *T E B Clarke*, G [b-d''(b')], Chester Collected.
Dialogue between Tom Filuter and his man, *Anon*, [d'-f''], Chester Collected.
Lullaby, *Thomas Dekker*, Fm [d'-f''], Chester Collected.
Red roses and red noses, *Lord Berners*, B*b* [b-f''], Chester Collected.
The green-eyed monster, *E L Duff*, [c'-g''](f), Chester Collected.
The lady visitor in the pauper ward, *Robert Graves*, [e'*b*-f''#], Chester Collected.
The Rio Grande, *Traditional*, [d'*b*-a''](m), Chester Collected.
Theodore or The Pirate King, *John Masefield*, [c'#-f''], Chester Collected.

Maurice Besley. 1888 - 1945. 90 more songs, B&H archive.
The second minuet, *Aubrey Dowdon*, G [d'-d''], B&H; (B*b*, B&H).
(An epitaph, *Walter de la Mare*, D*b* [c'*b*(a*b*)-e''*b*], Curwen.)

Judith Bingham. (BMIC). 1952 -

Henry Bishop. 1786 - 1855. 12 more songs, Cramer archive.
By the simplicity of Venus's doves, *Shakespeare*, E*b*, [e'*b*-g''], Novello (Bush) *Ballad Operas*, S&B (Bush & Temperley) *MB 43*.
Come live with me, *Marlowe* adapted *Reynolds*, G [c'#-g''], S&B (Bush & Temperley) *MB 43*.
Deep in my heart, *Anon*, E*b* [e'*b*-g''], B&H (Alec Rowley) *Imperial 2*.
Home sweet home, *John Howard Payne*, E [e'-e''], Cramer *Drawing Room Songs*.
Lo! here the gentle lark, *Shakespeare*, F [e'-a''(c''')](f), B&H (Woolfenden) *Shakespeare, Souvenirs,* Cramer.
Should he upbraid, *Shakespeare*, G [c'#-g''](f), B&H (Northcote) *Imperial 1*.
Take O take those lips away, *Shakespeare*, E*b* [d'-f''], S&B (Bush & Temperley) *MB 43, Recitalist 3*.

David Blake. 1936 -
Beata l'alma (cantata), *Herbert Read*, [a(b*b*)-b''], Novello.
The bones of Chuang Tzu (cantata), *Chang Heng* tr. *Arthur Waley*, [A-g'](m), Novello.

Howard Blake. 1938 -
(Three Sussex Songs, *Judith Garrett*, [mezzo soprano], Faberprint)
(Shakespeare Songs, *Shakespeare*, [medium voice], Faberprint)
(The Land of Counterpane, *Robert Louis Stevenson*, [medium voice] Faberprint).
Walking in the air, *Howard Blake*, [c'#-d''], Faber.

Arthur Bliss. 1891 - 1975.
Collections: *The Ballads of the Four Seasons*, Novello 1924; *Seven American Poems*, B&H 1942; (*Angels of the Mind*, Novello 1969); (*Two American Poems*, B&H 1980); *Nine Songs*, (Preface by George Dannatt) Novello 1983; *Two Love Songs* OUP.

A child's prayer, *Siegfried Sassoon*, [f'-f''], Novello 9 Songs.

Autumn, *Li Po* tr. *Shigeyoshi Obata*, [b♭(f)-a''], Novello 4 Seasons.

Auvergnat, *Hilaire Belloc*, [high voice], Novello.

Being young and green, *Edna St. Vincent Millay*, [b-e''], B&H 7 American; [e'♭-a''♭] B&H *Heritage* 3, B&H.

Fair Annet's song, *Elinor Wylie*, Gm [b-e''♭], B&H 7 American.

Fair is my love, *Edmund Spencer*, [b♭-f''](m), OUP 2 Love Songs.

Feast, *Edna St. Vincent Millay*, Dm [a-d''#], B&H 7 American.

Gone, gone again is summer, *Edna St. Vincent Millay*, E♭ [b♭-e''♭], B&H 7 American, B&H; (G, B&H).

(Harvest, *Kathleen Raine*, [a'-a''](f), Novello Angels.)

(Humoresque, *Edna St. Vincent Millay*, [e'-g''#](f), B&H 2 American.)

(In the beck, *Kathleen Raine*, [d'-g''](f) Novello Angels.)

In praise of his Daphnis, *John Wotton*, [c'#-f'#], OUP 2 Love Songs.

Leisure, *W H Davies*, G [g'-g''], Novello 9 Songs.

(Lenten flowers, *Kathleen Raine*, [d'-f''], Novello Angels.)

Little elegy, *Elinor Wylie*, D♭ [c'-f''], B&H 7 American, B&H; (E, B&H).

Lovelocks, *Walter de la Mare*, [d'-f''#], Novello 9 Songs.

(Nocturne, *Kathleen Raine*, [d'-g''](f), Novello Angels.)

Rain comes down, *Edna St. Vincent Millay*, C#m [b#-f#], B&H 7 American; (Bm, B&H).

Rich or poor, *W H Davies*, [e'-f''], Novello 9 Songs.

(Seed, *Kathleen Raine*, [d'-a''♭](f) Novello Angels.)

Siege, *Edna St. Vincent Millay*, Am [c'-g''], B&H 7 American; (Gm, B&H).

Simples, *James Joyce*, [e'♭-f''#], OUP.

(Spring, *Li Po* tr. *Shigeyoshi Obata*, A♭ [c'-f''], Novello 4 Seasons.)

(Storm, *Kathleen Raine*, [c'#-g''#](f), Novello Angels.)

(Summer, *Li Po* tr. Shigeyoshi Obata, [c'#-d''#], Novello 4 Seasons.)

The buckle, *Walter de la Mare*, A [b-f''#], Novello 9 Songs.

The fallow deer at the lonely house, *Thomas Hardy*, E [e'-g''#], Novello 9 Songs, Thames *Hardy Songbook*.

The hare, *Walter de la Mare*, [e'-g''#], Novello 9 Songs.

(The return from town, *Edna St. Vincent Millay*, G [e'-f''#](f), B&H 2 American.)

(The tramps, *Robert Service*, A♭ [e'♭-g''](m), B&H.)

This night, *W H Davies*, E♭ [c'-g''], Novello 9 Songs.

Thunderstorms, *W H Davies*, Bm [d'-f''#], Novello 9 Songs.

Tune on my pipe *see* In praise of his Daphnis.

(Winter, *Li Po*, tr. *Shigeyoshi Obata*, [d'-a''], Novello 4 Seasons.)

(Worry about money, *Kathleen Raine*, C [b-a''♭](f), Novello Angels.)

John Blow. 1649 - 1708.

Collections: *Ten Songs* (edited Michael Pilkington) S&B 1979.

Boasting fops, *Peter Anthony Motteux*, F [c'-a''], S&B 10 Songs.

Clarona, lay aside your lute, *Anon*, Cm [d'-a''], S&B 10 Songs.

Fain would I, Chloris, *Anon*, Dm [d'-a''](m), S&B 10 Songs.

Grant me, ye gods, *Anon*, Gm [c'-f''], S&B 10 Songs.

Horace to his lute, *Anon*, C [G-f'](m), Thames (Bevan) *6 Restoration*.

Of all the torments, *Anon*, Fm [c'-g''](m), S&B 10 Songs, *Recitalist 3*.

Peaceful is he, and most secure, *Thomas Flatman*, Am [c'-f''], Thames (Bevan) *6 Divine*.

Philander, do not think of arms, *Anon*, C [e'-a''](f), S&B 10 Songs, *Recitalist 1*.

Tell me no more, *Anon*, G [c'#-f'#](m); S&B 10 Songs, Schott (Tippett & Bergmann).

(The grove: why does Laura shun me?, *Anon*, Eb, B&H (Anthony Bernard).)

The perfection, *Thomas D'Urfey*, Dm [d'-a''], S&B 10 Songs.

The self banished, *Edmund Waller*, G [d'-g''], S&B 10 Songs, Schott (Tippett & Bergmann); *D*, B&H (Northcote) *Imperial 6*, Schott, Paterson (Diack) *100 Best 4*.

What is't to us, *Howe*, Gm [c'-a''](m), S&B 10 Songs.

Carey Blyton. 1932 -
Collections (*Mixed Bag* (words Enid Blyton), B&H 1965.) (See also BMIC.)

(Symphony in yellow, *Oscar Wilde*, [c'#-g], B&H).

Rutland Boughton. 1878 - 1960.
(A Song of Lyonesse, *Thomas Hardy*, Em [d'-g''](m), S&B; Dm, S&B.)

(At Grafton, *John Drinkwater*, F [c'-f''], B&H; G, B&H.)

(Evensong, *Thomas Hardy*, Dm [d'-g''], S&B.)

Faery song, *Fiona Macloed*, Eb [e'*b*-a''*b*], S&B *Recitalist 3*, S&B; (Db, S&B.)

(Foreboding, *Thomas Hardy*, [e'*b*-f''], S&B; [d'*b*-e''*b*], S&B.)

(In prison, *William Morris*, B&H.)

(Lorna's song, *R D Blackmore*, Bb, B&H.)

(The Feckenham men, *John Drinkwater*, Eb, B&H; Ab, B&H.)

York Bowen. 1884 - 1961.
Collection: *Three Royal Lyrics* (with Philip York Bowen), Weinberger.

A moonlight night, *Robert Southey*, Bb [a-e''*b*], Weinberger.)

(Cordovan love song, *George Leveson Gower*, C [d'-a''](m), Weinberger; *A*, Weinberger.)

(England's monarch, *Olive Maitland Marsh*, G [d'-e''], Weinberger *3 Royal*.)

(England's rose, *Olive Maitland Marsh*, Em [b-e''], Weinberger *3 Royal*.)

(England's ambassador, *Olive Maitland Marsh*, C [c'-f''], Weinberger *3 Royal*.)

(If you should frown, *George Leveson Gower*, Gm [f'-a''*b*], Weinberger.)

(In June, *George Leveson Gower*, F [e'-d''], Weinberger.)

(Love and death, *George Leveson Gower*, Ab [d'-f''(a''*b*)], Weinberger.)

(Love's reckoning, *George Leveson Gopwer*, F [e'-a''], Weinberger.)

(Storm song, *George Leveson Gower*, Bm [b-d''#(f'#)], Weinberger.)

(The fairies' lullaby, *Alexander Field*, Bb [d'-f''], Weinberger.)

(The wind's an old woman, *Wilfrid Thorley*, Em [b-e''], Weinberger.)

(To Myra, *James Thomson*, Eb [bb-e''*b*](m), Weinberger.)

William Boyce. 1711 - 1779.
Collections: (*Five Songs* (edited Michael Mullinar), S&B 1955; *Ten Songs* (edited Michael Pilkington), S&B 1979.

Amour sans soucis, *Colley Cibber*, A [e'-f'#](m), S&B 10 Songs.

(Balmy sweetness ever flowing, *E Moore*, F [d'-f''](m), OUP (Taylor).)

(Boast not, mistaken swain, *Anon*, G [f'#-g''](f), OUP (Taylor).)

By the banks, gentle Stour, *Anon*, Db [d'-*b*-a''*b*], OUP (Poston) *Solo Soprano*, (Bb, OUP).

(Declare my pretty maid, *Anon*, D [a-d''](m), S&B 5 Songs.)
For the Lord hath pleasure, [soprano], Schott (Bevan).
Goddess of the dimpling smile, *Anon*, Eb [d'-f''](f), S&B 10 Songs.
How unhappy's the nymph, *Anon*, Gm [f'#-f''], S&B 10 Songs.
Idleness, *Anon*, G [d'-g''], Thames (Copley & Reitan) *Gentleman's Magazine*.
(Of all the torments, *Anon*, D [c'#-d''], S&B 5 Songs.)
On a bank beside a willow, *Anon*, Cm [e'-b-g''](f), S&B 10 Songs, (Curwen (Poston)).
Orpheus and Euridice, *Anon*, Dm [d'-a''](m), S&B 10 Songs.
(Rail no more, ye learned asses, *Anon*, Am [g'-d''](m); OUP (Jacob).)
Spring Gardens, *John Lockman*, D [d'-a''], S&B 10 Songs, (S&B Mullinar); (Db OUP (Franklin)).
Tell me lovely shepherd, *Anon*, Db [d'-b-a''b], OUP (Poston); (Bb, OUP).
Tell me no more, *George Etheridge*, Bb [d'-a''b](m), S&B 10 Songs.
Tell me, ye brooks, *Anon*, Eb [d'-g''](f), S&B 10 Songs.
(The fatal blessing, *George Grenville (Lord Lansdowne)*, Cm [G-e'b](m), OUP (Taylor).)
(The happy pair, *Anon*, C [b-e''](m), S&B 5 Songs.)
The non-pareil, *Anon*, G [d'-g''](m), S&B 10 Songs.
The pleasures of Spring Gardens, *see* Spring Gardens.
The song of Momus to Mars, *John Dryden*, Eb, [bb-e''b](m), OUP (Arkwright) *Solo Baritone*.
(Tho' Chloe out of fashion, *Anon*, E [b-e''](m), S&B 5 Songs.)
(Venus to soothe my heart, *Anon*, Em [b-c''], S&B 5 Songs.)
Well judging Phyllis, *John Lockman*, Gm [d'-a''], S&B 10 Songs.
(What beauties my nymph doth disclose, *Mendez*, A [c'#-f''#](m), OUP (Taylor).)
(Whether I grow old or no, *Abraham Cowley*, Cm [F(Bb-f')(m), Elkin (Bevan).)

John Braham. 1774 - 1856.
The death of Nelson, *Anon*, Cm [f'-a''b], Cramer *Drawing Room Songs*.

Mary H Brahe (Mary Hannah Morgan). 1885 - 1956.
Bless this house, *Helen Taylor*, Eb [d'-a''b], B&H *Ballad Album 1*.

David Branson. 1909 -
Collections: (*Three Elizabethan Poems*, Elkin 1946.)
(Look not in my eyes, *A E Housman*, Ab [d'-b-f'](m), OUP.)
(Music, *Anon*, E [e'-g''#(f''#)], Elkin 3 Elizabethan.)
(Phillida, *Anon*, F [d'-f''](m), OUP.)
(The mortal glance, *Anon*, F [e'-f''], Elkin 3 Elizabethan.)
(The unseen spring, *A E Housman*, Eb [e'-b-a''b], OUP.)
(The wily lover, *Thomas Campion*, Eb [e'-b-f''](m), Elkin 3 Elizabethan.)

Thomas Brewer. 1611 - ?c1660-70.
Mistake me not, I am as cold as hot, *Anon*, Gm [d'-f'], S&B (Spink) *MB 33*.
O that mine eyes could melt into a flood, *Anon*, Cm [g'-g''], S&B (Spink) *MB 33*.

Frank Bridge. 1889 - 1941.
Collections: *Songs* (introduction by John Bishop), B&H 1971; *Four Songs by Frank Bridge* (introduction by Peter J. Pirie), S&B 1973; *Five Early Songs* (edited with introduction by Paul Hindmarsh), Thames 1981; *Six Songs*, Thames 1989.

A dead violet, *Shelley*, F#m [e'#-f''#], Thames 5 Early Songs.

A dirge, *Shelley*, Fm [c'-f''], Thames 5 Early Songs.

Adoration, *Keats*, C [c'-g''], B&H Songs.

All things that we clasp, *Heinrich Heine* tr. *Emma Lazarus*, Am [e'-g''], B&H Songs; (Fm, B&H).

Berceuse, *Dorothy Wordsworth*, Em [e'-g''#](f), Thames 6 Songs.

Blow, blow, thou winter wind, *Shakespeare*, Cm [c'-f''], B&H Songs, *Shakespeare*; (Dm, B&H).

Blow out, you bugles, *Rupert Brooke*, Bb [f'-b''b](m), B&H Songs.

Come to me in my dreams, *Matthew Arnold*, Eb [d'-f''], B&H Songs; (Db, B&H).

Dawn and evening, *Heinrich Heine* tr. *C. A.*, Gm [d'-f''#], B&H Songs; (Fm, B&H).

Day after day, *Rabindrinath Tagore*, [e'b-e''](f), S&B 4 Songs.

Dweller in my deathless dreams, *Rabindrinath Tagore*, [c'-a''], S&B 4 Songs.

E'en as a lovely flower, *Heinrich Heine* tr. *Kate Kroeker*, G [e'-g''], B&H Songs, *Imperial 4*; E, B&H, Mayhew *Collection 1*.

Fair daffodils, *Robert Herrick*, G [d'-e''], B&H Songs; (A, F, B&H).

Go not, happy day, *Alfred Lord Tennyson*, A [c'-f''#(a'')](m), B&H Songs, *Heritage 4*; (G, B&H).

Goldenhair, *James Joyce*, E [e'-g''], Thames 6 Songs; (C, Chappell *English Recital 2*.)

Into her keeping, *H D Lowry*, Eb [d'-f''#], B&H Songs; (F, Db, B&H).

Isobel, *Digby Goddard-Fenwick*, F#m [c'#-e''](m), Thames 6 Songs, (Chappell *English Recital 1*; Fm, Am, Chappell).

Journey's end, *Humbert Wolfe*, Gm [d'-e''], S&B 4 Songs.

Love went a-riding, *Mary Coleridge*, Gb [f'-g''], B&H Songs, *Heritage 3*, Banks, B&H; (E, B&H *Love and Affection*, B&H).

Mantle of blue, *Padraic Colum*, Dm [d'-f''], B&H Songs; (C, B&H).

My pent-up tears, *Matthew Arnold*, Ebm [d'-e''], Thames 5 Early Songs.

Night lies on the silent highways, *Heinrich Heine* tr. *Kate Kroeker*, Bm [b-e''b], Thames 5 Early Songs.

O that it were so, *W S Landor*, C [c'-f''(a')], Thames 6 Songs; (Bb, D, Chappell)

So early in the morning, *James Stephens*, E [e'-a''], B&H Songs.

So perverse, *Robert Bridges*, F [f'-e''(f')](m), B&H Songs, *Heritage 4*.

Speak to me, my love, *Rabindrinath Tagore*, [d''-g''](f), S&B 4 Songs.

Strew no more red roses, *Matthew Arnold*, Em [e'-f''#](m), B&H Songs; (C#m, B&H).

Tears, idle tears, *Alfred Lord Tennyson*, Am [c'-e''], Thames 5 Early Songs.

The Devon maid, *John Keats*, G [d'-e''](m), B&H Songs.

The last invocation, *Walt Whitman*, D [e'-f''#], B&H Songs; (E, C, B&H).

The violets blue, *Heine*, trans. *James Thompson*, F#m [e'#-g''], B&H Songs (Em, B&H).

Thy hand in mine, *Mary Coleridge*, G [f'#-g''#], B&H Songs; (Eb, B&H)

Tis but a week, *Gerald Gould*, Bm [f'#-f''#], B&H Songs; (C#m, Am, B&H).

What should I your true love tell, *Francis Thompson*, E [f'#-f''#], B&H Songs; (D, B&H).

When you are old and grey, *W B Yeats*, E [d'-g''], Thames 6 Songs, (Chappell *English Recital 1*).

Where she lies asleep, *Mary Coleridge*, D [d'-e''], B&H Songs.

Arrangement:

Easter hymn, *17th century German*, tr. *Wagemann*, Eb [e'b-e''b], Thames 6 Songs.

Benjamin Britten. 1913 - 1976. Collections: *On This Island*, B&H 1938; *The Holy Sonnets of John Donne*, B&H 1946; *A Charm of Lullabies*, B&H 1949; *Winter Words*, B&H 1954 (reissued 1994 with 2 extra songs); *Six Hölderlin Fragments*, B&H 1963; *The Poet's Echo*, Faber 1967; *Tit for Tat*, Faber 1969;

Who are these Children? Faber 1972; *Four Burns Songs* (piano version by Colin Matthews of songs from *A Birthday Hansel*), Faber 1978; *Cabaret Songs*, Faber 1980; *Beware*, Faber 1985; *Evening, Morning, Night*, B&H 1988; *The Red Cockatoo and Other Songs* (high & low keys), Faber 1995.

A charm, *Thomas Randolph*, Dm [a#-e''](f), B&H Charm of Lullabies, *Heritage 3*.
A laddie's sang, *William Soutar*, D [d'-g''](m), Faber Who are these Children?
A poison tree, *William Blake*, Dm [c'#-f'#], Faber Cockatoo; Cm, Cockatoo.
A riddle (the earth), *William Soutar*, G [c'-f'#](m), Faber Who are these Children?
A song of enchantment, *Walter de la Mare*, Ab [c'-f''], Faber Tit for Tat.
Afton Water, *Robert Burns*, E [b-g''#], Faber 4 Burns.
Angel, *Alexander Pushkin* tr. *Peter Pears*, [c'-g''], Faber Poet's Echo.
As it is, plenty, *W H Auden*, D [d'-g''], B&H On This Island.
At day-close in November, *Thomas Hardy*, Dm [d'-a''b], B&H Winter Words.
At the railway station, Upway, *Thomas Hardy*, [e'-g''], B&H Winter Words.
At the round earth's imagined corners, *John Donne*, D [d'-a''], B&H Holy Sonnets.
Autumn, *Walter de la Mare*, Fm [e'b-e''b], Faber Tit for Tat.
Batter my heart, *John Donne*, Cm [c'#-a''], B&H Holy Sonnets.
Bedtime, *William Soutar*, [d'b-g''b](m), Faber Who are these Children?
Before life and after, *Thomas Hardy*, D [d'-g''], B&H Winter Words.
Beware, *Henry Wadsworth Longfellow*, Fm [e'b-e''b], Faber Beware.
Black day, *William Soutar*, Am [d'#-g''](m), Faber Who are these Children?
Calypso, *W H Auden*, G [bb-b''], Faber Cabaret Songs.
Corpus Christi Carol, *Anon.*, [c'-d''], OUP *Solo Baritone; [f'-g'']*, OUP).
Cradle song, *William Blake*, Eb [bb-e''](f), B&H Charm of Lullabies.
Cradle Song, *Louis MacNeice*, Bbm [bb-a''(f'#)], Faber Cockatoo; Am, Cockatoo.
Death, be not proud, *John Donne*, B [d'#-g''], B&H Holy Sonnets.
Echo, *Alexander Pushkin* tr. *Peter Pears*, [c'-a''b], Faber Poet's Echo.
Epigram, *Alexander Pushkin* tr. *Peter Pears*, [e'-g''], Faber Poet's Echo.
Epitaph: the clerk, *Herbert Asquith*, F [c'-f''], Faber Beware.
Evening, *Ronald Duncan*, B [f'#-e''b], B&H Evening, Morning, Night.
Fish in the unruffled lakes, *W H Auden*, F# [c'#-a''#], B&H *Heritage 3*, B&H.
Funeral blues, *W H Auden*, Fm [c'-a''b], Faber Cabaret Songs.
If it's ever spring again, *Thomas Hardy*, [e'-a''b], B&H Winter Words 1994.
If thou wilt ease thy heart, *Thomas Lovell Beddoes*, D [d'-a''], Faber Cockatoo; Bb, Cockatoo.
Home, *Friedrich Hölderlin* tr. *Mayer & Pears*, A [e'b-g''], B&H 6 Hölderlin.
Johnny, *W H Auden*, F [f-c'''], Faber Cabaret Songs.
Let the florid music praise, *W H Auden*, D [c'#-a''], B&H On This Island.
Lines of life, *Friedrich Hölderlin* tr. *Mayer & Pears*, Ebm [e'b-g''b], B&H 6 Hölderlin.
Lines written during a sleepless night, *Alexander Pushkin* tr. *Pears*, [c'-a''b], Faber Poet's Echo.
Midnight on the Great Western, *Thomas Hardy*, Cm [c'-g''], B&H Winter Words.
Morning, *Ronald Duncan*, G [e'-d''], B&H Evening, Morning, Night.
My heart... *Alexander Pushkin* tr. *Pears*, [d'b-f'#], Faber Poet's Echo.
My hoggie, *Robert Burns*, Cm [c'-a''b], Faber 4 Burns.
Night, *Ronald Duncan*, Bm [c'-f''], B&H Evening, Morning, Night.
Nightmare, *William Soutar*, Dm [c'-a''b](m), Faber Who are these Children?
Nocturne, *W H Auden*, C#m [c'#-g''#], B&H On This Island, *Heritage 4*, B&H.
Not even summer yet, *Peter Burra*, D [c'#-f'#], Faber Cockatoo; C, Cockatoo.

Now the leaves are falling fast, *Auden*, Fm [a*b*(c')-b"*b*(a"*b*], B&H On This Island.
O might those sighs and tears, *John Donne*, Em [g'-a''], B&H Holy Sonnets.
O that I had ne'er been married, *Robert Burns*, G [d'-g''](m), Faber Beware.
Oh my blacke soule, *John Donne*, Bm [c'g''], B&H Holy Sonnets.
Oh to vex me, *John Donne*, F#m [c'-g''], B&H Holy Sonnets.
Proud songsters, *Thomas Hardy*, Eb [f'-g''], B&H Winter Words.
Riddle (the child you were), *William Soutar*, [d'-f''](m), Faber Who are these Children?
Seascape, *W H Auden*, C [c'-a''*b*], B&H On This Island.
Sephestia's lullaby, *R Greene*, Em [a-e''](f), B&H Charm of Lullabies, *Heritage 4*.
Silver, *Walter de la Mare*, [b-f''], Faber Tit for Tat.
Since she whom I loved, *John Donne*, Eb [e'-a''*b*], B&H Holy Sonnets, *Heritage 4*.
Slaughter, *William Soutar*, Cm [c'-a''*b*](m), Faber Who are these Children?
Socrates and Alcibiades, *Friedrich Hölderlin* tr. *Mayer & Pears*, D [c'#-a''*b*], B&H 6 Hölderlin.
Songs and Proverbs of William Blake (cycle), *William Blake*, [g#-g''*b*], Faber.
Supper, *William Soutar*, B [d'#-e''*b*](m), Faber Who are these Children?
Tell me the truth about love, *W H Auden*, D [a-a''], Faber Cabaret Songs.
The applause of men, *Friedrich Hölderlin* tr. *Mayer & Pears*, F [e'*b*-g''], B&H 6 Hölderlin.
The auld aik, *William Soutar*, Eb [e'*b*-g''*b*](m), Faber Who are these Children?
The birds, *Hilaire Belloc*, E [b-f''], B&H.
The children, *William Soutar*, [b-a''*b*](m), Faber Who are these Children?
The children and Sir Nameless, *Thomas Hardy*, C [d'-g''], B&H Winter Words 1994.
The choirmaster's burial, *Thomas Hardy*, Bb [g'-g''], B&H Winter Words, *Heritage 4*.
The highland balou, *Robert Burns*, B [b#-e''#](f), B&H Charm of Lullabies.
The larky lad, *William Soutar*, Dm [d'-g''*b*](m), Faber Who are these Children?
The little old table, *Thomas Hardy*, Em [e'-g''], B&H Winter Words.
The middle of life, *Friedrich Hölderlin* tr. *Mayer & Pears*, Bb [e'-a''*b*], B&H 6 Hölderlin.
The nightingale and the rose, *Alexander Pushkin* tr. *Pears*, [d'#-a''], Faber Poet's Echo.
The nurse's song, *John Philip*, Bb [a-e''](f), B&H Charm of Lullabies.
The red cockatoo, *Po Chü-i* tr. *Waley*, [c'#-g''#], Faber Cockatoo; [a'#-e''#], Cockatoo.
The ship of Rio, *Walter de la Mare*, [e'*b*-e''*b*], OUP.
The winter, *Robert Burns*, [b#-g''#], Faber 4 Burns.
Thou hast made me, *John Donne*, Bbm [e'*b*-a''*b*], B&H Holy Sonnets.
Tit for tat, *Walter de la Mare*, Am [b-e''], Faber Tit for Tat.
Youth, *Friedrich Hölderlin* tr. *Mayer & Pears*, G [c'#-a''], B&H 6 Hölderlin.
Vigil, *Walter de la Mare*, Dm [c'-e''], Faber Tit for Tat.
Wagtail and baby, *Thomas Hardy*, Am [e'-a''], B&H Winter Words, *Heritage 3*.
Wee Willie, *Robert Burns*, G, [c'#-g''], Faber 4 Burns.
What if this present, *John Donne*, Gm [d'-b''*b*], B&H Holy Sonnets.
When you're feeling like expressing your affection, *W H Auden*, F [c'-f''], Faber Cockatoo; E, Cockatoo.
Who are these children? *W Soutar*, Em [d'-g''](m), Faber Who are these Children?
Wild with passion, *Thomas Lovell Beddoes*, [d'*b*-a''*b*], Faber Cockatoo; [b*b*-f''], Cockatoo.
Arrangements: Folksong Arrangements: *Volume 1* (high & medium keys), B&H 1943; *Volume 3*, (high & medium keys), B&H 1947; *Volume 4, Moore's Irish Melodies*, B&H 1960; *Volume 5*, B&H 1961; *8 Folk Song Arrangements* (piano version of harp accompaniment by Colin Matthews), Faber 1980.

At the mid hour of night, *Thomas Moore*, E*b* [e'*b*-g''], B&H Folksong 4.
Avenging and bright, *Thomas Moore*, Bm [d'-f'#], B&H Folksong 4.
Bird scarer's song, *Anon*, G [d'-e''], Faber 8 Folksong.
Bonny at morn, *Anon*, Em [d'-e''], Faber 8 Folksong.
Ca' the yowes, *Robert Burns*, Bm [d'-f'#], B&H Folksong 5.
Come you not from Newcastle? *Anon*, F [d'-g''](f), B&H Folksong 3; D Folksong 3.
David of the White Rock, *Anon*, Fm [c'-a''*b*], Faber 8 Folksong.
Dear harp of my country, *Thomas Moore*, F [c'-g''], B&H Folksong 4.
Early one morning, *Anon*, G*b* [d'*b*-g''*b*], B&H Folksong 5.
How sweet the answer, *Thomas Moore*, B [f'#-f'#], B&H Folksong 4.
I was lonely and forlorn, *Anon*, E*b* [d'-f''](m), Faber 8 Folksong.
Lemady, *Anon*, B [b-f'#](m), Faber 8 Folk Song.
Little Sir William, *Anon*, F [f'-f''], B&H Folksong 1; D, Folksong 1.
Lord! I married me a wife, *Anon*, Em [e'-e''](m), Faber 8 Folksong.
O can ye sew cushions? *Anon*, A*b* [e'*b*-a''*b*], B&H Folksong 1; E*b*, Folksong 1, *Imperial 3*.
O the sight entrancing, *Thomas Moore*, C [b-g''], B&H Folksong 4.
O waly, waly, *Anon*, A [e'-e''](f), B&H Folksong 3; G, Folksong 3.
Oft in the stilly night, *Thomas Moore*, A*b* [e'*b*-a''*b*], B&H Folksong 4.
Oliver Cromwell, *Anon*, E*b* [e'*b*-e''*b*], B&H Folksong 1; C, Folksong 1.
Rich and rare, *Thomas Moore*, D [d'-f'#], B&H Folksong 4.
Sail on, sail on, *Thomas Moore*, F [f'-f''], B&H Folksong 4.
Salley in our alley, *Henry Carey*, D [d'-g''](m), B&H Folksong 5.
She's like the swallow, *Anon*, Dm [d'-f''](m), Faber 8 Folksong.
Sweet Polly Oliver, *Anon*, E [c'#-f'#], B&H Folksong 3; D, Folksong 3.
The ash grove, *Anon*, A*b* [d'*b*-f''], B&H Folksong 1; F, B&H Folksong 1.
The bonnie Earl o' Moray, *Anon*, E*b* [g'-g''], B&H Folksong 1; C, Folksong 1.
The brisk young widow, *Anon*, D [d'-f'#], B&H Folksong 5.
The false knight upon the road, *Anon*, E [b-e''], Faber 8 Folksong.
The foggy, foggy dew, *Anon*, A*b* [e'*b*-e''*b*](m), B&H Folksong 3; G, Folksong 3.
The last rose of summer, *Thomas Moore*, E*b* [e'*b*-a''*b*], B&H Folksong 4.
The Lincolnshire poacher, *Anon*, C [e'-g''](m), B&H Folksong 5.
The miller of Dee, *Anon*, Am [e'-e''], B&H Folksong 3; G, Folksong 3.
The minstrel boy, *Thomas Moore*, F# [c'#-f'#], B&H Folksong 4.
The plough boy, *Anon*, B*b* [g'-f''], B&H Folksong 3, B&H; G, Folksong 3.
The salley gardens, *W B Yeats*, G*b* [g'*b*-a''*b*], B&H Folksong 1; D*b*, Folksong 1.
The trees they grow so high, *Anon*, Am [c'-e''](f), B&H Folksong 1; Gm, Folksong 1.
There's none to soothe, *Anon*, D*b* [d*b*-f''], B&H Folksong 3; B*b*, Folksong 3.

Christopher Brown. (BMIC.) 1943 -

James Brown. 1923 -

Silent spring, *V C Staples*, [e'-f''], Banks.
The lass for a sailor, *Thomas Dibdin*, D [d'-e''](m), Banks.

Thomas Brown.

Shepherd! thy demeanour vary, *Anon*, F [e'-e''](f), B&H (Lane Wilson) *Old English*.

W Denis Browne. 1888 - 1915.

Collections: (*Two Songs*, S&B 1909); *Six Songs*, Thames 1989.

Arabia, *Walter de la Mare*, Gm [f′b-a″b], Thames 6 Songs.

Diaphenia, *Constable* or *Chettle*, Bb, [f′-f″](m), Thames 6 Songs; (Ab, B&H).

Dream-tryst, *Francis Thompson*, Bm [d′-e″](m), Thames 6 Songs.

Epitaph on Salathiel Pavey, *Ben Jonson*, Em [d′-g″], Thames *Century 3*; *F#* Thames 6 Songs, B&H Heritage 1.

(Move eastward, happy earth, *Alfred Lord Tennyson*, D [c′#-g″], S&B 2 Songs.)

The isle of lost dreams, *William Sharp (Fiona Macleod)*, Gb [f′-f″], Thames 6 Songs.

(The snowdrop, *Alfred Lord Tennyson*, Am [e′-g″], S&B 2 Songs.)

To Gratiana dancing and singing, *Richard Lovelace*, G [d′-g″], Thames 6 Songs; (F, B&H).

M Campbell Bruce. 1914 -

Migratory birds at Sennen, *Michael Gardiner*, [c′-f″], Banks.

(The rain, *W H Davies*, C [c′-e″], Curwen.)

(The snow, *Walter de la Mare*, Am [d′-f″(e″)], Curwen.)

Robert Bryan. 1858 - 1920.

A song of Cambria, [baritone], Snell.

Abide with me, *Henry Francis Lyte*, [contralto/baritone], Snell.

Adieu, [tenor], Snell.

Annabel Lee, *Edgar Allan Poe*, [contralto], Snell.

Ave Maria, [soprano/tenor], Snell.

Beloved maid, [tenor], Snell.

Come, my love, [tenor], Snell.

My dear, [tenor], Snell.

How sweet the moonlight sleeps, *Shakespeare*, [tenor], Snell.

I will come to thee, [tenor], Snell.

O love that wilt not let me go, *G Matheson*, [contralto/baritone], Snell.

Parting, [soprano/tenor], Snell.

Somebody, [tenor], Snell.

Song of the cradle, [mezzo/contralto], Snell.

Sweet and low, *Alfred Lord Tennyson*, [contralto/baritone], Snell.

Alan Bullard. 1947 - (BMIC.)

Geoffrey Burgon. 1941 -

(Hymn to Venus, *Edith Sitwell*, [a#-g″](f), Chester.)

Benjamin Burrows. 1891 - 1966. (See also BMIC.)

Collection: *Six Songs*, Thames 1978.

(How long and dreary, *Robert Burns*, Cramer.)

Lake isle of Innisfree, *W B Yeats*, [c′-g″#], Thames 6 Songs.

Love was true to me, *J Boyle O'Reilly* , [c′#-g″], Thames 6 Songs.

Queen Djenira, *Walter de la Mare*, [e′-a″], Thames 6 Songs.

Robin Goodfellow, *Anon*, Am [e′-a″], Thames 6 Songs.

The bride cometh, *Confucius* tr. *Anon*, Gb [d′b-a″b], Thames 6 Songs.

The kiss, *Charles D'Orleans*, [d'-g''], Thames 6 Songs.
(The dusty miller, *Robert Burns*, Cramer.)

Mervyn Burtch. (See also BMIC.)
Long barren, *Christina Rossetti* [c'-f''], Welsh Music.
Ozymandias, *P B Shelley*, [A-c'#](m), Welsh Music *Songs from Wales 2*.
When Satan fell, *D H Lawrence*, [c'-e''], Welsh Music.

William Busch. 1901 - 1945.
Collection: (*Two Songs of William Blake*, OUP 1944; *Two Songs*, Chester 1944.)
(Come, O come, my life's delight, *Thomas Campion*, E [d'#-g''#], OUP.)
(If thou wilt ease thy heart, *Thomas Lovell Beddoes*, G#m [d'#-e''], OUP.)
(Laughing song, *William Blake*, F#m [f#(a)-e''], Chester 2 Songs.)
(Memory, hither come, *William Blake*, [g#-b'], Chester 2 Songs.)
(Rest, *A E (George W Russell)*, Ab [c'b-e''b], OUP.)
(The centaurs, *James Stephens*, Dm [c'-f''], Chester.)
(The echoing green, *William Blake*, E [d'-g''#], OUP 2 Songs.)
(The shepherd, *William Blake*, G#m [b(e')-g''#], OUP 2 Songs.)

Alan Bush. 1900 - 1996. (BMIC.)

Geoffrey Bush. 1920 -
Collections: *Three Elizabethan Songs*, Novello 1948; *Four Songs from 'Hesperides'*, Novello 1951; *Three Songs of Ben Jonson*, Novello 1959; *Songs of Wonder*, Novello 1962; *Seven Greek Love Songs*, S&B 1969; *Five Mediaeval Lyrics*, Novello 1971; *Eight Songs for High Voice*, Novello 1979; *Eight Songs for Medium Voice*, Novello 1981; *Eight Songs for Medium Voice*, S&B 1984; *Two Stevie Smith Songs*, Novello 1990; *Old Rhymes Reset*, S&B 1990; *Yesterday*, Thames 1993.
A curse, *Melager* tr. *Fitts*, [Bb-f'](m), S&B Greek Love Songs.
A rebuke, *Ben Jonson*, [c-a''](m), Novello 3 Songs.
A song of praise, *George Herbert*, C [c'-g''], S&B 8 Songs.
An encounter, *Traditional*, [d'-a''], S&B Old Rhymes Reset.
Aubade, *Anon*, [c'#-a''], S&B Old Rhymes Reset.
Avondale, *Stevie Smith*, [c'#-a''], Novello 2 Stevie Smith.
By the Tamar, *Charles Causley*, [d'-g''], Thames Yesterday.
archy at the zoo (cycle), *don marquis*, [d'-a''], Thames.
Carol, *Anon*, [A-f'](m), Novello 5 Mediaeval; [a-f''] 8 Medium.
Colloquy, *Anon*, [A#-f'](m), Novello 5 Mediaeval.
Confession, *Anon*, [G#-e''](m), Novello 5 Mediaeval.
Cuisine Provençale, *Virginia Woolf* adapted *Geoffrey Bush*, [c'-g''(a')], S&B 8 Songs.
Daniel Brent, *Charles Causley*, C [c'-g''], Thames Yesterday.
(Diaphenia, *Constable* or *Chettle*, [e'b-g''](m), Novello.)
Echo's lament for Narcissus, *Ben Jonson*, Dm [e'-f''], Novello 8 High, Novello 3 Songs.
(Fain would I change that note, *Anon*, G [f'-a''], Elkin.)
Fanfare, *Melager* tr. *Fitts*, [f-f'](m), S&B Greek Love Songs.
Far-darting Apollo, *Kathleen Raine*, [c'-g''], S&B 8 Songs.
Fire, fire, *Thomas Campion*, G [d'-g''], Novello 3 Elizabethan.
Flowers, *Melager* tr. *Fitts*, [B-f'](m), S&B Greek Love Songs.

Here comes a lusty wooer, *Anon*, Bm [b(c')-a''], Novello Wonder.

Introspection, *Kathleen Raine*, [b♭-g''], S&B 8 Songs.

It was a lover and his lass, *Shakespeare*, D [c'-d''], Novello 8 Medium.

Lady Jane Grey, *Charles Causley*, Am [d'-a''], Thames Yesterday.

Lament, *Kathleen Raine*, [c'-g''], S&B 8 Songs.

Lay a garland on my hearse, *John Fletcher*, Am [e'-g''(a'')], Novello.

Love for such a cherry lip, *Thomas Middleton*, F, [c'#-f''#](m), S&B 8 Songs, *Recitalist 1*.

Lullaby, *Melager* tr. *Fitts*, [e♭-e''](m), S&B Greek Love Songs.

Merciless beauty, *Geoffrey Chaucer*, [c'#-f''](m), Novello.

Mirabile Misterium (cycle), *various*, [c'-a''] Novello.

Mistletoe, *Charles Causley*, Em [c'-g''], Thames Yesterday.

Morwenstow: a dialogue, *Charles Causley*, C [c'-a''♭], Thames Yesterday.

My cats, *Stevie Smith*, Am [e'-a''], Novello 2 Stevie Smith.

My true love hath my heart *Philip Sidney*, [f'-g''](f), Novello 8 High.

Night, *Melager* tr. *Fitts*, [c#-f'](m), S&B Greek Love Songs.

Nonsense song, *Geoffrey Bush*, [c'-g''], S&B Old Rhymes Reset.

Now the lusty spring is seen, *John Fletcher*, Am [d'-a''], Novello 8 High.

O, the month of May, *Thomas Dekker*, F [c'-f''](m), Novello 8 Medium.

Old Abram Brown, *Anon*, [e'-a''♭], Novello Wonder.

Polly Lillicote, *Anon*, [c'-a''], Novello Wonder.

Rutterkin, *Anon*, [G-f''](m), Novello 5 Mediaeval; [g-f''], Novello 8 Medium.

She hath an eye, *Anon*, F [c'-e''♭(f')](m), Novello 8 Medium.

Sigh no more, ladies, *Shakespeare*, F [f'-a''], Novello 8 High, 3 Elizabethan.

Sleigh ride, *Charles Causley*, Am [e'-a''], Thames Yesterday.

Songs of the Zodiac (cycle), *David Gascoigne*, [b-a''], Novello.

Smuggler's song, *Charles Causley*, Cm [c'-a''♭], Thames Yesterday.

Sweet, stay awhile, *John Donne*, Am [e'-g''], Novello 3 Elizabethan.

The end of love, *Kathleen Raine*, [c'-f''], S&B 8 Songs, *Recitalist 2*.

The impatient lover, *Robert Herrick*, [d'-e''](m), Novello 8 Medium.

The kiss, *Ben Jonson*, [c'-g''], Novello 3 Songs.

The little nut tree, *Traditional*, [e'-g''], Novello 8 Songs high, Wonder.

The mosquito, *Melager* tr. *Fitts*, [A-g'](m), S&B Greek Love Songs.

The poet's epitaph, *Melager* tr. *Fitts*, [B-f'](m), S&B Greek Love Songs.

The test, *Traditional*, B♭ [c'-g''], S&B Old Rhymes Reset, *Recitalist 3*.

The wonder of wonders, *Traditional*, [c'(b)-g''], Novello 8 Songs high, Wonder.

The vanity of human wishes, *Anon*, [D-f''](m), Novello 5 Mediaeval.

There is a garden in her face, *Thomas Campion*, Gm [c'-f''], S&B 8 Songs; (Am, Elkin).

To Electra, *Robert Herrick*, [d'b-g''♭](m), Novello 8 Medium.

Transience, *Charles Causley*, Dm [d'-g''], Thames Yesterday.

Venus and Adonis, *Robert Greene*, [c'-f''], Novello.

Weep you no more sad fountains, *Anon*, [f'-g''#(a''#)], Novello 8 High.

What thing is love, *George Peel*, [d'-a''], Novello.

When daffodils begin to peer, *Shakespeare*, A [f'-a''](m), Novello 8 High.

When May is in his prime, *Richard Edwardes*, D [b-f''], Novello 8 Medium.

Wishes, *Charles Causley*, C [c'-b''♭(a''♭)], Thames Yesterday.

James Butt. 1929 - (see also BMIC.)
(Ariel's song, Cramer.)
Virtue, *George Herbert*, Em [c'#-f''#], Thames *Century 4*.

George Butterworth. 1885 - 1916.
Collections: *A Shropshire Lad and other songs* (introduction by Peter J Pirie), S&B 1974; *Folk Songs from Sussex and other songs* (introduction by Peter J Pirie), S&B 1974; *Love blows as the wind blows* (introduction by John Bishop),Thames 1982).
Bredon Hill, *A E Housman*, F [c'-g''](m), S&B Shropshire Lad; (*G*, S&B).
Fill a glass with golden wine, *W E Henley*, [c'#-d''#], Thames Love Blows.
I fear thy kisses, *Shelley*, Fm [bb-e''](m), S&B Folk Songs.
I will make you brooches, *R L Stevenson*, D [c'-f'](m), S&B Folk Songs.
In the year that's come and gone, *W E Henley*, [c'-e''*b*], Thames Love Blows.
Is my team ploughing? *A E Housman*, Bb [e'*b*-e''b](m), S&B Shropshire Lad; (*Db* S&B).
Life in her creaking shoes, *W E Henley*, [c'-f''], Thames Love Blows.
Look not in my eyes, *A E Housman*, F [c'-f''](m), S&B Shropshire Lad.
Loveliest of trees, *A E Housman*, E [c'#-e''](m), S&B Shropshire Lad, Mayhew *Collection 1*.
O fair enough are sky and plain, *A E Housman*, Gm [a-e''](m), S&B Shropshire Lad.
On the idle hill of summer, *A E Housman*, A [c'#-f''](m), S&B Shropshire Lad.
On the way to Kew, *W E Henley* [c'#-f''], Thames Love Blows.
Requiescat, *Oscar Wilde*, Fm [c'-f''], S&B Folk Songs.
The lads in their hundreds, *A E Housman*, F# [c'#-e''](m), *G*, Mayhew *Collection 1*.
Think no more, lad, *A E Housman*, G#m [c'#-f''](m), S&B Shropshire Lad.
When I was one-and-twenty, *A E Housman*, [d'-e''](m), S&B Shropshire Lad, Mayhew *Collection 2*.
When the lad for longing sighs, *A E Housman*, Em [d'-e''], S&B Shropshire Lad.
With rue my heart is laden, *A E Housman*, F#m [c'#-e''], S&B Shropshire Lad.
Arrangements:
A blacksmith courted me, *Anon*, C#m [e'-f''#](f), S&B Folk Songs, Mayhew *Collection 2*.
A brisk young sailor courted me, *Anon*, E [e'-e''](f), S&B Folk Songs, Mayhew*Collection 1*.
A lawyer he went out, *Anon*, Am [c'-e''], S&B Folk Songs.
Come my own one, *Anon*, Ab [c'-f''], S&B Folk Songs.
Roving in the dew, *Anon*, Eb [e'*b*-e''*b*](m), S&B Folk Songs, Mayhew *Collection 2*.
Seventeen come Sunday, *Anon*, D [d'-e''](m), S&B Folk Songs.
Sowing the seeds of love, *Anon*, F [c'-d''](f), S&B Folk Songs.
Tarry trousers, *Anon*, Gm [d'-e''], S&B Folk Songs.
The cuckoo, *Anon*, [d'-d''], S&B Folk Songs.
The true lover's farewell, *Anon*, Gm [d'-e''*b*](m), S&B Folk Songs.
Yonder stands a lovely creature, *Anon*, A [c'#-e''](m), S&B Folk Songs.

William Byrd. 1543 - 1623.
Cradle song, *Anon*, C [b'-b''*b*]; *D* Thames (Hodgson) *Countertenors 1*; *G*, OUP (Willcocks) *Solo Christmas*; *Eb*, *Solo Christmas*; *F*, (Fellowes) S&B.

C

John Camidge. 1790 - 1859.
Put thou thy trust in the Lord, *Psalm 37 vv. 3-8*, F [e'-a''(f'#)], B&H (Patrick) *Sacred Songs 1.*

Thomas Campion. 1567 - 1620. All Campion's songs are obtainable in original keys from S&B.
Collections: *Songs from Rosseter's Book of Ayres* (edited David Scott), S&B 1969 [Rosseter]; *The First Book of Ayres* (edited David Scott), S&B 1979 [1st Book]; *The Second Book of Ayres* (edited David Scott), S&B 1979 [2nd Book]; *The Third Book of Ayres* (edited Thurston Dart), S&B 1969 [3rd Book]; *(The Fourth Book of Ayres* (edited E H Fellowes), S&B 1926 [4th Book]). Note that in the following: Pilking-ton = *English Lute Songs Book 1*, S&B; Keel 1/2 = *Elizabethan Lovesongs Books 1 and 2* (high & low keys), B&H. Only songs available in anthologies are listed individually here.
   A secret love or two, *Campion*, Gm [d'-e''♭](f), 2nd Book, Pilkington.
   Author of light, *Campion*, Gm [d'-e''♭], 1st Book, Pilkington.
   Beauty is but a painted hell, *Campion*, A [g'-f'#], (4th Book), Keel 2; F, Keel 2.
   Beauty since you so much desire, *Campion*, G [d'-e''](m), (4th Book), Pilkington.
   Break now, my heart, *Campion*, Gm [c'-e''♭](m), 3rd Book, Keel 2; Bm, Keel 2.
   Come you pretty false-eyed wanton, *Campion*, Gm [e'-e''], 2nd Book, Pilkington, Keel 2; Fm, Keel 2.
   Every dame affects good fame, *Campion*, F [e'-g''], (4th Book), Keel 2; D, Keel 2.
   Follow thy fair sun, *Campion*, Gm [d'-d''], Rosseter; F#m, Pilkington.
   Follow your saint, *Campion*, Gm [f'-f''], Rosseter, Pilkington.
   Her rosy cheeks, *Campion*, G [d'-e''](m), 2nd Book, A, Keel 2; F, Keel 2 .
   I must complain, *Campion*, Gm [g'-f''](m), (4th Book), Pilkington.
   If Love loves truth, *Campion*, G [d'-d''](m), 3rd Book, Pilkington.
   If thou long'st so much to learn, *Campion*, Cm [c'-e''♭](f), 3rd Book, Pilkington.
   It fell on a summer's day, *Campion*, G [f'#-e''], Rosseter, Pilkington, *Recital 4.*
   Love me or not, *Campion*, Gm [g'-f''](m), (4th Book), Pilkington.
   Move now with measured sound, *Campion*, G [d'-e''], S&B (Greer) *Printed.*
   My sweetest Lesbia, *Campion*, g [d'-e''](m), Rosseter, Pilkington.
   Never love unless you can, *Campion*, B♭ [f'-f''], 3rd Book, Pilkington.
   Now hath Flora robb'd her bowers, *Campion*, G [d'-e''], S&B (Greer) *Printed.*
   O dear, that I with thee might live, *Campion*, Gm [d'-d''], 2nd Book, Keel 2, Bm, Keel 2.
   O what unhoped for sweet supply, *Campion*, Fm [f'-f''], 2nd Book, Pilkington.
   Oft have I sighed, *Campion*, Dm [d'-d''](f), 3rd Book, Pilkington, Keel 2, B&H (Northcote) *Imperial 3;* Fm, Keel 2.
   So sweet is thy discourse, *Campion*, Gm [f'#-g''], (4th Book), B&H (Northcote) *Imperial 1.*
   The cypress curtain of the night, *Campion*, Gm [g'-f''], Rosseter, Pilkington.
   The peaceful western wind, *Campion*, G [d'-e''], 2nd Book, Pilkington, Keel 2; B♭, Keel 2.
   There is a garden in her face, *Campion*, G [d'-e''], (4th Book), Pilkington; A♭, Paterson (Diack) *100 Best 2.*
   Thrice toss these oaken ashes, *Campion*, Gm [d'-f''](m), 3rd Book; Am, Keel 2; Fm, Keel 2.
   Vain men whose follies, *Campion*, F [f'-f''](m), 2nd Book, Pilkington.

Veil, love, my eyes, *Campion*, Gm [f'#-e''*b*](m), (4th Book), Pilkington.
When to her lute Corinna sings, *Campion*, Gm [d'-f''], Rosseter; *Em*, Pilkington.
Where she her sacred bow'r adorns, *Campion*, G [d'-d''](m), 2nd Book, Keel 1; *Bb*, Keel 1.
Woo her and win her, *Campion*, Gm [d'-e''], S&B (Greer) *Printed*.
Your fair looks, *Campion*, Gm [d'-d''](m), (4th Book), Pilkington.

J M Capel.
Love, could I only tell thee, *Clifton Bingham*, F [d'(c')-g''(a'')], Cramer *Drawing Room*.

Cornelius Cardew. 1936 - 1981. (BMIC.)

Clive Carey. 1883 - 1968.
Collection: (*Three Songs of Faery* (words Algernon Blackwood), B&H 1926.)
   (I have loved flowers that fade, *Robert Bridges*, Cm, B&H.)
   (In the highlands, *R L Stevenson*, D [c'#-d''], OUP.)
   Love on my heart from heaven fell, *Robert Bridges*, Eb [d'-a''*b*], B&H *Heritage 2*.
   Melmillo, *Walter de la Mare*, B [d'#-f''#], B&H *Imperial 2*.
   (Since thou, O fondest and truest, *Robert Bridges*, B, B&H.)
   (Song of the sirens, *W Browne*, Bb, B&H.)
   (The spring, *William Barnes*, Eb [c'-e''], OUP.)
   (Thrice happy she, *Edmund Spenser*, B&H.)
   (To a poet a thousand years hence, *James Elroy Flecker*, D [b-f''#], OUP.)
   (To violets, *Robert Herrick*, Bb, B&H.)
   (When June is come, B&H.)
   (While the sun was going down, *Christina Rossetti*, B&H.)

Henry Carey. 1690 - 1743.
A pastoral (Flocks are sporting), *Anon*, F [c'-a''], B&H (Lane Wilson) *Old English*; G, Paterson
   (Diack) *100 Best 1*.
The friendly advisor, *Anon*, Cm [g'-a''*b*], Roberton (Cockshott).

Lewis Carey (Lucy Johnstone). ? - 1925.
Nearer, my God, to Thee, *Sarah Flower Adams*, G [d'-e''(g'')], B&H *Ballad Album 2*.

Andrew Carter. 1939 -
Pancake Tuesday, *Eleanore Farjeon*, [medium], Banks.

John Carol Case. 1923 -
Arrangements:
   King Herod and the cock, *Traditional*, Bbm [f'-f''], OUP *Solo Christmas*; Gm, *Solo Christmas*.
   Rocking, *Czech traditional*, tr. *Percy Dearmer*, Ab [e'*b*-f''] , OUP *Solo Christmas*, F, *Solo Christmas*.
   The two shepherd boys, *German folk-song*, tr. *John Carol Case*, A [e'-f''#], OUP *Solo Christmas*; F,
   OUP *Solo Christmas*.

John Casken. 1949 -
Ia Orana, Gauguin, *John Casken*, [b-b''*b*](f), Schott.

Michael Cavendish. *c.*1565 - 1628.
Collection: *Fourteen Ayres* (edited E H Fellowes), S&B 1926.) Only songs available in anthologies are listed individually here.
  Love is not blind, *Anon*, G [f'#-e''], S&B (Pilkington) *Lute Songs 1.*
  Stay, Glycia, stay, *Anon*, G [g'-e'']m, S&B (Pilkington) *Lute Songs 1.*
  The heart to rue, *Anon*, Gm [d'-e''*b*], S&B (Pilkington) *Lute Songs 1.*
  Wanton, come hither, *Anon*, Gm [c'-f''](m), S&B (Pilkington) *Lute Songs 1.*

Brian Chapple. 1945 -
Collection: *Five Blake Songs* Chester 1979.
  A robin redbreast in a cage, *William Blake*, [f'-a''], Chester 5 Blake.
  Every night and every morn, *William Blake*, [f'-g''], Chester 5 Blake.
  He who mocks the infant's faith, *William Blake*, [d'-a''], Chester 5 Blake.
  Joy and woe are woven fine, *William Blake*, [d'*b*-b''*b*], Chester 5 Blake.
  (Light breaks where no sun shines, [soprano], Chester.)
  To see a world in a grain of sand, *William Blake*, [c'#-g''#], Chester 5 Blake.

John Church. 1675 - 1741.
  King of all joys, *Anon*, Gm [d'-g''], Thames (Bevan) *6 Divine.*
  O God for ever blest, *Anon*, Fm [c'-a''*b*], Thames (Bevan) *6 Divine.*

Jeremiah Clarke. 1670 - 1707.
Collections: *Six Songs* (edited Maurice Bevan), Thames 1990.
  A gentle warmth comes o'er my heart, *Anon*, Dm [c'-a''](m), Thames 6 Songs.
  Alas, here lies the poor Alonso slain, *Thomas Shadwell*, Dm [c'-f''], Thames 6 Songs.
  An evening hymn, *Anon*, Gm [d'-f''], Thames 6 Songs.
  Cease that enchanting song, *Anon*, Cm [d'-a''*b*], Thames 6 Songs.
  Sleep betray'd the unhappy lover, *Anon*, Am [e'-a''], Thames 6 Songs.
  The bonny grey-ey'd morn, *Thomas D'Urfey*, B*b* [c'-g''](f), Thames 6 Songs.

Rebecca Clarke. 1886 - 1979.
Collections: *Song Album* (introduction by Calum MacDonald), B&H 1995.
  A dream, *W B Yeats*, Gm [d'-g''], B&H Song Album; (Fm, B&H).
  Cradle song, *William Blake*, G [e'-g''](f), OUP.
  Down by the salley gardens, *W B Yeats*, Em [d'-e''], B&H Song Album.
  Eight o'clock, *A E Housman*, [e'*b*-g''], B&H Song Album.
  Greeting, *Ella Young*, F [f'-a''], B&H Song Album; (D, B&H).
  Infant joy, *William Blake*, F [c'#-f''], B&H Song Album; (E*b*, B&H).
  June twilight, *John Masefield*, F [c'-f''#], B&H Song Album; (E*b*, B&H).
  · Shy one, *W B Yeats*, F [c'-a''](m), B&H Song Album.
  (The aspidistra, *Claude Flight*, G [d'-g''], Chester.)
  The cherry-blossom wand, *Anna Wickham*, Em [c'#-g''], Thames *Century 1.*
  The cloths of heaven, *W B Yeats*, Am [b-f''], B&H Song Album.
  The seal man, *John Masefield*, [c'-g''], B&H Song Album.

John Clarke-Whitfield. 1770 - 1836.
  Here's the vow she falsely swore, *Anon*, D [f'#-a''](m), S&B (Bush & Temperley) *MB 43.*

One struggle more, and I am free, *Lord Byron*, Fm [c'-f''](m), S&B (Bush & Temperley) *MB 43*.
What voice is this? *Joanna Baillie*, Am [d'#-a''], S&B (Bush & Temperley) *MB 43*.

John Clements. ? - 1986.
Blessed is the man, *Psalm 1*, Lengnick.
(Blue and white, *Mary Coleridge*, B&H.)
(Crossing the bar, *Alfred Lord Tennyson*, Cramer.)
(Early one morning, *Anon*, Cramer.)
(Elizabeth's song, *Lascelles Abercrombie*, G [f'#-b''](f), Keith Prowse.)
(Gibberish, Cramer.)
(Herself a rose, *Christina Rossetti* C [c'-g''], Chester.)

Eric Coates. 1886 - 1957. 20 more songs in B&H archive.
(By Mendip side, *P J O'Reilly*, Eb [e'b(b)-g''], Chappell *English Recital 1*.)
Orpheus with his lute, *Shakespeare*, Eb [d'-g''], B&H *Shakespeare*; (Db, B&H).
(Sigh no more, ladies, *Shakespeare*, G [d'-g''], Chappell *English Recital 2*.)
Stonecracker John, *Fred E Weatherly*, Eb [bb-f''(e''b)], B&H *Souvenirs*.
(The green hills of Somerset, *Fred E Weatherly*, Eb [d'-g''(b')], Chappell *English Recital 1*.)
Under the greenwood tree, *Shakespeare*, C [c-g''], B&H *Shakespeare*.
Who is Sylvia, *Shakespeare*, D [d'-f'''], B&H *Shakespeare*; (C, E, B&H.)

Gerald Cockshott. 1915 - 1979.
Arrangement:
Somebody fetch me a flute, *Anon* tr. *Gerald Cockshott*, G [g'-e''], Roberton.
(Threshing song, *Anon* tr. *Gerald Cockshott*, Bb [f'-g''], OUP.)

Samuel Coleridge-Taylor. 1875 - 1912.
Collections: (*Southern Love Songs Op 12*, S&B 1896); (*African Romances Op 17* (high & low keys), S&B 1897); (*Little Songs for Little Folks Op 19/2*, B&H 1898); (*In Memoriam Op 24*; S&B 1898); (*Three Songs Op 29*, S&B 1898); (*Six Sorrow Songs Op 57*, S&B 1904); (*Five Fairy Ballads* (high & low keys, B&H 1909); (*Songs of Sun and Shade* (high & low keys), B&H 1911).
(A birthday, *Christina Rossetti*, Bb, Cramer; Ab, Cramer.)
(A corn song, *P L Dunbar*, C, B&H; Eb, B&H.)
(A king there lived in Thule, *Goethe* tr. *Stephen Phillips & J Comyns Carr*, Dm, B&H.)
(A lovely little dream, *Sorojini Naidu*, Dm, Cramer; Gm, Cramer.)
(A prayer, *P L Dunbar*, A [d'#-g''], S&B Op 17.)
(A starry night, *P L Dunbar*, Am [e'-g''], S&B Op 17.)
(An African love song, *P L Dunbar*, F [f'-a''b](m), S&B Op 17.)
(Alone with mother, *Kathleen Easmon*, C, B&H 5 Fairy, B&H; Eb, 5 Fairy, B&H.)
(Ballad, *P L Dunbar*, G [f'#-g''],Op 17.)
(Big Lady Moon, *Kathleen Easmon*, F, B&H 5 Fairy, B&H; Eb, 5 Fairy, B&H; Db, B&H.)
(Candle lightin' time, *P L Dunbar*, Em, B&H; Gm, B&H.)
(Come in! *Alfred Noyes*, F, B&H; Ab, B&H.)
(Dawn, *P L Dunbar*, Ab [f'-a''b], S&B Op 17.)
(Earth fades! heaven breaks on me, *Robert Browning*, Gm [d'-e''b], S&B Op 24.)
Eleänore, *Eric Mackay*, D [f#'-g''](m), B&H *Ballad Album 1*; (Bb, B&H.)
(Eulalie, *Alice Parson*, G, B&H; A, B&H.)

(Fairy roses, *Kathleen Eamon*, A♭, B&H 5 Fairy, B&H; C, 5 Fairy, B&H.)

(Five-and-twenty sailor men, *Greville E Matheson*, Gm, B&H; Am, B&H.)

(How shall I woo thee? *P L Dunbar*, G♭ [g'♭-g''♭](m), S&B Op 17.)

(If thou art sleeping, maiden, *Henry Wadsworth Longfellow*, Dm [f'-f''](m), S&B Op 12.)

(Jessy, *Robert Burns*, C [d'-g''](m), S&B Op 29.)

(Life and death, *Jessie Adelaide Middleton*, A♭ [b-e''♭], S&B.)

(Long years ago, *P L Dunbar*, B&H.)

(Lucy, *William Wordsworth*, E♭ [e'♭-a''♭], S&B Op 29.)

(Mary, *William Wordsworth*, A [f'#-g''], S&B Op 24.)

(Minguillo, *Anon* tr. *Lockhart*, E♭ [e'♭-a''♭](f), S&B Op 12.)

(My doll, *Charles Kingsley*, D♭, B&H.)

(My love, *Henry Wadsworth Longfellow*, A [e'-g''#](m), S&B Op 12.)

(Oh, my lonely pillow, *Lord Byron*, Am [e'-a''](f), S&B Op 12.)

(Oh, roses for the flush of youth, *Christina Rossetti*, E♭m [b♭-e''♭], S&B Op 57; Fm, Op 57.)

(Oh what comes over the sea, *Christina Rossetti*, Dm [a-e''], S&B Op 57; Em, Op 57.)

Onaway, awake, beloved, *Henry W Longfellow*, G♭ [f'-b''♭](m), B&H *Ballad Album 2*.

(Over the hills, *P L Dunbar*, D [d'-f'#], S&B Op 17.)

(Red o' the dawn, *Alfred Noyes*, Bm, B&H.)

(She rested by the broken brook, *R L Stevenson*, E♭ [b♭-e''♭], B&H; G, B&H.)

(She sat and sang alway, *Christina Rossetti*, G [g(b)-e''], S&B Op 57; A, Op 57.)

(Song of the Nubian girl, *Thomas Moore*, Dm [a-e''](f), S&B.)

(Substitution, *Elizabeth Barrett Browning*, Bm [b-e''], S&B Op 24.)

(Sweet baby butterfly, *Kathleen Easmon*, F, B&H 5 Fairy, B&H; A♭, 5 Fairy, B&H.)

(Tears, *Anon*, D♭ [f'-g''♭], S&B Op 12.)

(The gift rose, *F Peterson*, B♭, B&H.)

(The rainbow child, *Marguerite Radclyffe-Hall*, Dm, B&H Sun & Shade, B&H; Em, Sun & Shade, B&H.)

(The Shoshone's adieu, *Brice Fennell*, A, B&H; B♭, B&H.)

(The stars, *Kathleen Easmon*, G, B&H 5 Fairy.)

(The willow song, *Shakespeare*, Cramer.)

(This is the island of gardens, *Marguerite Radclyffe-Hall*, C, B&H Sun & Shade, B&H; D♭, Sun & Shade, B&H.)

(Thou art risen, my beloved, *Marguerite Radclyffe-Hall*, Dm, B&H Sun & Shade, B&H; Fm, Sun & Shade, B&H.)

(Thou hast bewitched me, beloved, *Marguerite Radclyffe-Hall*, A, B&H Sun & Shade; G, Sun & Shade.)

(Too late for love, *Christina Rossetti*, Fm [b-e''♭], S&B Op 57; Gm, Op 57.)

(Unmindful of the roses, *Christina Rossetti*, D [a-d''], S&B Op 57; E, Op 57.)

(Until, *F Dempster Sherman*, G, B&H.)

(Waiting, *Alfred Noyes*, Dm, B&H; Em, B&H.)

(Weep not, beloved friends, *Chiabrera* tr. *Wordsworth*, E♭ [c'-d''], S&B Op 24.)

(When I am dead, my dearest, *Christina Rossetti*, F [c'-e''♭], S&B Op 57; G, Op 57.)

(You lay so still in the sunshine, *Marguerite Radclyffe-Hall*, C, B&H Sun & Shade; B♭, Sun & Shade.)

(Your heart's desire, *Alfred Noyes*, B&H.)

Arrangement:

(The three ravens, *Anon*, Em, B&H; Gm, B&H.)

Lawrance Collingwood. 1887 - 1982. (BMIC.)

Justin Connolly. 1933 - (BMIC.)

Arnold Cooke. (BMIC.) 1906 -

Ian Copley. 1926 -
(Twelfth Night, *Hilaire Belloc*, Bm [c'#-d''#], Roberton; Dm, Roberton.)

John Coprario. *c.*1575 - 1627.
Collection: *Funeral Tears, Songs of Mourning* and *The Masque of Squires* (edited Gerald Hendrie and Thurston Dart), S&B 1969.

William Corkine. *fl.*1610 - 1612.
Collection: (*Ayres* (edited E H Fellowes), S&B 1926.) Only songs available in anthologies are listed individually here.

> Dear, though your mind, *Anon, A* [d'#-f'#], B&H (Keel) *Lovesongs 1; F, Lovesongs 1.*
> He that hath no mistress, *Anon*, F [c'-e''*b*](m), S&B (Pilkington) *Lute Songs 1.*
> Shall a smile or guileful glance? *Anon*, G [g'-g''](m), B&H (Keel) *Lovesongs 2; Eb, Lovesongs 2.*
> Sweet Cupid, *Anon*, B*b* [f'-f''](m), S&B (Pilkington) *Lute Songs 1; B*, B&H (Keel) *Lovesongs 1; G, Lovesongs 2.*
> Sweet, let me go, *Anon*, C [c'-a''](f), S&B (Pilkington) *Lute Songs 1.*

Raphael Courteville. *fl* 1687 - *c*1735.
Cease Hymen, cease, *Thomas D'Urfey*, D [F#-e'](m), Thames (Bevan) *6 Restoration.*

Edward Cowie. 1943 - (BMIC.)

David Cox. 1916 - 1997.
Fine English days! *Anon*, E*b*, [b*b*-e''*b*], Thames *Century 4.*

William Croft. 1678 - 1727.
> A song to Celia's spinet, *R Steele*, Dm [g-b'*b*], Thames (Newton) *Countertenors 2.*
> Ah, how sweet, *Thomas D'Urfey*, Gm [d'-a''], S&B (Pilkington) *Georgian 2*; (*Fm*, B&H (Keel) *12 18th Century*).
> How severe is my fate, *Martin*, Cm [d'-a''*b*](m), S&B (Pilkington) *Georgian 2.*
> My heart is ev'ry beauty's prey, *Anon*, Am [e'-a''], Roberton (Diack Johnston).

Gordon Crosse. 1937 -
Collection: (*The Cool Web*, OUP hire.)
> (Allie, *Robert Graves*, [d'-a''], OUP Cool Web.)
> (The cool web, *Robert Graves*, [d'-a''*b*], OUP The Cool Web.)
> (The frog prince, *Stevie Smith*, [c'#-a''], OUP Cool Web.)
> The New World (cycle), *Ted Hughes*, [g-a''*b*], OUP; (a version for high voice on hire).
> (The voice from the tomb (cycle) *Stevie Smith*, [a*b*-f'#], OUP hire.)
> (Vanity, *Robert Graves*. [d'-g''], OUP Cool Web.)

Peter Crossley-Holland. 1916 -
Collection: *Two Songs*, Lengnick 1956; *Songs*, Forsyth 1997.

Cradle song, *Padraic Colum*, Bm [d'-g''], Forsyth Songs.
Evening is over the land, *Laurence Binyon*, B♭ [g-d''], Forsyth Songs.
Into the twilight, *W B Yeats*, E [g#-g''#], Forsyth Songs.
Night ride, *Ernest Rhys*, Em [B-e'](m), Forsyth Songs.
Now all is ready for Pentecost, *Henrik Ibsen* tr. *Anon*, E [e'-f''#](f), Forsyth Songs.
Sleep, my boy, *Henrik Ibsen* tr. *Anon*, E [d-g''#](f), Forsyth Songs.
The land of the west, *Samuel Lover*, D♭ [c'-f''](m), Forsyth Songs.
The mariner, *Winthrop MacWorth Praed*, Dm [d-e''](m), Forsyth Songs.
The nightingales, *Robert Bridges*, F [c'-a''], Forsyth Songs.
The piper, *Seumas O'Sullivan*, G [d'-g''], Lengnick 2 Songs, Forsyth Songs..
The weather the cuckoo likes, *Thomas Hardy*, G [d'-g''], Lengnick 2 Songs, Forsyth Songs.
Twilight it is, *John Masefield*, F [c'-g''(a')], Forsyth Songs.
Wanderer's night song, *Goethe* tr. *Percy Pinkerton*, A♭ [a♭-a'♭], Forsyth Songs.
When woods were green, *Henry Wadsworth Longfellow*, G [g-d''], Forsyth Songs.

Adrian Cruft. 1921 - 1987. (BMIC.)

Edric Cundell. 1893 - 1961.
(Gold o' the world, *Crosbie Garstin*, E♭ [f'-g''](m), Chappell *English Recital 2*.)

D

Martin Dalby. 1942 -
Collections: *Eight Songs from the Chinese*, Lengnick 1968; (*A Muse of Love*, B&H 1968).
Antoinette alone (scena), *Jean Rhys*, [mezzo soprano], Novello.
A soldier's song, *Anon*, tr. *Anon*, [b-d''](m), Lengnick 8 from the Chinese.
Cupid and Campaspe, *John Lyly*, [d'-a''](m), B&H *Heritage 3* (B&H Muse).
Flood, *T'ao Chien* tr. *Arthur Waley*, [a-e''], Lengnick 8 from the Chinese.
New corn, *T'ao Ch'ien* tr. *Arthur Waley*, [e'-e''*b*], Lengnick 8 from the Chinese.
(O gentle love, *George Peele*, B&H Muse.)
Plucking the rushes, *Anon* tr. *Waley*, [c'-c''], Lengnick 8 from the Chinese.
(Take, O take those lips away, *Shakespeare*, B&H Muse.)
The herd boy, *Lu Yu* tr. *Waley*, [b*b*-c''], Lengnick 8 from the Chinese.
The little cart, *Tzû-Lung* tr. *Waley*, [c'*b*-e''*b*], Lengnick 8 from the Chinese.
The little lady of Ch'ing-hsi, *Anon* tr. *Waley*, [g-c''], Lengnick 8 from the Chinese.
The pedlar of spells, *Lu Yu* tr. *Waley*, [b*b*-d''], Lengnick 8 from the Chinese.
(What thing is love? *George Peele*, B&H Muse.)
(When to her lute Corinna sings, *Thomas Campion*, B&H Muse.)

Benjamin Dale. 1885 - 1943.
O mistress mine, *Shakespeare*, F, Novello; (D, Novello).
(Come away, death, *Shakespeare*, D*b*, Novello; E, Novello.)

Mervyn Dale. 1922 - 1985.
Collection: *Four English Lyrics*, Roberton 1968.
Back and side go bare, *Anon*, F [c'-c''](m), Roberton 4 English.
Come live with me, *Christopher Marlowe*, F [c'-d''](m), Roberton 4 English.
Come night and lay thy velvet hand, *George Chapman*, F [c'-b'*b*], Roberton 4 English.
Fie diddle dee and fie on me, Roberton.
Footprints in the snow, F [c'-d''], Roberton.
Snowie the snowman, F [c'-d''], Roberton.
Where be ye, my love, *Anon*, C [b-c''], Roberton 4 English.

John Danyel. 1564 - after 1625.
Collection: *Songs*, (edited David Scott), S&B 1970. Only songs available in anthologies are listed individually here.
Dost thou withdraw thy grace? *Anon*, Gm [g'-f''], S&B (Pilkington) *Lute Songs 1*.
I die whenas I do not see, *Anon*, Am [c'-e''](m), S&B (Pilkington) *Lute Songs 1*.
Like as the lute delights, *Samuel Daniel*, Cm [c'-e''*b*], S&B (Pilkington) *Lute Songs 1*.
Why canst thou not? *Anon*, G [e'-f''], S&B (Pilkington) *Lute Songs 1*.

Royston Darlow. 1943 -
(Nocturnes for voice (cycle), *Wordsworth, Campion, Moore, Goethe*, B&H 1966.)

Malcolm Davidson.
A Christmas carol, *John Masefield*, Am [f'-a''](m), B&H *Heritage 3*; (Fm, B&H)
(A lake and a fairy boat, *Thomas Hood*, E, B&H.)
(At the turn of the burn, *Sylvia Townsend Warner*, D, B&H; F, B&H.)
(Conjuration, [high], Cramer.)
(Rain on the down, *Arthur Symons*, D, B&H.)
(Sorrow of Mydath, *John Masefield*, Bb, B&H; D, B&H.)
(Stay O sweet, *John Donne?*, [high], Cramer; [low], Cramer.)
(The bargain, *Philip Sidney*, D, B&H; E, B&H.).

Eiluned Davies. 1913 -
For Ann Gregory, *W B Yeats*, [c-f'](m), Welsh Music *Songs from Wales 2.*
Will you be as hard? *Lady Gregory*, [c#-e'](m), Gwynn.

Janet Davies.
Collection: *Four Christmas Songs, Lengnick.*
Festive carol, Lengnick
Jesus, infant Jesus, Lengnick.
The angel's warning, Lengnick
The star light carol, Lengnick.

Walford Davies. 1869 - 1941.
(Hame, *Alan Cunningham*, Bb [bb-d''], Chappell; C, D, Chappell.)
(I vow to thee, my country, *Cecil Spring-Rice*, Cramer.)
(The seal's lullaby, *Rudyard Kipling*, Novello.)
When childer plays, *T E Brown*, A [a-d''], Banks; (C, D, B&H).
Arrangements:
My loved one's grave, Gwynn.
O blackbird blithe, Gwynn.

William Davies. 1859 - 1907.
Starless crown, [soprano/tenor], Snell.

William Defesch. 1687 - 1761.
(Colin's success, *William Boyce*, D, [d'-g''](f), Curwen (Poston).)
(Oh! fie, shepherd, fie, *William Boyce*, D [d'-g''](f), Curwen (Poston).)
(Polly of the plain, *William Boyce*, D [d'-g''], Curwen (Poston).)

Frederick Delius. 1862 - 1934.
Collections: *Song Album*, B&H 1968; *Ten Songs*, S&B 1973; *Twenty-two Songs*, S&B 1987; *Sixteen Songs*, B&H 1987; *Nineteen Songs*, OUP 1987; *Four Posthumous Songs*, Universal 1992.
Autumn, *Holstein* tr. *Delius*, Eb [c'(bb)-a''], B&H Album, 16 Songs.
Black roses, *Josephson*, tr. *Delius*, Bb [c'-bf''], OUP 19 Songs.
Cradle song, *Ibsen* tr. *Peter Pears*, Db [c'-f''], OUP 19 Songs.
Dreamy nights, *Drachmann* tr. *Delius*, Eb [c'-g''], S&B 10 Songs, 22 Songs.
Hidden love, *Bjørnson* tr. *Peter Pears*, F [c'-a''], OUP 19 Songs.
In the garden of the seraglio, *Jacobsen* tr. *Delius*, Eb [d'-bg''b], B&H Album, 16 Songs.

I hear in the night, *Drachmann* tr. *Jelka Rosen*, Db [b-g"*b*], Universal 4 Posthumous.
I once had a newly cut willow pipe, *Krag* tr. *Lionel Carley*, Gb [a-g"*b*], Universal 4 Posthumous.
I-Brasîl, *Fiona Macleod*, [c'-f''], OUP 19 Songs.
In bliss we walked with laughter, *Drachmann* tr. *Addie Funk*, Fm [c'-f''], Universal 4 Posthumous.
Indian love song, *P B Shelley*, Eb [e'b-b''*b*], OUP 19 Songs.
Irmelin, *Jacobsen* tr. *Delius*, F#m [b-g''], B&H Album, 16 Songs.
It was a lover and his lass, *Shakespeare*, [c'#-a''], B&H Album, 16 Songs.
Let springtime come, *Jacobsen* tr. *Delius*, A [c'-g''#], OUP 19 Songs.
Longing, *Kjerulf* tr. *W Grist*, D [c'*b*(a)-f''#], S&B 10 Songs, 22 Songs.
Love's philosophy, *P B Shelley*, G [d'#-g''#(a'')], OUP 19 Songs.
Over the mountains high, *Bjørnson* tr. *Anon*, C [c'-e''], S&B 22 Songs.
Silken shoes, *Jacobsen* tr. *Delius*, F [c'-f''](m), B&H Album, 16 Songs.
Slumber song, *Bjørnson* tr. *W Grist*, G [d'-f''], S&B 10 Songs, 22 Songs.
So white, so soft, so sweet is she, *Ben Jonson*, F [b-f''#], B&H Album, 16 Songs, *Songs of Love and Affection*; (D, B&H).
Softly the forest murmurs, *Bjørnson* tr. *Lionel Carley*, F#m [c'#-f'#], Universal 4 Posthumous.
Spring, the sweet Spring, *Thomas Nashe*, [d'-a''], B&H Album, 16 Songs.
Summer eve, *Paulsen* tr. *W Grist*, F# [d'#-f''x], S&B 10 Songs, 22 Songs.
Summer nights, *Drachmann* tr. *Delius*, Ab [c'-g''*b*], S&B 10 Songs, 22 Songs.
Sunset, *Munch* tr. *W Grist*, Gb [d'*b*(bb)-g''*b*], S&B 10 Songs, 22 Songs.
The birds' story, *Ibsen* tr. *Peter Pears*, F [d'a-g''#], OUP 19 Songs.
The homeward way, *Vinje* tr. *Peter Pears*, Ab [e'*b*-f''], OUP 19 Songs.
The minstrel, *Ibsen* tr. *Peter Pears*, A [b-f''#](m), OUP 19 Songs.
The nightingale, *Kjerulf* tr. *W Grist*, Eb [bb-e''*b*], S&B 22 Songs; G, 10 Songs, S&B.
The nightingale has a lyre of gold, *W E Henley*, Dm [c'#-g''], OUP 19 Songs, OUP.
The page sat in the lofty tower, *Jacobsen* tr. *Delius*, Gm [d'-e''*b*], S&B 10 Songs, 22 Songs.
The violet, *Holstein* tr. *Delius*, G [b-g''], B&H Album, 16 Songs.
They are not long, the weeping and the laughter, *Ernest Dowson*, Bb [d*b*-g''], B&H 16 Songs.
Through long long years, *Jacobsen*, tr. *Delius*, Db [bb-f''], S&B 10 Songs, 22 Songs.
To daffodils, *Robert Herrick*, [c'#-g''#], B&H Album, 16 Songs, *Heritage 2*.
To the queen of my heart, *P B Shelley*, B [d'#-a''#], OUP 19 Songs.
Twilight fancies, *Bjørnson* tr. *F S Copeland*, Bm [d'-f'#], OUP 19 Songs, OUP; *Gm*, OUP *Solo Contralto*, OUP.
Wine roses, *Jacobsen* tr. *Delius*, C#m [c'#-e''], S&B 10 Songs, 22 Songs.
Young Venevil, *Bjørnson* tr. *Peter Pears*, C [c'-g''(e')], OUP 19 Songs.

Edward J Dent. 1876 - 1957.
The oxen, *Thomas Hardy*, E [e'-f''], Thames *Hardy Songbook*.

J Michael Diack. 1869 - 1946. (16 songs, 2 albums of songs, 6 arrangements and 2 volumes of arrangements, all at SMIC.)

Charles Dibdin. 1745 - 1814.
Collections: (*Five Dibdin Airs* (edited Robert Chignell), B&H 1927.)
Come, every man now give his toast, *Charles Dibdin*, F [c'-g''](m), Novello (Bush) *Ballad Operas*.
(I locked up all my treasure, *Anon*, Db, [c'-d''*b*](m) B&H 5 Dibdin.)

Nothing like grog, [baritone], Gwynn (Ian Parrott).

(Peggy Perkins, *Anon*, B♭[e'♭-g''](m), OUP (Cockshott).)

(The anchorsmiths, *Anon*, G [g-e''](m), B&H 5 Dibdin.)

(The jolly young waterman, *Anon*, F [c'-d''], B&H 5 Dibdin.)

(The sailor's journal, *Anon*, G [g-e''](m), B&H 5 Dibdin.)

The tinker's song, *Charles Dibdin*, D♭, [d'♭-f''(e''♭)](m), B&H (Lane Wilson) *Old English*.

(Then farewell my trim-built wherry, *Anon*, D♭[a♭-d''♭](m), B&H 5 Dibdin.)

Peter Dickinson. 1934 -

Collection: (*Three Comic Songs*, Novello 1972); (*Four Auden Songs*, Novello). (See also BMIC.)

A Dylan Thomas cycle, *Dylan Thomas*, [baritone], Novello

(An e e cummings Song Cycle, [g#-g''♭], Novello.)

(Carry her over the water, *W H Auden*, [e'♭-g''](f), Novello 4 Auden.)

Extravaganzas (cycle), *Gregory Corso*, [a♭-g''], Novello.

(Eyes look into the well, *W H Auden*, [d'-e'' *or* f'-g''](f), Novello 4 Auden.)

(Happy ending, *W H Auden*, [d'-g''], Novello 3 Comic.)

(Look, stranger, *W H Auden*, [c'-g''](f), Novello 4 Auden.)

(My second thoughts, *W H Auden*, [e'♭-g''♭], Novello 3 Comic.)

(Over the heather, W H Auden, [e'♭-f''#](m), Novello 3 Comic.)

Stevie's Tunes (cycle), *Stevie Smith*, [b-g''], Novello.

Three songs from 'The Unicorns' (cycle), *John Heath-Stubbs*, [soprano], Novello.

(What's in your mind, *W H Auden*, [d'#-g''#(f''#)](f), Novello 4 Auden.)

Bernard van Dieren. 1884 - 1936

Collection: *Seven Songs,* Thames 1983.

(A new-blown rose a message brings, *Otto Julius Bierbaum* tr. *Calvocoressi*, [b-f''], OUP.)

(Alone in the wood, *Heine* tr. *Oliver Strachey*, c'#-f''#], OUP.)

(Balow, my babe, *Anon*, [c'-f''](f), OUP.)

(Come, I will sing with you, *P B Shelley*, [c'#-e''], OUP.)

Dream pedlary, *Thomas Lovell Beddoes*, [d'♭-f''], Thames 7 Songs.

(Every day the wondrous, *Heine* tr. *Calvocoressi*, [b-f''#], OUP.)

Last days, *Walter Savage Landor*, [d'-e''♭], Thames 7 Songs.

(Lavana and our ladies of sorrow, *Thomas da Quincey*, [d'#-f''#](f), OUP.)

(Love must be gone, *Walter Savage Landor*, [d'-g''], OUP.)

(Mild is the parting year, *Walter Savage Landor*, [c'#-f''], OUP.)

(She I love, *Walter Savage Landor*, [d'-g''](m), OUP.)

Spring, *Thomas Nashe*, [e'-a''],Thames 7 Songs.

Spring song of the birds, *King James I of Scotland*, [e'♭-g''] Thames 7 Songs.

Take O take those lips away, *Shakespeare*, [e'-f''], Thames 7 Songs.

(The touch of love, *Walter Savage Landor*, [d'#-f''], OUP.)

(The holy three Magi, *Goethe* tr. *Calvocoressi*, [c'-a''♭], OUP.)

Weep you no more, sad fountains, *Anon*, [d'♭-a''♭], Thames 7 Songs.

Weeping and kissing, *Sir Edward Sherburne*, [d'#-g''](m), Thames 7 Songs.

(What is good King Ringang's daughter's name? *Mörike* tr. *Calvocoressi*, [b-a''], OUP.)

(With margeraine gentle, *Philip Skelton*, [e'-e''#], OUP.)

J Airlie Dix. A further 20 songs in B&H archive.
The trumpeter, *J Francis Barron*, C [e'-g''](m), B&H *Ballad Album 1*, G, *Souvenirs*, Bb, Cramer *Drawing Room Songs*.

Stephen Dodgson. (BMIC.) 1924 -

John Dowland. 1563 - 1626.
Collections: *The First Book of Ayres* (edited Thurston Dart), S&B 1965 [1st Book]; *The Second Book of Songs* (edited Thurston Dart), S&B 1970 [2nd Book]; *The Third Book of Songs* (edited Thurston Dart), S&B 1970 [3rd Book]; *A Pilgrim's Solace* (edited Thurston Dart), S&B 1979 [Pilgrim]; *Fifty Songs Books 1 and 2* (high & low keys) (edited David Scott), S&B 1970 [50/1, 50/2]. Note that in the following: Pilkington = *English Lute Songs Book 2*, S&B; Keel 1/2 = *Elizabethan Lovesongs Books 1 & 2* (high & low keys,) B&H. Only songs available in anthologies are listed individually here.
A shepherd in a shade, *Anon*, G [d'-d''], 2nd Book, 50/1, Keel 1; *B*, 50/1; *Bb*, Keel 1.
Awake sweet love, *Anon*, F [e'-f''](m), 1st Book, 50/1, Pilkington; *D*, 50/1.
Away with these self-loving lads, *Fulke Greville*, G [d'-e''], 1st Book; *A*, *F*, Keel 2.
Burst forth, my tears, *Anon*, Gm [d'-d''](m), 1st Book, 50 Songs 1; *Bm*, 50/1.
By a fountain where I lay, *Anon*, Gm [f'#-f''](m), 3rd Book, 50/2; *Em*, 50/2.
Can she excuse my wrongs? *Anon*, Dm [d'-d''](m), 1st Book, 50/1; *Fm*, 50/1.
Clear or cloudy, *Anon*, G [d'-e''](m), 2nd Book; *Bb*, 50/2; *F*, 50/2, Pilkington.
Come again, sweet love doth now invite, *Anon*, G [d'-e''], 1st Book, Keel 1, B&H *Im-perial 5*; *Ab*, 50/1; *A*, Keel 1, Paterson (Diack) *100 Best 2*; *F*, 50/1, Pilkington.
Come away, come sweet love, *Anon*, Gm [f'#-f''], 1st Book, 50/1, Pilkington, Chester (Shavitz) *Celebrated*; *Em*, 50/1; *Am*, *Fm*, Keel 2.
Come heavy sleep, *Anon*, G [d'-e''], 1st Book; *A*, *Eb*, 50/1.
Daphne was not so chaste, *Anon*, F [e'-f''], 3rd Book, Pilkington.
Dear, if you change, *Anon*, Am [d'-e''], 1st Book; *Bm*, 50/1, Keel 1, *Gm*, 50/1, Keel 1.
Disdain me still, *Anon*, G [d'-e''](m), Pilgrim; *Bb*, *F*, 50/2.
Far from triumphing court, *Sir Henry Lee*, G [d'-e''], Pilgrim; *A*, 50/2; *F*, 50/2, Pilkington.
Farewell, unkind, farewell, *Anon*, G [f'#-e''], 3rd Book; *Bb*, 50/2; *F*, 50/2, Keel 2; *A*, Keel 2.
Fie on this feigning, *Anon*, F [f'-g''], 3rd Book, Pilkington.
Fine knacks for ladies, *Anon*, F [e'-f''](m), 2nd Book, 50/1, Pilkington; Keel 1; *D*, 50/1; *Eb*, Keel 1, Paterson (Diack) *100 Best 4*.
Flow my tears, *Anon*, Am [d'-e''], 2nd Book; *Cm*, 50/1; *Gm*, 50/1, Pilkington; *Bm*, B&H *Dol-metsch 2*.
Flow not so fast ye fountains, *Anon*, Gm [g'-g''], 3rd Book, 50/2, Pilkington; *Dm*, 50/2; *F#m*, *Em*, Keel 1.
Go, crystal tears, *Anon*, Cm [g'-e''b](m), 1st Book; *Dm*, *Bm*, 50/1.
His golden locks, *Anon*, G [f'#-d''], 1st Book; *Bb*, *F*, 50/1.
I saw my lady weep, *Anon*, Am [e'-e''], 2nd Book; *Cm*, 50/2; *Gm*, 50/1, Pilkington.
If my complaints could passions move, *Anon*, Gm [f'#-f''], 1st Book, Pilkington, 50/1, *Em*, 50/1.
If that a sinner's sighs, *Anon*, Gm [f'#-g''], Pilgrim, 50/2; *Dm*, 50/2.
In darkness let me dwell, *Anon*, Am [c'-e''], Pilgrim, 50/2; *Cm*, 50/2; *Gm*, 50/2, Pilkington.
It was a time when silly bees, *Anon*, Dm [d'-e''b], 3rd Book; *Em*, *Cm*, 50/2.
Lady, if you so spite me, *Anon*, Cm [g'-f''](m), Pilgrim, 50/2, Pilkington; *Am*, 50/2.

Love those beams, *Anon*, Gm [f'#-g''], Pilgrim, 50/2; *Em*, 50/2.

Me, me, and none but me, *Anon*, G [g'-e''], 3rd Book; *Bb*, *F*, 50/2.

Mourn! day is with darkness fled, *Anon*, D [d'-d''], 2nd Book; *F*, *C*, 50/1.

My heart and tongue were twins, *Anon*, Dm [f'-a''], Pilgrim; *Bm*, *Gm*, 50/2.

My thoughts are winged with hopes, *Anon*, Cm [g'-g''](m), 1st Book, 50/1, *Gm*, 50/1.

Now cease my wandering eyes, *Anon*, F [f'-f''], 2nd Book, 50/1; *D*, 50/1.

Now, O now I needs must part, *Anon*, G [e'-e''], 1st Book; *A*, 50/1, Keel 2; *F*, 50/1, Keel 2, Pilkington.

O what hath overwrought? *Anon*, Gm [f'#-f''], 3rd Book, 50/2; *Em*, 50/2.

Rest awhile, you cruel cares, *Anon*, G [f'#-d''], 1st Book; *Bb F*, 50/1.

Say love if ever thou didst find, *Anon*, G [f'#-d''], 3rd Book, 50/2; *Bb*, 50/2.

Shall I strive with words to move? *Anon*, Em [e'-d''](m), Pilgrim, 50/2; *Am*, 50/2.

Shall I sue? *Anon*, Gm [g'-g''], 2nd Book, 50/2, Pilkington; *Dm*, 50/2, Keel 2; *F#m*, Keel 2.

Sleep, wayward thoughts, *Anon*, G [g'-e''], 1st Book; *A*, 50/1; *Eb*, 50/1, Pilkington.

Sorrow, stay, *Anon*, Gm [d'-d''], 2nd Book, Keel 2; *Bm*, 50/1, Keel 2; *Fm*, 50/1, Pilkington.

Stay time awhile thy flying, *Anon*, Am [e'-d''], Pilgrim, Keel 2; *Cm*, Keel 2.

Sweet stay awhile, *John Donne?*, Am [e'-e''], Pilgrim; *Cm*, 50/2; *Gm*, 50/2, Pilkington.

Tell me, true love, *Anon*, Gm [d'-d''], Pilgrim, 50/2; *Bm*, 50/2.

The lowest trees have tops, *Anon*, Gm [d'-d''], 3rd Book; *Bm*, *F#m*, 50/2.

Time stands still, *Anon*, G [g'-d''](m), 3rd Book; *Bb*, 50/2; *F*, 50/2, Pilkington.

To ask for all thy love, *Anon*, Gm [e'-g''], Pilgrim, Pilkington.

· Toss not my soul, *Anon*, Gm [f'#-f''], 2nd Book, Pilkington.

Unquiet thoughts, *Anon*, Gm [f'-e''*b*], 1st Book; *Am*, 50/1, 50/1.

Weep you no more, sad fountains, *Anon*, Gm [d'-g''], 3rd Book, 50/2, Pilkington; *Em*, 50/2, Keel 2; *F#*, Keel 2.

Were every thought an eye, *Anon*, Cm [g'-g''], Pilgrim, 50/2; *Gm*, 50/2.

What if I never speed?, *Anon*, Am [e'-f''], 3rd Book, 50/2, Pilkington; *Fm*, 50/2; *Bm*, *Gm*, Keel 2.

When Phoebus first did Daphne love, *Anon*, G [g'-e''](m), 3rd Book, Pilkington.

Where sin sore wounding, *Anon*, Gm [a'-a''], Pilgrim; *Fm*, 50/2; *Dm*, 50/2.

White as lilies was her face, *Anon*, Gm [g'-f''], 2nd Book, 50/1; *Em*, 50/1.

Whoever thinks or hopes of love, *Fulke Greville*, Gm [f'-g''], 1st Book, 50/1; *Dm*, 50/1.

Wilt thou, unkind, thus reave me? *Anon*, Am [e'-e''], 1st Book; *Bm*, 50/1; *Fm*, 50/1.

Madeleine Dring. 1923 - 1977.

Collections: *Five Betjeman Songs*, Weinberger 1980; *Three Shakespeare Songs*, Lengnick ; *Seven Shakespeare Songs*, Thames 1992; *Dedications*, Thames 1992; *Four Night Songs*, Thames 1992; *Seven Songs*, Thames 1993; *Love and Time*, Thames 1994. (See also BMIC.)

A bay in Anglesey, *John Betjeman*, C [b-f''(g')], Weinberger 5 Betjeman.

A devout lover, *Thomas Randolph*, F [a-c''#](m), Thames 7 Songs.

Ah, how sweet it is to love, *John Dryden*, [d'-a''](f), Thames Love and Time.

Blow, blow thou winter wind, *Shakespeare*, Gm [d'*b*-f''], Thames 7 Shakespeare, Lengnick 3 Shakespeare.

Business girls, *John Betjeman*, D [d'-f''#], Weinberger 5 Betjeman.

Come away, come sweet love, *Anon*, C [c'#-d''], Thames 7 Songs.

Come away, death, *Shakespeare*, Am [d'-e''], Thames 7 Shakespeare, Lengnick 3 Shakespeare.

Crabbed age and youth, *Shakespeare*, F [f'-f''](f), Thames 7 Shakespeare.

Encouragements to a lover, *Sir John Suckling*, E [b-e''], Thames 7 Songs.
Frosty night, *Michael Armstrong*, Gm [c'#-g''], Thames 4 Night Songs.
Holding the night, *Michael Armstrong*, [d'(b♭)-g''(b''♭)], Thames 4 Night Songs.
I feed a flame within, *John Dryden*, Gm [d'-a''](f), Thames Love and Time.
It was a lover, *Shakespeare*, E [b-e''(g''#)], Thames 7 Shakespeare.
Melisande, The far-away Princess, *D F Aitken*, Gm [f'-f''](m), Thames 7 Songs.
My proper Bess, *John Skelton*, [b♭-d''](m), Thames 7 Songs.
Separation, *Michael Armstrong*, Cm [d'-g''], Thames 4 Night Songs.
Sister, awake, *Anon*, [f'-b''♭](f), Thames Love and Time.
Song of a nightclub proprietress, *John Betjeman*, Gm [b-e''♭](f), Weinberger 5 Betjeman.
Take O take those lips away, *Shakespeare*, [g-d''], Thames 7 Shakespeare.
The cuckoo, *Shakespeare*, F [b-g''♭], Thames 7 Shakespeare.
The faithless lover, *Anon*, Dm [c'-g''♭](m), Thames 7 Songs.
The reconcilement, *John Sheffield, Duke of Buckinghamshire*, [c'-a''](f), Thames Love and Time.
Through the centuries, *Michael Armstrong*, E♭ [b♭-g''#], Thames 4 Night Songs.
To daffodils, *Robert Herrick*, [f'-f''], Thames Dedications.
To music - to becalm a sweetsick youth, *Robert Herrick*, [d'-g''], Thames Dedications.
To Phyllis - to love and live with him, *Robert Herrick*, A [e'-g''](m), Thames Dedications.
To the virgins - to make much of time, *Robert Herrick*, D [c'#-g''], Thames Dedications.
To the willow tree, *Robert Herrick*, G [f'-g''♭], Thames Dedications.
Undenominational, *John Betjeman*, Gm [d'-g''], Weinberger 5 Betjeman.
Under the greenwood tree, *Shakespeare*, C [b♭-f''], Thames 7 Shakespeare, Lengnick 3 Shakespeare.
Upper Lambourne, *John Betjeman*, B♭ [d'-g''(b''♭)], Weinberger 5 Betjeman.
Weep you no more, sad fountains, *Anon*, Cm [c'-c''], Thames 7 Songs.

David Dubery. (see also BMIC.)
The birds, *Hilaire Belloc*, [a#-c''#], Banks.

Thomas Dunhill. 1877 - 1946.
(A child's song of praise, *Lizette Woodworth Reese*, F [f'-d''], Cramer.)
(A visit from the moon, Cramer.)
April, *Margaret Rose*, F [f'-f''], Cramer; (A♭, Cramer).
(Child o' mine, F, B&H; A♭, B&H.)
(Evening, Cramer.)
(Gifts, *James Thomson*, E♭ [b♭-e''♭(m), Cramer.)
(Go, pretty birds, D, Cramer.)
(How soft upon the evening air, *Irene Gass*, E [b-c'#], Curwen; G, A, Curwen.)
(I can hear a cuckoo, *Margaret Rose*, F [f'-g''], Cramer.)
(I remember, Cramer.)
(I think of you, Cramer.)
(In the dawn, *Ida M Stenning*, F#m [d'#-f''#], Cramer.)
(John Peel, Cramer.)
(Little town of Bethlehem, *John Greenleaf Whittier*, E♭, Cramer.)
(Quiet night, Cramer.)
(Ride straight, Cramer.)
(Sweet July, *Margaret Rose*, F [e'-f''], Cramer.)

The cloths of heaven, *W B Yeats*, E♭[E♭-g''], S&B; *C*, S&B.
(The dandelion song, *Anon*, G [d'-g''], S&B; *F*, S&B.)
(The happy man, *Harvey Braban*, C [b(g)-e''](m), Chappell; B♭, Chappell.)
(The haymakers' roundelay, *Anon*, D [c'#-f'#], S&B.)
(The holy babe, *William Canton*, E♭[d'-g''], Cramer.)
(The Suffolk owl, *Anon*, A♭[e'♭-f''], Cramer; B♭, Cramer.)
Three fine ships, *Margaret Rose*, D [a-d''(f'#)], *Cramer Song Folio 1*; (C, Cramer).
(To dance and sing, Cramer.)
To the Queen of Heaven, *Anon*, Dm [c'-g''], Thames *Century 3*.

George Dyson. 1883 - 1964.
(A poet's hymn, *Robert Herrick*, C [c'-g''(e'')], Cramer.)
(Sea music, Cramer.)

E

Leslie East. 1949 -
Collections: *Three Betjeman Songs*, S&B 1984.
    Harrow-on-the-hill, *John Betjeman*, [c'#-g''], S&B 3 Betjeman.
    Middlesex, *John Betjeman*, Ab [c'-a''b], S&B 3 Betjeman.
    The Metropolitan Railway, *John Betjeman* [c'-f''], S&B 3 Betjeman.

John Eccles. 1650 - 1735.
Collections: *Eight Songs* (edited Michael Pilkington), S&B 1978.
    A nymph and a swain, *William Congreve*, D [d'-g''], S&B 8 Songs.
    Ah, whither shall I fly, *Anon*, Em [d'-g''](f), S&B 8 Songs.
    (As Cupid roguishly one day, *the Hon. C B*, F [c'-g''], B&H (Keel) *12 18th Cenruty*.)
    Belinda, *Anon*, C [b-f''](m), S&B (Pilkington) *Early Georgian 1*.
    (Fair Amoret is gone astray, *William Congreve*, C [c'-f''], B&H (Keel) *12 18th Century*.)
    Find me a lonely cave, *Porter*, Gm [bb-f''], S&B (Pilkington) *Early Georgian 1, Recitalist 4*.
    I burn, I burn, *Thomas D'Urfey*, Em [d'#-g''](f), Thames (Bevan) *8 Restoration*.
    I gently touched her hand, *Anon*, Fm [e'b-f''](m), S&B 8 Songs.
    If I hear Orinda swear, *Burnaby*, Em [d'-g''], S&B 8 Songs.
    Love's but the frailty of the mind, *William Congreve*, Dm [c'-g''](f), S&B (Pilkington) *Early Georgian 2*.
    Nature framed thee, *William Congreve*, Gm [d'-g''], S&B 8 Songs.
    So well Corinna likes the joy, *Lord Lansdowne*, Am [e'-g''], S&B 8 Songs.
    Sylvia, how could you, *John Dryden*, Am [d'#-g''], S&B 8 Songs.
    The foolish maid, *John Crowne*, Am [e'-g''], S&B 8 Songs.
    The jolly jolly breeze, *Anon*, G [b-e''], S&B (Pilkington) *Early Georgian 1*; (Bb, B&H (Keel) *12 18th Century*).

Oliver Edwards. 1902 - 1979.
    The fiddler of Pendine, [mezzo/baritone], Gwynn.
    The winter it is past, *Anon*, Gm, d'-e''b, Gwynn.

Edward Elgar. 1857 - 1934.
Collections: *Sea Pictures*, B&H 1899; *An Elgar Song Album*, Novello 1984; *Thirteen Songs Books 1 & 2*, Thames 1987.
    A child asleep, *E B Browning*, Eb [d'-e''b], Novello Album.
    A song of Autumn, *Adam Lindsay Gordon*, F [f'-a''(f')], Thames 13 Songs 1.
    (A song of flight, *Christina Rossetti*, Ab, B&H.)
    (A war song, *C Flavell Hayward*, C, B&H; D, B&H.)
    (After, *Philip Bourke Marston*, F, B&H; G, A, B&H.)
    (Always and everywhere, *Zygmunt Krasinski* tr. *F E Fortey*, C, B&H.)
    (Arabian serenade, *Margery Lawrence*, Gm [f'-g''](m), B&H.)
    (Come, gentle night, *Clifton Bingham*, C, B&H; D, Eb, B&H.)
    Dry those fair, those crystal tears, *Henry King*, G [f'#-e''], Thames 13 Songs 2.
    In haven, *Caroline Alice Elgar*, C [c'-c''](f), B&H Sea Pictures, (B&H; Eb, B&H).

In moonlight, *P B Shelley*, F [c'(f')-f'')], Novello Album.

In the dawn, *Arthur C Benson*, C [c'-e''](m), Thames 13 Songs 2; (E*b*, B&H).

Is she not passing fair? *Louisa Stuart Costello*, G [f'#-a''], B&H *Heritage 2, Imperial 4*; F, Thames 13 Songs 2; (D, B&H).

Land of hope and glory, *Arthur C Benson*, C [c'-f''], B&H; (B*b*, D, B&H.)

Like to the damask rose, *Simon Wastell*, B*b*m [d'*b*(b*b*)-g''], Thames 13 Songs 1, (Chappell *English Recital 2*).

Modest and fair, *Ben Jonson*, E*b* [d'-e''*b*], Novello Songs.

My old tunes, *Algernon Blackwood*, B*b* [d'-e''*b*], Novello Songs.

Oh, soft was the song, *Gilbert Parker*, E [b-f''#], Novello Album.

Pleading, *Arthur L Salmon*, G [d'-f'#], Novello Album, Novello; (F, A*b*, Novello.)

Queen Mary's song, *Tennyson*, Gm [d'-a''](f), Banks, Thames 13 Songs 1.

Rondel, *Longfellow*, B*b* [e'(d')-a''(g'')], Banks, Thames 13 Songs 1.

Sabbath morning at sea, *E B Browning*, C [b(c')-g''(e'')](f), B&H Sea Pictures; (B*b*, B&H).

Sea slumber song, *Roden Noel*, Em [g(b)-d''](f), B&H Sea Pictures, (B&H).

Speak, music, *Arthur C Benson*, B*b* [e'*b*-f''], B&H *Heritage 1*; A, Thames 13 Songs 2; (C, B&H), (Speak, my heart, *C H Benson*, C, B&H.)

Still to be neat, *Ben Jonson*, E [b'-e''], Novello Songs.

The blue-eyes fairy, *Algernon Blackwood*, E*b* [b*b*-f''(e''*b*)], Novello Songs.

(The chariots of the Lord, *Brownlie*, C, B&H; D*b*, D, E*b*, B&H.)

(The King's way, *Alice Elgar*, F, B&H.)

The pipes of Pan, *Adrian Ross*, Am [c'-e''(d'')](m), Thames 13 Songs 2; (Gm, Bm, B&H).

The poet's life, *Ellen Burroughs*, F [d'-a''(g'')], Thames 13 Songs 1.

The river, *Pietro d'Alba*, Am [e'*b*(b)-g''](m), Novello Album.

The shepherd's song, *Barry Pain*, F [e'-a''], Banks, Thames 13 Songs 1, (Chappell *English Recital 1*; Eb, Chappell).

(The song of liberty, *A P Herbert*, E*b*, B&H.)

The swimmer, *Adam Lindsay Gordon*, D [a(b)-a''(f)](f), B&H Sea Pictures, (B&H).

The torch, *Pietro d'Alba*, G [d'-e''(g'')], Novello Album, Novello; (A, F, Novello).

The wind at dawn, *C Alice Roberts*, Fm [c'-g''(a'')], Thames 13 Songs 2, (B&H).

There are seven that pull the thread, *W B Yeats*, Em [e'-g''], Novello Album.

Through the long days, *John Hay*, C [g'-a''](m), Thames 13 Songs 1.

To the children, *Algernon Blackwood*, B*b* [c'-f''(e'')], Novello Album.

Twilight, *Gilbert Parker*, Bm [e'-d''], Novello Album.

Was it some golden star? *Gilbert Parker*, C#m [c'#-e''](m), Novello Album.

Where corals lie, *Richard Garnett*, Bm [b(d')-d''](f), B&H Sea Pictures, (B&H; Dm, B&H).

Brian Elias. 1948 -

At the edge of time (cycle) , *Mervyn Peake*, [c'-b''*b*](m), Chester.

Dilys Elwyn-Edwards. 1918 -

Collection: *Bro a Mynydd*, Welsh Music; *Six Songs for Children* (text I D Hooson, tr. Wil Ifan) [d*b*-f''], Gwynn; *In Faery*, Gwynn.

A fairy hunt, *Francis Ledwidge*, F [d'-g''], Gwynn In Faery.

Berwyn, *Robert Ellis* tr. *John Stoddart*, C [c'-g''(e'')], Welsh Music Bro a Mynydd.

Eifionydd, *R Williams Parry* tr. *John*Stoddart, Dm [a-e''], Welsh Music Bro a Mynydd, *Songs from-Wales 2* .
Merry Margaret, *John Skelton*, F [f'-g''], Gwynn.
Sweet Suffolk owl, *Thomas Vautor*, [soprano/tenor], Gwynn.
The cloths of heaven, *W B Yeats*, D [d'-e''], Roberton.
The find, *Francis Ledwidge*, Gm [d'-a''], Gwynn In Faery.
The wife of Lleu, *Francis Ledwidge*, C [e'-a''*b*], Gwynn In Faery.

David Evans. 1874 - 1948.
Awake, [contralto], Snell.

D Pughe Evans. 1866 - 1897.
Sweet memories, [soprano/tenor], Snell.
The old minstrel, [soprano/tenor], Snell; [contralto/baritone], Snell.
Wreckers of Dunraven, [baritone], Snell.

T Hopkin Evans. 1879 - 1940.
Aphrodite, *Sappho*, tr. *H Idris Bell*, E*b* [c'(b)-b'], Gwynn.
Jesus, lover of my soul, [any voice], Snell.

F

Ernest Bristow Farrar. 1885 - 1918.
Collection: (*Vagabond Songs Op 10*, S&B 1911); (*Two Pastorals*, Novello 1921).
Brittany, *E V Lucas*, Eb [bb'-e''b], Thames *Century 4*; G, Novello; (F, Novello).
(Come you, Mary, Novello 2 Pastorals.)
(O mistress mine, *Shakespeare*, Ab [e'b-a''b](m), Novello.)
(Silent noon, *D G Rossetti*, [bb-d''], S&B Op 10.)
(The roadside fire, *Robert Louis Stevenson*, Bb [d'-f''], S&B Op 10.)
(The wanderer's song, *Arthur Symons*, A [c'-e''](m), S&B Op 10.)
(Who would shepherd pipes forsake, Novello 2 Pastorals.)

Howard Ferguson. 1908 -
Collections: (*Three Mediaeval Carols*, Curwen 1934); *Discovery*, B&H 1952.
(A lyke-wake dirge, *Anon*, [baritone], B&H.)
Babylon, *Denton Welch*, Gm [g'-e], B&H Discovery.
Discovery, *Denton Welch*, Ebm [f'-g''], B&H Discovery.
Dreams melting, *Denton Welch*, Dm [f'#-g''(a')], B&H Discovery.
(I saw three ships, *Anon*, Bb [e'-g''], Curwen 3 Carols.)
Jane Allen, *Denton Welch*, Dm [f'#-g''], B&H Discovery.
Love and reason, *William Golding*, G [b-b''](m), Banks; C, Banks.
(The cherry-tree carol, *Anon*, Gm [f'-a''b], Curwen 3 Carols.)
(The falcon, *Anon*, Fm [e'b-g''], Curwen 3 Carols.)
The freedom of the city, *Denton Welch*, Am [e'-f'#], B&H Discovery.
(Twa corbies, *Anon*, [baritone], B&H.)
Arrangements: *Five Irish Songs*, B&H 1956.
Calen-o, *Anon*, F [c'-c''], B&H 5 Irish Songs.
I'm from over the mountain, *Anon*, Ab [e'b-e''b](m), B&H 5 Irish Songs.
My grandfather died, *Anon*, Db [bb-d''b], B&H 5 Irish Songs.
The apron of flowers, *Anon*, Db [c'-d''b](f), B&H 5 Irish Songs, B&H.
The swan, *Anon*, Bb [bb-e''b](m), B&H 5 Irish Songs.

Alfonso Ferrabosco. *c.*1575 - 1628.
Collection: (*Ayres* (edited E H Fellowes), S&B 1927.) Only songs available in anthologies are listed individually here.
Drown not with tears, *Anon*, G [d'-f''], S&B (Pilkington) *Lute Songs 1.*
Fain I would, *Anon*, G [d'-f''](m), S&B (Pilkington) *Lute Songs 1.*
Like hermit poor, *Sir Walter Raleigh?* Gm [d'-e''b], S&B (Pilkington) *Lute Songs 1.*
Unconstant love, *Anon*, Cm [g'-g''], S&B (Pilkington) *Lute Songs 1.*
Young and simple though I am, *Thomas Campion*, G [g'-g''](f), S&B (Pilkington) *Lute Songs 1.*

T P Fielden. (BMIC.)

Stuart Findlay.
Collection: (*Five Shakespeare Songs*, B&H 1949.)

(How sweet the moonlight, *Shakespeare*, B&H 5 Shakespeare.)
It was a lover and his lass, *Shakespeare*, [d'-e''*b*], B&H *Shakespeare* (5 Shakespeare).
(The current with the gentle murmer glides, *Shakespeare*, B&H 5 Shakespeare.)
The poor soul sat sighing, *Shakespeare*, [d'-e''], B&H *Shakespeare* (5 Shakespeare).
(Under the greenwood tree, *Shakespeare*, B&H 5 Shakespeare.)

Michael Finnissy. 1946 - (BMIC.)

Gerald Finzi. 1901 - 1956.
Collections: *A Young Man's Exhortation*, B&H 1933; *Earth and Air and Rain*, B&H 1936; *Let us Gar-lands Bring*, B&H 1942; *Before and After Summer*, B&H 1949; *I Said to Love*, B&H 1958; *Till Earth Outwears*, B&H 1958; *To a Poet*, B&H 1965; *Oh Fair to See*, B&H 1966.
A young man's exhortation, *Thomas Hardy*, A*b* [c'(d')-a''](m), B&H Exhortation.
Amabel, *Thomas Hardy*, E*b* [b*b*-e''*b*](m), B&H Before and After.
～ As I lay in the early sun, *Shanks*, E [c'#-g''#], B&H O Fair to See.
＼ At a lunar eclipse, *Thomas Hardy*, Bm [e'-a''], B&H Till Earth Outwears.
At middle-field gate in February, *Thomas Hardy*, G#m [b-e''](m), B&H I Said to Love.
Before and after summer, *Thomas Hardy*, D*b* [a*b*-f''(e''*b*)](m), B&H Before and After.
Budmouth dears, *Thomas Hardy*, F#m [c'#-a''](m), B&H Exhortation.
Channel firing, *Thomas Hardy*, Cm [g(b*b*)-f''](m), B&H Before and After, *Heritage 3*.
Childhood among the ferns, *Thomas Hardy*, E*b* [b*b*-f''](m), B&H Before and After.
～ Come away, come away, death, *Shakespeare*, Bm [a#-d''], B&H Garlands, *Heritage 3*.
Ditty, *Thomas Hardy*, G [d'-g''](m), B&H Exhortation.
Epeisodia, *Thomas Hardy*, G [b-e''](m), B&H Before and After.
＼ Fear no more the heat o' the sun, *Shakespeare*, B*b* [b*b*-e''*b*], B&H Garlands, *Heritage 3*.
For life I had never cared greatly, *Thomas Hardy*, D [a-f''#(d'')](m), B&H I Said to Love.
Former beauties, *Thomas Hardy*, Em [d'-a''](m), B&HExhortation.
＼ Harvest, *Edmund Blunden*, Dm [c'-a''*b*], B&H O Fair to See.
He abjures love, *Thomas Hardy*, Bm [a-d''](m), B&H Before and After.
Her temple, *Thomas Hardy*, E*b* [d'-a''](m), B&H Exhortation.
～ I look into my glass, *Thomas Hardy*, [c'-g''], B&H Till Earth Outwears.
～ I need not go, *Thomas Hardy*, E [c'#-e''], B&H I Said to Love.
～ I said to love, *Thomas Hardy*, C [c'-e''*b*], B&H I Said to Love.
I say I'll seek her, *Thomas Hardy*, Em [d'-a''](m), B&H O Fair to See.
— In a churchyard, *Thomas Hardy*, [a-d''], B&H Earth and Air and Rain.
— In five-score summers, *Thomas Hardy*, Gm [c'#-e''], B&H I Said to Love.
In the mind's eye, *Thomas Hardy*, Gm [d'-f''](m), B&H Before and After.
In time of the breaking of nations, *Thomas Hardy*, B*b*m [A*b*-d'*b*](m), Banks.
～ In years defaced, *Thomas Hardy*, Dm [c'-a''], B&H Till Earth Outwears.
～ Intrada, *Thomas Traherne*, [b*b*-f''], B&H To a Poet.
～ It never looks like summer, *Thomas Hardy*, F [c'-g''], B&H Till Earth Outwears.
— It was a lover and his lass, *Shakespeare*, E [a-e''], B&HGarlands.
— June on Castle Hill, *F L Lucas*, Gm [a-e''*b*], B&H To a Poet.
＼ Let me enjoy the earth, *Thomas Hardy*, G*b* [d'*b*-a''*b*], B&H Till Earth Outwears.
～ Life laughs onward, *Thomas Hardy*, G [c'-g''], B&H Till Earth Outwears.
＼ O fair to see, *Christina Rossetti*, Cm [e'*b*-g''], B&H O Fair to See.

O mistress mine, *Shakespeare*, E♭ [b♭-e"♭](m), B&H Garlands.
～ Ode, on the rejection of St Cecilia, *George Barker*, Gm [a♭(c'♭)-f"], B&H To a Poet.
— On parent knees, *William Jones*, Em [d'-e"], B&H To a Poet.
— Only the wanderer, *Ivor Gurney*, Fm [e'♭-f"], B&H O Fair to See.
Overlooking the river, *Thomas Hardy*, E♭ [d'-e"♭](m), B&H Before and After.
╱ Proud songsters, *Thomas Hardy*, Bm [b-d"], B&H Earth and Air and Rain.
～ Rollicum-rorum, *Thomas Hardy*, D [a-e"], B&H Earth and Air and Rain, *Heritage 4*.
Shortening days, *Thomas Hardy*, Dm [d'-a"](m), B&H Exhortation.
～ Since we loved, *Robert Bridges*, G [g'-g"], B&H O Fair to See.
— So have I fared, *Thomas Hardy*, F [a-d"], B&H Earth and Air and Rain.
Summer schemes, *Thomas Hardy*, D [a-e"](m), B&H Earth and Air and Rain.
～ The birthnight, *Walter de la Mare*, D♭ [d'b-e], B&H To a Poet.
— The clock of the years, *Thomas Hardy*, Am [f#(a)-f'#(e)], B&H Earth and Air and Rain.
The comet at Yell'ham, *Thomas Hardy*, [d'-g"](m), B&H Exhortation.
The dance continued, *Thomas Hardy*, Dm [c'(d')-g"](m), B&H Exhortation.
ᴗ The market-girl, *Thomas Hardy*, F [c'-a"](m), B&H Till Earth Outwears.
— The phantom, *Thomas Hardy*, Dm [c'-f"], B&H Earth and Air and Rain.
The self-unseeing, *Thomas Hardy*, Am [g(a)-f"](m), B&H Before and After.
— The sigh, *Thomas Hardy*, G [d'-g"](m), B&H Exhortation, *Heritage 4*.
The too short time, *Thomas Hardy*, [a-f"](m), B&H Before and After.
━. To a Poet a thousand years hence, *James Elroy Flecker*, Cm [g-f"#], B&H To a Poet, *Heritage 4*.
⚬ To Joy, *Edmund Blunden*, Fm [f'b-a"b], B&H O Fair to See.
To Lizbie Browne, *Thomas Hardy*, E♭ [b♭-e"♭], B&H Earth and Air and Rain.
Two lips, *Thomas Hardy*, Fm [c'-f"](m), B&H I Said to Love.
～ Waiting both, *Thomas Hardy*, E♭ [c'-f"], B&H Earth and Air and Rain.
Transformations, *Thomas Hardy*, G [d'-a"](m), B&H Exhortation.
━ When I set out for Lyonnesse, *Thomas Hardy*, Em [b♭-e"], B&H Earth and Air and Rain.
━ Who is Sylvia, *Shakespeare*, F [a-d"], B&H Garlands.

Roger Fiske. 1910 - 1987.
(Done for, *Walter de la Mare*, Gm [e'#-e"♭], OUP.)
Weathers, *Thomas Hardy*, G [d'-e"], OUP.
(Miss Cherry, *Walter de la Mare*, G [c'#-g"], OUP.)

David Fligg. (BMIC).

Eric Fogg. 1903 - 1939.
Collection: (*Songs of Love and Life* (high & low keys), Elkin.)
Carol of the little king, Bosworth.
(Free me from the bonds of your sweetness, *Rabindranath Tagore*, [b-e"], Elkin Love and Life.)
(In the dusky path of a dream, *Rabindranath Tagore*, [a♭-d"], Elkin Love and Life.)
(It was in May, *Rabindranath Tagore*, D♭ [a-d"♭], Elkin; E♭, Elkin Love and Life.)
(One morning in the flower garden, *Rabindranath Tagore*, E [b-e"], Elkin Love and Life; G, Elkin.)
(Peace, *Rabindranath Tagore*, F [b-f"], Elkin Love and Life; E♭, G, Elkin.)

Andrew Ford. (BMIC.) 1957 -

Thomas Ford. *c.*1580 - 1648.
Collection: *Ten Airs from Musicke of Sundrie Kindes* (edited Thurston Dart), S&B 1966. Only songs available in anthologies are listed individually here.

Come Phyllis, come into these bowers, *Anon*, Gm [f#-f''](m), *Am*, B&H (Keel) *Lovesongs 1*; *Em*, *Lovesongs 1*.

Fair, sweet, cruel, *Anon*, Gm [d'-f''], B&H (Keel) *Lovesongs 1*; *Fm*, *Lovesongs 1*; *Em*, S&B (Pilkington) *Lute Songs 1*.

Not full twelve years, *Henry Morrice*, Dm [d'-a''], *Am*, S&B (Pilkington) *Lute Songs 1*.

Now I see thy looks were feigned, *Thomas Lodge*, Gm [d'-f''], *Em*, S&B (Pilkington) *Lute Songs 1*.

Since first I saw your face, *Anon*, C [c'-c''], S&B (Pilkington) *Lute Songs 1*; *Eb*, Paterson (Diack) *100 Best 4*.

Unto the temple of thy beauty, *Anon*, Gm [d'-f''](m), S&B (Pilkington) *Lute Songs 1*.

Hubert J Foss. 1899 - 1953.
Collection: (*Six Songs from Shakespeare*, OUP (two are unaccompanied duets).)
(As I walked forth, *William Blake*, Bb [f'-f''], OUP.)
(Castlepatrick, *G K Chesterton*, Dm [c'-f''](m), OUP.)
(Clouds, *Rupert Brooke*, Eb, B&H.)
(Fear no more the heat o' the sun, *Shakespeare*, Fm [c'-f''], OUP 6 Shakespeare.)
(Infant joy, *William Blake*, Bbm [e'*b*-f''], OUP.)
(O mistress mine, *Shakespeare*, F [d'-f''](m), OUP 6 Shakespeare.)
(Rioupéroux, *James Elroy Flecker*, [b-e''], OUP.)
(She sauntered by the swinging seas, *W E Henley*, Db [f'-g''*b*], OUP.)
(The new mistress, *A E Housman*, F [a-f''], OUP.)
(The nurse's song, *William Blake*, [c'-a''](f), OUP.)
(The sergeant's song, *Thomas Hardy*, F#m [c'#(b)-e''](m), OUP.)
(Unrest, *John Davidson*, [d'-f''#], OUP.)
(When daisies pied, *Shakespeare*, G [d'-g''], OUP 6 Shakespeare.
Arrangement:
(The trees they do grow high, *Anon*, [c-e''](f), OUP.)

Ivor Foster. 1904 -
Collection: *Three Songs* Lengnick 1947.
Let me enjoy, *Thomas Hardy*, Eb [d'-g''](m), Lengnick 3 Songs.
Rose-Ann, *Thomas Hardy*, Cm [e'*b*-g''](m), Lengnick 3 Songs.
The voice of the thorn, *Thomas Hardy*, Dm [f'-f''], Lengnick 3 Songs.

Myles B Foster. 1851 - 1922.
Under the greenwood tree, *Shakespeare*, Eb [c'-f''], B&H *Shakespeare*.
(Unity, *Helen Marion Burnside*, Eb, B&H.)
John Foulds. 1880 - 1939. (See also BMIC.)
(Eileen Aroon, *Gerald Griffin*, D [d'-e''], Chappell; E, F, Chappell.)
(The reed player, *Fioan Macleod*, Bm [a*b*-d''], Curwen.)

Benjamin Frankel. 1906 - 1973.
Collection: *Eight Songs*, Novello 1963.
Drop, drop, slow tears, *Phineas Fletcher*, [d'*b*-g''], Novello 8 Songs.

Faery Song, *John Keats*, [c'-g''#], Novello 8 Songs.
Hornpipe, *Cecil Day Lewis*, [c'-g''#], Novello 8 Songs.
I had a dove, *John Keats*, [a#-f'#], Novello 8 Songs.
O solitude, *John Keats*, [c'#-b''♭], Novello 8 Songs.
Retort to a clarion call, *John Scott of Amwell*, [e'-b''♭], Novello 8 Songs.
Stay, O sweet, *John Donne*, [c'#-g''], Novello 8 Songs.
The knight of the grail, *Anon*, [e'♭-a''♭], Novello 8 Songs.

Norman Fraser. 1904 - 1986.
(Venice twilight, *Logan Pearsall Smith*, Bm [b♭-f''], OUP.)

Herbert Fryer. 1877 - 1957.
The Virgin's cradle-hymn, *Anon* tr. *Arthur Charlton*, F [f'-f''], B&H *Heritage 1*.

Norman Fulton. 1910 - 1980.
Collection: (*Two Songs of Thomas Lodge, Two Songs from Twelfth Night*, OUP 1943); (*Three Songs for High Voice*, S&B 1952); (*Two Christmas Songs*, OUP 1973.)
(A lament in spring, *Thomas Lodge*, Am [d'-e''], OUP 2 Thomas Lodge.)
(Christ keep the hollow land, *William Morris*, [e'-f''], S&B 3 Songs.)
(Come away, death, *Shakespeare*, E♭ [d'-e''♭](m), OUP 2 Twelfth Night.)
(Love in my bosom, *Thomas Lodge*, F#m [c'#-f'#], OUP 2 Thomas Lodge.)
Make we merry, *Richard Hill*, D [d'-f'#], OUP *Solo Christmas*; B♭, *Sing Christmas*; (2 Christmas).
(Never look back, *Will Redgrave*, [d'-a''♭], S&B 3 Songs.)
(No room at the inn, *F N Robert*, G [d'-e''♭], OUP 2 Christmas.)
(O mistress mine, *Shakespeare*, D [c'#-d''](m), OUP 2 Twelfth Night.)
(The cakewalk, *Wilfrid Wilson Gibson*, B♭m [e♭-e'♭](m), OUP.)
(The willow song, *Shakespeare*, Gm [d♭-f''], OUP.)
(To the moon, *Thomas Hardy*, [e'♭-f'#], S&B 3 Songs.)

G

H Balfour Gardiner. 1877 - 1950.

The stranger's song, *Thomas Hardy*, C [c'-e''](m), Thames *Hardy Songbook*.

(Winter, *Shakespeare*, F [c'-f''], Ascherberg.)

Roberto Gerhard. 1896 - 1970.

Arrangement: (*Six Catalan Folksongs*, B&H 1933.)

(Dancing in a sack, *Anon* tr. *J B Trend*, [a'-b-f''], B&H 6 Catalan.)

(Death and the maiden, *Anon* tr. *J B Trend*, [g'-g''], B&H 6 Catalan.)

(Old Cotilo, *Anon* tr. *J B Trend*, [a'-b-g''b](m), B&H 6 Catalan.)

(The lark, *Anon* tr. *J B Trend*, [g'#-f''#](m), B&H 6 Catalan.)

(The ploughboy, *Anon* tr. *J B Trend*, [a'-b-f''], B&H 6 Catalan.)

(The woman-hater, *Anon* tr. *J B Trend*, [f-e''](m), B&H 6 Catalan.)

Edward German. 1862 - 1936.

Collection: (*The Just So Song Book*, Novello)

(All the world awakes today, Cramer.)

Big steamers, *Rudyard Kipling*, D [c'#-f''#(e'')], *Cramer Song Folio 1*; (C, Cramer).

Charming Chloe, *Robert Burns*, Eb [c'-e''b], Novello.

(Dew upon the lily, Cramer.)

Dream o' Day Jill, *Chas. H Taylor*, Eb [c'-f''](f), Chappell/Elkin; F, Chappell/Elkin.

Glorious Devon! *Harold Boulton*, F [e'-g''](m), B&H *Ballad Album 1*; C, *Souvenirs*, (D, B&H).

(I am the most wise Baviaan, *Rudyard Kipling*, D, [b-f''#], Novello Just So.)

(I keep six honest serving-men, *Rudyard Kipling*, Eb, [bb-e''b], Novello Just So.)

(Kangaroo and Dingo, *Rudyard Kipling*, A, [e'-f''#(e'')], Novello Just So.)

(Merrow Down, *Rudyard Kipling*, E, [b-e''], Novello Just So.)

(My song is of the sturdy north, Dm, Cramer; Cm, Cramer.)

(Of all the tribe of Tegumai, *Rudyard Kipling*, F, [b-f''], Novello Just So.)

(Rolling down to Rio, *Rudyard Kipling*, Am, [a-e''], Novello Just So.)

(Sea lullaby, *Harold Boulton*, F [c'-g''], Chappell *English Recital 2*.)

(The camel's hump, *Rudyard Kipling*, Eb, [c'-e''b], Novello Just So.)

The English Rose, *Basil Hood*, Bb [e'-g''](m), B&H *Ballad Album 1*.

(The first friend, *Rudyard Kipling*, G, [d'-e''], Novello Just So.)

(The riddle, *Rudyard Kipling*, Dm, [d'-d''], Novello Just So.)

(There was never a Queen like Balkis, *Rudyard Kipling*, A, [e'-e''], Novello Just So.)

(This unhabited island, *Rudyard Kipling*, Gm, [d'-d''], Novello Just So.)

(What 'Dane-geld' means, *Rudyard Kipling*, A, Cramer; G, Cramer.)

(When the cabin portholes, *Rudyard Kipling*, Dm, [c'-f''], Novello Just So.)

Who'll buy my lavender, *Caryl Battersby*, D [d'-f''#], B&H *Ballad Album 2*; (C, E, B&H).

Alan Gibbs.

Collection: *Five Elizabethan Songs*, Bardic.

And if I did what then? *George Gascoigne*, [A#-e''](m), Bardic 5 Elizabethan.

Even such is time, *Walter Raleigh*, [G-e''b](m), Bardic 5 Elizabethan.

Follow a shadow, *Ben Jonson*, [d-e''](m), Bardic 5 Elizabethan.

Mark when she smiles, *Edmund Spenser*, [G-e'*b*](m), Bardic 5 Elizabethan.
Sir Patrick Spens, *Anon*, [G#-f'](m), Bardic.
With how sad steps, *Philip Sidney*, [B-f'](m), Bardic 5 Elizabethan.

Armstrong Gibbs. 1889 - 1960.

Collections: (*Two Songs*, B&H 1932); (*Old Wine in New Bottles, Five Children's Songs from 'Peacock Pie'*, B&H 1933); (*A Voice in the Dusk Op 91*, B&H 1938); (*Joan of Arc Op 102*, B&H 1947); (*Songs of the Mad Sea-Captain Op 111*, B&H 1946); (*Two Old English Lyrics*, Chappell 1949); (*Three Lyrics by Christina Rossetti*, OUP 1953); *Ten Songs* (introduction by Mollie Petrie), Thames 1989.

(A ballad-maker, *Padraic Colum*, Cm [c'-e''*b*](m), B&H; E*b*m, B&H.)
(A birthday, *Christina Rossetti*, C [e'-a''](f), OUP 3 Lyrics.)
A song of shadows, *Walter de la Mare*, E*b* [e'*b*-g''*b*], Thames *Century 1*, B&H.
(Abel Wright, *Bernard Martin*, C [a*b*-d''#](m), B&H Sea-Captain.)
(Amaryllis, *Anon*, A [e'-f'#(a')](m) Chappell *English Recital 1*; F, 2 Old English).
(Ann's cradle song, *Walter de la Mare*, C#m [d'*b*-e''*b*](f), Curwen.)
(Arrogant poppies, *Clifford Bax*, Em [g'-g''](f), Curwen.)
(As I lay in the early sun, *Edward Shanks*, F [d'-f''](m), B&H.)
(Beggar's song, *Walter de la Mare*, Em [b-e''](m), Curwen.)
(By a bier-side, *John Masefield*, C#m [c'#-e''], Curwen.)
(Chloris in the snow, *Anon*, Am [d'-e''*b*], Chappell 2 Old English; Cm, 2 Old English.)
Covent Garden, *Eileen Carfrae*, C [c'-e''], Roberton; D, E, Roberton.
(Crowning, *Mordaunt Currie*, A [c'#-a''](f), B&H Joan of Arc.)
(Danger, *Mordaunt Currie*, [d'*b*-d''], Curwen.)
(Defeat, *Mordaunt Currie*, Am [d'-f''](f), B&H Joan of Arc.)
(Down in yonder meadow, *Anon*, D [c'-f''], B&H 2 Songs.)
(Dream song, *Walter de la Mare*, A*b*, B&H.)
(Dusk, *Anon*, F [c'-e''*b*], B&H.)
(Evening in summer, *John Fletcher*, D*b* [d'*b*-f''], OUP.)
(February, *Mordaunt Currie*, Am [c'-f''], B&H.)
Five eyes, *Walter de la Mare*, Gm [d'-d''], B&H; B*b*m, B&H.
(For remembrance, *Edward Shanks*, D [d'-g''], B&H.)
Fulfilment, *Mordaunt Currie*, D [d'-a''], Thames 10 Songs.
(Gipsies, *H H Bashford*, Cm [c'-f''], OUP; Em, OUP.)
(Gone is my love, *Edith Harrhy*, B&H.)
(Gone were but the winter, *Christina Rossetti*, G [d'-g''], OUP 3 Lyrics.)
(Hidden treasure, *Bernard Martin*, Gm [g(b*b*)-d''](m), B&H Sea-Captain.)
Hypochondriacus, *Charles Lamb*, [b*b*-e''], Thames 10 Songs.
(If music be the food of love, *Henry Heveningham*, G*b* [a*b*-e''*b*](m), B&H Old Wine.)
(Immortality, *Mordaunt Currie*, Am [e'-a''], B&H.)
(In the faery hills, *John Irvine*, E*b* [d'-g''], B&H A Voice.)
(In the highlands, *R L Stevenson*, E*b* [e'*b*-a''*b*], Curwen.)
(In the woods in June, *Mordaunt Currie*, A, B&H.)
(Jenny Jones, *Doris Rowley*, Bm [a-e''], Curwen.)
(John Mouldy, *Walter de la Mare*, Cm [c'-e''*b*], B&H.)
(Juliet Anne, *Mordaunt Currie*, D [b-d''], B&H; A, B&H.)
(Lily-bright and shine-a, *Anon*, Em [e'-g''], B&H 2 Songs.)

(Love's prisoner, *William Blake*, B♭ [b-f''], B&H; D, B&H.)
(Love's wisdom, *Mordaunt Currie*, B♭, B&H; D, A, B&H.)
(Lullaby, *Walter de la Mare*, Gm [e'-f''], Curwen.)
Lyonesse, *Thomas Hardy*, Am [a-f''](m), Thames *Hardy Songbook*; (Cm, B&H).
(Maritime invocation, *A C Boyd*, Cm [b-f''](m), B&H; Dm, E♭m, B&H.)
(Midnight, *Jeffery Lang*, B♭m [c'-f''], B&H.)
(Moon magic, *John Irvine*, [e'-g''], B&H A Voice.)
(Mors Janua Vitae, *Mordaunt Currie*, [c'-b''♭](f), B&H Joan of Arc.)
(Neglected moon, *Clifford Bax*, E♭ [e'♭-a''♭](f), Curwen.)
(Nightfall, *Harry Dawson*, C [d'-g''], Curwen.)
Nod, *Walter de la Mare*, D [d'-f''#], B&H *Heritage 3*, Chester *Celebrated 1*.
(Oh, nightingale upon my tree, *Mordaunt Currie*, B♭ [c'-e''♭], B&H.)
(Padraic the fiddler, *Padraic Gregory*, [e'-f''], Curwen.)
Philomel, *Richard Barnfield*, Bm [e'♭-g''], Thames 10 Songs.
(Philomela, *Philip Sidney*, E♭ [b♭-e''♭], B&H.)
(Picture me love, *Westlake & Ridley*, B&H.)
(Pious Celinda goes to prayers, *William Congreve*, Gm [d'-d''](m), B&H Old Wine.)
(Rest in the Lord, *Edmund Beale Sargant*, Gm [b-e''♭], B&H.)
(Revelation, *Mordaunt Currie*, D♭ [c'-g''#](f), B&H Joan of Arc.)
(Sailing homeward, *Chan Fang Shen*, tr. *Arthur Waley*, Bm [d'-g''#], B&H; Gm, B&H.)
Silver, *Walter de la Mare*, F#m [c'#-f''#], B&H *Heritage 4*, B&H.
(Sledburn Fair, *Anon*, B♭ [c'-e''♭], B&H.)
Slow, horses, slow, *Thomas Westwood*, Cm [f'-g''], Roberton.
(Spring, *John Irvine*, B♭ [f'-g''], B&H A Voice.)
(Summer night, *Margery Agrell*, C#m [f'-g''], Curwen.)
(Summertime, *Benedict Ellis*, B♭, B&H.)
(Sussex ways, *Mordaunt Currie*, E♭ [c'-e''♭], B&H.)
(Sweet sounds, begone, *Walter de la Mare*, B♭ [d'♭-f''#], B&H.)
(Take heed, young heart, *Walter de la Mare*, Em [e'-g''], Curwen.)
The ballad of Semmerwater, *William Watson*, Gm [g♭-e''♭] Thames *Century 4*, (Curwen).
(The birch tree, *Georgina Mase*, Am [a'-a''], Curwen.)
(The cherry tree, *Margaret Rose*, Bm [b-e''], Curwen.)
(The exile, *Walter de la Mare*, Am [c'-e''], Chester.)
The fields are full, *Edward Shanks*, E♭m [d'♭-g''♭], Thames 10 Songs, B&H *Heritage 4*, B&H.
(The golden ray, *Bernard Martin*, D [b-d''](m), B&H Sea-Captain.)
(The hawthorn tree, *Hilda Maude*, Gm, B&H; Em, B&H.)
(The lamb and the dove, *Christina Rossetti*, Em [e'-a''♭], OUP 3 Lyrics.)
(The little green orchard, *Walter de la Mare*, F [e'♭-f'], B&H.)
(The little salamander, *Walter de la Mare*, Gm [g'♭-f''], Curwen.)
(The love talker, *Ethna Carbery*, [mezzo], B&H.)
(The orchard sings to the child, *Margaret Cropper*, A [e'-f''#], Curwen.)
The oxen, *Thomas Hardy*, Fm [d'♭-f''], Thames 10 Songs.
(The rejected lover, *Clifford Bax*, G [d'-g''](m), Curwen.)
(The scarecrow, *Walter de la Mare*, Bm [a-f''#], Curwen.)
The ship of Rio, *Walter de la Mare*, E♭ [a♭-e''♭], B&H *Heritage 3*.
The splendour falls, *Alfred Lord Tennyson*, Cm [a♭-e''], Thames 10 Songs.

(The starlighters, *Ann Gibbs*, B&H.)
(The summer palace, *Benedict Ellis*, E*b*, B&H.)
The wanderer, *Walter de la Mare*, B*b*m [d'*b*-f''], Thames 10 Songs.
(The wind comes softly, *John Irvine*, F [e'-f''#], B&H A Voice.)
The witch, *Mordaunt Currie*, Em [d'-g''], Thames 10 Songs.
(Tis wine that inspires, *Anon*, C [g-e''](m), B&H Old Wine.)
Titania, *Mordaunt Currie*, E*b* [b*b*-f''], Thames 10 Songs.
(To Anise, *Nathaniel Downes*, D [a-d''], B&H.)
(To one who passed whistling through the night, *Margery Agrell*, C [f'-g''], Curwen.)
(Toll the bell, *Bernard Martin*, Dm [a-d''](m), B&H Sea-Captain.)
Tom o' Bedlam, *Anon*, Am [g-e''*b*], Thames 10 Songs.
(Victory, *Mordaunt Currie*, C#m [e'-g''#](f), B&H Joan of Arc.)
(When Arthur first in Court began, *Anon*, Cm [a-e''](m), B&H Old Wine.)
(When I was one-and-twenty, *A E Housman*, G [d'-f''#](m), Curwen.)
Why do I love, *Ephelia (Joan Philips?)*, [c'-a''*b*(g''*b*)], B&H New Imperial 1.
Arrangements: (*Four Songs by Edward Miller*, B&H 1933); (*Two Songs*, B&H 1938.)
(Fyre, fyre, *Anon*, *Elizabeth Rogers Virginal Booke*, G [d'-e''], B&H 2 Songs.)
(I prithee, send me back my heart, *John Suckling*, B&H 4 Miller.)
(Lye still, my deare, *Anon*, *Elizabeth Rogers Virginal Booke*, Am [g'#-f''], B&H 2 Songs.)
(The despairing shepherd, *Air Carr Scroope*, B&H 4 Miller.)
(The happy pair, *Pilkington*, B&H 4 Miller.)
(To Althea, from prison, *Richard Lovelace*, B&H 4 Miller.)

Thomas Giles, *fl.* 1607.
Triumph now with joy and mirth, *Thomas Campion*, G [d'-d''], S&B (Greer) *Printed*.

Harry Gill. 1897 - 1987.
Collection: (*3 Songs*, OUP 1941.)
(A Saxon song, *Vera Sackville-West*, G [b-e''], OUP.)
(About my father's farm, *Edward Wright*, [b*b*-g''](f), OUP.)
In memoriam, *H Percy Dixon*, D [b-e''], Thames *Century 2*, (OUP 3 Songs).
(Love forsaken, *H Percy Dixon*, B*b*m, [a-f''], OUP 3 Songs.)
(Obsequy, *H Percy Dixon*, A [b-e''], OUP 3 Songs.)
(The night, *Hilaire Belloc*, C [c'-e''*b*], OUP.)

Ruth Gipps. 1921 - (BMIC.)

Gareth Glyn. 1951 -
Hymn to the Virgin, *Ieuan ap Hywel Swrdwal*, [A#-f''](m) Welsh Music *Songs from Wales 2*.

Alexander Goehr. 1932 -
Collection: *Four Songs from the Japanese*, Schott 1971.
Do torrents spare the fressh bloom flower? *Anon* tr. *Lafcadio Hearn*, [c'-f''], Schott 4 Songs.
I love and I love, *Anon* tr. *Lafcadio Hearn*, [c'-g''*b*], Schott 4 Songs.
The truth is, *Anon* tr. *Lafcadio Hearn*, [c'-f''#], Schott 4 Songs.
Things have never changed, *Anon* tr. *Lafcadio Hearn*, [d'-a''#](m), Schott 4 Songs.

A M Goodhart. 1866 - ?
The bells of Clermont Town, *Hilaire Belloc*, Dm [a-d''], B&H *Heritage 1*.

Eugène Goossens. 1893 - 1962.
Collections: *Chamber Music*, Lengnick 1930; *Four Songs*, Chester.
A winter night idyll, *Bettie F Holmes*, [high], Chester 4 Songs.
A woodland dell, *Bettie F Holmes*, [high], Chester 4 Songs.
All day I hear the noise of waters, *James Joyce*, [d'*b*-e''*b*], Lengnick Chamber Music.
Dear heart, why will you use me so, *James Joyce*, [b-e''], Lengnick Chamber Music.
(Don Juan's serenade, *Arnold Bennett*, [e*b*-d'(g')](m), Chester.)
Gentle lady, do not sing sad songs, *James Joyce*, [c'#-e''], Lengnick Chamber Music.
I hear an army, *James Joyce*, [d'-f'#], Lengnick Chamber Music.
Melancholy, *John Fletcher*, [d'-e''], Chester.
Now, O now, *James Joyce*, [c#-f'#], Lengnick Chamber Music.
O cool is the valley now, *James Joyce*, [f'-e''*b*], Lengnick Chamber Music.
Philomel, *John Fletcher*, [medium],Chester.
Seascape *Bettie F Holmes*, [high], Chester 4 Songs.
The appeal, *Thomas Wyatt*, [medium],Chester.
Threshold, *Bettie F Holmes*, [high], Chester 4 Songs.
When thou art dead, *Margaret Kennedy*, [f'#-e''*b*], Curwen.
(Arrangements: *Old Scottish Folksongs*, Chester.)
Searching for lambs, *Anon*, Chester.

David Gow. 1924 - 1993.(BMIC.)
(A West Sussex drinking song, *Hilaire Belloc*, B&H.)

Ella Grainger.
Crying for the moon, *Ella Grainger*, [b*b*-e''*b*], Bardic.
Farewell to an atoll, *Ella Grainger*, [e'*b*-a''*b*], Bardic.
Honey pot bee, *Ella Grainger*, [c'#-f'#], Bardic.
Love at first sight, *Ella Grainger*, [a-e''], Bardic.
The mermaid, *Ella Grainger*, [c'-e''*b*], Bardic.
To echo, *Ella Grainger*, [c'-f''], Bardic.

Percy Grainger. 1882 - 1961.
Anchor song, *Rudyard Kipling*, [c'#-f'#](m), Bardic.
Dedication, *Rudyard Kipling*, [e'-c''], Bardic.
Ganges pilot, *Rudyard Kipling*, [c'-f''](m), Bardic.
Lukannon, *Rudyard Kipling*, [c'-g''], Bardic (realised B P Ould).
Merciful Town, *Rudyard Kipling*, [e'*b*-e''*b*], Bardic.
Northern ballad, *Rudyard Kipling*, [b*b*-f''](m), Bardic.
Ride with an idle whip, *Rudyard Kipling*, [g-f'#](m), Bardic.
Sailor's chanty, *Arthur Conan Doyle*, [g'-e''], Bardic.
Soldier, soldier (1), *Rudyard Kipling*, [e'*b*-c''](m), Bardic.
Soldier, soldier (2), *Rudyard Kipling*, [c'#-f'#], Bardic.
The first chanty, *Rudyard Kipling*, [a#-f'#], Bardic.
The sea-wife, *Rudyard Kipling*, [c'#-f''], Bardic.

The secret of the sea, *Henry Wadsworth Longfellow*, [e'-e''](m), Bardic.
The young British soldier, *Rudyard Kipling*, [c'#-e''], Bardic.
Variations on 'The harmonious blacksmith', *vocalise*, [b-g''#], Bardic.
Arrangements: *Thirteen Folksongs Volume 1* (introduction by Peter Pears, notes on the songs by David Tall), Thames 1981; *Volume 2*, Thames 1982; *Songs of the North*, Bardic.
Afton Water, *Robert Burns*, [c'-e''], Bardic.
Bold William Taylor, *Anon*, [d'-e''*b*], Thames Folksongs 2.
Bonnie George Campbell, *Anon*, [d'-e''], Bardic North.
British waterside, *Anon*, [e'-e''], Thames Folksongs 1.
Creeping Jane, *Anon*, G [c'#-e''], Thames Folksongs 2, Bardic.
Died for love, *Anon*, [e'-e''](f), Thames Folksongs 1.
Drowned, *Rev. A Stewart*, [d'-d''], Bardic North.
Early one morning, *Anon*, Fm [c'-c'''(f')], Thames Folksongs 2, Bardic.
Evan Banks, *Robert Burns*, [e'*b*-g''], Bardic.
Fair young Mary, *Mairi Bhan Og (A C Macleod)*, [d'-f'#], Bardic North.
Hard hearted Barb'ra (H)ellen, *Anon*, F# [c'#-f'#](m), Thames Folksongs 2, Bardic.
Leezie Lindsay, *Anon*, [e'*b*-e''*b*], Bardic North.
Lord Maxwell's goodnight, *Anon*, F [c'-a''](m), Thames Folksongs 2, Bardic.
My faithful fond one, *Anon (Gaelic)* tr. *Blackie*, [d'-e''], Bardic North.
O'er the moor, *A C Macleod*, [B*b*-c''], Bardic North.
Six dukes went afishing, *Anon*, [e'-f'#], Thames Folksongs 1.
Skye boat song, *Harold Boulton*, [d'-d''], Bardic North.
The power of love, *Anon*, [g'#-g''](f), Thames Folksongs 2, Bardic.
The pretty maid milking her cow, *Anon*, [d'-g''], Thames Folksongs 1.
The sprig of thyme, *Anon*, A [e'-f'#](f), Thames Folksongs 1.
The twa corbies, *Anon*, Gm [b*b*-g''](m), Thames Folksongs 1.
The woen are a' gane wud, *Anon*, [e'-e''], Bardic North.
This is not my plaid, *W Haley*, [d'-d''], Bardic North.
Turn ye to me, *Christopher North (John Wilson)*, [b-e''], Bardic North.
Weaving song, *Anon*, [c'-c''], Bardic North.
Willie's gane to Melville Castle, *Anon*, [d'-d''], Bardic North.
Willow, willow, *Anon*, Em [e'-e''], Thames Folksongs 1.
Yon wild mossy mountains, *Robert Burns*, [b*b*-b'*b*], Bardic.

Thomas Greaves. *fl.* 1604.
Collection: *Songes of Sundrie Kindes* (edited Ian Spink), S&B 1962). Only songs available in anthologies are listed individually here.
Shaded with olive trees, *Anon*, F [d'-f''], B&H (Keel) *Lovesongs 1*; Eb, *Lovesongs 1*.
Ye bubbling springs, *Anon*, Gm [d'-f''], S&B (Pilkington) *Lute Songs 1*.

Maurice Greene. 1696 - 1755.
Collections: *Seven Sacred Solos* (edited Stanley Roper) (high & low keys), Bosworth 1911.
Blessed are they that dwell in thy house, *Psalm 84*, D [d'-f'#], Bosworth 7 Sacred; E, 7 Sacred.
(Fair Sally, *Anon*, Cm [c'-ef''(g')], OUP (Fiske).)
Go, rose, my Chloe's bosom grace, *Gay*, G [d'-e''], S&B (Pilkington) *Early Georgian 1*.
I laid me down and slept, Bosworth (Roper).

I will lay me down in peace, *Psalm 4, v. 9*, E♭[d'-e''♭], Bosworth 7 Sacred, Bosworth, B&H (Patrick) *Sacred Songs 2*; F, Bosworth 7 Sacred.

Like the young god of wine, *Anon*, E♭[B♭-e'♭](m), Elkin (Taylor).

(My lips shall speak the praise, *Psalm?*, C[d'-f''], OUP (Roper).)

(O give me the comfort, *Psalm?*, Em[c'#(b)-e''], OUP (Roper).)

O praise the Lord, *Psalm 103*, G[d'#-f''#(g)], Bosworth 7 Sacred, Bosworth; B♭, 7 Sacred.

O that my ways, *Psalm 119*, D♭[d'b-f''♭], Bosworth 7 Sacred; F, 7 Sacred.

Orpheus with his lute, *Shakespeare*, B♭[c'-g''], S&B (Pilkington) *Early Georgian 2*.

Praise the Lord, O my̆ soul, *Psalm 103*, E♭[d'-f''], Bosworth 7 Sacred.

(Praised be the Lord, *Psalm?*, Cm[c'-f''], OUP (Roper).)

(Salvation belongeth unto the Lord, *Psalm?*, B♭[f'-e''♭], OUP (Roper).)

The gentiles shall come to thy light, *Isaiah 60, v. 3*, F[c'-f''], B&H (Patrick) *Sacred Songs 2*.

(The eyes of all / Thou openest thine hand, *Psalm?*, F[e'-f''], OUP (Roper).)

The Lord's name is praised, *Psalm 113*, D[c'#-e''], Bosworth 7 Sacred; F, 7 Sacred.

The sun shall be no more thy light, *Psalm?*, Cm[d'-f''], Bosworth 7 Sacred, Bosworth; Dm, 7 Sacred.

Edward Gregson. 1945 - (BMIC.)

Ivor Gurney. 1890-1937. Collections: (*Lights Out*, S&B 1926); (*A First Volume of Ten Songs, Twenty Songs Volume 2*, OUP 1938); (*A Third Volume of Ten Songs*, OUP 1952); (*A Fourth Volume of Ten Songs*, OUP 1959); (*A Fifth Volume of Ten Songs*, OUP 1979); *Five Elizabethan Songs*, B&H, 1920; *Ludlow and Teme*, S&B, 1923, rev. edition (Pilkington) 1982; *The Western Playland*, S&B, 1926, rev. edition (Pilkington) 1982; *Twenty Favourite Songs* (Neil Jenkins), OUP 1996.

(A cradle song, *W B Yeats*, E♭[e'b-f''♭], OUP Songs 4.)

(A sword, *Robin Flower*, Dm[d'-e''](m), OUP Songs 2.)

A piper in the streets today, *Seumas O'Sullivan*, G[g'-e''], OUP 20 Favourite, (Songs 4).

All night under the moon, *Wilfrid Gibson*, G#[d'#-f''#], OUP 20 Favourite, (Songs 1).

An epitaph, *Walter de la Mare*, D[d'-e''], OUP 20 Favourite, (Songs 2); C, *Solo Baritone*.

Black Stichel, *Wilfrid Gibson*, F[d'b-e''], OUP 20 Favourite, (Songs 1).

(Blaweary, *Wilfrid Gibson*, F[d'-d''], OUP Songs 2.)

Bread and cherries, *Walter de la Mare*, Em[e'-f''#], OUP 20 Favourite, (Songs 2), Mayhew *Collection 2*.

Bright clouds, *Edward Thomas*, G[d'-f''], Thames *Century 4* (S&B Lights Out).

Brown is my love, *Anon*, D♭[d'b-g''♭](m), OUP 20 Favourite, (Songs 4).

(By a bierside, *John Masefield*, C, [a-f''], OUP Songs 5.)

(Captain Stratton's fancy, *John Masefield*, G[c'-e''](m), S&B.)

(Cathleen ni Houlihan, *W B Yeats*, Am[c'b-f''], OUP Songs 1.)

Carol of the Skiddaw yowes, *Ernest Casson*, Am[d'-e''], B&H *Heritage 1*.

(Come, O come, my life's delight, *Thomas Campion*, A♭[b♭-f''#], B&H.)

Desire in spring, *Francis Ledwidge*, E[b-e''], OUP 20 Favourite, (Songs 5; G, OUP).

Down by the salley gardens, *W B Yeats*, A♭[d'b-f''], OUP 20 Favourite, (Songs 1), Mayhew *Collection 2*.

(Edward, Edward, *Anon*, Dm[c'-f''], S&B.)

(Epitaph in old mode, *John Squire*, D♭[d'b-f''♭], OUP Songs 2.)

Even such is time, *Walter Raleigh*, Em[b-e''], OUP 20 Favourite, (Songs 4).

Far in a western brookland, *A E Housman*, Db [d'b-g''b](m), S&B Ludlow and Teme.
Golden friends, *A E Housman*, Ab [e'b-e''b](m), S&B The Western Playland.
(Goodnight to the meadow, *Robert Graves*, Eb [c'-e''b], OUP Songs 3.)
(Ha'nacker mill, *Hilaire Belloc*, F [f'-e''b], OUP 1.)
Hawk and buckle, *John Doyle (Robert Graves)*, Gm [d'-e''b], Mayhew *Collection 1*.
I praise the tender flower, *Robert Bridges*, F [c'#-e''], OUP 20 Favourite, (Songs 3).
(I shall ever be maiden, *Bliss Carman*, G [d'b-g''](f), OUP 3.)
I will go with my father a-ploughing, *MacCathmhaoil*, Em [d'-e''], B&H *Heritage 1*.
(In Flanders, *F W Harvey*, Eb [c'#-f''], OUP Songs 4.)
Is my team ploughing, *A E Housman*, Dm [a(b)-e''](m), S&B The Western Playland.
(Last hours, *John Freeman*, Em, [bb-e''], OUP Songs 2.)
Lights out, *Edward Thomas*, Db [d'b-e''], Thames *Century 2*, (S&B Lights Out).
(Love shakes my soul, *Bliss Carman*, Bm, [b-f''#](f), OUP Songs 4.)
Loveliest of trees, *A E Housman*, Db [d'b-f''](m), S&B The Western Playland.
Ludlow Fair, *A E Housman*, Cm [e'b-g''](m), S&B Ludlow and Teme.
March, *A E Housman*, F [c'-f''](m), S&B The Western Playland.
Most holy night, *Hilaire Belloc*, Eb, [e'b-e''], OUP 20 Favourite, (Songs 4).
Nine of the clock, *John Doyle (Robert Graves)*, G, [d'-e''], Mayhew *Collection 1*.
(On the downs, *John Masefield*, Gm, [c'-e''], OUP Songs 4.)
On the idle hill of summer, *A E Housman*, F [e'b-a''](m), S&B Ludlow and Teme.
Orpheus, *Shakespeare*, E [d'#-g''], B&H 5 Elizabethan.
(Ploughman singing, *John Clare*, B [d'-g''], OUP Songs 3.)
Reveille, *A E Housman*, F [d'-f''](m), S&B The Western Playland.
(Scents, *Edward Thomas*, Db, [d'b-e''], S&B Lights Out.)
Severn meadows, *Ivor Gurney*, D [b-d''], OUP 20 Favourite, (Songs 5).
(Shepherd's song, *Ben Jonson*, Db [c'-f''b], OUP Songs 3.)
(Since thou O fondest and truest, *Robert Bridges*, E [d'#-e''], B&H.)
Sleep, *John Fletcher*, Db [d'b-a''b], B&H 5 Elizabethan, *New Imperial 4*, B&H; Bb, B&H *Heritage 1*.
Snow, *Edward Thomas*, Fm [e'b-g''], OUP 20 Favourite, (Songs 3).
(Song of Ciabhan, *Ethna Carbery*, D [d'-e''b], OUP Songs 5.)
(Sowing, *Edward Thomas*, Cm [c'-e''], S&B).
Spring, *Thomas Nashe*, E [c'-g''#], B&H 5 Elizabethan, *Heritage 1*.
(Star-talk, *Robert Graves*, D [b'-f''#], S&B.)
Tears, *Anon*, C#m [c'#-e''], B&H 5 Elizabethan.
The apple orchard, *Bliss Carman*, Eb [d'#-e''b], OUP 20 Favourite, (Songs 5).
The aspens, *A E Housman*, F [c'-e''](m), S&B The Western Playland.
(The boat is chafing, *John Davidson*, Db [d'b-e''], OUP Songs 2.)
The bonnie Earl of Murray, *Anon*, Dm [d'-f''], B&H *New Imperial 5*.
(The cherry trees bend over, *Edward Thomas*, E [e'-e''], OUP Songs 3.)
The cloths of heaven, *W B Yeats*, Eb [e'b-g''], OUP 20 Favourite, (Songs 5).
(The County Mayo, *James Stephens*, Em [c'-f''](m), B&H.)
The far country, *A E Housman*, F# [c'#-d''#](m), S&B The Western Playland.
(The fiddler of Dooney, *W B Yeats*, Eb [bb-f''](m), OUP Songs 4.)
(The fields are full, *Edward Shanks*, E [c'#-e''], OUP 20 Favourite, (Songs 5).
(The folly of being comforted, *W B Yeats*, C#m [c'#-g''#](m), OUP Songs 2.)
(The happy tree, *Gerald Gould*, E [e'-e''], OUP Songs 3.)

(The Latmian shepherd, *Edward Shanks*, Eb [c'-e''], OUP Songs 1.)
The Lent lily, *A E Housman*, A [e'-a''](m), S&B Ludlow and Teme.
(The night of Trafalgar, *Thomas Hardy*, Dm [d'-f''](m), OUP Songs 5.)
(The penny whistle, *Edward Thomas*, Dm [c'#-f''], S&B Lights Out.)
The Scribe, *Walter de la Mare*, Bm [bb-e''], OUP 20 Favourites, (Songs 2).
(The ship, *John Squire*, Db [d'b-e''], OUP Songs 3.)
The singer, *Edward Shanks*, Bm [d'b-f''], OUP 20 Favourite, (Songs 1).
(The trumpet, *Edward Thomas*, Ab [d'b-f''], S&B Lights Out).
(The twa corbies, *Anon*, Am [c'-f''], OUP Songs 5.)
(Thou didst delight my eyes, *Robert Bridges*, Db [d'b-e''b], OUP Songs 3.)
Tis time, I think, *A E Housman*, F [e'b-g''b](m), S&B Ludlow and Teme.
To violets, *Robert Herrick*, G [c'-e''], OUP 20 Favourite, (Songs 4).
Twice a week, *A E Housman*, Bm [b-f''](m), S&B The Western Playland.
Under the greenwood tree, *Shakespeare*, Am [c'-f''#], B&H 5 Elizabethan.
Walking song, *F W Harvey*, F [c'-f''], OUP 20 Favourite, (Songs 5).
(West Sussex drinking song, *Hilaire Belloc*, F [c'-f''](m), Chappell.)
(When death to either shall come, *Robert Bridges*, Db [d'b-e''b], OUP Songs 1.)
When I was one-and-twenty, *A E Housman*, Am [e'-g''](m), S&B Ludlow and Teme.
When smoke stood up, *A E Housman*, A [d'b-a''](m), S&B Ludlow and Teme.
(Will you come, *Edward Thomas*, F [c'-e''], S&B Lights Out.)
(You are my sky, *John Squire*, Db [c'-f''], OUP Songs 1.)

John Guthrie. 1912 - 1986. (SMIC.)

H

Patrick Hadley. 1899 - 1973.
Scene from 'The Woodlanders', *Thomas Hardy*, [d-g''](f), Thames *Hardy Songbook*.

Robert Hales. *fl.* 1583.
O eyes, leave off your weeping, *Nicholas Breton?* Cm [e'*b*-e''*b*], S&B (Stroud) *Banquet*.

Richard Hall. 1903 - 1982. (BMIC.)

Alasdair Hamilton.
Collection: *The Plumes of Time* Roberton 1973.
Autumnal, *Lewis Spence*, [a-e''], Roberton Plumes.
Pieces of eight, *Lewis Spence*, [a-e''], Roberton Plumes.
The plumes of time, *Lewis Spence*, [b*b*-e''*b*], Roberton Plumes.
The silken heart, *Lewis Spence*, [a-f''], Roberton Plumes.

Colin Hand. 1929 - (BMIC.)

George Frideric Handel. 1685 - 1759.
Collection: *Songs and Cantatas* (edited Donald Burrows), OUP 1988.
An answer to Colin's complaint, *Anon*, Em [d'#-e''](f), OUP Songs.
(Come to me, soothing sleep, *Arthur Somervell*, E*b* [d'-f''], Curwen (Somervell).)
Dear Adonis, beauty's treasure, *John Hughes*, Gm [d'-a''](f), OUP Songs.
I like the am'rous youth, *James Miller*, F [e'-g''](f), OUP Songs.
(Lost love, *Arthur Somervell*, Gm [c'-f''], Curwen.)
Love's but the frailty of the mind, *William Congreve*, F [e'-g''](f), OUP Songs.
Quite unconcerned, tr. *Anon*, Dm [d'-f''](f), OUP Songs.
Silent worship, *Arthur Somervell*, A [e'-f''#], Chester (Somervell) *Celebrated 1*, (Curwen (Somervell);
 F, Curwen.)
(Spring, *Arthur Somervell*, E [d'#-f''#], Curwen (Somervell); D, Curwen.)
The forsaken maid's complaint, *Anon*, A [e'-b''](f), OUP Songs.
The forsaken nymph, *Anon*, F [d'-f''](f), OUP Songs.
The poor shepherd, *John Gay*, Em [d'-g''](f), OUP Songs.
(The trumpet is calling, *Arthur Somervell*, B*b* [d'-g''], Curwen (Somervell).)
The unhappy lovers, *Anon*, Dm [c'#-g''](f), OUP Songs.
Transporting joy, *John Hughes*, Cm [d'-g''](f), OUP Songs.
Twas when the seas were roaring, *John Gay*, Gm [c'-g''](f), OUP Songs.

George Handford. 1582 - 1647.
Collections: *Ayres, Books 1 & 2* (edited Anthony Rooley), S&B.

David Harries. 1933 -
Last night, *Alun Jones*, tr. *John Stoddart*, Am [e'-g''], Welsh Music *Songs from Wales 1*.

Denham Harrison.
Give me a ticket to heaven, *Richard Elton*, E*b* [d'-e''*b*], Cramer *Drawing Room*.

Julius Harrison. 1885 - 1963.
Collection: (*Four Songs of Chivalry*, B&H 1915); (*Four Narratives from the Ancient Chinese*, B&H 1917); (*Three Sonnets from Boccaccio*, Enoch 1919); (*Five English Songs*, Enoch 1921); *Songs from Twelfth Night*, Lengnick 1948.
   (A cavalier to his lady, *William Strode*, D [c'-e''](m), B&H; F, B&H.)
   (Ave mors, *Margery Hamilton-Fellowes*, Cm, [c'-a''*b*], B&H.)
   (Boot, saddle, to horse, *Robert Browning*, G [d'-f''](m), B&H; A, B&H.)
   (By a clear well, *Boccaccio* tr. *D G Rossetti*, [d'-g''], Enoch 3 Boccaccio.)
   Clown's Song, *Shakespeare*, Em [e'-g''](m), Lengnick Twelfth Night.
   Come away death, *Shakespeare*, Fm [f'-a''*b*], Lengnick Twelfth Night.
   (Fiammetta singing, *Boccaccio* tr. *D G Rossetti*, [e'*b*-a''*b*](m), Enoch 3 Boccaccio.)
   (Heliodore, *Meleager* tr. *Andrew Lang*, F#m [e'#-f'#], Enoch 5 English.)
   (Guendolen, *William Morris*, E*b* [d'-g''(b''*b*)](m), B&H 4 Chivalry, B&H; C, B&H.)
   (I heard a music sweet today, *Thomas MacDonagh*, E [d'#-g''(f'#)], Enoch 5 English.)
   I know a bank, *Shakespeare*, E [d'#-f'#(g''#)], B&H *Shakespeare*; (D, B&H).
   (In prison, *William Morris*, Cm [c'-f''], Enoch 5 English.)
   Jolly Robin, *Shakespeare*, A*b* [e'*b*-a''*b*], Lengnick Twelfth Night.
   (King Charles, *Robert Browning*, Am [c'-e''](m), B&H; Cm, B&H.)
   (Marching along, *Robert Browning*, Dm [c'#-f''](m), B&H; Fm, B&H.)
   (Memory island, *Paul Askew*, F [d'-f'#](m), B&H; D, B&H.)
   (Merciless beauty, *Chaucer*, [d'-f''], Enoch 5 English.)
   O mistress mine, *Shakespeare*, E [e'-f'#(g'')](m), Lengnick Twelfth Night.
   Philomel, *Shakespeare*, B*b* [f'-b''(a''*b*)], B&H *Heritage 1*; (G, B&H).
   (Sea winds, *Paul Askew*, G [c'-e''], B&H; F, B&H.)
   (Sir Giles' War Song, *William Morris*, Gm [d'-a''(b''*b*)](m), B&H 4 Chivalry.)
   (The escape from love, *Chaucer*, [d'-g''*b*], Enoch 5 English.)
   (The eve of Crecy, *William Morris*, E [e'(d'#)-a''](m), B&H 4 Chivalry.)
   (The gilliflower of gold, *William Morris*, A [e'-a''](m), B&H 4 Chivalry.)
   (The last revel, *Ch'en Tzu-ang* tr. *Anon*, Gm [c'-f''], B&H 4 Narratives.)
   (The last sight of Fiammetta, *Boccaccio* tr. *D G Rossetti*, [c'#-a''](m), Enoch 3 Boccaccio.)
   (The recruiting sergeant, *Tu Fu* tr. *Anon*, Dm [c'-g''*b*(f'')], B&H 4 Narratives.)
   (The soldier, *Confucius* tr. *Anon*, Fm, [e'*b*-g''*b*(f'')](m), B&H 4 Narratives.)
   (There was a King of Liang, *Kao-Shih* tr. *Anon*, F#m [c'#-f'#(d'')], B&H 4 Narratives.)

Pamela Harrison. 1915 -
Collection: (*Two Songs*, OUP 1954); (*Eight Poems of Walter de la Mare*, OUP 1956.)
   (A goldfinch, *Walter de la Mare*, [d'-e''], OUP 2 Songs, 8 Walter de la Mare.)
   (Blindman's in, *Walter de la Mare*, [d'-e''], OUP 8 Walter de la Mare.)
   (Dreamland, *Walter de la Mare*, [d'-g''], OUP 8 Walter de la Mare.)
   (Nicoletta, *Walter de la Mare*, [d'-f'#], OUP 8 Walter de la Mare.)
   (The horseman, *Walter de la Mare*, [d'-f'#], OUP 8 Walter de la Mare.)
   (Where, *Walter de la Mare*, [d'-d''], OUP 8 Walter de la Mare.)
   (White, *Walter de la Mare*, [c'-g''], OUP 2 Songs, 8 Walter de la Mare.)
   (Why? *Walter de la Mare*, [d'-d''], OUP 8 Walter de la Mare.)

Jonathan Harvey

James Hart. 1647 - 1718.
Adieu to the pleasures and follies of love, *Thomas Shadwell*, Dm [c'-f''](f), Thames (Bevan)
8 Restoration.
Honest shepherd, since you're poor, *Anon*, Am [e'-f''](f), Thames (Bevan) *8 Restoration.*

Walter Hartley.
Love song of the bride, *Song of Solomon*, [a-b''](f), Bardic.
Shall I compare thee? *Shakespeare*, [d'-a''], Bardic.

Hamilton Harty. 1879 - 1941.
Collections: (*Three Flower Songs*, B&H 1906); (*Six Songs of Ireland*, B&H 1908); (*Antrim and Donegal*,
B&H 1926); (*Five Irish Poems*, B&H 1938).
(A drover, *Padraic Colum*, Cm [c'-f''](m), Novello.)
A lullaby, *Cahal O'Byrne*, Bbm [e'-g''b], B&H *Imperial* 1, (6 Songs); *Gm*, *Heritage 1.*
(A Mayo love song, *Alice Milligan*, [f'-a''](m), B&H 5 Irish.)
(A rann of wandering, *Padraic Colum*, Novello.)
(Across the door, *Padraic Colum*, Novello.)
(An Irish love song, *Katherine Tynan*, Chappell.)
(At Easter, *Helen Lanyon*, C#m [c'#-g''#(e'')], B&H 5 Irish, B&H.)
(At sea, *Moira O'Neill*, C [c'-a''], B&H 6 Songs.)
(Bonfires, *W L Bultitaft*, C, B&H; Eb, B&H.)
(By the bivouac's fitful flame, *Walt Whitman*, Eb [a-e''b], B&H.)
(Come, O come, my life's delight, *Thomas Campion*, Eb [d'-g''(a''b)], B&H.)
(Cradle song, *Padraic Colum*, Novello.)
(Denny's daughter, *Moira O'Neill*, Gb [e'b-g''b(b''b)](m), B&H 5 Irish.)
(Dreaming, *Cahir Healy*, Bb [c'-g''], B&H 6 Songs.
(Flame in the skies of sunset, *Lizzie Twigg*, [c'-e''], B&H 6 Songs.)
(Gorse, *L B Hay Shaw*, Eb [e'b-g''](m), B&H 3 Flower.)
(Grace for light, *Moira O'Neill*, G [c'-g''], B&H 6 Songs, B&H.)
(Herrin's in the bay, *Elizabeth Shane*, D [d'-g''](f), B&H Antrim.)
(Hush Song, *Elizabeth Shane*, Am [e'-f''](f), B&H Antrim.)
(Lane o' the thrushes, *Cathal O'Byrne* and *Cahir Healy*, E [e'-f''#], B&H.)
(Lookin' back, *Moira O'Neill*, Dm [d'-g''], B&H 6 Songs.)
(Lullaby, *Cathal O'Byrne*, Gm, B&H 6 Songs.)
(Mignonette, *L B Hay Shaw*, Eb [bb-g''], B&H 3 Flower.)
(Now is the month of maying, *Anon*, G, B&H.)
(Poppies, *L B Hay Shaw*, Db [d'b-f''], B&H 3 Flower.)
Scythe song, *Riccardo Stephens*, F [c'-e''], B&H *Heritage 2.*
Sea wrack, *Moira O'Neill*, Bb [bb-e''b](f), B&H *Heritage 1*, *Imperial 3*: (C, D, B&H).
(Song of the three mariners, *Anon*, G [d'-e''(g'')](m), B&H.)
(Tell me not, sweet, I am unkind, *Richard Lovelace*, Db, B&H.)
(The fiddler of Dooney, *W B Yeats*, Bm, B&H 5 Irish.)
(The little Son, *Moira O'Neill*, B [b-e''](f), B&H Antrim.)
(The ould lad, *Moira O'Neill*, Db [ab-d''b](m), B&H.)
(The Rachray man, *Moira O'Neill*, Novello.)
(The sailor man, *Moira O'Neill*, Dm [d'-e''](m), B&H 5 Irish, B&H.)

(The sea gypsy, *Richard Hovey*, C [e'-f''](m), B&H; E*b*, B&H.)
(The song of Glen Dun, *Moira O'Neill*, G [e'*b*-g''](f), B&H.)
(The stranger's grave, *Emily Lawless*, Novello.)
(The two houses, *Moira O'Neill*, Am [e'-g''](f), B&H Antrim.)
(The wake feast, *Alice Milligan*, Dm [c'#-e''](m), Novello.)
Arrangements: (*Three Traditional Ulster Airs* (high & low keys), B&H 1903; *Three Irish Folksongs*, OUP 1929.)
(Black Sheela of the silver eye, *Seosamh MacCathmhaoil*, E*b* [c'-e''*b*](m) B&H 3 Ulster; G*b*, 3 Ulster.)
My Lagan love, *Seosamh MacCathmhaoil*, C [b*b*-e''*b*](m), B&H *Imperial 6, McCormack*; (E, 3 Ulster).
(The blue hills of Antrim, *Seosamh MacCathmhaoil*, B*b* [b*b*-d''], B&H 3 Ulster; D, 3 Ulster.)
(The fairy king's courtship, *P W Joyce*,, E*b* [e'*b*-f''], OUP 3 Irish.)
(The game played in Erin-go-Bragh, *P W Joyce*, Cm [c'-e''*b*](m), OUP 3 Irish.)
(The lowlands of Holland, *P W Joyce*, Em [d'-e''](f), OUP 3 Irish.)

Jonathan Harvey. 1939 -
Lullaby for the unsleeping, *John V Taylor*, [d'-g''](f), Faber.

Philip Hattey.
Collection: (*Seven Poems of Robert Graves*, B&H 1969.)
(Horizon, *Robert Graves*, E [b-d''], B&H 7 Graves.)
(Is now the time? *Robert Graves*, [c'-e''*b*], B&H 7 Graves.)
(Lift-boy, *Robert Graves*, [b-f''], B&H 7 Graves.)
(She tells her love while half asleep, *Robert Graves*, F#m [c'-e''], B&H 7 Graves.)
(The sharp ridge, *Robert Graves*, Cm [b-e''*b*], B&H 7 Graves.)
(The two witches, *Robert Graves*, Gm [b*b*-e''], B&H 7 Graves.)
(Variables of green, *Robert Graves*, F [d'-d''*b*], B&H 7 Graves.)

John Liptrot Hatton. 1808 - 1886.
Collection: *A Herrick Cycle* (Graves), Thames 1997.
Gather ye rosebuds, *Robert Herrick*, E [e'-e''](m), Thames Cycle.
(I'm conquered, love, by thee, C, Cramer.)
(In her garden, Cramer)
(It is early in the morning, Cramer.)
(Student's serenade, F, Cramer; A, Cramer.)
The deluge, *Robert Herrick*, Am [e'-e''](m), Thames Cycle.
The enchantress, *Robert Herrick*, Am [f'#-e''](f), B&H *New Imperial 3.*
The hag, *Robert Herrick*, Dm [a-f''], S&B *Recitalist 2. MB 43.*
The rock of rubies, *Robert Herrick*, E [e'-e''](m), Thames Cycle.
(The sands of Dee, *Charles Kingsley*, Cramer.)
The teare, *Robert Herrick*, C [e'-f''](m), Thames Cycle.
To Anthea, *Robert Herrick*, E [d'#-f'#](m), Thames Cycle, S&B *Recitalist 4, MB 43*; E*b*, B&H *New Imperial 5*, Paterson *100 Best 3*; (F, Cramer).
To Julia, *Robert Herrick*, F#m [c'#-f'#](m), Thames Cycle.
To the rose, *Robert Herrick*, D [d'-e''](m), Thames Cycle.
To the willow tree, *Robert Herrick*, C#m [c'#-e''](m), Thames Cycle.
(Uncle Jack, Cramer.)

(Wanderer, Cramer.)

Hawkins of Liverpool.
Ode on the morning, *Anon*, Em [c'-g''], Thames (Copley & Reitan) *Gentleman's Magazine.*

George Hayden. ? - 1722.
(A cypress grove, *Anon*, Bbm [d'*b*-g], OUP (Taylor).)

Michael Head. 1900 - 1976.
Collections: *Over the rim of the moon* (high & low keys), B&H, 1919; (*Three Songs of Fantasy* (high, medium & low keys), B&H 1925); (*Songs of the Countryside*, 1929); (*More Songs of the Countryside*, B&H 1933); (*Three Cotswold Songs*, B&H 1938); (*Five Songs*, B&H 1938); (*Song Album for Soprano or Tenor*, [Album high], (*Song Album for Mezzo-soprano or Baritone*, [Album low] B&H 1947); (*Six Sea Songs*, B&H 1948); (*Three Songs of Venice*, B&H 1977); *Song Album 1 — Songs of the Countryside*, *Song Album 2 — Songs of Romance and Delight*, *Song Album 3 — Songs for Male Voice* , B&H 1985.
    A blackbird singing, *Francis Ledwidge*, E [b-e''], B&H Over the rim, (B&H); A*b*, Over the rim, (B&H).
    A dog's life, *Cecily Fox Smith*, Dm [a-f''(d'')](m), B&H Album 3, (6 Sea, B&H).
    (A funny fellow, *Frank Dempster Sherman*, E*b* [b*b*-e''*b*], B&H Album Low; G, 3 Fantasy; F, 3 Fantasy, B&H.)
    A green cornfield, *Christina Rossetti*, F, [d'-f''], B&H Album 1, *Heritage 3*, B&H, (E*b*, B&H).
    (A love rhapsody, *Martin MacDermott*, F [f'-a''](m), B&H.)
    A piper, *Seumas O'Sullivan*, Dm [c'-e''], B&H Album 1, Album 3, B&H; Fm, B&H.
    (A sea burthen, *Cecily Fox Smith*, Gm [d'-f''], B&H 6 Sea, B&H.)
    A slumber song of the Madonna, *Alfred Noyes*, C [c-e''](f), B&H; (B*b*, B&H.)
    A summer idyll, *Richard le Gallienne*, F [c'-f''](m), B&H Album 3; (A*b*, Album High).
    (A vagabond song, *John Drinkwater*, C#m [g#-e''(m), B&H 3 Cotswold, B&H.)
    (Acquaint now thyself with Him, *Job 22, Psalms 99, 96, Micah*, adapted *Denice Koch*, E*b* [b*b*-e''*b*], B&H; G, B&H.)
    (Autumn's breath, *R W Dixon*, B [b-d''], B&H.)
    (Ave Maria, *Latin* tr. *Nancy Bush*, Am [a'e''], B&H; Cm, B&H.)
    (Back to Hilo, *Cecily Fox Smith*, Em [b'-e''](m), B&H, Album Low, 6 Sea.)
    Be merciful unto me, O God, *Psalm 57*, C [a'-g''(f')], Roberton; E*b*, Roberton.
    (Behold, I send an angel, *Exodus & Isaiah*, adapted *Denice Koch*, G [b-d''], B&H.)
    Beloved, *Francis Ledwidge*, B*b* [b*b*-f''(g'')], B&H Over the rim, (Album Low); C, Over the rim.
    (Beloved, let us love one another, *John 4*, adapted *Denice Koch*, F [a-f''], B&H.)
    (Bird-song, *Marjorie Rayment*, Fm [c'#-c'''(b'' or f'')](f), B&H.)
    Child on the shore, *Nancy Bush*, D [b*b*-e''], Roberton.
    (Claribel, *Alfred Lord Tennyson*, F [c'-f''], B&H; D, B&H.)
    (Come take your lute, *Helen Taylor*, Dm [a-d''(c')], B&H.)
    (Constancy, *Ruth Pitter*, [a-f''], B&H.)
    (Cotswold love, *John Drinkwater*, D*b*, B&H; D, B&H.)
    Dear delight, *Walter de la Mare*, A*b* [e'*b*-a''*b*], B&H Album 2.
    (Elizabeth's song, *Lascelles Abercrombie*, G [d'-b''](f), B&H.)
    (Fallen veils, *D G Rossetti*, [c'-f''], B&H 5 Songs, B&H.)
    Foxgloves, *Mary Webb*, C [g'-g''], B&H Album 1; A*b*, Album Low, B&H, (B&H More Countryside).

Michael Head

(Gaite and Orior, *Alastair Miller*, Fm [e'*b*-g''], B&H Album High.)
(Give a man a horse he can ride, *James Thomson*, Eb [b*b*(c')-e''*b*(g'')], B&H.)
Green rain, *Mary Webb*, [c'-f''], B&H Album 1, (5 Songs).
(Had I a golden pound, *Francis Ledwidge*, C [b-e''(d''), B&H.)
(Hail, bounteous May, *John Milton*, Db [e'*b*-f''(a''*b*)], B&H.)
Holiday in heaven, *Ruth Pitter*, Am [e'-a''], B&H Album 2.
(Holy and most blessed Virgin, *St Augustine* tr. *Nancy Bush*, Em [e'-g''#], B&H.)
(How sweet the moonlight sleeps, *Shakespeare*, Db [a(b*b*)-f''(e''), B&H.)
(I arise from dreams of thee, *P B Shelley*, G [d'-g''], B&H.)
I will lift up mine eyes, *Psalm 121*, C [b-e''], Roberton; F, Roberton.
Lavender Pond, *Cecily Fox Smith*, Ab, [c'*b*-e''*b*], B&H *Heritage 3*, (6 Sea).
(Lean out of the window, *James Joyce*, Eb [c'-e''*b*], B&H.)
(Limehouse Reach, *Cecily Fox Smith*, G [b-e''](m), B&H, Album Low, 6 Sea, B&H).
Lone dog, *Irene McCleod*, Cm [c'-e''*b*](m), B&H Album 3.
Love not me for comely grace, *Anon*, F [c'-g''(a'')](m), B&H Album 2; (G, Album High).
Love's lament, *Christina Rossetti*, Fm [c'-f''], B&H Album 2.
(Ludlow Town, *A E Housman*, E [b-e''](m), B&H, Album Low; G, B&H.)
Make a joyful noise unto the Lord, *Psalm 100*, E [b-e''(g''#)], Roberton; G, Roberton.
Mamble, *John Drinkwater*, Bb [b*b*-d''](m), B&H Album 3, (Album Low, 3 Cotswold).
Money, O, *W H Davies*, Gm [b*b*(g)-d''](m), B&H *Heritage 4, Imperial 6*, B&H; (Bm, B&H).
My sword for the king, *Helen Taylor*, Em [b-g''(f''#)](m), B&H Album 3; (Dm, B&H).
(Nature's friend, *W H Davies*, Dm [c'-f''#(d'')], B&H Countryside, B&H; Fm, B&H.)
Nocturne, *Francis Ledwidge*, Ebm [c'-e''], B&H Over the rim (B&H); G, Over the rim.
(O blessed virgin, *Latin* tr. *Nancy Bush*, G [d'-g''], B&H.)
O let no star compare with thee, *Henry Vaughan*, F [c'-f''], B&H Album 2; (*A*, B&H).
O to be in England, *Robert Browning*, F [d'-a''(g'')], B&H Album 1.
(October valley, *Nancy Bush*, [c'#-e''*b*], B&H.)
Oh, for a March wind, *Winifred Williams*, A [c'#-a''], B&H Album 1.
(On a lady singing, *Edward Quillinan*, F [d'-a''], B&H Album High.)
On the wings of the wind, *Alastair Miller*, Eb [c'-a''(a''*b*)], B&H Album 1.
(Rain storm, *Nancy Bush*, F#m [c'#-f''#], B&H 3 Venice.)
(Robin redbreast, *W H Davies*, Am [c'-e''], B&H Countryside, B&H; Cm, B&H.)
(Saint Mark's Square, *Nancy Bush*, D [b*b*-f''#], B&H 3 Venice.)
(Small Christmas tree, *Mona Gould*, Ab [f'-a''*b*(f'')], B&H.)
Star candles, *Margaret Rose*, Dm [c'-f''], B&H, (Album Low).
Sweet almond blossom, *Samuel Waddington*, G [d'-g''], B&H Album 1.
Sweet chance, that led my steps abroad, *W H Davies*, F [c'-f''], B&H Album 1, *Heritage 4*, B&H; D, B&H.
(Sweet day, so cool, *George Herbert*, F [e'*b*-a''*b*], B&H.)
(Sweethearts and wives, *Cecily Fox Smith*, G[d'-e''](m), B&H 6 Sea, B&H.)
Tewkesbury Road, *John Masefield*, Em [b-f''](m), B&H Album 1; (B&H, Dm, B&H).
(The blunder, *Jan Struther*, Dm [a-f''], B&H 5 Songs, B&H.)
(The carol of the field mice, *Kenneth Grahame*, D [d'-e''*b*(f''#)], B&H.)
(The comet, *Ruth Pitter*, Dm [b*b*-f''], B&H.)
(The dove, *John Keats*, Gm [f'-g''](f), B&H.)
(The dreaming lake, *Elizabeth Evelyn Moore*, C [c'-e''], B&H; E, B&H.)

The estuary, *Ruth Pitter*, E♭, [b♭-f''], B&H *Heritage 3,* (Album Low).

The fairies' dance, *Frank Sherman*, G [d'-g''], B&H Album 2, (3 Fantasy, Album High; E♭, B&H).

(The fairy tailor, *Rose Fyleman*, G [d'-g''(e'')], B&H Album High.)

(The garden seat, *Thomas Hardy*, [b-c''#], B&H Album Low, More Countryside.)

(The gondolier, *Nancy Bush*, Bm [b-e''♭], B&H 3 Venice.)

(The happy wanderer, *Helen Taylor*, F [f'-a''], B&H Album High.)

(The homecoming of the sheep, *Francis Ledwidge*, C#m [c'#-d''#], B&H.)

(The King of China's daughter, *Edith Sitwell*, F [c'-f''](m), B&H 5 Songs, B&H.)

(The little dreams, *Eileen M Reynolds*, E♭ [e'♭(b♭)-g''(f')], B&H 3 Fantasy; C, D♭, B&H.)

The little road to Bethlehem, *Margaret Rose*, A♭ [e♭-a''♭], B&H; F, *Souvenirs*, B&H.

The Lord's Prayer, E♭, [b♭-e''♭], B&H.

The matron cat's song, *Ruth Pitter*, Am [a-e''](f), B&H Album 3, (Album Low, B&H).

(The primrosy gown, *Edward Lockton*, A♭ [g-e''♭](m), B&H.)

The robin's carol, *Patience Strong*, A♭ [c'-a''♭(f')], B&H.

The sea gypsy, *Richard Hovey*, Cm [c'-e''(e''♭)](m), B&H Album 3; (Bm, Em, B&H).

The ships of Arcady, *Francis Ledwidge*, B♭ [b♭-e''♭], B&H Over the rim, B&H; D, Over the rim.

The singer, *Bronnie Taylor*, Fm [c'-a''♭](f), B&H Album 2, *Imperial 1*, (Album High).

(The temper of a maid, *W H Davies*, B [f'#-g''#], B&H Album High, Countryside.)

(The three mummers, *Helen Taylor*, A♭ [e'♭-f''], B&H.)

The twins, *H S Leigh*, C [c'-e''♭](m), B&H Album 2.

(The viper, *Ruth Pitter*, F [c'-e''], B&H Album Low.)

(The woodpath in spring, *Ruth Pitter*, D [a(b)-f'#(d'')], B&H.)

There's many will love a maid, *Penvel Grant Ross*, D [a-d''(e'')](m), B&H *Love and Affection*; (G♭, B&H).

(Thus spake Jesus, *John 17*, Gm [b-e''], B&H; Bm, B&H.)

(Weathers, *Thomas Hardy*, A♭ [e'♭-a''♭], B&H Album High, More Countryside, B&H.)

(What Christmas means to me, *Joan Lane*, F [c'-f''], B&H; A♭, B&H.)

(When I came forth this morn, *W H Davies*, G [d'-e''], B&H, Countryside, B&H; B♭, B&H.)

When I think upon the maidens, *Philip Ashbrooke*, C [b-e''](m), B&H Album 3; (D♭, B&H).

When sweet Ann sings, *Margaret Rose*, E♭ [b♭-e''♭(g')], B&H Album 3; F, B&H, (Album High).

Why have you stolen my delight? *Francis Brett Young*, A♭ [f'-a''♭], B&H Album 2, (Album High, More Countryside; F, B&H).

(You cannot dream things lovelier, *Humbert Wolfe*, [c'-g''], B&H.)

You shall not go a-maying, *Mordaunt Currie*, E♭ [e'♭-g''], B&H Album 2; (C, B&H).

Anthony Hedges. 1931 - (BMIC.)

Victor Hely-Hutchinson. 1901 - 1947.

Collection: (*Three Nonsense Songs*, Paterson 1927); (*Alice Songs*, Elkin 1931).

(Adam lay i-bounden, *Anon*, F [c'-c''], Elkin; A, Elkin.)

Cuckoo song, C [high voice], Novello.

(Dream Song, *Walter de la Mare*, B♭ [e'♭-f''], OUP.)

(Father William, *Lewis Carroll*, C [e'♭-g''], Elkin Alice.)

(Humpty Dumpty, *Lewis Carroll*, E♭ [e'♭-d''♭], Elkin Alice.)

(Jabberwocky, *Lewis Carroll*, C [b-a''], Elkin Alice.)

Old mother Hubbard, *Anon*, E [b-e''], Paterson; (G, Paterson).

(Silver, *Walter de la Mare*, F [c'-e''], OUP.)
(The duck and the kangaroo, *Edward Lear*, F [c'-f''], Paterson 3 Nonsense.
(The huntsman, *Walter de la Mare*, G [d'-g''], OUP.)
(The old soldier, *Walter de la Mare*, Eb [c'-f''], OUP.)
(The owl and the pussy-cat, *Edward Lear*, G [d'-f''], Paterson 3 Nonsense.)
The song of soldiers, Bb, [high voice], Novello
(The table and the chair, *Edward Lear*, Eb [e'b-e''b], Paterson 3 Nonsense.)
(To the looking-glass world, *Lewis Carroll*, Eb [bb-e''b], Elkin Alice.)
(Tweedledum and Tweedledee, *Lewis Carroll*, F [c'-c''], Elkin Alice.)

Henry VIII. 1491 - 1547.
Pastyme with good companye, *Anon*, [e'-c''], Thames (Hodgson) *Countertenors 2.*
Whereto shuld I expresse? *Anon*, [d'b'b], Thames (Hodgson) *Countertenors 2.*

Dalwyn Henshall. 1957 -
To... *P B Shelley*, Db [e'b-e''], Welsh Music *Songs from Wales 2.*

Gary Higginson. (BMIC.)

Ian Higginson.
Fear no more the heat o' the sun, *Shakespeare*, Em [d'-e''], B&H *Shakespeare.*
It was a lover and his lass, *Shakespeare*, G [d'-g''], B&H *Shakespeare.*
O mistress mine, *Shakespeare*, Bb [d'-g''](m), B&H *Shakespeare.*

John Hilton. 1599 - 1657.
Hang golden sleep upon her eyelids fair, *Anon*, Gm [d'-d''], S&B (Spink) *MB 33, Recitalist 4.*
Wilt thou forgive the sin where I begun, *John Donne*, Gm [d'-g''], S&B (Spink) *MB 33, Recitalist 3,*
    Cavalier, B&H (Patrick) *Sacred Songs 2.*

Alun Hoddinott. 1929 -
Collections: *Landscapes*, OUP 1976; *Ancestor worship*, OUP 1979.
Ancestor worship, *Emyr Humphreys*, [B-f'#](m), OUP Ancestor.
Din Lligwy, *Emyr Humphreys*, [d'-g''#], OUP Landscapes.
From father to son, *Emyr Humphreys*, [c#-f'](m), OUP Ancestor.
Hen Gapel, *Emyr Humphreys*, [e'b-a''], OUP Landscapes.
Llys Dulas, *Emyr Humphreys*, [e'-a''b], OUP Landscapes.
Marro's only son, *Emyr Humphreys*, [Bb-f'#](m), OUP Ancestor.
Master plan, *Emyr Humphreys*, [c-f'#(m)], OUP Ancestor.
(Medieval carol, *Anon* adapted *Jacqueline Froom*, [d'-e''], OUP.)
Mynydd Bodafon, *Emyr Humphreys*, [f'-g''b], OUP Landscapes.
The silver hound (cycle), *Ursula Vaughan Williams*, [c'-g''#](m), Lengnick.
Traeth Bychan, *Emyr Humphreys*, [e'-a''b], OUP Landscapes.
Arrangements: *Six Welsh Folksongs*, OUP.
Ap Shenkin, *Anon* tr. *Rhiannon Hoddinott*, [e'b-g''], OUP 6 Welsh.
Fairest Gwen, *Anon* tr. *Rhiannon Hoddinott*, [f'-g''](m), OUP 6 Welsh.
If she were mine, *Anon* tr. *Rhiannon Hoddinott*, [f'-g''b](m), OUP 6 Welsh.
O gentle dove, *Anon* tr. *Rhiannon Hoddinott*, [e'-g''](m), OUP 6 Welsh.

The golden wheat, *Anon* tr. *Rhiannon Hoddinott*, [f'-g''](m), OUP, 6 Welsh.
Two hearts remain, *Anon* tr. *Rhiannon Hoddinott*, [f'-f''](m), OUP, 6 Welsh.

Anthony Holborne. *fl.* 1584.
My heavy sprite, *George Clifford*, Gm [f'#-g''], S&B (Stroud) *Banquet.*

Josef Holbrooke. 1878 - 1958.
(An outsong, *T E Ellis*, E♭[c'♭-a''♭(f''♭)], Cramer; C, Cramer.)
(Killary, *Herbert Trench*, C, Cramer; E♭, Cramer.)
(Long ago, *N Malloch*, Weinberger.)
(Where be ye going, *John Keats*, [low], Cramer; [high], Cramer.)

Trevor Hold. 1939 -
Collection: *Something Rich and Strange*, Banks 1982; (see also BMIC).
Come unto these yellow sands, *Shakespeare*, [e'-g''], Banks Something Rich.
Full fathom five, *Shakespeare*, [e'♭-f''], Banks Something Rich.
Song at night, Am [c'-e''], Banks, Thames *Century 4*; Cm, Banks.
Where the bee sucks, *Shakespeare*, [f'-g''], Banks Something Rich.

Robin Holloway. 1943 -
(A Medley of Nursery Rhymes and Conundrums (cycle), *Anon*, [mezzo soprano], B&H.)
(Author of Light (cycle), *Quarles, A W, Campion*, [f(g)-g''(e''♭)(f), B&H.)
(Banal Sojourn (cycle), *Wallace Stevens*, [high voice], B&H.)
(Four Housman Fragments(cycle), *A E Housman*, [soprano], B&H.)
(From High Windows (cycle), *Philip Larkin*, [G-e'](m), B&H.)
(Georgian Songs (cycle), *Blunden, Stephens, Housman, Cornford, Walter de la Mare*, [A-g'](m), B&H.)
(In the Thirtieth Year (cycle), [c'-b''♭](m), B&H.)
(Lights Out (cycle), *Edward Thomas*, [F-g'(f')](m), B&H.)
(The Leaves Cry (cantata), *Wallace Stevens, Christina Rossetti*, [c'-c'''](f), B&H.)
(The Lover's Well (cycle), *Geoffrey Hill*, [baritone], B&H.)
Three Georgian Songs (part of cycle), *Cornford, Walter de la Mare*, [A-e'](m), B&H.
This is just to say (cycle), *Carlos Williams*, [d'-a''](m), B&H.
Wherever we may be (cycle), *Robert Graves*, [b(c')-a''](f), B&H 1982.

Gustav Holst. 1874 - 1934.
Collections: *Hymns from the Rig Veda, Op 24*, Chester; *Twelve Humbert Wolfe Songs* (Introduction by Imogen Holst), S&B 1969.
A little music, *Humbert Wolfe*, [d'-g''], S&B 12 Humbert Wolfe.
(Awake my heart, *Robert Bridges*, B♭[b♭-d''](m), Enoch; D, Enoch.)
Betelgeuse, *Humbert Wolfe*, [b-f''], S&B 12 Humbert Wolfe, *Recitalist 2.*
Creation, *Humbert Wolfe*, [b♭-f''], Chester Vedic Hymns.
Envoi, *Humbert Wolfe*, [c'-g''], S&B 12 Humbert Wolfe.
Faith, *Gustav Holst*, F [d'-e''♭], Chester Vedic Hymns.
In a wood, *Thomas Hardy*, [b(g#)-f''#], Thames *Hardy Songbook.*
In the street of lost time, *Humbert Wolfe*, [e'-g''], S&B 12 Humbert Wolfe, Mayhew *Collection 2.*
Indra (God of storm and battle), *Gustav Holst*, C [e'-f''], Chester Vedic Hymns, Mayhew *Collection 2.*
Journey's end, *Humbert Wolfe*, [c'-g''♭], S&B 12 Humbert Wolfe.

(Lovely kind and kindly loving, *Nicholas Breton*, G [c#-g''], B&H, Chappell *English Heritage 2*; F, A*b*, B&H.)

Margrete's cradle song, *Henrik Ibsen* tr. *William Archer*, F [f'-g''](f), Bosworth.

Maruts (Stormclouds), *Gustav Holst*, Am [d'*b*-f''], Chester Vedic Hymns.

Now in these fairylands, *Humbert Wolfe*, [d'-f''], S&B 12 Humbert Wolfe.

Persephone, *Humbert Wolfe*, [d'-g''*b*], S&B 12 Humbert Wolfe, *Recitalist 1*.

Rhyme, *Humbert Wolfe*, [d'-g''], S&B 12 Humbert Wolfe.

(She who is dear to me, *Walter E Grogan*, F [f'-g''](m), Enoch; D, Enoch.)

Slumber song, *Charles Kingsley*, D [d'-f'#](f), Bosworth.

Soft and gently, *Heinrich Heine* tr. *Anon*, Bosworth.

Song of the frogs, *Gustav Holst*, Em [b-d''], Chester Vedic Hymns.

The dream-city, *Humbert Wolfe*, [d'-g''*b*], S&B 12 Humbert Wolfe.

The floral bandit, *Humbert Wolfe*, [c'#-a''*b*], S&B 12 Humbert Wolfe.

The heart worships, *Alice Buckton*, Dm [b*b*-d''], S&B; Em, S&B.

The sergeant's song, *Thomas Hardy*, Gm [g-d''](m), Thames *Hardy Songbook*; (Am, Ashdown).

The thought, *Humbert Wolfe*, [c'#-f'#], S&B 12 Humbert Wolfe.

Things lovelier, *Humbert Wolfe*, [d'-g''], S&B 12 Humbert Wolfe, Mayhew *Collection 1*.

Ushas (Dawn), *Gustav Holst*, B*b* [b*b*-f''(d')], Chester Vedic Hymns.

Vac (Speech), *Gustav Holst*, E*b* [d'-f''], Chester Vedic Hymns.

Varuna I (Sky), *Gustav Holst*, C [b*b*-d''*b*], Chester Vedic Hymns.

Varuna II (The Waters), *Gustav Holst*, C [c'-e''], Chester Vedic Hymns.

Arrangements:

Masters in this hall, *William Morris*, Dm [c'#-f''], OUP *Solo Christmas*; C, *Solo Christmas*.

James Hook. 1746 - 1827.

Collections: *Eight Songs for High Voice* (edited Michael Pilkington), S&B 1979.

(Awake my fair, *Anon*, G [b'-a''], S&B (Ivimey).)

Mary of Allendale, *Anon*, E*b* [e'*b*-a''*b*](m), B&H (Lane Wilson) *Old English*.

(Hail, lovely rose, *Anon*, C [c'-g''], S&B (Ivimey).)

No, no, no, it must not be, *Anon*, A [e'-a''](m), S&B 8 Songs.

O listen to the voice of love, *Anon*, D [d'-g''](m), S&B 8 Songs.

Softly lulling, sweetly thrilling, *Dr Houlton*, E*b* [e'*b*-e''*b*], Novello (Bush) *Ballad Operas*.

Take me, take me, some of you, *John Dryden*, B*b* [f'-g''](f), S&B 8 Songs.

(The cautious maid, *Anon*, A [e'-a''](f), S&B (Ivimey).)

The emigrant, *Mrs Amelia Opie*, E*b* [e*b*-g''], S&B 8 Songs, OUP (Roberts) *Tuneful Voice*.

The lad wha lilts sae sweetly, *Charles Dibdin*, B*b* [d'-g''](f), S&B 8 Songs.

(The silver moon, *Anon*, G [d'-g''](f), S&B (Ivimey).)

The steadfast shepherd, *George Wither*, C [g'-g''](m), S&B 8 Songs.

(Sweet are the banks, *William Woty*, F [c'-f''], S&B (Ivimey).)

The sweet little girl that I love, *Anon*, F [f'-a''](m), B&H (Lane Wilson) *Old English*.

The turtle dove coos round my cot, *Anon*, D [d'-f''](f), S&B 8 Songs.

The warning, *Mrs Rowley*, A [e'-a''], S&B 8 Songs.

(Think it not strange, *Anon*, B*b* [d'-g''(b')], S&B (Ivimey).)

Donald Geoffrey Hope.

Lullay thou little tiny child, *Anon*, E [c'#-g''#], B&H *Heritage 4*.

Antony Hopkins. 1921 -
(A humble song to the birds, *Rosencreutz* tr. *Harries*, [c'-a''], Chester.)
A melancholy song, *Anon*, D [d'-f''#](f), Thames *Century 1*, Chester.

Mervyn Horder.
Collections: *Six Betjeman Songs*, Lengnick 1967; *A Shropshire Lad*, Lengnick 1980; *7 Shakespeare Songs*, Lengnick 1987; *Black Diamonds I*, Bardic; *Black Diamonds II*, Bardic; *Five Burns Songs*, Bardic. (See also BMIC.)
A red, red rose, *Robert Burns*, [d'-b''], Bardic 5 Burns.
A subaltern's love-song, *John Betjeman*, G [b-e''(a'')](m), Lengnick 6 Betjeman.
And is it true, *John Batjeman*, [a-g''], Bardic.
Blow, blow thou winter wind, *Shakespeare*, B♭m [b♭-f''], Lengnick 7 Shakespeare.
Bohemia, *Dorothy Parker*, [B♭-f''], Bardic Diamonds I.
Bric-à-brac, *Dorothy Parker*, [d'-g''], Bardic Diamonds II.
Caprice, *John Betjeman*, D♭ [c'-f''](m), Lengnick 6 Betjeman.
Convalescent, *Dorothy Parker*, [b-g''], Bardic Diamonds II.
Fear no more the heat o' the sun, *Shakespeare*, E♭ [b♭-f''], Lengnick 7 Shakespeare.
Goldcups, *A E Housman*, G [d'-g''], Lengnick Shropshire Lad.
How to get on in society, *John Betjeman*, C [g-c''](f), Lengnick 6 Betjeman.
In Westminster Abbey, *John Betjeman*, E♭ [c'-e''♭](f), Lengnick 6 Betjeman.
John Anderson, my jo, *Robert Burns*, [d'-g''], Bardic 5 Burns.
Loveliest of trees, *A E Housman*, G [e'-a''], Lengnick Shropshire Lad.
My Jean, *Robert Burns*, [c'-a''], Bardic 5 Burns.
My own dear love, *Dorothy Parker*, c'-f''], Bardic Diamonds I
O mistress mine, *Shakespeare*, C [b-e''♭](m), Lengnick 7 Shakespeare.
O whistle and I'll come to you, *Robert Burns*, [c'-f''], Bardic 5 Burns.
Sigh no more ladies, *Shakespeare*, E [a-f''#], Lengnick 7 Shakespeare.
The church's restoration, *John Betjeman*, F [b-f''], Lengnick 6 Betjeman.
The Lenten lily, *A E Housman*, A [e'-a''], Lengnick Shropshire Lad.
The winter it is past, *Robert Burns*, [e'-e''], Bardic 5 Burns.
Under the greenwood tree, *Shakespeare*, D [c'#-e''], Lengnick 7 Shakespeare.
Unfortunate coincidence, *Dorothy Parker*, [c'-f''], Bardic Diamonds I.
Wail, *Dorothy Parker*, [c'-e''], Bardic Diamonds II.
Westgate-on-Sea, *John Betjeman*, G [b-e''], Lengnick 6 Betjeman.
When daisies pied, *Shakespeare*, G [d'-e''], Lengnick 7 Shakespeare.
When I was one-and-twenty, *A E Housman*, A [e'-f''#], Lengnick Shropshire Lad.
White in the moon, *A E Housman*, F [c'-g''], Lengnick Shropshire Lad.
Who is Sylvia? *Shakespeare*, B♭ [d'-f''(g')], Lengnick 7 Shakespeare.

Charles Edward Horn. 1786 - 1849.
(Cherry ripe, *Robert Herrick*, E♭ [e'♭-a''♭(b''♭)], Chappell (Lehmann).)

David Horne. 1970 -
Collection: (*Days now Gone*, B&H 1992.)
(Burned ships, *Henrik Ibsen* tr. *Michael Meyers*, [d'-f''#], B&H 4 Songs.)
(Gone, *Henrik Ibsen* tr. *Michael Meyers*, [e'-g''#], B&H 4 Songs.)
(In the picture gallery, *Henrik Ibsen* tr. *Michael Meyers*, [b♭(c')-g''♭], B&H 4 Songs.)

(Rikke Holst, *Henrik Ibsen* tr. *Michael Meyers*, [d'-g''*b*], B&H 4 Songs.)
(The letter, *Walt Whitman*, [high voice], B&H.)

Joseph Horowitz. 1926 -
Lady Macbeth (Scena), *Shakespeare*, [d'-f''#](f), Novello.

John Horton. 1905 -
Arrangements:
The robin's last will, *Traditional*, A*b* [c'-c''], Thames *Countertenors 1*.
The sweet nightingale, *Traditional*, E*b* [b-c''], Thames *Countertenors 2*.

Samuel Howard. 1710 - 1782.
Hymen and fashion, *Anon*, B*b* [c'-g''], Thames (Copley & Reitan) *Gentleman's Magazine*.
Love in thy youth, *W Porter*, B [g#-d''#], Paterson (Coleman) *100 Best 4*.
Soft invader of my soul. *Anon*, B*b* [d'-g''](m), Elkin (Bevan).
The nut-brown maid, *Anon*, E [e'-a''](m), Thames (Copley & Reitan) *Gentleman's Magazine*.

Herbert Howells. 1892 - 1983.
Collections: (*Three Rondeaux*, S&B 1918); (*Peacock Pie*, Chester 1923); *In Green Ways*, Thames 1928; *Songs* (Introduction by Christopher Palmer), B&H 1986; *A Garland for Walter de la Mare*, (Introduction by Christopher Palmer, edited Michael Pilkington), Thames 1996.
A madrigal, *Austin Dobson*, E*b* [e'-b-e''*b*], B&H Songs, *Heritage 4*.
A queer story, *Walter de la Mare*, [b*b*-a''], Thames A Garland.
(A rondel of rest, *Arthur Symons*, D*b* [d'-b-e''*b*], S&B 3 Rondeaux.)
(Alas, alack, *Walter de la Mare*, [d'-b-f''], Chester Peacock Pie.)
Andy Battle, *Walter de la Mare*, Bm [c'-f''], Thames A Garland.
Balulalow *see* O my deir hert.
Before dawn (1), *Walter de la Mare*, [c'#-f''#], Thames A Garland.
Before dawn (2), *Walter de la Mare*, [c'#-f''#], Thames A Garland.
Come sing and dance, *Anon*, A*b* [d'-a''*b*], OUP.
(Flood, *James Joyce*, [e'-b-a''*b*], OUP.)
(Full moon, *Walter de la Mare*, Em [c'-d''#], Chester Peacock Pie.)
Gavotte, *H Newbolt*, G [d'-g''], OUP *Solo Soprano*, OUP, Thames *Century 1*.
Girl's song, *Wilfrid Gibson*, G [e'-e''](f), B&H Songs, *Heritage 3, Imperial 2*.
Goddess of night, *F W Harvey*, E [e'-g''], B&H Songs.
(Her scuttle hat, *Frank Dempster Sherman*, C [c'-d''], S&B 3 Rondeaux.)
King David, *Walter de la Mare*, [c'#-f''], Thames A Garland, B&H Songs, *Heritage 4*, B&H.
(Little boy lost, *William Blake*, Em [d'-e''], OUP.)
Lost love, *Clifford Bax*, Dm [c'-g''], B&H Songs.
(Mally O! *Anon*, F#m [c'#-c''#], S&B.)
Merry Margaret, *John Skelton*, F [d'-a''], Thames In Green Ways.
(Miss T, *Walter de la Mare*, C [c'-d''*b*], Chester Peacock Pie.)
(Mrs MacQueen, *Walter de la Mare*, G [d'-e''], Chester Peacock Pie.)
O, my deir hert, *Luther* tr. *Wedderburn*, Am [b-e''], B&H Songs, *Imperial 3*, B&H.
(Old Meg, *W W Gibson*, E*b* [d'-b-e''*b*], OUP.)
(Old skinflint, *Wilfrid Wilson Gibson*, [d'-f''], Curwen.)
On the merry first of May, *Parker & Aveling*, C [d'-a''], Thames In Green Ways.

(Roses, *Charles Camp Tarelli*, D [b*b*-d''], S&B 3 Rondeaux.)
Some one, *Walter de la Mare*, [c'-e''], Thames A Garland.
(The dunce, *Walter de la Mare*, [c'-e''*b*], Chester Peacock Pie.)
The goat paths, *James Stephens*, [c'-a''], Thames In Green Ways.
The Lady Caroline, *Walter de la Mare*, G [d'-a''*b*], Thames A Garland.
The mugger's song, *Wilfrid Gibson*, D [d'-e''*b*](m), B&H Songs.
The old house, *Walter de la Mare*, [d'-g''#], Thames A Garland.
The old soldier, *Walter de la Mare*, [c'-f''#], Thames A Garland.
The old stone house, *Walter de la Mare*, [b-e''], Thames A Garland.
(The restful branches, *W A Byrne*, D*b* [a-d''], S&B.)
The song of the secret, *Walter de la Mare*, [d'*b*-f''], Thames A Garland.
The three cherry trees, *Walter de la Mare*, [d'-g''], Thames A Garland.
The widow bird, *Shelley*, Em [e'-e''], B&H Songs.
There was a maiden, *W L Courtney*, Cm [c'-e''*b*], B&H Songs.
(Tired Tim, *Walter de la Mare*, Cm [c'-e''*b*], Chester Peacock Pie.)
Under the greenwood tree, *Shakespeare*, F [e'-b''], Thames In Green Ways.
Wanderers, *Walter de la Mare*, B*b*m [b-f''], Thames A Garland.
Wanderer's night song, *Goethe* tr. *Howells*, A [e'*b*-g''], Thames In Green Ways.
Arrangements: *Two English Folksongs*, Thames 1996.
I will give my love an apple, *Anon*, Am [c'-e''], Thames 2 English Folksongs.
The brisk young widow, *Anon*, C [c'-e''], Thames 2 English Folksongs.

Elaine Hugh-Jones. 1927 - (see also BMIC.)
Futility, *Wilfred Owen*, E*b* [f'-g''*b*], Thames *Century 3*.

Arwel Hughes. 1909 - 1988.
Birds of Rhiannon, *Gwenallt*, tr. *John Stoddart*, [d'-f''], Welsh Music *Songs from Wales 1*.
Good Friday, *Rhiannon Bowen Thomas* tr. *H Idris Bell*, Am [e'-a''], Gwynn.
Romany, *Crwys* tr. *G Crwys Williams*, G [d'-a''], Gwynn.

Herbert Hughes. 1882 - 1937.
(I cannot change as others do, *John Wilmot, Earl of Rochester*, A*b* [e*b*-a''*b*(f'')](m), B&H.)
O men from the fields, *Padraic Colum*, B*b*m [d'*b*-f''], B&H *Heritage 2*.
Arrangements: *Irish Country Songs Vol 1*, B&H 1909; *Irish Country Songs Highlights*, B&H 1995.
A Ballynure ballad, *Anon*, Cm [b*b*-d''], B&H Irish Country 1, Highlights.
A good roarin' fire, *Anon*, E [e'-e''](m), B&H Highlights.
A young maid stood in her father's garden, *Anon*, A*b* [e'*b*-f''], B&H Highlights.
An Irish elegy, *Thomas Moore*, F [d'-g''], B&H Highlights.
An island spinning song, *Padraic Colum*, B [f'#-f''#], B&H Irish Country 1.
B for Barney, *Anon*, F [c'-d''](f), B&H Irish Country 1.
Down by the salley gardens, *Yeats*, D*b* [d'*b*-e''*b*], B&H Irish Country 1, Highlights, B&H; E*b*, McCormack.
I have a bonnet trimmed with blue, *Anon*, F [f'-d''](f), B&H Highlights.
I know my love, *Anon*, F [c'-f''], B&H Irish Country 1, Highlights.
I know where I'm goin', *Anon*, E*b* [g'-e''*b*], B&H Irish Country 1, Highlights; G, B&H.
I will walk with my love, *Anon*, A*b* [e'*b*-f''](f), B&H Highlights.
I wish I had the shepherd's lamb, *P W Joyce*, G [c'-e''](m), B&H Irish Country 1.

Innisfree, *Anon*, Em [d'-e''], B&H Highlights.
Johnny, I hardly knew ye, *Anon*, Am [e'-e''](f), B&H Highlights.
Kitty my love, will you marry me? *Anon*, Eb [c'-f''](m), B&H *McCormack*.
Monday, Tuesday, *Anon*, Gb [d'b-c''], B&H Highlights.
Must I go bound, *Anon*, Cm [c'-c''](m), B&H Irish Country 1.
My bonny labouring boy, *Anon*, Eb [e'b-f''], B&H Highlights.
My love, oh, she is my love, *Douglas Hyde*, Bb [e'b-f''](m), B&H Irish Country 1.
Oh, breathe not his name, *Thomas Moore,* Eb [c'-e''b], B&H Highlights.
Reynardine, *Anon*, A [c'#-f''], B&H Irish Country 1.
Rich and rare, *Thomas Moore*, Db [d'b-f''], B&H Highlights.
Róisín Dubh, *Thomas Furlong*, Cm [c'-f''], B&H Highlights.
She moved thro' the fair, *Padraic Colum*, Db [d'b-e''b](m), B&H Irish Country 1, Highlights; G,
   B&H.
Shule Agra, *Anon*, Am [c'-e''](f), B&H Highlights.
Slow by the shadows, *Seosamh MacCathmhaoil*, F [d'-d''](m), B&H Irish Country 1.
The bard of Armagh, *Anon*, Ab [e'b-f''], B&H Highlights.
The black ribbon-band, *Anon*, G [d'-e''](m), B&H Highlights.
The bonny wee mare, *Anon*, Dm [c'#-e''](m), B&H Irish Country 1.
The Fanaid Grove, *Anon*, Bm [b-d''], B&H Irish Country 1.
The Gartan mother's lullaby, *Anon*, D [b-e''](f), B&H Irish Country 1, Highlights.
The leprehaun, *P W Joyce*, Am [d'-g''], B&H Highlights.
The little rose of Gartan, *Seosamh MacCathmhaoil*, Ab [e'b-e''b], B&H Irish Country 1.
The lover's curse, *Anon*, Db [bb-e''b](f), B&H Irish Country 1.
The magpie's nest, *Anon*, Bb [a-d''], B&H Highlights.
The next market day, *Anon*, Dm [a-c''], B&H Irish Country 1, Highlights.
The old turf fire, *Anon*, Dm [b-e''], B&H Highlights.
The star of the County Down, *Anon*, F#m [c'#-e''](m), B&H Highlights.
The verdant braes of Skreen, *Anon*, Bb [f'-f''], B&H Irish Country 1.
The weaver's daughter, *Anon*, F [e'b-e''b], B&H Irish Country 1.
Tigaree Torum Orum, *Anon*, E [d'#-e''], B&H Highlights.
When thro' life unblest we rove, *Thomas Moore*, C [c'-g''], B&H Irish Country 1.
You couldn't stop a lover, *Anon*, F [c'-e''], B&H Irish Country 1.

Hugh Hughes. 1876 - 1946.
   The shepherd's song, *Richard Crashaw*, Fm [e'-a''b], Gwynn.

R S Hughes. 1855 - 1893.
   Sailor boy's dream, [soprano/tenor], Snell.
   The warrior's return, [any voice], Snell.

Llifon Hughes-Jones. 1918 - 1996.
   The mill at Trefin, *Crwys* tr. *R Gerallt Jones*, Cm [a-e''b] Welsh Music, *Songs from Wales 2*.

Tobias Hume. *c.* 1569 - 1645.
   Fain would I change that note, *Anon*, G [d'-g''] S&B (Greer) *Printed*; F, B&H (Keel) *Lovesongs 1*;
      Eb, *Lovesongs 1*.
   The soldier's song, *Anon*, C [g-g''](m), S&B (Greer) *Printed*.

Tobacco, tobacco, *Anon*, Dm [d'-f''], S&B (Greer) *Printed*; B♭m, B&H *Imperial 6.*
What greater grief, *Anon*, Gm [d'-f''], S&B (Greer) *Printed.*

Pelham Humfrey. 1647 - 1674.

A hymn to God the father, *John Donne*, Gm [c'#-f''], Thames (Bevan) *6 Divine Hymns*, OUP *Solo Tenor*; Fm, Schott (Tippett).
Oh! that I had but a fine man, *Anon*, Gm [d'-d''](f), Thames (Bevan) *8 Restoration.*
Where the bee sucks, *Shakespeare*, Am [e'-g''], Thames (Bevan) *8 Restoration.*

Michael Hurd. 1928 -
Collection: *Shore leave*, Novello 1968.

Able Seaman Hodge remembers Ceylon, *Charles Causley*, C [c'-f''](m), Novello Shore leave.
Convoy, *Charles Causley*, Dm [c'-f''](m), Novello Shore leave.
Elizabethan sailor's song, *Charles Causley*, F [c'-f''](m), Novello Shore leave.
Sailor's carol, *Charles Causley*, Dm [d'-f''](m), Novello Shore leave.
Shore leave, *Charles Causley*, D [d'-e''](m), Novello Shore leave.
The day's alarm (cycle), *Paul Dehn*, [b-e''](m), Novello.

William Yeates Hurlstone. 1876 - 1906.
Collection: *Two Miniature Ballads*, Banks.

(A litany, *Phineas Fletcher*, Am, B&H.)
Darkness, *Olive C Malvery*, [medium], Banks 2 Miniature.
Morning, *Olive C Malvery*, [medium], Banks 2 Miniature.
(The Derby Ram, *Anon*, Cm [c'-d''], Ashdown.)
(Wilt thou be my dearie, *Robert Burns*, G [c'-d''](m), Ashdown.)

John Hywel. 1941 -
Farewell to Snowdonia, [mezzo/baritone], Gwynn.

I

John Ireland. 1879 - 1962.

Collections: *Three Arthur Symons Songs*, Chester 1920; *Songs Sacred and Profane*, Schott 1934; *Five XVIth Century Poems*, Braydeston Press 1938; *Eleven Songs* (Preface and Notes, John Longmire), S&B 1970; *The Land of Lost Content and other songs* (Preface and Notes, John Longmire), S&B 1976; *Complete Works for Voice and Piano volumes 1 — 5*, S&B 1981.

A report song, *Nicholas Breton*, Eb [e'-e''b], S&B Complete 3, Braydeston 5 Poems.

A song from o'er the hill, *P J O'Reilly*, Ab [d'-e''b], S&B Complete 5.

A thanksgiving, *William Cornish*, D [b-e''], S&B Complete 3, Braydeston 5 Poems.

All in a garden green, *Richard Edwardes*, F [d'-e''], S&B Complete 3, Braydeston 5 Poems.

An aside, *Anon*, Bb [bb-e''b], S&B Complete 3, Braydeston 5 Poems.

Bed in summer, *R L Stevenson*, F [c'-d''], S&B Complete 5.

Blind, *Eric Thirkell Cooper*, Dm [d'-d''], S&B Complete 5.

Blow out, ye bugles, *Rupert Brooke*, Eb [e'-e''b], S&B Complete 4.

During music, *D G Rossetti*, Eb [bb-g''b], S&B Complete 2, OUP.

Earth's call, *Harold Munro*, Eb [b-f''#], S&B Complete 4.

English May, *D G Rossetti*, Eb [bb-e''b], S&B Complete 4.

Epilogue, *A E Housman*, Db [b'-bg''b], S&B Complete 1, Lost Content.

Five poems by Thomas Hardy, (cycle) [bb-e''(g''b)](m), S&B Complete 3, OUP.

Friendship in misfortune, *Anon*, Db [d'b-f''], S&B Complete 5, 11 Songs.

Goal and wicket, *A E Housman*, Em [e'-g''](m), S&B Complete 1, Lost Content.

Great things, *Thomas Hardy*, C [c'-e''(d'')](m), S&B Complete 3, 11 Songs; (D, S&B).

Hawthorn time, *A E Housman*, C [d'-g''], S&B Complete 1; (Bb, B&H)

Her song, *Thomas Hardy*, Dm [c'-d''](f), S&B Complete 3; *Dm, F#m*, B&H; (Em, Fm, Cramer).

Hope the hornblower, *Henry Newbolt*, Bb [f'-g''], S&B Complete 5, 11 Songs; (C, A, G, B&H).

Hymn for a child, *Sylvia Townsend Warner*, A [c'#-f''], S&B Complete 1, Schott Sacred.

I have twelve oxen, *Anon*, F [c'-f''], S&B Complete 5, B&H *Heritage 3*; G, *New Imperial 1*.

I was not sorrowful, *Arthur Symons*, C [c'-e''b], S&B Complete 4.

I will walk the earth, *James Vila Blake*, C [c'-e''(g'')], S&B Complete 4.

If there were dreams to sell, *Thomas Lovell Beddoes*, Eb [c'-f''], S&B Complete 5; Db, B&H; (F, B&H).

If we must part, *Ernest Dowson*, G [d'-e''], S&B Complete 5, Lost Content.

Ladslove, *A E Housman*, Ab [f'-a''b], S&B Complete 1, Lost Content.

Love and friendship, *Emily Bronte*, [c'-g''], S&B Complete 5, 11 Songs, *Junior Recitalist 3*.

Love is a sickness full of woes, *Samuel Daniel*, Gb [e'b-g''], S&B Complete 1, B&H *Heritage 4*; (F, Eb, B&H).

Memory, *William Blake*, D [b-d''], S&B Complete 4.

Mother and child (8 short songs), *Christina Rossetti*, [d'-f''], S&B Complete 2.

My fair, *Alice Meynell*, B [e'-g''], S&B Complete 1, Schott Sacred.

My true love hath my heart, *Philip Sidney*, E [d'#-f''#], S&B Complete 1, 11 Songs; (G, S&B).

Penumbra, *D G Rossetti*, [a-f''], S&B Complete 4.

Remember, *Mary Coleridge*, D [e'b-g''], S&B Complete 1; (C, Bb, B&H).

Rest, *Arthur Symons*, Db [e'b-f''], S&B Complete 2, Chester 3 Symons.

Santa Chiara, *Arthur Symons*, Gm [c'-e''*b*], S&B Complete 2, 11 Songs; (*Cm*, S&B).

Sea fever, *John Masefield*, Em [b-d''](m), S&B Complete 2, 11 Songs; Am, Gm, Fm, Em, S&B.

Spleen, *Ernest Dowson*, [c'#-c''#], S&B Complete 4.

Spring sorrow, *Rupert Brooke*, F [c'-d''], S&B Complete 4, B&H *Heritage 3*; F, A*b*, B&H.

Summer schemes, *Thomas Hardy*, A*b* [c'-f''], S&B Complete 3; (*G*, B&H *Cramer Song Folio 1*).

The adoration, *Arthur Symons*, A*b*m [d'*b*-f''], S&B Complete 2, Chester 3 Symons; (*Bm*, *F#m*, Chester).

The advent, *Alice Meynell*, Dm [d'-g''], S&B Complete 1, Schott Sacred.

The bells of San Marie, *John Masefield*, Gm [c'-d''], S&B Complete 2, 11 Songs; (*Cm*, *Am*, S&B).

The cost, *Eric Thirkell Cooper*, Fm [c'-f''], S&B Complete 5.

The East Riding, *Eric Chilman*, Cm [e'*b*-g''], S&B Complete 1.

The encounter, *A E Housman*, C [g'-g''], S&B Complete 1, Lost Content.

The heart's desire, *A E Housman*, D*b* [f'-a''*b*], S&B Complete 1, B&H *Heritage 4*; (*B*, *Bb*, B&H).

The holy boy, *Herbert S Brown*, E*b* [c'-f''(g'')], B&H, Mayhew *Holy Night*; F, B&H *Ballad Album 2*, OUP *Solo Christmas*; D, *Solo Christmas*; (*G*, B&H).

The journey, *Ernest Blake*, C [d'-f''], S&B Complete 5.

The lent lily, *A E Housman*, Em [g'-f''#], S&B Complete 1, Lost Content.

The merry month of May, *Thomas Dekker*, E [c'#-f''#], S&B Complete 5; (*G*, *D*, B&H).

The one hope, *D G Rossetti*, [b*b*-f''#], S&B Complete 5, 11 Songs.

The rat, *Arthur Symons*, Bm [b-e''], S&B Complete 2, Chester 3 Symons.

The sacred flame, *Mary Coleridge*, C [d'*b*-a'*b*], S&B Complete 1; (*Bb*, B&H).

The salley gardens, *W B Yeats*, Em [e'-e''], S&B Complete 1, Schott Sacred; *D*, Schott.

The scapegoat, *Sylvia Townsend Warner*, G [e'-f''], S&B Complete 1, Schott Sacred.

The soldier, *Rupert Brooke*, F [d'-f''], S&B Complete 4; (*Gb*, *Eb*, B&H).

The soldier's return, *Sylvia Townsend Warner*, Gm [d'-e''], S&B Complete 1, Schott Sacred.

The sweet season, *Richard Edwardes*, D [d'-e''], S&B Complete 3, Braydeston 5 Poems.

The trellis, *Aldous Huxley*, A*b* [c'-g''], S&B Complete 1, 11 Songs.

The vain desire, *A E Housman*, Am [e'-a''*b*], S&B Complete 1, Lost Content.

Tryst (In Fountain Court), *Arthur Symons*, [d'-f''#], S&B Complete 2, OUP.

Tutto e sciolto, *James Joyce*, [e'-e''], S&B Complete 5.

Vagabond, *John Masefield*, B*b* [f'-f''](m), S&B Complete 2, 11 Songs; (A*b*, *G*, *F*, S&B).

What art thou thinking of? *Christina Rossetti*, A*b* [e'*b*-g''*b*], S&B Complete 2, Lost Content.

Weathers, *Thomas Hardy*, C [c'-d''], S&B Complete 3; *E*, D, C, B&H.

We'll to the woods no more (2 songs and a piano solo), *A E Housman*, [c'*b*-f''](m), S&B Complete 3, OUP.

When daffodils begin to peer, *Shakespeare*, C [b-e''(e''*b*)](m), S&B Complete 4, B&H *Shakespeare*.

When I am dead, my dearest, *Christina Rossetti*, F [d'-d''], S&B Complete 2.

When lights go rolling round the sky, *James Vila Blake*, D [d'-f''#(e'')], S&B Complete 5, Lost Content, (Chappell *English Recital 1*; C, Chappell).

Youth's spring-tribute, *D G Rossetti*, E*b* [b*b*-g''(f')], S&B Complete 4.

Arrangement:

The three ravens, *Anon*, Fm [c'-e''*b*], S&B Complete 5 (G, B&H).

Simon Ives. 1600 - 1662.

Go bid the swan in silence die, *Anon*, G [e'-g''], S&B (Spink) *MB 33*.

Will Chloris cast her sun-bright eyes? *Anon*, Am [g'#-f''](m), S&B (Spink) *MB 33*.

Grayston Ives. 1948 -
   The falcon, *Anon*, [d'-g''], Roberton.

J

Francis Jackson. 1917 -
Tree at my window, *Robert Frost*, [high], Banks.

William Jackson. 1730 - 1803.
Let no mortal sing to me, *Anon*, A [c'#-f'#], OUP (Roberts) *Tuneful Voice.*

Gordon Jacob. 1895 - 1984.
Collection: *Three Songs of Innocence*, OUP 1926.
(Adlestrop, *Edward Thomas*, E [e'-e''], OUP.)
(Cam' ye by? *Anon*, Am [c'-f''](f), S&B.)
(Helen of Kirkconnell, *Anon*, Gm [B-f'](m), S&B.)
(Laughing song, *William Blake*, G [d'-g''], OUP 3 Songs.)
(Love me not for comely grace, *Anon*, C [e'-f''], S&B.)
Mother, I will have a husband, *Anon*, G [d'-e''](f), Thames *Century 4.*
(The lamb, *William Blake*, Em [e'-g''], OUP 3 Songs.)
(The shepherd , *William Blake*, F#m [e'-f'#], OUP 3 Songs.)
Arrangement:
(Golden slumbers kiss your eyes, *Anon*, Bb [d'-f''], OUP)
(Pull away home, *Anon*, F [c'-f''], OUP.)
(The Londonderry Air, *Anon*, Eb [bb-g''], OUP.)
(Widdecombe Fair, *Anon*, G [d'-d''], OUP.)

Maurice Jacobson. 1896 - 1976.
(Boys, *W M Letts*, F#m [e-f'#], Curwen; Em, Curwen.)
(Jolly good ale and old, *William Stevenson*, [bb-e''b], Curwen.)
(Last hours, *John Freeman*, D [e'b-f'#], Curwen.)
(Mamble, *John Drinkwater*, [db-f'#], Curwen.)
(Queen Mab, *Thomas Hood*, [c'-e''], Curwen.)
(The Lord is my shepherd, *Psalm 23*, A [f'#-d''], Elkin.)
(The Roman Road, *Peggy Laing*, Gm [e'-a''b], Curwen.)
(The savoury seal, *Edward A Parry*, Am [e'-c''#], Curwen.)
The Song of Songs, *Song of Solomon*, Bm [a-f''], Lengnick.
Arrangements:
(A song for Christmas, *Hermon Ould*, Bm [b-d''], Curwen.)
(In praise of Isla, *Anon* tr. *Thomas Pattison*, C [c'-e''], Curwen.)
(Jota, *Anon* tr. *Whyte Monk*, D [f'#-g''#], Curwen.)
(Swansea Town, *Anon*, D [c'#-e''](m), Curwen.)
(Willow Song, *Shakespeare*, Em [e'-e''], Curwen.)

George Jeffreys. ? - 1685.
Cruel! but once again, *Peter Hausted*, Am [g'-f''], S&B (Spink) *MB 33.*
Have pity, grief, I cannot pay, *Peter Hausted*, Gm [d'-f''], S&B (Spink) *MB 33.*

John Jeffreys. 1927 -
Collections: *Book of Songs*, Roberton 1983; *Second Book of Songs, When I was Young*, Roberton 1984; *Third and Last Book of Songs, When I was Young Part Two, When I was Young Part Three*, Roberton 1990; *New Brooms*, Thames 1994. Note that the ranges given for the songs in Roberton's volumes are sometimes in error; they have been corrected here.

A light wind, *Barry Duane Hill*, [d'-f''#](m), Roberton 2nd Book.

A lyke-wake dirge, *Anon*, Gm [d'-e''#], Roberton Book of Songs.

A true woman's eye, *Anon*, Eb [e'-b-e''b](m), Roberton 3rd Book.

A white rose, *John Boyle O'Reilly*, C [g-a'](m), Thames New Brooms.

Amaryllis, *Thomas Campion*, G [d'-e''](m), Roberton 2nd Book.

Ambulance train, *Wilfrid Gibson*, [c'#-e''], Roberton Book of Songs.

And would you see my mistress' face, *Rosseter*, Bb [f'-e''b](m), Roberton Book of Songs.

At the cry of the first bird, *Anon* tr. *H M Jones*, [e'-b-a''], Roberton 2nd Book.

Awake thee my Bessy, *J J Callanan*, G [d'-g''](m), Roberton 3rd Book.

Be you blithe and bonny, *Shakespeare*, Eb [e'-b-g''b], Roberton 2nd Book.

Black Stichel, *Wilfrid Gibson*, Bm [d'-f''#], Roberton 2nd Book.

Brown is my love, *Anon*, Db [d'-b-e''b](m), Roberton 3rd Book.

Candle Gate, *Wilfrid Gibson*, [d'-d''], Roberton 2nd Book.

Christ's Nativity, *Anon*, Bb [f'-f''], Roberton 2nd Book.

Corpus Christi, *Anon*, Em [e'-g''], Roberton 3rd Book.

Cruel and bright, *Wilfrid Gibson*, [c'#-e''](m), Roberton 2nd Book.

Curlew calling, *Wilfrid Gibson*, F#m [f'#-e''], Roberton Book of Songs.

Dapple Grey, *Anon*, Eb [d'-e''b], Roberton When I was Young 3.

Ding dong bell, *Anon*, Eb [e'-b-e''b], Roberton When I was Young 2.

Fill me O stars, *Joseph Campbell*, A [d'-e''], Roberton 3rd Book.

Drop, drop slow tears, *Phineas Fletcher*, Em [g-g'](m), Thames New Brooms.

Four and twenty tailors, *Anon*, [d'-f''], Roberton When I was Young 3.

From Omiecourt, *Ivor Gurney*, F#m [e'-f''#](m), Roberton Book of Songs.

Full fathom five, *Shakespeare*, Bm [d'-c''#], Roberton Book of Songs.

Gather ye rosebuds, *Robert Herrick*, A [e'-e''], Roberton 3rd Book.

Golden slumbers, *Thomas Dekker*, Ab [e'-b-f''], Roberton 2nd Book.

Gone is my love from the silver stream, *Barry Duane Hill*, [d'-f''], Roberton.

Goosey goosey gander, *Anon*, [d'-e''], Roberton When I was Young 2.

Ha'nacker Mill, *Hilaire Belloc*, Am [d'-f''](m), Roberton 3rd Book.

Hill song, *Barry Duane Hill*, Am [d'-e''](m), Roberton 2nd Book.

Horror follows horror, *Ivor Gurney*, C#m [f'#-e''], Roberton Book of Songs.

How many miles to Babylon? *Anon*, Gm [d'-e''b], Roberton When I was Young 1.

How should I your true love know? *Shakespeare*, [e'-e''], Roberton 2nd Book.

Humpty Dumpty, *Anon*, Gm [d'-d''], Roberton When I was Young 3.

I am the gilly of Christ, *Joseph Campbell*, Gm [d'-d''], Roberton 3rd Book.

I love little kitty, *Anon*, G [d'-e''], Roberton When I was Young 2.

I was young and foolish, *W B Yeats*, E [c'#-e''](m), Roberton Book of Songs.

I will go with my father a-ploughing, *Joseph Campbell*, G [d'-f''], Roberton.

I will make you brooches, *R L Stevenson*, E [b-e''](m), Roberton 2nd Book.

If it chance your eye offend you, *A E Housman*, Fm [c'-d''b], Roberton Book of Songs.

If there were dreams to sell, *Thomas Lovell Beddoes*, [d'-e''], Roberton 2nd Book.

In a boat, *Hilaire Belloc*, Gm [f'-f''], Roberton 3rd Book.
In Marley Wood, *Hugh S Roberton*, [d'-f''(g')], Roberton 3rd Book.
In pride of May, *Anon*, G [d'-e''](m), Roberton 2nd Book; E, Roberton 2nd Book.
In youth is pleasure, *Robert Wever*, D [d'-d''](m), Roberton Book of Songs.
It is winter, *Walter de la Mare*, [d'-e''], Roberton Book of Songs.
It was a lover and his lass, *Shakespeare*, E [e'-e''], Roberton Book of Songs.
Jack and Jill, *Anon*, E [e'-e''], Roberton When I was Young 1.
Jillian of Berry, *Anon*, F [d'-f''](m), Roberton Book of Songs.
Little trotty wagtail, *John Clare*, G [d'-g''], Roberton 2nd Book.
Love me not for comely grace, *Anon*, E [e'-e''](m), Roberton 3rd Book.
Lovely playthings, *Ivor Gurney*, [b-d''](m), Roberton 2nd Book.
Lullaby, *Thomas Dekker*, [f'-e''*b*], Roberton 3rd Book.
Maid of Kent, *William Wager*, E [g#-a'](m), Thames New Brooms.
Matthew Mark Luke and John, *Anon*, [d'-e''], Roberton When I was Young 2.
Merry eye, *Wilfrid Gibson*, Fm [c'(f')-f''*b*], Roberton 3rd Book.
My lady, *Anon*, E*b* [e'*b*-e''*b*](m), Roberton 3rd Book.
My little pretty one, *Anon*, E [e'-e''], Roberton Book of Songs.
My Master hath a garden, *Anon*, B [f#-f'#], Roberton 3rd Book.
My mistress frowns, *Anon*, G [d'-f''](m), Roberton 2nd Book.
My pretty honey one, *Anon*, F [f'-f''](m), Roberton 2nd Book.
Northumberland, *Wilfrid Gibson*, E [e'-e''], Roberton 3rd Book, Roberton.
Now is the time of Christemas, *Anon*, G [g-g'](m), Thames New Brooms.
Now wolde, *Anon*, E [b-e''](m), Roberton 2nd Book.
O good ale, *Anon*, D [d'-d''](m), Roberton 2nd Book.
O mistress mine, *Shakespeare*, A*b* [d'*b*-f''](m), Roberton Book of Songs.
O my dere hert, *Martin Luther* tr. *Wedderburn*, E*b* [e'*b*-e''*b*], Roberton 2nd Book.
Old Mother Hubbard, *Anon*, Fm [e'*b*-e''*b*], Roberton When I was Young 3.
Omens, *James H Cousins*, [f'#-e''], Roberton Book of Songs.
Otterburn, *Wilfrid Gibson*, Bm [f'#-f'#], Roberton Book of Songs.
Passing by, *Anon*, G [f'#-g''](m), Roberton Book of Songs.
Peter the pumpkin-eater, *Anon*, D [d'-d''], Roberton When I was Young 1.
Pippen Hill, *Anon*, B*b* [f'-d''], Roberton When I was Young 1.
Requiem, *Ivor Gurney*, [d'-e''], Roberton Book of Songs.
Robin Redbreast, *W H Davies*, [f'-g''], Roberton 2nd Book.
Romance, *R L Stevenson*, F [c'-f''](m), Roberton Book of Songs.
Sally, *Barry Duane Hill*, A [d'-a''](m), Roberton 3rd Book.
Seals of love, *Shakespeare*, B*b*m [a'*b*-e''*b*], Roberton 2nd Book.
Severn meadows, *Ivor Gurney*, [d'-f'#], Roberton Book of Songs.
She is all so slight, *Richard Aldington*, E*b* [b*b*-e''*b*](m), Roberton 2nd Book.
She is ever for the new, *Anon*, G [d'-g''](m), Roberton 2nd Book.
Sigh no more ladies, *Shakespeare*, G [e'-g''], Roberton Book of Songs.
Six badgers, *Robert Graves*, A*b* [d'*b*-e''*b*](m), Roberton 3rd Book.
Sleep, *John Fletcher*, A*b* [e'*b*-a''*b*], Roberton Book of Songs.
Snow, *Edward Thomas*, [f'-f'#], Roberton Book of Songs.
Stow-on-the-Wold, *Wilfrid Gibson*, Gm [d'-d''], Roberton Book of Songs.
Sweeney the mad, *Anon* tr. *J G O'Keefe*, Gm [d'*b*-d''](m), Roberton 3rd Book.

Take O take those lips away, *Shakespeare*, B♭ [f'-g''], Roberton Book of Songs.

That ever I saw, *Anon*, D [d'-e''](m), Roberton 3rd Book.

The appeal, *Sir Thomas Wyatt*, B [b-d''], Roberton Book of Songs.

The birds, *Hilaire Belloc*, E♭m [d'♭-e''♭], Roberton 3rd Book.

The cuckoo, *Anon*, G [d'-e''], Roberton 2nd Book.

The falcon, *Anon*, Em [d'-g''], Roberton 2nd Book.

The farewell, *Robert Burns*, G [d'-e''](m), Roberton 3rd Book.

The hag, *Robert Herrick*, Bm [d'-f'♯], Roberton Book of Songs.

The high hills, *Ivor Gurney*, [c'♯-f'♯], Roberton Book of Songs.

The little milkmaid, *Thomas Nabbes*, G [d'-g''](‘tenor’), Roberton 2nd Book.

The little milkmaid, *Thomas Nabbes*, G [d'-g''](‘lower voices’), Roberton 2nd Book.

The little pretty nightingale, *Anon*, E♭ [e'♭-e''♭](m), Roberton 2nd Book.

The lone bird, *Emily Brontë*, [e'-g''♯], Roberton 3rd Book.

The milkmaid, *Thomas Nabbes*, G [d'-e''], Roberton Book of Songs.

The poacher's dog, *Louis Mayerling*, Em [d'-f'♯](m), Roberton.

The Queen of Hearts, *Anon*, [d'-d''], Roberton When I was Young 1.

The reaper, *Barry Duane Hill*, [d'♯-d''♯], Roberton 3rd Book.

The reaper, *Barry Duane Hill*, Bm [g♯-b'](m) Thames New Brooms.

The salley gardens, *W B Yeats*, G♭ [d'♭-g''♭](m), Roberton 2nd Book.

The songs I had, *Ivor Gurney*, Fm [d'-f''], Roberton Book of Songs.

There is a lady sweet and kind, *Anon*, E [e'-e''](m), Roberton Book of Songs.

There was a crooked man, *Anon*, F [d'-f''], Roberton When I was Young 2.

Thirteen pence a day, *A E Housman*, [d'-d''](m), Roberton Book of Songs.

This is the weather, *Thomas Hardy*, [b-e''], Roberton 2nd Book.

This little pig, *Anon*, E [e'-e''], Roberton When I was Young 2.

This night, *Padraic Pearse*, E♭m [e'♭-a''♭], Roberton Book of Songs.

Thomas MacDonagh, *Francis Ledwidge*, [c'♯-f'♯], Roberton 2nd Book.

Through the streets of Picardy, *Anon*, G [d'-e''], Roberton When I was Young 1.

'Tis time I think, *A E Housman*, Cm [e'♭-f''], Roberton Book of Songs.

To bed, to bed, *Anon*, F [c'(f')-f''(d')], Roberton When I was Young 3.

To make my mistress kind, *Patrick Hannay*, F [e'-f''](m), Roberton 3rd Book.

Tom the piper's son, *Anon*, E [d'-e''], Roberton When I was Young 3.

Under the blossom, *Shakespeare*, E♭ [e'♭-f''], Roberton Book of Songs.

Under the leaves green, *Anon*, C [g-a''](m), Thames New Brooms.

Weep you no more, *Anon*, G [g-g''](m), Thames New Brooms.

What evil coil of fate, *Ivor Gurney*, F♯m [d'-e''], Roberton Book of Songs.

What thing is love, *Anon*, G [d'-d''](m), Roberton 3rd Book.

Welcome to spring, *John Lyly*, Bm [a-a'](m) Thames New Brooms.

When daisies pied, *Shakespeare*, A [c'♯-e''], Roberton Book of Songs.

When I came at last to Ludlow, *A E Housman*, F♯m [f'♯-e''♯](m), Roberton 3rd Book.

When I was one-and-twenty, *A E Housman*, E [b(e')-e''](m), Roberton 3rd Book.

When that I was and a little tiny boy, *Shakespeare*, G [d'-g''](m), Roberton Book of Songs.

When that I was and a little tiny boy, *Shakespeare*, C [g-a'](m), Thames New Brooms.

Whenas I wake, *Patrick Hannay*, F [e'-e''♭](m), Roberton 3rd Book.

Whether men do laugh or weep, *Anon*, C [g-g'](m), Thames New Brooms.

White was the way, *Barry Duane Hill*, F [d'-f''](m), Roberton 2nd Book.

Who is at my window? *Anon*, Gm [d'-e''*b*], Roberton Book of Songs.
With rue my heart is laden, *A E Housman*, Fm [c'-d''](m), Roberton 3rd Book.
Yet will I love her, *Anon*, A*b* [f'-f''](m), Roberton 3rd Book.

David Jenkins. 1848 - 1915.
Home for ever, [contralto/baritone], Snell.
Speak, I pray thee, gentle Jesus, [soprano/tenor], Snell; [contralto/baritone], Snell.
The Lord is my shepherd, *Psalm 23*, [soprano/tenor], Snell.

John Jenkins. 1592 - 1678.
Cease not, thou heav'nly-voiced glorious creature, *Anon*, Cm d'-f''], S&B (Spink) *MB 33*.

Robert Johnson. 1583 - 1633.
Collection: *Ayres, Songs and Dialogues* (edited Ian Spink), S&B 1974. Only songs available in anthologies are listed individually here.
As I walked forth, *Anon*, Gm [d'-g'']; (*Fm*, B&H *Dolmetsch 1*); Dm, Paterson (Diack), *100 Best 4*.
Dear, do not your fair beauty wrong, *Anon*, Gm [c'-g''], S&B (Pilkington), *Lute Songs 1*.
Have you seen but the bright lily grow? *Ben Jonson*, F [e'-f''], (B&H *Dolmetsch 1*).

Maurice Johnston. 1900 - 1976.
Collection: (*Two Songs*, OUP 1944.)
(At night, *Alice Meynell*, D [d'-e''], OUP 2 Songs.)
Dover Beach, *Matthew Arnold*, F [b-f''], Lengnick.
(Hush! *James Walker*, [d'-e''], OUP 2 Songs.)
So are you to my thoughts, *Shakespeare*, D*b* [d'*b*-e''*b*], Lengnick.

Kenneth V Jones. 1924 - (BMIC.)

Richard Elfyn Jones. 1944 -
Ascension Thursday, *Saunders Lewis*, tr. *Anthony Conran*, [d'-g''], Welsh Music *Songs from Wales 1*.

Richard Roderick Jones. 1947 -
The oak-tree, *William Thomas* tr. *John Stoddart*, [G(A)-d'](m), Welsh Music *Songs from Wales 2*.

Robert Jones. *c.* 1570 - after 1610.
Collections: (*The First Book of Songs* (edited Thurston Dart) [1st Book], S&B 1959); (*The Second Book of Songs* (edited E H Fellowes) [2nd Book], *Ultimum Vale* (edited E H Fellowes) [Ultimum], S&B 1926); (*A Musicall Dreame* (edited E H Fellowes), *The Muses Gardin for Delights* (edited E H Fellowes) [Muses], S&B 1927). Only songs available in anthologies are listed individually here. Note that in the following: Pilkington = *English Lute Songs Book 2*, S&B; Keel 1/2 = *Elizabethan Lovesongs Books 1 and 2*, B&H (high & low keys).
Fie, what a coil is here, *Anon*, G [d'-g''](f), (2nd Book), Pilkington.
Go to bed, sweet muse, *Anon*, Gm [d'-f''], (Ultimum), Pilkington, Paterson (Diack) *100 Best 2*; *Am*, Keel 1; *Fm*, Keel 1.
My father fain would have me take, *Anon*, G [g'-g''](f), (Muses), Pilkington.
My love hath her true love betrayed, *Anon*, G [g'-f''](m), (Muses), Pilkington.
What if I seek for love of thee? *Anon*, Gm [d'-f''], (1st Book), Pilkington; *Am*, Keel 1; *F#m*, Keel 1.
What if I speed? *Anon*, Gm [d'-f''](m), Ultimum; *Am*, Keel 2; *Fm*, Keel 2.

W Bradwen Jones. 1892 - 1970.

Blow, bugle, blow, *Alfred Lord Tennyson*, [baritone], Snell.
Calling, love, for you, *Anon*, E♭[d'-f''], Gwynn.
Llanarmon, *Cynan*, Dm [d'-a''], Gwynn.
My love has a garden, *Eifion Wyn* tr. *Brendan Dunne*, E [c'#-e''(g''#)], Gwynn.
Now praise we the famous men, *Ecclesiasticus 44* adapted *Brendan Dunne*, E [c#-e''(g''#)], Gwynn.

Wilfred Josephs. 1927 -

Collection: *Four Japanese Lyrics*, Novello 1975.

If I had known, *Anon*, tr. *Bownas & Thwaite*, [e'-e''], Novello 4 Japanese.
. Lullaby, *Anon*, tr. *Bownas & Thwaite*, [b'-a''](f), Novello 4 Japanese.
Silent, but.... *Tsuboi Shigeji*, tr. *Bownas & Thwaite*, f#-f''(f), Novello 4 Japanese.
Tourist Japan, *Takenaka Iku*, tr. *Bownas & Thwaite*, [b'-a''], Novello 4 Japanese.

John Joubert. 1927 -

Collection: *Two Invocations*, Novello 1960; *Six Poems of Emily Brontë*, Novello 1971; *The Turning Wheel*, Novello 1982.

Autumn jig, *Ruth Dallas*, [d'#-g''](f), Novello Turning Wheel.
Caged bird, *Emily Brontë*, [f'#-a''], Novello 6 Poems.
Fain would I change that note, *Anon*, [c'#-a''♭](m), Novello.
Harp, *Emily Brontë*, [f'-a''♭], Novello 6 Poems.
Headlands in summer, *Ruth Dallas*, [c'-g''](f), Novello Turning Wheel.
Immortality, *Emily Brontë*, [b-b♭], Novello 6 Poems.
Love me not for comely grace, *Anon*, [c'-g''](m), Novello.
Meditation in winter, *Ruth Dallas*, [e'♭-a''♭](f), Novello Turning Wheel.
My love in her attire, *Anon*, [c'-a''♭](m), Novello.
Narcissus, *Ruth Dallas*, [f'#-g''#](f), Novello Turning Wheel.
O come, soft rest of cares, *George Chapman*, [c'-b''♭](m), Novello.
Oracle, *Emily Brontë*, [b♭-a''], Novello 6 Poems.
Sleep, *Emily Brontë*, [b♭-a''], Novello 6 Poems.
Song in Spring, *Ruth Dallas*, [f'-a''](f), Novello Turning Wheel.
Stay, O sweet, and do not rise, *John Donne?*, [b#-a''](m), Novello.
Storm, *Emily Brontë*, [b♭(a)-a''], Novello 6 Poems.
The remarkables, Queenstown, *Ruth Dallas*, [d'-a''](f), Novello Turning Wheel.
The sea, *Ruth Dallas*, [g'-a''](f), Novello Turning Wheel.
To Spring, *William Blake*, [f'-b''♭](m), Novello 2 Invocations.
To Winter, *William Blake*, [d'#-a''#](m), Novello 2 Invocations.

K

Percy B Kahn. 1880 - 1966.
Springtime, *Marshall Roberts*, Lengnick.

Frederick Keel. 1871 - 1954. 20 more songs in Cramer archive.
Collections: (*Three Salt-Water Ballads*, B&H 1919); (*Four Salt-Water Ballads*, B&H 1920); (*Three Old English Lyrics*, B&H); (*Four Songs of Childhood*, B&H).
(A sailor's prayer, *John Masefield*, Cm [b♭-e''](m), B&H 4 Salt-Water.)
(A wanderer's song, *John Masefield*, Am [c'-e''](m), B&H 4 Salt-Water.)
(Cape Horn Gospel, *John Masefield*, C [c'-c''](m), B&H 4 Salt-Water.)
(Had I a golden pound to spend, E♭, B&H.)
(If she forsake me, *Anon*, F, B&H; A, B&H.)
(It was a lover and his lass, *Shakespeare*, E♭, B&H, F; B&H.)
(Hell's pavement, *John Masefield*, Dm [c'-d''](m), B&H 4 Salt-Water.)
(Lullaby, *Alfred Noyes*, D♭ [d'-b♭-e''bb], S&B; E, S&B.)
(Mother Carey, *John Masefield*, Cm [b♭-e''b](m), B&H 3 Salt-Water.)
(On Eastnor knoll, F, B&H.)
(Port of many ships, *John Masefield*, Dm [c'-e''b](m), B&H 3 Salt-Water.)
(The merry month of May, *Thomas Dekker*, F, B&H.)
(The rose and the nightingale, G, B&H.)
(Tell me not, sweet, *Richard Lovelace*, F, B&H.)
(There is a garden in her face, *Thomas Campion*, G, B&H; B♭, B&H.)
(To Althea from prison, *Richard Lovelace*, F, B&H; A♭, B&H.)
Trade winds, *John Masefield*, E♭ [b♭-e''b(m), B&H, (B&H 3 Salt-Water; F, G, B&H.)
(With the pride of the garden, G, B&H.)

Marjorie Kennedy-Fraser. 1857 - 1930. 75 more songs in B&H archive (see also SMIC).
An Eriskay love lilt, *Kenneth Macleod*, A [e'-f'#], B&H *Ballad Album 2*; G, *Souvenirs*.

James Kent. 1700 - 1776.
My song shall be of mercy and judgment, *Psalms 101, vv.1-3, 108, vv. 3-4*, G [d'-f'#], B&H (Patrick) *Sacred Songs 1*.
It is a good thing to give thanks to the Lord, *Psalm 92, vv. 1-3*, D [d'-e''], B&H (Patrick) *Sacred Songs 2*.

Robert King. fl.1676 - 1728.
Urge me no more, unhappy swain, *Anon*, B♭ [f'-g''](f), Thames (Bevan) *8 Restoration*.

Antoinette Kirkwood.
High seriousness, *Richard Phibbs*, [d'-g''], Bardic.
Morning in Bengal, *Anthony Heyward*, [b-d''], Bardic.
Must she go? *James Forsyth*, [G-c'](m), Bardic.
Remembrance, *Eddie McGrory*, [g-c''], Bardic.

Remorse, *Michael O'Hagen*, [g-d''], Bardic.
Snowflake, *Eddie McGrory*, [d'-d''], Bardic.
Song of the fishermen of Cacru, *James Forsyth*, [c'-e''], Bardic.
The barrel organ, *Michael Ashe*, [b-c''], Bardic.
The fly, *William Blake*, [d'-a''], Bardic.
The oyster catcher's song, *James Forsyth*, [c'-f''], Bardic.
The tourney, *Anthony Heyward*, [b-f''#], Bardic.
Visit to the killing fields, *Eddie McGrory*, [a-f''], Bardic.

Howard Kleyn.
Collections: *Offerings*, Lengnick; *A Sheaf of Sonnets*, Lengnick.
A supplication, *Abraham Cowley*, [medium], Lengnick Offerings.
Hers will I be, *F Petrarca* tr. *Henry Hoard*, [medium], Lengnick Sheaf.
Remember me, *Christina Rossetti*, [medium], Lengnick Sheaf.
The country faith, *N Gale*, [medium], Lengnick Offerings.
Time is flying, *Ronsard* tr. *Andrew Lang*, [medium], Lengnick Sheaf.
To a young lady, *William Cowper*, [medium], Lengnick Offerings.
To Lucasta, *Richard Lovelace*, [medium], Lengnick Offerings.

Oliver Knussen. 1952 -
Collection: *Whitman Settings*, Faber 1993.
A noiseless patient spider, *Walt Whitman*, [b-b''*b*](f), Faber Whitman.
The dalliance of the eagles, *Walt Whitman*, [c'#-b''](f), Faber Whitman.
The voice of the rain, *Walt Whitman*, [b*b*-b''*b*](f), Faber Whitman.
When I heard the learn'd astronomer, *Walt Whitman*, [c'-b''](f), Faber Whitman.

L

Constant Lambert. 1905 - 1951.
Collection: (*Four Poems by Li-Po*, OUP 1927); *Three Poems of Li-Po* Chester.
(A summer day, *Li-Po* tr. *Shigeyoshi Obata*, C [c'-f''], OUP 4 Li-Po.)
(Lines, *Li-Po* tr. *Shigeyoshi Obata*, [c'-e''], OUP 4 Li-Po.)
(Nocturne, *Li-Po* tr. *Shigeyoshi Obata*, [d'-e''], OUP 4 Li-Po.)
On the city street, *Li-Po* tr. *Shigeyoshi Obata*, [medium], Chester 3 poems.
The intruder, *Li-Po* tr. *Shigeyoshi Obata*, [medium], Chester 3 Poems.
(The long-departed lover, *Li-Po* tr. *Shigeyoshi Obata*, [d'b-f''], OUP.)
The ruin of the Ku-Su palace, *Li-Po* tr. *Shigeyoshi Obata*, [medium], Chester 3 Poems.
(With a man of leisure, *Li-Po* tr. *Shigeyoshi Obata*, [b-f'#], OUP 4 Li-Po.)

John Lambert. 1926 -(BMIC.)

Henry Lamb.
The volunteer organist, *W B Glenroy*, Eb [d'-e''b], Cramer *Drawing Room Songs*.

John Frederick Lampe. 1703 - 1751.
By the beer as brown as a berry, *Henry Carey*, Dm [c-d'](m), Novello (Bush) *Ballad Operas*.

Nicholas Lanier. 1588 - 1666.
Collections: *Six Songs* (edited Edward Huws Jones), S&B 1976.
Bring away this sacred tree, *Thomas Campion*, G [d'-f''], S&B (Greer) *Printed*.
Come, come thou glorious object, *William Killigrew*, Dm [f'-f''], S&B Six Songs.
Fire! fire! lo here I burn, *Thomas Campion*, G [d'-e''], S&B (Spink) *MB 33*.
Like hermit poor, *Walter Raleigh*, Gm [d'-d''], S&B (Spink) *MB 33*, Six Songs.
Love and I of late did part, *Anon*, Gm [d'-e''b](m), S&B (Spink) *MB 33*.
Mark how the blushful morn, *Thomas Carew*, Dm [d'-f''], S&B Six Songs, (Spink) *MB 33*, *Cavalier Songs*.
Neither sighs, nor tears, nor mourning, *Anon*, Dm [c'-d''], S&B (Spink) *MB 33*.
No more shall meads be deck'd with flowers, *Thomas Carew*, G [b-g''](m), S&B (Spink) *MB 33*.
Nor com'st thou yet, my slothful love, *Anon*, Dm [c-g''](f), S&B (Spink) *MB 33*.
Silly heart forbear, *Anon*, F [g'-f''], S&B (Spink) *MB 33*.
Silly heart forbear, *Anon*, G [g'-g''], S&B (Spink) *MB 33*.
Stay, silly heart, and do not break, *Anon*, Gm [d'-f''](m), S&B (Spink) *MB 33*, *Cavalier Songs*.
Thou art not fair, *Thomas Campion*, G [d'-g''](m), S&B Six Songs.
Though I am young, *Ben Jonson*, Gm [d'-e''b], S&B Six Songs.
Weep no more my wearied eyes, *Anon*, F [c'-f''](m), S&B (Spink) *MB 33*.
Young and simple though I am, *Thomas Campion*, Gm [f'#-d''](f), S&B Six Songs.

Henry Lawes. 1596 - 1662.
Collections: (*Ten Ayres* (edited Thurston Dart), S&B 1956); (*Hymns to the Holy Trinity* (edited Gwilym Beechey), OUP 1973); *Six Songs* (edited Gwilym Beechey), Peters.
A beautiful mistress, *Thomas Carew*, F [e'-f''](m), Peters 6 Songs.
(A complaint against Cupid, *Mr Cartwright*, Em [c'-d''], S&B 10 Ayres.)

(A lady to a young courtier, *Henry Hughes*, F [e'-d''](f), S&B 10 Ayres.)

(A young maid's resolution, *Henry Hughes*, Bb [c'-d''](f), S&B 10 Ayres.)

(Amintor's welladay, *Henry Hughes*, Bb [c'-d''], S&B 10 Ayres.)

(Among rosebuds, *John Berkenhead*, Gm [e'-e''b], S&B 10 Ayres.)

(About the sweet bag of a bee, *Robert Herrick*, Gm [g'-f''], B&H *Dolmetsch 1*.)

(Amidst the mirtles as I walk, *Robert Herrick*, G [e'-e''](m), B&H *Dolmetsch 1*.)

(Ask me why I send you here, *Robert Herrick*, Cm [e'b-a''b], B&H *Dolmetsch 2*.)

Beauty and love once fell at odds, *Anon*, F [e'-g''], S&B (Spink) *MB 33*.

Bid me but live and I will live, *Robert Herrick*, Cm [g'-f''](m), S&B (Spink) *MB 33*, *Cavalier Songs*, (B&H *Dolmetsch 1*).

Break heart in twain, *Anon*, Dm [f'-a''](m), S&B (Spink) *MB 33*.

Come my sweet while ev'ry strain, *William Cartwright*, C [e'-g''], S&B (Spink) *MB 33*.

Cupid as he lay, *Robert Herrick*, Cm [e'b-g''], Peters 6 Songs.

(Dissuasion from presumption, *Henry Harrington*, F [c'-d''], S&B 10 Ayres.)

(I am confirm'd a woman can, *John Suckling*, C [c'-e''](m), B&H *Dolmetsch 1*.)

I do confess thou'rt smooth and fair, *Robert Ayton*, F [c'-c''], Paterson (Diack) *100 Best 4*.

(I prethee sweet to me be kind, *Anon*, Dm [d'-f''], B&H *Dolmetsch 2*.)

Go thou gentle whisp'ring wind, *Thomas Carew*, Dm [d'-f''](m), S&B (Spink) *MB 33*.

Hard-hearted fair, if thou wilt not consent, *Anon*, Cm [c'-e''b], S&B (Spink) *MB 33*.

Happy youth, that shalt possess, *Thomas Carew*, C [d'-f''], Peters 6 Songs.

Have you e'er seen the morning sun? *Henry Hughes*, C [d'-d''](m), S&B (Spink) *MB 33*.

(I am confirm'd a woman can, *John Suckling*, C [c'-e''](m), B&H *Dolmetsch 1*.)

(I prethee send me back my heart, *Henry Hughes*, Am [c'-c''], S&B 10 Ayres.)

I rise and grieve, *Anon*, Cm [c'-g''], S&B (Spink) *MB 33*.

(No constancy in man, *Henry Lawes*, Dm [d'-d''](f), S&B 10 Ayres.)

No, no, fair heretic, it cannot be, *John Suckling*, Dm [e'-f''](m), S&B (Spink) *MB 33*, *Cavalier Songs*.

O let me groan one word into your ear, *William Herbert*, Gm [d'-f''], S&B (Spink) *MB 33*.

O tell me love! O tell me fate, *Henry Hughes*, Dm [e'-g''](m), S&B (Spink) *MB 33*.

O turn away those cruel eyes, *Thomas Stanley*, Dm [c'#-g''], S&B (Spink) *MB 33*.

Or you, or I, nature did wrong, *Anon*, F [f'-g''], S&B (Spink) *MB 33*.

Out upon it, I have lov'd, *John Suckling*, C [c'-d''](m), S&B (Spink) *MB 33*, *Cavalier Songs*.

(Parting, *Henry Reynolds*, Cm [b-e''b], S&B 10 Ayres.)

Persuasions to enjoy, *Thomas Carew*, [f'#-f'#], Peters 6 Songs.

Read in these roses, *Thomas Carew*, Cm [g'-g''], Peters 6 Songs.

Seest thou those diamonds, *Robert Herrick*, Dm [e'-g''], Peters 6 Songs.

Sleep soft, you cold clay cinders, *Anon*, Gm [d'-f''], S&B (Spink) *MB 33*.

Slide soft you silver floods, *W Brown*, Gm [d'-f''], S&B (Spink) *MB 33*.

Speak, speak, at last reply, *Anon*, Cm [c'-e''b], S&B (Spink) *MB 33*.

(Sufferance, *Aurelian Townsend*, F [d'-d''], S&B 10 Ayres.)

Sweet stay awhile, why do you rise, *John Donne?*, Gm [d'-g''], S&B (Spink) *MB 33*, *Cavalier Songs*.

(The angler's song, *Isaak Walton*, F [f'-f''](m), B&H *Dolmetsch 1*.)

(The lark, *Anon*, F [d'-g''](f), B&H *Dolmetsch 2*.)

Tis but a frown, I prithee let me die, *Anon*, Dm [d'-f''], S&B (Spink) *MB 33*.

(To God the Father, *John Crofts*, Gm [d'-f''], OUP Hymns.)

(To God the Holy Ghost, *John Crofts*, Gm [d'-g''], OUP Hymns.)

(To God the Son, *John Crofts*, Gm [c'#-f''], OUP Hymns.)
Wert thou yet fairer than thou art, *Walter Montague?*, C [g'-g''](m), S&B (Spink) *MB 33*.
When thou, poor excommunicate, *Thomas Carew*, Gm [g'-g''], S&B (Spink) *MB 33*.
Whither are all her false oaths blown, *Robert Herrick*, Gm [d'-a''](m), S&B (Spink) *MB 33*.
Will you know my mistress' face, *Anon*, Eb [e'b-f''](m), S&B (Spink) *MB 33*, *Cavalier Songs*.

William Lawes. 1602 - 1645.
Collections: *Six Songs* (edited Edward Huws Jones), Schott 1971.
Faith, be no longer coy, *Anon*, F [f'-g''](m), S&B (Spink) *MB 33*, *Cavalier Songs*.
Come Adonis, come away, *John Tatham*, C [e'-f''], S&B (Spink) *MB 33*.
Faith, be no longer coy, *Anon*, F [f'-g''](m), S&B (Spink) *MB 33*, *Cavalier Songs*.
No no, fair heretic, it needs must be, *John Suckling*, G [f'#-f''](m), S&B (Spink) *MB 33*.
(O my Clarissa, *Anon*, Bm [d'-f'#](m), B&H *Dolmetsch 2*.)
On the lilies, *Robert Herrick*, G [e'-e''], Schott 6 Songs.
Persuasions not to love, *Robert Herrick*, Gm f'-g''], Schott 6 Songs.
Pleasures, beauty, youth attend thee, *John Ford*, C [e'-e''], S&B (Spink) *MB 33*.
To pansies, *Robert Herrick*, Gm [g'-f''], Schott 6 Songs.
To sycamores, *Robert Herrick*, Cm [e'b-f''], Schott 6 Songs.
To the dews, *Robert Herrick*, G [d'-f'#], Schott 6 Songs.
To the virgins, to make much of time (Gather ye rosebuds), *Robert Herrick*, G [g'-e''], S&B (Spink)
   MB 33, Schott 6 Songs, (B&H *Dolmetsch 1*).
To whom should I complain? *Anon*, Dm [d'-f''], S&B (Spink) *MB 33*.
Why should great beauty virtuous fame desire? *Sir William Davenant?* Dm [d'-g''], S&B (Spink) *MB*
   33.
Why so pale and wan, fond lover? *John Suckling*, Cm [b-e''b], S&B (Spink) *MB 33*.

Thomas Lawrence. (BMIC.)

Martin Leadbetter. (BMIC.)

Edward Lear. 1812 - 1888.
A farewell, *Alfred Lord Tennyson*, A [c'#-f'#], Cramer *Drawing Room Songs*.
Sweet and low, *Alfred Lord Tennyson*, B [d'#-e''](f), Cramer *Drawing Room Songs*.

Nicola LeFanu. 1947 -
A penny for a song (cycle), [g-b''b], Novello.

Christopher Le Fleming. 1908 - 1985.
(Three sisters, *Walter de la Mare*, [c'-f''], Cramer.)
(Egypt's might is tumbled down, *Mary Coleridge*, F#m [c'#-e''], Chester.)
(Hymnus, *Sarum Primer*, Gm [d'-f''], Chester.)
If it's ever spring again, *Thomas Hardy*, Ab [e'b-f''](m), Chester, *Celebrated 1*, Chester.
(In a sleepless night, *W H H*, Gb [bb-f''], Chester.)
(Once in a while, *Bruce Sevier*, B&H.)
Arrangement:
(Sheep shearing, *Anon*, Dm [c'-d''], Chester.)

Liza Lehmann. 1862 - 1918. 50 more songs in B&H archive; 10 more in Cramer archive.
A widow bird sate mourning, *P B Shelley*, F#m [c'#-f'#], S&B *MB 56*.
Ah, moon of my delight, *Omar Khayyam* tr. *Fitzgerald*, G [c'-a''](m), B&H; *F*, B&H.
(Evensong, *Constance Morgan*, Bb [c'-g''b(e''b)], Chappell *English Recital 2*.)
I will make you brooches, *R L Stevenson*, C [g-e''], S&B *MB 56*.
If I built a world for you, *Herbert Fordwych*, F [f'-f''(a')], B&H *Ballad Album 2*.
(Magdalen at Michael's gate, *Henry Kingsley*, Am [e'-a''(g')], Chappell *English Recital 1*.)
Myself when young, *Omar Khayyam*, tr. *Fitzgerald*, F [f(c')-e''](m), B&H *Cramer Song Folio 1*.
Oh, tell me, nightingale, sweet bird, *Friedrich Bodenstedt*, tr. *Anon*, Dm [d'-f''], S&B *MB 56*.
Within a rose love sleeping lay, *Hoffmann von Fallersleben*, tr. *Anon*, Db [d'b-g''b(b''b)], S&B *MB 56*.

Laura G Lemon. 1865 - 1924.
My ain folk, *Wilfrid Mills*, G [d'-g''] B&H *Ballad Album 1*; (*Eb*, F, B&H).

Richard Leveridge. 1670 - 1758.
Oft I'm by the women told, *Abraham Cowley*, Am [G-d'](m), Thames (Bevan) *6 Restoration*; (Cm, B&H (Keel) *12 18th Century*).
The beggar's song, *Anon*, G [g(a)-d''](m), B&H (Lane Wilson) *Old English Melodies*.
The cure of care, *Anon*, F major [g(a)-e''](m), S&B (Pilkington) *Georgian 1*.
When dull care, *Anon*, G [b-e''(g')](m), B&H (Lane Wilson) *Old English Melodies*.
Whilst I'm carousing, *Anon*, Gm [g-e''b](m), Keith Prowse; Am, Keith Prowse.
(Who is Sylvia? *Shakespeare*, Eb [e'b-g''], B&H (Keel) *12 18th Century*.)

Claire Liddell. ca 1940 - (see also SMIC.)
Collections: *Five Orkney Scenes*, Roberton 1975.
Beachcomber, *George Mackay Brown*, Eb [bb-g''](f), Roberton 5 Orkney.
Country girl, *George Mackay Brown*, [d'b-g''](f), Roberton 5 Orkney.
Fine flowers in the valley, Brunton.
Fisherman's bride, *George Mackay Brown*, [b-e''](f), Roberton 5 Orkney.
Old fisherman with guitar, *George Mackay Brown*, Em [d'-g''#](f), Roberton 5 Orkney.
Roads, *George Mackay Brown*, D [d'-f''#](f), Roberton 5 Orkney.
The rhythm of life, (f), Brunton.
Arrangements: *The Kindling Fire*, Roberton 1974.
A rosebud by my early walk, *Robert Burns*, Eb [c'-g''], Roberton Kindling Fire.
Ca' the yowes to the knowes, *Robert Burns*, Em [d'-f''#], Roberton Kindling Fire.
Comin' thro' the rye, *Robert Burns*, Ab [e'b-f''](f), Roberton Kindling Fire.
Go fetch to me a pint o' wine, *Robert Burns*, D [d'-g''](m), Roberton Kindling Fire.
I dreamed I lay, *Robert Burns*, F [d'-g''], Roberton Kindling Fire.
I'm o'er young to marry ~~yet~~, *Robert Burns*, Bb [bb-g''](f), Roberton Kindling Fire.
On Cessnock Banks, *Robert Burns*, F [c'-g''], Roberton Kindling Fire.
Scots wha hae, *Robert Burns*, Bb [d'-f''](m), Roberton Kindling Fire.
Talk not of love, *Robert Burns*, C [c'-g''], Roberton Kindling Fire.
To a blackbird, *Robert Burns*, Em [e'-g''], Roberton Kindling Fire.
Wee Willie Gray, *Robert Burns*, F [c'-f''], Roberton Kindling Fire.
Ye banks and braes, *Robert Burns*, Ab [e'b-f''](f), Roberton Kindling Fire.

Samuel Liddle. 1867 - 1951. 40 more songs in B&H archive.
Abide with me, *Henry Francis Lyte*, Eb[bb-g''], B&H *Ballad Album 1*; (C, Db, F, B&H).
How lovely are thy dwellings, *Psalm 84*, Eb[e'b-a''b(g'')], B&H *Ballad Album 2*; (C, Db, B&H).

C A Lidgey. 10 more songs in B&H archive; 3 in Cramer archive.
See where my love a-maying goes, *Anon*, F [c'-f''](m), B&H *Heritage 2*.
Sunny March, *Norman Gale*, Eb[bb-f''], B&H *Heritage 1*.

Thomas Linley Snr. 1732 - 1795
Collections: *Songs of the Linleys* (edited Michael Pilkington), S&B 1979.
Alas, from the day my poor heart, *Anon*, Cm [c'-g''](f), OUP (Roberts) *Tuneful Voice*.
No flower that blows, *George Collier*, A [e'-f''#(g''#)], S&B Songs of the Linleys.
(Primroses deck the bank's green side, *Anon*, C [c'-g''], S&B (Ivimey).)
Still the lark finds repose, *Mark Lonsdale*, A [e'-f''#], S&B Songs of the Linleys, Ab [e'b-a''b(b''b)],
(Ivimey).
The lark sings high in the cornfield, *Anon*, A [e'-a''], OUP (Roberts) *Tuneful Voice*.
Think not, my love, *Anon*, G [d'-f''#], OUP (Roberts) *Tuneful Voice*.
When a tender maid, *R B Sheridan*, Cm [c'-g''], S&B Songs of the Linleys.

Thomas Linley Jnr. 1756 - 1778.
Collections: *Songs of the Linleys*, (Michael Pilkington), S&B 1979.
Awake my lyre, *Anon*, A [e'-g''#](m), S&B Songs of the Linleys.
Flora, *Abraham Portal*, G [d'-a''], S&B Songs of the Linleys.
O mighty judge, *Abraham Portal*, G [d'-g''](f), S&B Songs of the Linleys.
The rill, *Anon*, Eb[d'-g''], S&B Songs of the Linleys.
Though cause for suspicion appears, *R B Sheridan*, Bb[f'-g''](m), Novello (Bush) *Ballad Operas*.
When I was a dyer, *Abraham Portal*, Gm [g'-g''](m), S&B Songs of the Linleys.

William Linley. 1767 - 1835.
While the foaming billows roll, *Anon*, Ab[bb(ab)-e''b](m), B&H (Lane Wilson) *Old English*.
(Orpheus, *Shakespeare*, G [b-e''], OUP (Denis Arundell).)

Malcolm Lipkin. 1932 - (BMIC.)

David de Lloyd. 1883 - 1948.
Collection: *Two Songs*, Gwynn.
Dainty little maiden, *Lord Tennyson*, [mezzo/baritone], Gwynn 2 Songs.
You are old, father William, *Lewis Carroll*, [mezzo/baritone], Gwynn 2 Songs..
Arrangement:
The banks of Conway, *Anon*, [mezzo/baritone], Gwynn.

John Morgan Lloyd. 1880 - 1960.
Dilys, *Rhosyr* tr. *Edgar Jones*, Bbm [d'b-g''b], Gwynn.
Saint Govan, *A G Prys-Jones*, Em [a-e''b], Gwynn.
The golden hour, *Crwys* tr. G *Crwys Williams*, Em [d'#-g''], Gwynn.

Richard Lloyd. 1933 -
The ballad of the Judas tree, *Ruth Etchells*, [soprano], Banks.

William Lloyd Webber. 1914 – 1982.
Collection: *The Songs of William Lloyd Webber*, Kevin Mayhew 1995.
A rent for love, *Ivronwy Morgan*, G [e'-f''](m), Mayhew Songs.
Eutopia, *Francis T Palgrave*, Bb [f'-g''], Mayhew Songs.
I looked out into the morning, *James Thomson*, D [e'-g''], Mayhew Songs.
How do I love thee? *Elizabeth Barrett Browning*, Eb [bb-f''], Mayhew Songs.
(Love, like a drop of dew, *W H Davies*, Ab [e'-b-a''](m), Chappell.)
Over the bridge, *James Thomson*, G [d'-g''], Mayhew Songs.
(Sleep, *John Fletcher*, G [d'-e''(g')], Chappell *English Recital 2.)*
So lovely the rose, *Joseph Murrells*, C [c'-g''(f)], Mayhew Songs.
The cottage of dreams, *Patience Strong*, Eb [bb-e''b], Mayhew Songs.
The forest of wild thyme, *Alfred Noyes*, D [e'-a''(f'#)], Mayhew Songs.
(The half loaf, *Helen Rowe Henze*, Bb [d'-f''], B&H.)
The pretty washer-maiden, *W E Henley*, Eb [e'-b-g''], Mayhew Songs.
To the Wicklow hills, *R G Leigh*, D [d'#-f''#(d'')], Mayhew Songs.

Matthew Locke. 1621 - 1677.
Collection: *Songs and Dialogues of Matthew Lock* (edited with introduction and notes by Mark Levy), S&B 1996.
Lucinda, wink or veil those eyes, *Anon*, C [e'-f''], S&B Songs and Dialogues.
The despondent lover's song, *Thomas Stanley*, Am [d'#-g''], S&B Songs and Dialogues.
Then from a whirlwind oracle, *Anon*, [G-e'](m), S&B Songs and Dialogues.
To a lady singing to herself by the Thames-side, *William Habington*, [f'-a''], S&B Songs and Dialogues.
Urania to Parthenissa: a dream, *Thomas Flatman*, [e'-g''], S&B Songs and Dialogues.
Wrong not your lovely eyes, *Anon*, Gm [e'-f''], S&B Songs and Dialogues.

Edward Loder. 1813 - 1865.
Dirge: Rough wind that moaneth loud, *P B Shelley*, Bm [d'-d''], S&B (Bush & Temperley) *MB 43*.
I heard a brooklet gushing, H *W Longfellow*, Ab [e'-b-g''], S&B (Bush & Temperley) *MB 43*, *Recitalist 3*; Gb, B&H (Northcote) *Imperial 4*, Cramer *Drawing Room Songs*.
Invocation to the deep, *Felicia Hemans*, Eb [bb-g''], S&B (Bush & Temperlay) *MB 43*.
The lamentation, *Michael Desmond Ryan*, F#m, [bb-f'#], S&B (Bush & Temperlay) *MB 43*.
Wake, my love, *George Soane*, Db [f'-b''b], S&B (Bush & Temperley) *MB 43*.

Bertram Luard-Selby. 1853 - 1918.
A widow bird sat mourning, *P B Shelley*, Gm [d'-d''], B&H *Heritage 1*.

Mark Lubbock.
The whispering poplar, *Christopher Hassall*, G [d'-g''], Schott.

Thomas Lupo. 1571 - 1628.
Shows and nightly revels, *Thomas Campion*, Gm [d'-e''b], S&B (Greer) *Printed.*
Time, that leads the fatal round, *Thomas Campion*, G [d'-e''], S&B (Greer) *Printed.*

Elizabeth Lutyens. 1906 - 1983. (See also BMIC.)
Refugee Blues, *W H Auden*, Bb [bb-f''], Thames *Century 2*.

M

John McCabe. 1939 -
Collection: (*Irish Songbook*, Novello 1994.)
(A question, *John M Synge*, [b♭-f'#], Novello Irish.)
(A white rose, *John Boyle O'Reilly*, [c'-d''], Novello Irish.)
(In ruin reconciled, *Aubrey de Vere*, [c'#-e''], Novello Irish.)
(Lullaby, *W B Yeats*, [b♭-g''b], Novello Irish.)
Requiem Sequence, *Catholic Rite*, [d'-a''](f), Novello.
(The lover's farewell, *James Clarence Mangan*, [c'#-e''], Novello Irish.)
(The mother, *Padraic Pearse*, [c'#-f'#](f), Novello Irish.)
(The nameless Doon, *William Larminie*, [d'b-g''b], Novello Irish.)

Hamish MacCunn. 1868 - 1916. (see also SMIC.)
Had I a cave on some wild distant shore, *Robert Burns*, Dm [c'#-f''](m), S&B (Bush) *MB 56*.
(In a palace garden, Cramer.)
(Lie there, my lute, *Charles H Taylor*, B♭ [b♭-f''], Chappell; A♭, Chappell.)
(Princess Helene, Cramer.)
Thine am I, my faithful fair, *Robert Burns*, A♭ [d'-f''](m), S&B (Bush) *MB 56*.
Wilt thou be my dearie? *Robert Burns*, F [c'-f''](m), S&B (Bush) *MB 56*.
(You are free, Cramer.)

Cecilia McDowell. 1951 - (BMIC.)

George Alexander Macfarren. 1813 - 1887. 9 more songs in Cramer archive.
Separation, *Edward William Lane*, Dm [c'#-g''b], S&B (Bush & Temperley) *MB 43*.

Alexander Mackenzie. 1847 - 1935.
A birthday, *Christina Rossetti*, F [d'#-g''(a')], S&B (Bush) *MB 56*.
The first Spring day, *Christina Rossetti*, E♭ [c'-g''], S&B (Bush) *MB 56*.
When I am dead, *Christina Rossetti*, A [e'-f'#], S&B (Bush) *MB 56*.

John McClain.
Our father, who art in heaven, *The Lord's Prayer*, [c'-d''], Bardic.

Dermot MacMurrough. 1872 - 1943.
Macushla, *Josephine V Rowe*, A♭ [e'b-g''b(a''b)](m) B&H *Ballad Album 1*; F, *McCormack*.

Walter MacNutt. 1910 -
O love, be deep, *H E Foster*, D♭ [d'b-e''b], Roberton.

Charles MacPherson. 1870 - 1927. (SMIC.)

Stephen Mace. ? - 1635.
Weep no more, nor sigh nor groan, *Beaumont & Fletcher*, Dm [d'-f''], S&B (Spink) *MB 33*.

Elizabeth Maconchy. 1907 - 1994.
Collections: (*Three Donne Songs*, Chester 1966; *Three Songs*, Chester 1982.) See also BMIC.
    (A hymn to God the Father, *John Donne*, [c'-a''], Chester.)
    (A meditation for his mistress, *Robert Herrick*, E♭m [e'♭-g''♭](m), OUP.)
    (Harp Song of the Dane Women, *Rudyard Kipling*, (f), Chester.)
    (Have you seen but a bright lily grow, *Ben Jonson*, Fm [e'♭-f''], OUP.)
    (In memory of W B Yeats, [soprano], Chester.)
    Ophelia's song, *Shakespeare*, [e'♭-g''](f), OUP.
    (The garland, Chester.)
    (Sun, moon and stars (cycle), *Elizabeth Machonchy*, [b♭-b''♭], Chester.)
Arrangement:
    Sho-heen sho-ho, *Anon*, A♭ [e'♭-e''♭], Lengnick.

Robert Marchant. 1916 - 1995.
Collection: *Four Songs*, Banks.
    Fish in the unruffled lakes, *W H Auden*, [high], Banks 4 Songs.
    Look, stranger, *W H Auden*, [high], Banks 4 Songs.
    The hidden law, *W H Auden*, [high], Banks 4 Songs.
    When Sir Beelzebub, *Edith Sitwell*, [high], Banks 4 Songs.

Alfonso Marsh. 1627 - 1681.
    Ah Chloris! would the gods allow, *Anon*, Gm [f'-g''], S&B (Spink) *MB 33*.

Charles Marshall. 13 more songs, B&H archive.
    I have a garden, *Thomas Moore*, [medium], Banks.
    I hear you calling me, *Harold Harford*, B♭ [f'-g''] B&H *Ballad Album 1*; E♭, *McCormack*; C, Cramer
    Drawing Room Songs; (G, A♭, B&H).

Richard Martin. ?1517 - ?1618.
    Change thy mind since she doth change, *Robert Devereux Earl of Essex*, Gm [g'-g''](m), S&B (Stroud)
    Banquet, (Pilkington) *Lute Songs 2*.

George Mason. *fl.* 1610 - 1617.
    Dido was the Carthage Queen, *Thomas Campion?* C [g'-g''], S&B (Pilkington) *Lute Songs 2*.

Colin Matthews. 1946 -
    (Aubade, *Paul Auster*, [high or low voice], Faberprint.)
    (Shadows in the water, *Thomas Traherne*, [high voice], Faberprint.)
    Strugnell's Haiku, *Wendy Cope*, Faber.

David Matthews. 1943 -
    (From Coastal Stations, *Maggie Hemingway*, [medium voice], Faberprint 1991.)
    (The golden kingdom (cycle), *Raine, Shelley, Blake*, [high voice], Faberprint.)

William Mathias. 1934 -
    (A vision of time and eternity, *Henry Vaughan*, [b♭-f''#(g''#)], OUP.)
    (The Fields of Praise (cycle), *Dylan Thomas*, [tenor], OUP hire.)

Caroline Maude.
Magdalen, *Henry Kingsley*, Gm, [b-e''], B&H *Heritage 2*.

Nicholas Maw. 1935 -
The voice of love (cycle), *Peter Porter*, [b♭-a''♭], B&H.
Arrangements: *Five American Folksongs,* Faber.

Frank Merrick. 1886 - 1981. (BMIC.)

Robin Milford, 1903 - 1959.
Collection: *Twelve Songs* Thames 1986.
Cradle song, *William Blake*, F [c'-f''], Thames 12 Songs.
Daybreak, *John Donne*, B♭ [f'-f''], Thames 12 Songs.
Epitaph, *de la Mare*, [d'-f''], Thames 12 Songs.
If it's ever spring again, *Thomas Hardy*, G [d'-g''], Thames 12 Songs.
Laus Deo, [high], Novello; [low], Novello.
Love on my heart, *Robert Bridges*, F♯ [f♯-f''♯], Thames 12 Songs.
Pleasure it is, *William Cornish*, G [g'-g''], Thames 12 Songs.
So sweet love seemed, *Robert Bridges*, B♭ [f'-f''], Thames 12 Songs, Novello.
The colour, *Thomas Hardy*, G [e'-g''], Thames 12 Songs.
The pink frock, *Thomas Hardy*, Em [e'-d''](f), Thames 12 Songs.
This endris night, *Anon*, B♭ [d'-f''], Thames 12 Songs.
Tolerance, *Thomas Hardy*, [c'-g''], Thames 12 Songs.
What pleasures have great princes, *Anon*, Dm [d'-f''], Thames 12 Songs.

Anthony Milner. 1925 -
Collection: *Our Lady's Hours*, Novello 1959.
Dawn, *Anon*, Em [e'-g''], Novello Our Lady, Novello.
Dusk, *Hilaire Belloc*, G♭ [d'♭-g''♭], Novello Our Lady.
Noon, *Gerard Manley Hopkins*, A [b-a''], Novello Our Lady.

E J Moeran. 1894 - 1950.
Collections: *Two Songs* Chester 1924; *(Ludlow Town*, OUP 1924); *(Seven Poems of James Joyce*, OUP 1930); *(Four English Lyrics*, B&H 1934); *Four Shakespeare Songs*, Novello 1940; *(Six Poems by Seumas O'Sullivan*, S&B 1946); *(Twelve Songs* (introduction by Peter Todd), Thames 1988; *Collected Solo Songs 1* (Preface by John Talbot), Thames 1994.
(A cottager, *Seumas O'Sullivan*, [d'♭-g''♭], S&B 6 Poems,)
(A dream of death, *W B Yeats*, [c'-e''♭], Thames 12 Songs, OUP.)
Blue-eyed Spring, *Robert Nichols*, G [d'-g''], Thames Collected 1.
(Bright cap, *James Joyce*, A [d'-e''], OUP 7 Poems.)
(Cherry-ripe, *Thomas Campion*, F [d'-a''](m), Thames 12 Songs).
(Come away, death, *Shakespeare*, Am [e'-e''](m), OUP.)
Diaphenia, *Constable*, A [e'-a''](m), Thames Collected 1, B&H *Heritage 4*.
(Donneycarney, *James Joyce*, [e'♭-e''♭](m), OUP 7 Poems.)
(Evening, *Seumas O'Sullivan*, A♭ [d'♭-g''♭], Thames 12 Songs, S&B 6 Poems.)
(Far in a western brookland, *A E Housman*, [c'-e''](m), B&H.)
(Farewell to barn and stack and tree, *A E Housman*, [c'-e''♭](m), OUP Ludlow Town).

Impromptu in March, *D A E Wallace*, [high], Chester 2 Songs.

Invitation in Autumn, *Seumas O'Sullivan*, G [d'-g''], Thames Collected 1, Novello.

In youth is pleasure, *Robert Wever*, F [f'-g''](m), Thames Collected 1, (12 Songs).

(Loveliest of trees, *A E Housman*, E [b-e''], Curwen.)

(Lullaby, *Seumas O'Sullivan*, Gm [d'*b*-b''*b*], S&B 6 Poems.)

(Now, O now, in this brown land, *James Joyce*, [c'-f''], OUP 7 Poems.)

Oh fair enough are sky and plain, *A E Housman*, Gm [d'*b*-e''*b*](m), Chester *Celebrated 2* .

(Rahoon, *James Joyce*, [c'-c''], OUP.)

(Rain has fallen, *James Joyce*, [c'#-f'#], OUP 7 Poems.)

Rosaline, *Thomas Lodge*, G [d'-a''](m), Thames Collected 1.

(Rosefrail, *James Joyce*, C#m [c'#-e''], Thames 12 Songs, *Em*, S&B).

(Say, lad, have you things to do, *A E Housman*, [d'-e''*b*](m), OUP Ludlow Town, Thames 12 Songs).

(Spring goeth all in white, *Robert Bridges*, F [f'-e''], Curwen.)

(Strings in the earth and air, *James Joyce*, Dm [d'-f''], OUP 7 Poems.)

The bean flower, *Dorothy L Sayers*, [high], Chester 2 Songs.

The constant lover, *William Browne*, G [d'-g''](m), Thames Collected 1, (12 Songs).

(The day of palms, *Arthur Symons*, Cramer.)

(The dustman, *Seumas O'Sullivan*, [e'*b*-f''], S&B 6 Poems.)

(The herdsman, *Seumas O'Sullivan*, Bm [d'-f''], S&B 6 Poems.)

(The lads in their hundreds, *A E Housman*, [c'#-e''](m), OUP Ludlow Town).

The lover and his lass, *Shakespeare*, E*b* [e'*b*-f''], Novello 4 Shakespeare.

(The merry green wood, *James Joyce*, [e'-e''], OUP 7 Poems.)

The merry month of May, *Thomas Dekker*, G [d'-g''](m), Thames Collected 1.

The monk's fancy, *H J Hope*, Cm [e'*b*-g''], Thames Collected 1.

The passionate shepherd, *Christopher Marlowe*, A [e'-a''](m), Thames Collected 1.

(The pleasant valley, *James Joyce*, F [c'-f''], OUP 7 Poems.)

(The poplars, *Seumas O'Sullivan*, A [a#-e''], Thames 12 Songs, S&B 6 Poems.)

The sweet o' the year, *Shakespeare*, G [d'-g''](m), Thames Collected 1, (12 Songs).

(Tis time, I think, by Wenlock Town, *A E Housman*, F [c'-f''], B&H.)

(Troll the bowl, *Thomas Dekker*, Bm [g'-f'#](m), Thames 12 Songs.)

(Twilight, *John Masefield*, [c'-d''], Thames 12 Songs.)

Weep you no more, sad fountains, *Anon*, Am [f'#-g''], Thames Collected 1.

When daisies pied, *Shakespeare*, F [c'-g''], Novello 4 Shakespeare.

When icicles hang by the wall, *Shakespeare*, [d'-g''], Novello 4 Shakespeare.

(When June is come, *Robert Bridges*, Curwen.)

(When smoke stood up from Ludlow, *A E Housman*, [c'#-e''](m) OUP Ludlow Town.)

Where the bee sucks, *Shakespeare*, E*b* [c'-f''], Novello 4 Shakespeare.

Willow song, *John Fletcher*, Gm [f'-g''](f), Thames Collected 1 (12 Songs).

Arrangements: *Collected Folksong Arrangements 1*, Thames 1994 (introduction by John Talbot); *(Six Suffolk Folksongs*, Curwen 1932); *(Songs from County Kerry*, S&B 1950).

(A seaman's life, *Anon*, [d'-d''], Curwen 6 Suffolk.)

(Blackberry fold, *Anon*, [c'-d''], Curwen 6 Suffolk.)

(Cupid's garden, *Anon*, [a-e''](m), Curwen 6 Suffolk.)

Down by the riverside, *Anon*, [d'-e''], Thames Collected Folksongs 1.

(Father and daughter, *Anon*, [f'-e''], Curwen 6 Suffolk.)

Gaol song, *Anon*, [g'-d''](m), Thames Collected Folksongs 1.
High Germany, *Anon*, [c'-f''], Thames Collected Folksongs 1.
(Kitty, I am in love with you, *Anon*, [d'-f'#](m), S&B Kerry.)
Lonely waters, *Anon*, [c'-d''](m), Thames Collected Folksongs 1.
(My love passed me by, *Anon*, [c'-e''](m), S&B Kerry.)
(Nutting Time, *Anon*, D [c'#-d''], Curwen 6 Suffolk, Curwen.)
(O sweet fa's the eve, *Robert Burns*, OUP.)
Parson and clerk, *Anon*, [d'-e''], Thames Collected Folksongs 1.
The bold Richard, *Anon*, [d'-e''](m), Thames Collected Folksongs 1.
(The dawning of the day, *Anon*, [c'#-e''], S&B Kerry.)
(The isle of Cloy, *Anon*, [d'-e''], Curwen 6 Suffolk.)
The jolly carter, *Anon*, [b-e''](m), Thames Collected Folksongs 1.
The little milkmaid, *Anon* [c'-d''], Thames Collected Folksongs 1.
(The lost lover, *Anon*, [d'-f''](f), S&B Kerry.)
(The murder of Father Hanratty, *Anon*, [e'-f''], S&B Kerry.)
The Oxford sporting blade, *Anon*, [d'-d''](m), Thames Collected Folksongs 1.
The pressgang, *Anon*, [c'-d''](m), Thames Collected Folksongs 1.
(The roving Dingle boy, *Anon*, [e'-f'#], S&B Kerry.)
The sailor and young Nancy, *Anon*, [c'#-e''], Thames Collected Folksongs 1.
The shooting of his dear, *Anon*, [d'-e''], Thames Collected Folksongs 1.
(The tinker's daughter, *Anon*, [c'-e''](m), S&B Kerry.)

Frank L Moir.
Down the vale, *Gunby Hadath*, F [e'-f''], B&H *Souvenirs*.

James Lynam Molloy. 1837 - 1909. 20 more songs in Cramer archive. 23 more songs in B&H archive.
Love's old sweet song, G *Clifton Bingham*, G [c'#-e''(g')], B&H *Ballad Album 1, McCormack*; (E♭, F, B&H).
The Kerry Dance, *J L Molloy*, E♭ [c'-f''], B&H *McCormack*.

Islwyn Morgan.
April, [soprano/mezzo/tenor/baritone], Gwynn.

Thomas Morley. 1557 - 1602.
Collection: *The First Book of Ayres* (edited Thurston Dart), S&B 1966 [1st Book]. Only songs available in anthologies are listed individually here. Note that in the following: Pilkington = *English Lute Songs Book 2*, S&B; Keel 1/2 = *Elizabethan Lovesongs Books 1 & 2* (high & low keys), B&H .
Absence, hear thou my protestations, *John Donne?*, G [d'-f''](m), 1st Book, Pilkington.
I saw my lady weeping, *Anon*, Am [d'-e''], 1st Book, Pilkington.
It was a lover and his lass, *Shakespeare*, G [g'-g''], 1st Book; F, Pilkington, Paterson (Diack) *100 Best 2*.
Love winged my hopes, *Anon*, G [f'-g''], 1st Book; F, (B&H *Dolmetsch 2*).
What if my mistress now, *Anon*, G [e'-g''](m), 1st Book, (B&H *Dolmetsch 2*).
With love my life was nestled, *Robert Southwell*, G [g'-g''], 1st Book, F, (B&H *Dolmetsch 2*).

David Moule-Evans. 1905 - 1988.
Collection: (*Two Celtic Songs*, S&B 1946)

(I-Brasîl, *Fiona Macleod*, F#m [c'#-g''#], S&B 2 Celtic.)
(When the dew is falling, *Fiona Macleod*, Bbm [c'-e''b], S&B 2 Celtic.)

Dominic Muldowney. 1952 -
Collection: *Songs from 'The Good Person of Sichuan*, Faber 1989.
(In Paris with you, *James Fenton*, Faber hire.)
(Never let me see you suffer, *James Fenton*, Faber hire.)
On suicide, *Bertolt Brecht* tr. *Michael Hofmann*, [g-g'], Faber Good Person.
Pigs'll fly, *Bertolt Brecht* tr. *Michael Hofmann*, [g-d''], Faber Good Person.
Song of the inadequacy of the Gods and the Good, *Bertolt Brecht* tr. *Michael Hofmann*, [bb-c''], Faber Good Person.
Song of the smoke, *Bertolt Brecht* tr. *Michael Hofmann*, [b-c''], Faber Good Person.
Song of the waterseller in the rain, *Bertolt Brecht* tr. *Michael Hofmann*, [b-a''b], Faber Good Person.
Trio of the vanishing Gods on the cloud, *Bertolt Brecht* tr. *Michael Hofmann*, [c'b-e''], Faber Good Person.

Michael Mullinar. 1895 - 1973.
Collection: (*Pippen Hill*, S&B 1951.)
(An epitaph, *de la Mare*, Db [bb-d''], OUP.)
(A farmer went trotting, *Anon*, D [d'-f''], S&B Pippen Hill.)
(A little cock sparrow, *Anon*, F [c'-e''b], S&B Pippen Hill.)
(I will go with my father a-ploughing, *Joseph Campbell*, C [d'-a''], OUP.)
(Over the water to Charlie, *Anon*, F [c'-d''], S&B Pippen Hill.)
(Pippen Hill, *Anon*, D [d'-d''], S&B Pippen Hill.)
(Pretty Polly Pillicote, *Anon*, F [c'-f''], S&B Pippen Hill.)
(The daisies, *James Stephens*, G [d'-g''], OUP.)
(The piper and the drummer, *Anon*, C [c'-e''](f), S&B Pippen Hill.)
(The seas are quiet, *Edmund Waller*, Db [d'b-c''], OUP.)
(Wee Willie Winkie, *Anon*, Em [d'-f''#], S&B Pippen Hill.)
(Where go the boats, *R L Stevenson*, B&H.)

George Munro. ? - 1731.
Celia the fair, *Anon*, G [d'-g''](m), S&B (Pilkington) *Georgian 2, Recitalist 3*; E, Paterson (Diack) *100 Best 3*.
Gold a receipt for love, *Anon*, D [d'-g''], S&B (Pilkington) *Georgian 2*.
My lovely Celia, *Anon*, G [d'-g''](m), B&H (Lane Wilson) *Old English*; E, Chester *Celebrated 3*.

Herbert Murrill. 1909 - 1952.
Collections: *Five Songs* (introduction by Carolyn Murrill), Thames 1989.
A thanksgiving to God, for his house, *Robert Herrick*, Cm [c'-a''], Thames 5 Songs.
In youth is pleasure, *Robert Wever*, Ab [e'b-a''](m), Thames 5 Songs.
Love is a sickness, *Samuel Daniel*, Am [e'-f''], Thames 5 Songs.
Piggësnye, *Anon*, A [f'#-a''](m), Thames 5 Songs.
To music, to becalm his fever, *Robert Herrick*, [e'b-a''], Thames 5 Songs.

Thea Musgrave. 1928 -
Collections: *A Suite O' Bairnsangs*, Chester 1962; *Songs for a Winter's Evening*, Novello 1997.

A bairn's prayer at nicht, *Maurice Lindsay*, [g'-d''], Chester A Suite.

A song for Christmas, *William Dunbar*, [b(g)-a''*b*], Chester.

Ca' the yowes to the knowes, *Robert Burns*, [c'#-b''(g'')](f), Novello Songs.

Daffins, *Maurice Lindsay*, [f'-f'#], Chester A Suite.

I am my Mammy's ae bairn, *Robert Burns*, [d'-g''*b*(g'')](f), Novello Songs.

Jamie, come try me, *Robert Burns*, [c'-c'''(a'')](f), Novello Songs.

John Anderson my jo, *Robert Burns*, [e'-a''](f), Novello Songs.

O whistle and I'll come to ye my lad, *Robert Burns*, [c'-a''*b*](f), Novello Songs.

Summer's a pleasant time, *Robert Burns*, [e'*b*-a''*b*](f), Novello Songs.

The gean, *Maurice Lindsay*, [f'-g''], Chester A Suite.

The man-in-the-mune, *Maurice Lindsay*, [e'*b*-f''], Chester A Suite.

Willie Wabster, *Maurice Lindsay*, [e'-e''], Chester A Suite.

Ye banks and braes o' bonnie Doon, *Robert Burns*, [c'-a''](f), Novello Songs.

N

James Nares. 1715 - 1783.
   O Lord my God, I will exalt thee, *Anon*, C [b-d''], B&H (Patrick) *Sacred Songs 2.*

Stuart Nash. 1914 -
   Sonnet No 104, *Shakespeare*, E [b(e')-e''], B&H *Songs of Love and Affection.*

Bernard Naylor. 1907 - 1986.
Collections: *Speaking from the snow*, Roberton 1973.
   A child's carol, *Arthur L Salmon*, A [c'#-f''], Roberton.
   Beauty's end is in sight, *C Day Lewis*, [e'*bb*-a''], Roberton Speaking.
   Come away death, *Shakespeare*, Dm [a-d''], Roberton; G, Roberton.
   Dreams of the sea, *W H Davies*, [g'-e''], Roberton.
   Gentle sleep, *S T Coleridge*, C [c'-b''*b*(g'')], Roberton.
   Now she is like the white tree-rose, *C Day Lewis*, [d'-g''], Roberton Speaking.
   Rest from loving and be living, *C Day Lewis*, [c'-a''], Roberton Speaking.
   Roseberries, *Mary Webb*, Em [e'-g''], Roberton.
   The ecstatic, *C Day Lewis*, Gm [c'-g''], Roberton; Am, Roberton.
   The fallen poplar, *Mary Webb*, Fm [f'-f''], Roberton.
   Twenty weeks near past, *C Day Lewis*, [d'-a''], Roberton Speaking.

Havelock Nelson. 1917 - 1996.
   Dirty work, *John o' the North*, [medium], Banks.
   I think it will be winter, *Helen Waddell*, C [c'-f''], Banks.
   Love is cruel, *Thomas MacDonagh*, [medium], Banks.
   The black cat, *John o' the North*, [high], Banks.
   The town tree, *Dorothy Roberts*, F [c'-f''], B&H.
Arrangements: *An Irish Folksinger's Album*, Roberton.

David Nevens. 1945 -
   Genesis, *David Cole*, [a#-g''], Welsh Music *Songs from Wales 2.*

C Newman. (BMIC.)

George Newson. (BMIC.)

George Nicholson. 1949 - (BMIC.)

Alfred Nieman. 1913 - 1997.
Collections: *Three Chinese Songs*, S&B 1967. (see also BMIC).
   How goes the night, *Shih King* tr. *Waddell*, [c'-g''], S&B 3 Chinese, Thames *Century 3.*
   Sailing homeward, *Anon* tr. *Waley*, [e'*b*-f''#], S&B 3 Chinese.
   The morning glory, *Confucius* tr. *Waddell*, [d'-g''](f), S&B 3 Chinese.

Harold Noble. 1903 -
Johnny, *Anon*, Lengnick.
Naples Bay, *Arthur Symons*, D♭ [b♭-e''], Lengnick.
The ballad of Semmerwater, *William Watson*, E♭ [g#-f''], Lengnick.
The road of evening, *de la Mare*, F [d'-f'#], Lengnick.

Thomas Tertius Noble. 1867 - 1953.
O sweet content, *Thomas Dekker*, [medium], Banks.

Ivor Novello. 1893 - 1951.
Collection: (*The Valley of Rainbows*, B&H.)
  If, *Edward Teschemacher*, Cm [c'-f''] B&H *Ballad Album 2*.
  (Little one, D, B&H.)
  (Megan, F, B&H; G, A, B&H.)
  (The little damozel, E♭, B&H; F, G, B&H.)
  (The valley, C, B&H.)

Michael Nyman. 1944 -
  (Ariel Songs (cycle), *Shakespeare*, [e'♭-b''#](f), Chester.)

O

Arthur Oldham. 1926 -
Collections: *Five Chinese Lyrics*, Novello 1951.
A gentle wind, *Fu Hsüan* tr. *Arthur Waley*, F [c'#-a''], Novello 5 Chinese.
Fishing, *Anon* tr. *E D Edwards*, [c'#-g''], Novello 5 Chinese.
The herd boy's song, *Anon* tr. *E D Edwards*, E [d'-g''], Novello 5 Chinese.
The pedlar of spells, *Lu Yu* tr. *Arthur Waley*, A [c'#-a''], Novello 5 Chinese.
Under the pondweed, *Anon* tr. *Helen Waddell*, [c'-a''], Novello 5 Chinese.

Norman O'Neill. 1875 - 1934.
Collection: (*Songs from the Fairy Play 'Through the Green Door'* (words by M Vernon), OUP
1920); (*Blossom Songs*, (Japanese, tr. S Kimura), Cramer, 1924.)
(Home of mine, *B Haddon*, Cramer.)
(I have a flaunting air, *Ashley Dukes*, Cramer.)
(Jewels, *Herbert Asquith*, Cm [d'-f''](m), B&H.)
(May lilies, *E Rutter Leatham*, Cramer.)
(Musette, *Anon* tr. *Rosa Newmarch*, A [e'-a''], Cramer.)
(On a grey day, *E Temple Thurston*, F [f'-a''], Cramer; D♭, Cramer.)
(The golden hour of noon, *Ashley Dukes*, Cramer.)
(The song of Lucius, *Shakespeare*, [d'-f''(e'')], OUP.)
(The warrior lover, *William Watson*, Cm [c'-f''](m), Schott.)
(When May walks by, *Betty Haddon*, E♭ [e'♭-a''♭], Cramer.)

Buxton Orr. 1924 - (See also BMIC.)
The Ballad of Mr and Mrs Discobolos, *Edward Lear*, [c'-a''](m), Eulenberg.

C W Orr. 1893 - 1976.
Collections: (*Two Songs from A Shropshire Lad*, Chester 1923); *Two Seventeenth Century
Poems*, Roberton 1930; (*Cycle of Songs from 'A Shropshire Lad'*, Chester 1934); (*Three Songs
from 'A Shropshire Lad'*, Chester 1940); (*Four Songs for High Voice*, OUP 1959); *Five Songs from
A Shropshire Lad*, Roberton 1959.
(Along the field, *A E Housman*, Em [b-e''](m), Chester Cycle.)
(Bahnhofstrasse, *James Joyce*, G [e'-g''], OUP 4 Songs.)
(Farewell to barn and stack and tree, *A E Housman*, Fm [b♭-f''](m), Chester Cycle.)
(Hughley steeple, *A E Housman*, F [b♭-f''](m), Chester Cycle.)
Hymn before sleep, *Prudentius*, tr. *Helen Waddell*, G [b-e''], Roberton.
In valleys green and still, *A E Housman*, E♭ [b♭-g''], Roberton.
(Into my heart, *A E Housman*, F [c'-f''](m), Chester 3 Songs.)
Is my team ploughing? *A E Housman*, [d'-g''](m), Roberton 5 Songs.
(Loveliest of trees, *A E Housman*, Fm [d'♭-f''], Chester 2 Songs.)
(O fair enough are sky and plain, *A E Housman*, F [c'-e''#](m), Chester Cycle.)
(Oh see how thick, *A E Housman*, E [c'#-g''#](m), Chester 3 Songs.)
Oh, when I was in love with you, *A E Housman*, Gm [d'-f''](m), Roberton 5 Songs.
On your midnight pallet lying, *A E Housman*, Dm [d'-g''](m), Roberton 5 Songs.

(Plucking the rushes, *Anon* tr. *Arthur Waley*, Bm [b-f''#], Chester.)
(Requiem, *Anon* tr. *Helen Waddell*, Ab [e'b-a''b], OUP 4 Songs.)
(Silent noon, *D G Rossetti*, E [c'#-e''#], Chester.)
(Since thou, O fondest and truest, *Robert Bridges*, Db [d'-b''b], OUP 4 Songs.)
Soldier from the wars returning, *A E Housman*, D [A-d'](m), Roberton.
The Carpenter's Son, *A E Housman*, Dm [e'b-a''](m), Chester.
The Earl of Bristol's farewell, *John Digby*, E [c'#-e''](m), Roberton Two 17th Century.
The Isle of Portland, *A E Housman*, Eb [c'#-e''](m), Chester.
The lads in their hundreds, *A E Housman*, F [c'-a''](m), Roberton.
(The Lent lily, *A E Housman*, F [c'-f''](m), Chester Cycle.)
(The time of roses, *Thomas Hood*, B [d'#-g''#], OUP 4 Songs.)
This time of year, *A E Housman*, G [d'-f''#](m), Roberton 5 Songs.
(Tis time I think by Wenlock Town, *A E Housman*, G [e'-f''#-], Chester 2 Songs.)
Tryste Noel, *Louise Imogen Guiney*, Cm [c'-g''], Roberton.
(Westward on the high-hilled plains, *A E Housman*, G [c'#-a''](m), Chester 3 Songs.)
Whenas I wake, *Patrick Hannay*, E [e'-e''](m), Roberton Two 17th Century.
When I was one-and-twenty, *A E Housman*, Dm [d'-g''](m), Chester.
(When I watch the living meet, *A E Housman*, Fm [c'b-f''](m), Chester Cycle.)
(When smoke stood up from Ludlow, *A E Housman*, E [b-e''](m), Chester Cycle.)
When the lad for longing sighs, *A E Housman*, E [d'-g''#], Chester.
While summer on is stealing, *Helen Waddell*, D [d'-e''](m), Roberton.
With rue my heart is laden, *A E Housman*, Bm [d'-f''#](m), Roberton 5 Songs.

Robin Orr. 1909 - (BMIC.)

James Oswald. 1711 - 1769.

The self banished, *Edmund Waller*, Em [e'-g''], Thames (Copley & Reitan) *Gentleman's Magazine.*

Morfydd Owen. 1891 - 1918.

Collections: (*Early Songs, Selected Songs*, OUP 1923); *Four Flower Songs*, Welsh Music 1996.
(A mother's lullaby, *Morfydd Owen*, F [d'-g''](f), OUP Early.)
(A noon-tide lullaby, *Ethel Newman*, Ab [g'b-g''b(a''b)], OUP Selected.)
(A serenade, *Anon*, Db [f'-a''b], OUP Early.)
A song of sorrow, *William Blake*, [f'-g''], Welsh Music.
(An Irish lullaby, *Anon*, G [g'-g''](f), OUP.)
Daisy's song, *John Keats*, D [d'-f'#], Welsh Music 4 Flower.
Foredoomed, *Philip Bourke Marston*, [c'#-f'#], Welsh Music.
God made a lovely garden, *Mabel Spence*, Db [d'b-g''#], Welsh Music 4 Flower.
(He prayeth best who loveth best, *S T Coleridge*, Gb [g'b-g''b], OUP Selected.)
(Impenitent, *Ethel Newman*, B&H.)
(In cradle land, *Eos Gwalia*, G [g'-g''], OUP Selected.)
Infant joy, *William Blake*, [e'-f'#], Welsh Music.
(Jesus, tender saviour, *Anon*, Ab [a'b-f''], OUP Selected.)
(Mister rain, *Richard Aldington*, E [f'#-g''#], OUP.)
(Orbits, *Richard le Gallienne*, Gm [e'b-f''], OUP Early.
(Patrick's your boy, *Anon*, Am, B&H; Bm, B&H.)

(Pippa's song, *Robert Browning*, F [f'-f'#], OUP Early.)

(Shepherd's love song, *A d Edwards*, B&H.)

Speedwell, *Atwyth Eversley*, Em [e'-g''#], Welsh Music 4 Flower.

Spring, *William Blake*, F [c'-f''], Welsh Music *Songs from Wales 1*.

Slumber song of the Madonna, *Alfred Noyes*, G [c'-a''♭], Welsh Music, Gwynn.

The lamb, *William Blake*, [c'-g''], Welsh Music.

(The weeping babe, *Katherine Tynan*, Em [g'-e''](f), OUP Selected.)

To Our Lady of Sorrows, *Wilfred Hinton*, [d'#-g''#], Welsh Music.

To violets, *Robert Herrick*, Fm [f'-f''], Welsh Music 4 Flower.

(When I came at last to Ludlow, *A E Housman*, B♭m [f'-g''♭], OUP Selected.)

(William, *Eric Hiller*, Fm [f'-f''](f), OUP Selected.)

P

Krinió Papastavrou.
Collection: *Seven Songs for a Child*, Bardic.
 Adoréd Spring, [d'-f''#], Bardic 7 Songs.
 Anemone, [d'-f''], Bardic 7 Songs.
 Buzz, buzz, buzz, [d'-e''], Bardic 7 Songs.
 Father time, [d'-e''], Bardic 7 Songs.
 Icon from abroad, [d'-e''], Bardic 7 Songs.
 Off to school, [d'-g''], Bardic 7 Songs.
 The wheel of life, [e'-g''], Bardic 7 Songs.

Dorothy Parke. 1904 - 1990.
Collection: *By Winding Roads* (words John Irvine), Roberton.
 (A song of good courage, *Gunby Hadath*, Eb, B&H.)
 (Kilkeel, *Richard Rowley*, Fm [c'-e''b], Paterson.)
 (Sing heigh-ho, *Charles Kingsley*, [d'-e''], Elkin.)
 Song in exile, *John Irvine*, Eb [bb-e''b], Roberton.
 The falling of the leaves, *W B Yeats*, F#m [e'-b-f''#], Roberton.
 The house and the road, *Josephine Peabody*, F [c'-f''], Roberton.
 The road to Ballydare, *John Irvine*, Cm [c'-e''b], Roberton.
 (The Lord is my refuge, *Psalm 91*, B&H.)
 The wish, *Winifred Letts*, Eb [e'-b-e''b], Roberton.
 (To the sailors, *John Irvine*, Ab, B&H.)
 Wee Hughie, *Elizabeth Shane*, C [c'-e''], Roberton; Eb, Roberton.

Ian Parrott. 1916 - (See also BMIC).
 I heard a linnet courting, *Robert Bridges*, A [c'#-f''#(e')], Lengnick.
 In Phæacia, *James Elroy Flecker*, [c'#-a''], Lengnick.
 Leaves, *Elizabeth Ward*, [b-g''], Lengnick.
 Absence, *John Donne*, Am [e'-f''](m), Welsh Music *Songs from Wales 1*.

C H H Parry. 1848 - 1918.
Collections: (*Three Odes of Anacreon*, S&B 1880); (*English Lyrics Sets 1 - 12*, Novello 1885 - 1920); *Seven Songs for High Voice* (edited Geoffrey Bush), S&B 1979; *Musica Britannica 49* (Bush) S&B 1982.
 (A contrast, *Anon*, Gm [d'-d''], B&H.)
 (A girl to her glass, *Julian Sturgis*, D [e'-g''](f), Novello English 5).
 (A fairy town (St Andrews), *Mary Coleridge*, G [c'#-g''], Novello English 9).
 (A hymn for aviators, *Mary C D Hamilton*, Eb [d'-e''b], B&H; F, B&H.)
 (A lover's garland, *A P Graves*, G [d'-d''](m), Novello English 6).
 (A moment of farewell, *Julian Sturgis*, D [f'#-a''(g''#)], Novello English 10).
 (A sea dirge, *Shakespeare*, Fm [c'-e''b], B&H.)
 A spring song, *Shakespeare*, G [d'-g''(e')], B&H *Heritage 1*.
 A stray nymph of Dian, *Julian Sturgis*, F [e'-b-a''b](f), S&B MB 49, (Novello English 5).

A Welsh lullaby, *Ceirog* tr. *E O Jones*, F [f'-f'']($), S&B MB 49, (Novello English 5).
And yet I love her till I die, *Anon*, G [c'#-e''](m), S&B MB 49, (Novello English 6).
Armida's garden, *Mary Coleridge*, Eb [d'-g''], S&B 7 Songs, MB 49, (Novello English 9).
(At the hour the long day ends, *A P Graves*, Eb [d'-d''b](m), Novello English 6).
(Away, away, ye men of rules, *Anacreon* tr. *Thomas Moore*, Dm [A-d'](m), S&B 3 Odes.)
Blow, blow, thou winter wind, *Shakespeare*, Em [e'-g''#](m), S&B 7 Songs, MB 49, (Novello English 2).
Bright star, *Keats*, Ab [e'b-a''b](m), Thames *Century 1*, S&B MB 49, (Novello English 4).
(Concerning love, *Samuel Daniel*, Cm [c'-e''b], B&H)
Crabbed age and youth, *Shakespeare?*, Eb [e'b-g''b(a''b)]($), Novello (Novello English 5); F, Novello.
Dirge in woods, *George Meredith*, G [g-e''], S&B, MB 49, *Recitalist 2*, (Novello English 8).
Dream pedlary, *Thomas Lovell Beddoes*, Bb [c'-g''b], S&B 7 Songs, MB 49, (Novello English 12).
Farewell, thou art too dear for my possessing, *Shakespeare*, Eb [d'-g''](m), S&B MB 49.
(Fill me, boy, as deep a draught, *Anacreon* tr. *Thomas Moore*, F [A-f'](m), S&B 3 Odes.)
(Follow a shadow, *Ben Jonson*, G [b-d''](m), Novello English 7).
From a city window, *Langdon Elwyn Mitchell*, D [b(c'#)-g''], Thames *Century 1*, (Novello English 10).
(Golden hues of life are fled, *Anacreon* tr. *Thomas Moore*, Cm [G-e'b](m), S&B 3 Odes.)
(Gone were but the winter cold, *Alan Cunningham*, Cm [c'-g''], Novello English 10).
Good night, *P B Shelley*, Bb [e'b-g''], Novello English 1, S&B MB 49.
Grapes, *Julian Sturgis*, F [c'-e''b], S&B MB 49, (Novello English 8).
(If I might ride on puissant wing, *Julian Sturgis*, G [c'#-e''], Novello English 11).
If thou would'st ease thine heart, *Thomas Lovell Beddoes*, G [c'#-d''#(e'')], S&B MB 49, (Novello English 3).
(Julia, *Robert Herrick*, G [d'-d''](m), Novello English 7).
Lay a garland on my hearse, *John Fletcher*, Gm [d'-f'']($), S&B MB 49, (Novello English 5).
(Looking backward, *Julian Sturgis*, Ab [b-e''b], Novello English 8).
(Love and laughter, *Arthur Gray Butler*, F [d'-g''b], Novello English 5).
Love is a bable, *Anon*, Eb [c'-e''b](m), S&B MB 49, Novello, (Novello English 6).
(Marian, *George Meredith*, F [c'-e''b](m), Novello English 8).
Merry Margaret, *John Skelton*, F [c'-f''], Banks.
My heart is like a singing bird, *Christina Rossetti*, F [c'-a'']($), S&B 7 Songs, MB 49, Novello, (Novello English 10).
My true love hath my heart, *Sir Philip Sidney*, F [d'-f'']($), Novello English 1, S&B MB 49.
Nightfall in winter, *Langdon Elwyn Mitchell*, Em [c'-e''(e''b)], S&B MB 49, (Novello English 8).
No longer mourn for me, *Shakespeare*, Fm [e'b(c')-a''b], S&B MB 49, (Novello English 2).
(O mistress mine, *Shakespeare*, F [d'-g''](m), Novello English 2.)
O never say that I was false of heart, *Shakespeare*, Eb [bb-f''b], S&B MB 49, (Novello English 7).
(O world, O life, O time, *P B Shelley*, F# [c'#-a''], Novello English 12).
(Of all the torments, *William Walsh*, G [d'-d''](m), Novello English 3).
On a day, alack the day, *Shakespeare*, Gm [f'-d''], Banks.
On a time the amorous Silvy, *Anon*, Eb [bb-e''b(g'')], S&B MB 49, (Novello English 7).
(One golden thread, *Julia Chatterton*, D [c'#-f''#], Novello English 11).
(One silent night of late, *Robert Herrick*, F [c'-g''], Novello English 10).
Proud Maisie, *Walter Scott*, Eb [d'-f''], S&B 7 Songs, MB 49, (Novello English 5).
Rosaline, *Thomas Lodge*, Eb [d'-a''b](m), S&B 7 Songs, MB 49, (Novello English 12).

Shall I compare thee to a summer's day? *Shakespeare*, E♭ [e'♭-a''♭](m), S&B MB 49.

(She is my love beyond all thought, *A P Graves*, E♭ [b-e''♭](m), Novello English 11).

Sleep, *Julian Sturgis*, D♭ [a♭-e''♭], S&B MB 49, (Novello English 7).

Take O take those lips away, *Shakespeare*, B♭ [c'-g''], S&B MB 49, (Novello English 2).

(The blackbird, *A P Graves*, G [c'#-e''], Novello English 11).

(The child and the twilight, *Langdon Elwyn Mitchell*, F [d'-g''], Novello English 10).

(The faithful lover, *A P Graves*, D [c'#-e''](m), Novello English 11).

(The Laird of Cockpen, *Lady Caroline Nairn*, F [g-d''], Novello.)

(The maiden, *Mary Coleridge*, A♭ [e'♭-a''♭], Novello English 9).

(The sound of hidden music, *Julia Chatterton*, G [c'#-g''], Novello English 12).

(The spirit of the spring, *A P Graves*, Em [c'♭-e''♭](m), Novello English 11).

(The witches' wood, *Mary Coleridge*, Gm [c'-g''], Novello English 9).

(There, *Mary Coleridge*, G [b-g''], Novello English 9).

There be none of beauty's daughters, *Lord Byron*, B♭ [f'-a''](m), S&B MB 49, (Novello English 4).

(Thine eyes still shined for me, *Ralph Waldo Emerson*, D [e'-f''#](m), Novello English 4).

(Three aspects, *Mary Coleridge*, E♭ [c'-a''♭], Novello English 9).

Through the ivory gate, *Julian Sturgis*, G [b-d''](m), Thames *Century 2*, (Novello English 3).

To Althea, from prison, *Richard Lovelace*, D♭ [b♭-e''♭], S&B MB 49, (Novello English 3).

To blossoms, *Robert Herrick*, A♭ [d'-g''], S&B MB 49, (Novello English 12).

To Lucasta, on going to the wars, *Richard Lovelace*, F [c'-e''](m), S&B MB 49, (Novello English 3).

Under the greenwood tree, *Shakespeare*, G [c'-e''](m), S&B MB 49, (Novello English 6).

Weep you no more, sad fountains, *Anon*, Gm [d'-g''], S&B MB 49, 7 Songs, *Recitalist 1;* Novello English 4).

(What part of dread eternity, *C H H Parry?*, Em [b-e''♭], Novello English 11).

When comes my Gwen, *Mynydog* tr. *E O Jones*, E♭ [d'-e''♭](m), S&B MB 49, (Novello English 6).

(When icicles hang by the wall, *Shakespeare*, B♭ [f'-g''], Novello English 2).

(When in disgrace with fortune and men's eyes, *Shakespeare*, Em [d'#-g''](m), S&B MB 49.

(When lovers meet again, *Langdon Elwyn Mitchell*, D [e'-g''], Novello English 4).

(When the dew is falling, *Julia Chatterton*, G♭ [d'♭-g''♭], Novello English 12).

(When the sun's great orb, *H Warner*, Fm [c'-a''], Novello English 12).

When to the sessions of sweet silent thought, *Shakespeare*, D [d'-g''](m), S&B MB 49.

(When we two parted, *Lord Byron*, E♭ [d'-g''](m), Novello English 4).

(Whence, *Julian Sturgis*, D [c'#(d')-e''♭], Novello English 8).

Where shall the lover rest? *Walter Scott*, E♭ [e'♭-a''(g'')], Novello English 1, S&B MB 49.

(Whether I live, *Mary Coleridge*, A♭ [c'-g''], Novello English 9).

Why art thou slow, *Philip Massinger*, Fm [b-g''♭](f), S&B MB 49, (Novello English 11).

Why so pale and wan, fond lover? *John Suckling*, G [c'#-e''](m), S&B MB 49, (Novello English 3).

Willow, willow, willow, *Shakespeare*, Em [d'-g''], Novello English 1, S&B MB 49.

Ye little birds that sit and sing, *Thomas Heywood*, A [d'#-d''](m), S&B MB 49, (Novello English 7).

Arrangement:

(Noble of air, *Anon* tr. *Paul England*, E♭ [c'-e''♭], B&H.)

Joseph Parry. 1841 - 1903.

Make new friends but keep the old, G, [soprano/tenor], Snell; E♭ [contralto/baritone].

My Blodwen, my darling, [tenor], Snell.

O ye that love the Lord, [contralto/baritone], Snell.

The mother and child, [tenor/mezzo/soprano], Snell.
The sailor's wife, [mezzo/contralto/baritone], Snell.

Robert Parsons. 1530 - 1570.
In youthly years, *Richard Edwards*, Dm [c'-c''](m), S&B (Greer) *Manuscript 1.*

Robert H Patterson.
The curtains now are drawn, *Thomas Hardy*, E♭ [c'-e''♭](m); Thames *Hardy Songbook.*

Anthony Payne. 1936 -
(Adlestrop, *Edward Thomas*, [soprano], Chester.)
(Evening land, [soprano], Chester.)

Graham Peel. 1877 - 1947. 13 more songs, B&H archive; 7 more songs, Cramer archive.
(In summertime on Bredon, *A E Housman*, E♭ [b♭-e''♭](m), Chappell *English Recital 1; F*, Chappell.)
In the highlands, *R L Stevenson*, D♭ [d'♭(b♭-f''], B&H *Heritage 1.*
Sorrow and Spring, *St John Lucas*, B♭ [f'-g''], B&H *Heritage 2.*
(Wind of the western sea, *Lord Tennyson*, D♭ [b♭-f''], Chappell *English Recital 2; C, E♭*, Chappell.)

Tom Pender.
(Fidele, *William Shakespeare*, Em [e'-a''♭], OUP.)
(Shall I compare thee? *William Shakespeare*, F [e'-a''], OUP.)

Morris Pert. 1947 -
Four Japanese Verses (cycle), tr. Bownas & Thwaite, [c'-f''](f), Weinberger.

Norman Peterkin. 1886 - 1982.
Collection: *Eight Songs,* Thames 1983.
Advice to girls, *Herbert A Giles*, F#m [c'#-f'#], Thames 8 Songs.
(All suddenly the wind comes soft, *Rupert Brooke*, F [d'-f''], OUP.)
Dubbuldideery, *Walter de la Mare*, Em [b-f''], OUP.)
(Goneril's lullaby, *Anon*, C, B&H.)
I heard a piper piping, *Seosamh MacCathmhaoèl*, Gm [g'-f''], OUP, Thames 8 Songs.
I love the din of beating drums, *Seosamh MacCathmhaoèl*, [d'-f''#(e'')], Thames 8 Songs.
(I wish and I wish, *Joseph Campbell*, E [b-e''], OUP.)
(If I be living in Erin, *J P McCall*, Am [c'#-f'#], OUP.)
(My fiddle is singing, *Joseph Campbell*, D♭ [d'♭-f''], OUP.)
(Never more, sailor, *Walter de la Mare*, [b-f''#], OUP.)
(Once and there was a young sailor, *Walter de la Mare*, Em [b-f''#], OUP.)
(Pierrette in memory, *William Griffith*, F#m [e'-f''], OUP.)
(Rune of the burden of the tide, *Fiona Macleod*, Am [b-e''], OUP.)
(She's me forgot, *Walter de la Mare*, Am [b-f''#], OUP.)
Sleep, white love, *Seosamh MacCathmhaoil*, D [d'-f''#], Thames 8 Songs.
(So we'll go no more a-roving, *Lord Byron*, [d'♭-d''], OUP.)
Song of Asano, *John Masefield*, B♭m [d'♭-f''], Thames 8 Songs.
Song of the water maiden, *Walter de la Mare*, [e'-f''#](f), Thames 8 Songs.
(The bees' song, *Walter de la Mare*, Em [c'-f''#], OUP.)
The chestnut blossom, *Wilfrid Gibson*, [c'-e''], Thames 8 Songs.

(The fiddler, *I M Maunder*, Fm [f'-a''], OUP.)
(The galliass, *Walter de la Mare*, Em [c'-e''], OUP.)
The garden of bamboos, *E Powys Mathers*, Db[e'b-f''], Thames 8 Songs.
(The little red hen, *J P McCall*, Em [b-e''], OUP.)
(The Palatine's daughter, *Anon* tr. *J P McCall*, C#m [b-e''], OUP.)
(The song of Fionula, *Fiona Macleod*, Am [c'-e''], OUP.)
(The song of the secret, *Walter de la Mare*, A [e'(c'#)-f'#(a')], OUP.)
(The tide rises, the tide falls, *Henry Wadsworth Longfellow*, Cm [c'#-g''], OUP.)
(There is a lady sweet and kind, *Anon*, E [c'-f'#](m), OUP.)
(Why Thomas Cam was grumpy, *James Stephens*, B&H.)
Arrangement:
(A little wind came blowing, *Marie Peterkin*, F [e'-f''], OUP.)

Montague Phillips. 1885 - 1969.
(Crab apple, *Nancie Marsland*, G [e'-a''], Chappell *English Recital 2.)*
(Sing, joyous bird, *Nora Usher*, C [d'-g''], Chappell *English Recital 1.*)
(The silent mill, *Beryl Cooper*, F [c'-f''], Chappell *English Recital 1.*)
(Wind of the wheat, *Harold Simpson*, Cm [c'-e''b], Chappell *English Recital 2.)*

John Pickard.
The Phoenix, *after Cynewulf* tr. *R K Gordon*, [b-c''''](f), Bardic.

Henry Hugo Pierson. 1815 - 1873.
All my heart's thine own, *Anon*, Am [c'-f'#], S&B (Bush & Temperley) *MB 43.*
Dirge: Fear no more the heat of the sun, *Shakespeare*, Am [g-d''], S&B (Bush & Temperley) *MB 43, Recitalist 4.*
John Anderson, my jo, *Robert Burns*, F#m [c'#-f'#](f), S&B (Bush & Temperley) *MB 43.*
Love and grief, *John Fletcher*, F [f'-a''](m), S&B (Bush & Temperley) *MB 43.*
The white owl, *Tennyson*, Am [c'(a)-e''], S&B (Bush & Temperley) *MB 43, Recitalist 1.*
Those evening bells, *Thomas Moore*, Ab [e'b-a''b], S&B (Bush & Temperley) *MB 43.*

Harry E Piggott. ? - 1966
Long ago I went to Rome, *Celia Furse*, [high], Lengnick; [low], Lengnick.

Lionel Pike. (BMIC.)

Francis Pilkington. *c.* 1570 - 1638.
Collection: *The First Booke of Songs* (edited Thurston Dart), S&B 1971 [1st Book]. Only songs available in anthologies are listed individually here. Note that in the following: Pilkington = *English Lute Songs Book 2*, S&B; Keel 1/2 = *Elizabethan Lovesongs Books 1 & 2* (high & low keys), B&H .
Diaphenia, *H Constable?* G [d'-d''](m), 1st Book, Keel 1; *Bb*, Keel 1; *F*, Pilkington.
Down-a-down, thus Phyllis sang, *Thomas Lodge*, G [d'-d''], 1st Book, Pilkington, Keel 2; *Bb*, Keel 2.
Now let her change, *Thomas Campion*, F [e'-f''](m), 1st Book, Pilkington.
Rest sweet nymphs, *Anon*, Gm [g'-f''], 1st Book, Pilkington, B&H (Northcote) *Imperial 4.*

James Holme Pilkington. 1856 - 1916.
Wynken, Blynken and Nod, *Eugene Field*, Eb [b'b-e''b], Thames *Century 4.*

Michael Pilkington. 1928 -
Collections: *Four Epigrams and a Prayer*, Thames 1993.
A love song, *Anon* tr. *T F Higham*, Gm [d'-f''], Thames 4 Epigrams.
Evening on the Moselle, *Ausonius* tr. *Helen Waddell*, Eb [bb-e''b], Thames 4 Epigrams.
Li Fu-Jen, *Wu-ti* tr. *Arthur Waley*, [e'b-e''], Thames 4 Epigrams.
Night, *Alcman* tr. *H T Wade-Grey*, [a-f''], Thames 4 Epigrams.
The spouse to the beloved, *William Baldwin*, Am [a-f''], Thames 4 Epigrams.

George Frederick Pinto. 1786 - 1806.
A shepherd lov'd a nymph so fair, *Anon*, G [d'-e''], OUP (Roberts) *Tuneful Voice*.
Eloisa to Abelard, *Alexander Pope*, Dm [d'-g''](f), S&B (Bush & Temperley) *MB 43*.
From thee, Eliza, I must go, *Robert Burns*, Eb [d'b-f''](m), OUP (Roberts) *Tuneful Voice*, S&B (Bush & Temperley) *MB 43*.
Invocation to Nature, *Anon*, Ab [d'-f''], OUP (Roberts) *Tuneful Voice*, S&B (Bush and Temperley) *MB 43*, *Recitalist 2*.

Thomas Pitfield. 1903 -
Collection: *Selected Songs*, Forsyth 1989.
Birds about the morning air, *Thomas Pitfield*, G [d'-g''(a')], Forsyth Selected.
By the Dee at night, *Thomas Pitfield*, Eb [e'b-e''b], Forsyth Selected.
Christmas lullaby, *Thomas Pitfield*, G [e'-e''], Forsyth Selected.
Cuckoo and chestnut time, *Robert Faulds*, G [e'-g''], Forsyth Selected.
(Desdemona's song, *Shakespeare*, Em [c'-g''](f), Cramer.)
In an old country church, *Thomas Pitfield*, Db [db-e''], Forsyth Selected.
(In the moonlight, Cramer.)
Lingering music, (1st setting), *Thomas Pitfield*, Bbm [f'-b''b(g''b)], Forsyth Selected.
Lingering music, (2nd setting), *Thomas Pitfield*, Am [bb-e''], Forsyth Selected.
Naiad, *Dennis Jones*, G [c'-g''(e')], Forsyth Selected.
September lovers, *Thomas Pitfield*, B [b-e''], Forsyth Selected.
Shadow march, *R L Stevenson*, Dm [c'-f''], Forsyth Selected.
Song of compassion, *Thomas Pitfield*, [d'-e''(g')], Forsyth Selected.
The child hears rain at night, *Thomas Pitfield*, Dm [d'-f''], Forsyth Selected.
The crescent boat, *John Grecon Brown*, Eb [bb-f''], Forsyth Selected.
The sands of Dee, *Charles Kingsley*, Cm [bb-f''], Forsyth Selected.
The unfulfilled, *Pushkin*, tr. *Pitfield*, Cm [c'-f''], Forsyth Selected.
The wagon of life, *Pushkin*, tr. *Pitfield*, Dm [a-f''], Forsyth Selected.
Willow song, *Shakespeare*, Bm [d'-f''#], Forsyth Selected.
Winter evening: Dunham Park, *Thomas Pitfield*, D [bb-a''], Forsyth Selected.
Winter song, *Katherine Mansfield*, Am [d'-e''], Forsyth Selected.
You frail sad leaves, *Thomas Pitfield*, Em [bb-e''], Forsyth Selected.
Arrangements:
(Donkey riding, *Anon*, E [e'b-e''], Cramer.)
Faithful Johnny, *Anon*, F [e'-g''], Forsyth Selected.
So far from my country, *Anon*, Eb [e'b-g''], Forsyth Selected.
The carrion crow, *Anon*, F [f'-f''], Forsyth Selected.

John Playford. 1623 - 1686.
On a quiet conscience, *Francis Quarles*, Dm [f'-g''], Thames (Bevan) *6 Divine*.

Mary Plumstead. 1905 - 1980.
(A forsaken lover's complaint, *Robert Johnson*, B&H.)
A grateful heart, *George Herbert*, Db [d'b-f''], Roberton.
Close thine eyes, *Francis Quarles*, Db [bb-d''b], Roberton, Thames *Century 2*; Gb Roberton.
(Come sweet lass, *Anon*, B&H.)
Down by the salley gardens, *W B Yeats*, Cm [a'b-e''b], Roberton.
Ha'nacker Mill, *Hilaire Belloc*, Cm [bb-e''b], Roberton.
He was the one, *Phyllida Garth*, Em [b-e''], Roberton.
(Sigh no more, ladies, *Shakespeare*, Bb [bb(f)-e''b], Curwen.)
Take O take those lips away, *Shakespeare*, Bm [b-e''], Roberton.
The grey wind, *Vera Wainwright*, Bb [d'b-e''b], Roberton.
The song of the cross, *Phyllida Garth*, Em [b-e''], Roberton; Gm, Roberton.
(The tale of the lamb, *Sarah Josepha Hale*, C [g-e''], Chappell.)
(Where are you going to, my pretty maid, *Anon*, B&H.)

Elizabeth Poston. 1905 - 1987.
(A little candle to St Anthony, *S J C Russell*, B&H.)
(Ardan Mor, *Francis Ledwidge*, B&H.)
(Aubade, *Sir William Davenant*, Bb, B&H.)
(Balulalow, *Luther* tr. *Wedderburn*, B&H.)
(Be still my sweet sweeting, *John Philip*, B&H.)
(Brown is my love, *Anon*, B&H.)
(Call for the robin redbreast, *John Webster*, B&H.)
(Dance to your daddie, *Anon*, B&H.)
(In praise of woman, *Anon*, B&H.)
(In youth is pleasure, *Robert Wever*, B&H.)
(Maid quiet, *W B Yeats*, F, B&H.)
(She is all so slight, *Richard Aldington*, Eb [e'b-e''b](m), B&H.)
(Sheepfolds, *Mary Madeleva*, G [d'-d''], Elkin.)
(Sweet Suffolk owl, *Thomas Vautor*, Ab [e'b-a''b], B&H, Ab, B&H.)
(The bellman's song, *Thomas Ravenscroft*, Bb, B&H.)
(The lake isle of Innisfree, *W B Yeats*, C, B&H.)
(The Queen of Sheba's song, *1 Kings 10*, [c'-f''](f), OUP.)
(The stockdoves, *Andrew Young*, [d'-g''], OUP.)
Arrangement:
(Bonny at morn, *Anon*, [c'-e''], OUP.)

Anthony Powers. 1953 -
High Windows (cycle), *Philip Larkin*, [f-f''](Counter-tenor or Mezzo soprano/Con-tralto), OUP.

Beryl Price.
Collection: (*Shepherd on a hill*, Curwen 1950.)
(In an arbour green, *Robert Wever*, C [c'-f''](m), Curwen Shepherd.)
(Jig, *Sir John Wotton*, C [c'-g''], Curwen Shepherd.)

(Phillis, *Thomas Lodge*, Am [d'-f''#](m), Curwen Shepherd.)

Humphrey Procter-Gregg. 1895 - 1980.
(In the highlands, *R L Stevenson*, G [d'-e''], B&H.)
(The Danube to the Severn, *Lord Tennyson*, A, B&H.)

Daniel Purcell. 1660 - 1717.
Cupid, make your virgins tender, *Anon*, Gm [d'-f''](m), S&B (Pilkington) *Georgian 1.*
Let not love on me bestow, *Richard Steele*, Ab [e'b-e''b], S&B (Pilkington) *Georgian 1.*

Henry Purcell. 1659 - 1695. Listed here are all songs, whether originally solo songs or songs from stage works, which are currently available in collections of solo songs. Solos occuring in larger works only available in complete scores are not covered, nor are songs available only in Purcell Society complete editions. Note that volumes are referred to under editor's names, publishers only being given in the case of anthologies.
Collections: (edited Britten), *Five Songs, Seven Songs* (high & medium keys), *Three Divine Hymns*, B&H 1947; *Six Songs* (high & medium keys), B&H 1948. *Two Divine Hymns and Alleluia*, B&H 1960; *A Miscellany of Songs*, Faber 1994; (edited Cooper), *Fifteen Songs and Airs Sets 1 & 2* (high & low keys), Novello no date; (edited Harley), *Selected Songs*, Cramer 1981; (edited Kagen), *Forty Songs volumes 1-4* (high & low keys), International 1958/9; *Six Songs for Bass, Four Sacred Songs* (high & low keys), International 1959; (edited Laurie), *Solo Songs volumes 1-4*, Novello 1993; (edited Tippett and Bergmann), *Songs volumes 1-5*, Schott 1947-59; (edited Roberts), *30 Songs, volumes 1 & 2* (high & low keys), OUP 1995; (edited Wishart), *Songs* volumes 1-3, S&B 1976. Note that B&H published some single songs edited by Britten, and the Tippett and Bergman editions all appeared separately.
A morning hymn, *William Fuller*, Gm [c'-g''], Britten 2 Divine, Thames (Bevan) *6 Divine.*
A thousand sev'ral ways I tried, *Anon*, Bb [d'-g''], Laurie 1.
Ah!, Belinda, *Nahum Tate*, Cm [c'-f''](f), Cooper 1, Kagen 2; *Bbm*, Cooper 1, Kagen 2.
Ah! cruel nymph! you give despair, *Anon*, Gm [d'-a''](m), Laurie 3.
Ah! how pleasant 'tis to love, *Anon*, C [g'-g''], Kagen 1, Laurie 3; *A*, Kagen 1.
Ah! how sweet it is to love, *John Dryden*, Gm [f'#-g''], Roberts 1, Tippett 2; *Fm*, Wishart, S&B *Recitalist 4*; *Em*, Roberts 1; *Dm*, Tippett 4.
Altisadora's song, *Thomas D'Urfey*, Cm [d'-g''](f), Cooper 1, Kagen 2, Tippett 2; *Bm*, Wishart 2; *Am*, Cooper 1, Kagen 2, Tippett 4.
Amidst the shades and cool refreshing streams, *Anon*, Am [d'-g''], Laurie 1.
Amintas, to my grief I see, *Anon*, Dm [d'-g''](f), Harley, Laurie 1.
Amintor, heedless of his flocks, *Anon*, Cm [c'-a''b], Laurie 1.
An Epithalamium, *Elkanah Settle?*, Gm [d'-g''](f), Cooper 1, Kagen 1; *Fm*, Tippett 1; *Em*, Cooper 1, Kagen 1; *Dm*, Tippett 4.
An evening hymn, *William Fuller*, G [d'-g''], Britten 3 Divine, Kagen 4, 4 Sacred, Roberts 2, Tippett 3, Wishart 3; *Eb*, Kagen 4, 4 Sacred, Roberts 2; *D*, Tippett 5.
Anacreon's defeat, *Anon*, C [F-e'](m), Kagen 6 for Bass, Laurie 3.
Ask me to love no more, *Anthony Hammond*, Bb [c'-g''](f), Laurie 4.
Bacchus is a pow'r divine, *Anon*, D [D-d'](m), Laurie 3, 4.
Bess of Bedlam, *see* Mad Bess.
Beware, poor shepherds, *Anon*, Dm [d'-g''](m), Laurie 2.

Bonvica's song, *Anon*, Cm [d'-a''*b*](f), Cooper 1, Harley, Kagen 4, Roberts 2; *Bm*, Tippett 2; *Am*, Cooper 1, Kagen 4, Roberts 2; *Gm*, Tippett.

Cease, anxious world, your fruitless pain, *George Etherege*, Gm [d'-g''](m), Laurie 2.

Cease, O my sad soul, *William Webbe*, Cm [g'-g''](m), Harley, Kagen 3; *Am*, Kagen 3.

Celia's fond, too long I've loved her, *Anthony Motteux*, Dm [d'-g''](m), Laurie 4.

Come all ye songsters, *Elkanah Settle?*, C [g'-a'']; *Bb*, Cooper 2, Kagen 4; *G*, Cooper 2, Kagen 4.

Corinna is divinely fair, *Anon*, Gm [d'-g''], Harley, Laurie 3.

Crown the altar, *Nahum Tate*, Gm [d'-d''], Tippett 2; *B*, Tippett 5.

Cupid, the slyest rogue alive, *Anon*, Gm [d'-g''], Laurie 2, Roberts 2; *Em*, Roberts 2.

Dear pretty youth, *Anon*, A [e'-g''](f) Thames (Bevan) *8 Restoration*, Roberts 2; *G*, Roberts 2, Wishart 1, S&B *Recitalist 2*.

Dido's lament, *Nahum Tate*, Cm [c'-g''](f), Cooper 1, Kagen 2, Wishart 2; *Am*, Cooper 1, Kagen 2.

Fairest isle, *John Dryden*, Bb [f'-a''], Britten 7 Songs, Roberts 1; *Ab*, Cooper 1, Kagen 1; *G*, Roberts 1; *F*, Britten 7 Songs, Cooper 1, Kagen 1.

Fly swift, ye hours, *Anon*, Dm [d'-g''](m), Laurie 3.

'From rosy bowers, *see* Altisadora's song.

From silent shades and the Elysian groves, *see* Mad Bess.

Hail to the myrtle shade, *Nathaniel Lee*, Bb [a'-g''], Harley; *A*, Cooper 2; *F*, Cooper 2.

Hark how all things in one sound rejoice, *Settle?*, G [d'-f''](f), Cooper 1, Wishart 2, S&B *Recitalist 1*; *A*, Cooper 1.

Hark the echoing air, *Elkanah Settle?*, C [e'-a''], Kagen 3; *Bb*, Britten 5 Songs, Paterson (Diack) *100 Best 1*; *Ab*, Kagen 3.

He himself courts his own ruin, *Anon*, F [c'-f''](m), Laurie 1.

Hear, ye gods of Britain, *Anon*, Cm [g-e''*b*](m), B&H (Northcote) *Imperial 6*.

Hears not my Phyllis, *see* The knotting song.

Hence with your trifling deity, *Thomas Shadwell*, Bb [F-e'*b*](m), Kagen 6 for Bass.

Here let my life, *Abraham Cowley*, Gm [d'-f''], Cooper 2, Fm, Cooper 2.

Here the deities approve, *Christopher Fishburn*, Em [g'-b''], Harley.

How blest are shepherds, *John Dryden*, G [d'-g''], Britten 5 Songs.

How I sigh when I think of the charms, *Anon*, Cm [c'-f''](f), Laurie 1.

I am come to lock all fast, *Elkanah Settle?*, Cm [d'-g''](f), Cooper 1, *A*, Cooper 1

I attempt from love's sickness, *Robert Howard*, A [d'#-f'#], Britten 5 Songs, Chester (Holloway) *Celebrated 3*, Cooper 1, Kagen 4, Roberts 2; *Ab*, B&H (Northcote) *Imperial 2; G*, Cooper 1, Roberts 2, Tippett 1, Wishart 3; *F*, Kagen 4; Paterson (Diack) *100 Best 4*.

I came, I saw, and was undone, *Abraham Cowley*, Am [d'-g''](m), Laurie 2.

I lov'd fair Celia, *Bernard Howard*, Dm [e'-a''](m), Laurie 3.

I love and I must, *Anon*, Cm [f#-a''*b*](m), Laurie 3.

I resolve against cringing, *Anon*, Am [e'-g''](m), Laurie 4.

I saw that you were grown so high, *Anon*, Dm [d'-f''], Kagen 1; *B*, Kagen 1.

I see she flies me, *John Dryden*, Gm, [d'-g''] Cooper 2, Roberts 1; *Em*, Cooper 2, Roberts 1.

I take no pleasure in the sun's bright beams, *Chamberlaine?* Am [d'-g''] Britten 5, Laurie 1.

If grief has any pow'r to kill, *Anon*, Dm [d'-g''], Laurie 2.

If music be the food of love (1), *Henry Heveningham*, Am [e'-a''], Laurie 3, Roberts 1, *Fm*, Roberts 1; *Em*, OUP Solo Contralto.

If music be the food of love (2), *Henry Heveningham*, Gm [d'-g''], Britten 6, Kagen 1, Laurie 3, Roberts 1; *F#m*, Tippett 1; *Em*, Britten 6, Roberts 1; *Ebm*, Kagen 1; *Dm*, Tippett 4.

If music be the food of love (3), *Henry Heveningham*, Gm [d'-a''], Britten 7, Kagen 1, Laurie 4, Roberts 1; *Em*, Britten 7, Kagen 1, Roberts 1.

If pray'rs and tears, *Anon*, Cm [c'-g''], Laurie 2.

I'll sail upon the dogstar, *Thomas D'Urfey*, C [d'-a''](m); *Bb*, Britten 7 Songs, B&H (Northcote) *Imperial 4*, Kagen 3, Wishart 3, S&B *Recitalist 3*; *G*, Britten 7 Songs, Kagen 3, Paterson (Diack) *100 Best 3*.

In the black dismal dungeon of despair, *William Fuller*, Em [c'#-g''], Britten 2 Divine.

In Chloris all soft charms agree, *John Howe*, G [d'-g''](m), Laurie 1.

In vain we dissemble, *Anon*, Dm [d'-g''](f), Laurie 2.

Incassum Lesbia, *see* The Queen's Epicedium.

Job's curse, *Jeremy Taylor*, Cm [c'-g''], Britten.

Let each gallant heart, *John Turner*, C [c'-g''](m), Laurie 1.

Let formal lovers still pursue, *Anon*, Am [e'-g''](m), Laurie 3.

Let the dreadful engines, *Thomas D'Urfey*, F [c-g'](m), Britten (Faber); *Eb*, B&H (Northcote) *Imperial 5*, Tippett 5.

Let the night perish, *see* Job's Curse.

Lord, what is man, *William Fuller*, Gm [d'-a''], Britten 3 Divine, Kagen 3, 4 Sacred, Roberts 2; *Em*, Roberts 2, Wishart 1; *Ebm*, Kagen 3, 4 Sacred.

Love arms himself in Celia's eyes, *Matthew Prior*, C [d'-a''b](m), Laurie 4.

Love is now become a trade, *Anon*, Gm [d'-g''](m), Harley, Laurie 2.

Love quickly is palled, *Anthony Motteux*, Bb [f-a'](m), *A*, Cooper 2; *F*, Cooper 2.

Love, thou can'st hear, *Robert Howard*, Cm [d'-a''](m), Laurie 4.

Lovely Albina's come ashore, *Anon*, C [d'-a''], Harley, Laurie 4.

Love's pow'r in my heart, *Anon*, C [g'-g''], Laurie 3.

Mad Bess, *Anon*, C [c'-g''](f), Britten 6 Songs, Kagen 3, Laurie 1, Tippett 3; *Bb*, Britten 6 Songs; *A*, Kagen 3, Tippett 5.

Man is for the woman made, *Anthony Motteux*, C [e'-g''], Britten 6 Songs, Cooper 2, Kagen 2, Roberts 2, Tippett 3; *Bb*, Britten 6 songs; *A*, Cooper 2; *Ab*, Kagen 2; *G*, Roberts 2, Tippett 5.

More love or more disdain I crave, *William Webbe*, G [e'-a'']; *F*, Kagen 2; *Db*, Kagen 2; *C*, Paterson (Diack) *100 Best 4*.

Music for a while, *John Dryden*, Cm [g'-a''b], Britten 7 Songs; *Bbm*, Cooper 2; *Am*, Kagen 1, Roberts 2, Tippett1; *Gm*, Britten 7 Songs, Cooper 2, Roberts 2; *Fm*, Kagen 1, Tippett 4.

My heart, whenever you appear, *Anon*, Dm [d'-g''](m), Laurie 2.

Next winter comes slowly, *Elkanah Settle?*, Am [A-e'](m), Kagen 6 for Bass.

Not all my torments, *Anon*, Cm [d'-a''b], Britten 6 Songs, Kagen 4, Laurie 3, Roberts 2, Tippett 2; *Am*, Britten 6 Songs, Kagen 4, Roberts 2; *Gm*, Tippett 5.

Now that the sun has veiled his light. *see* An evening hymn.

Nymphs and shepherds, come away, *Thomas Shadwell*, G [d'-g''], Kagen 4, Roberts 1, Wishart 3; *F*, Paterson (Diack) *100 Best 2*; *Eb*, B&H (Northcote) *Imperial 2*, Kagen 4, Roberts.

O! fair Cedaria, hide those eyes, *Anon*, C [d'-a''](m), Laurie 4.

O lead me to some peaceful gloom, *see* Bonvica's song.

Oh let me weep, *see* The plaint.

Oh solitude, my sweetest choice, *Katherine Philips*, Cm [c'-g''], Laurie 2, Britten Miscellany, Roberts 1; *Bbm*, Wishart 3; *Am*, Roberts 1.

Olinda in the shades unseen, *Anon*, G [d'-a''], Laurie 4.

On the brow of Richmond Hill, *Thomas D'Urfey*, Bb [f'-a''b], Britten 7 Songs, Laurie 3, Roberts 2; G, Britten 7 Songs, Roberts 2.

One charming night,Cm [g-a'], *Am*, Cooper 2; *F#m*, Cooper 2.

Pastora's beauties, when unblown, *Anon*, Cm [d'-g''](m), Laurie 1.

Phyllis, I can ne'er forgive it, *Anon*, Gm [e'-g''](m), Laurie 3.

Phyllis, talk no more of passion, *Anon*, Cm [d'-g''](m), Laurie 2.

Pious Celinda goes to pray'rs, *William Congreve*, Dm [d'-a''](m), Britten 7 Songs, Laurie 4, Roberts 1; *Cm*, Wishart 3; *Bm*, Roberts; *Am*, Britten 7 Songs.

Rashly I swore I would disown, *Anon*, Bb [e'-g''](m), Laurie 1.

Retired from any mortal sight, *Nahum Tate*, Gm [d'-f''], Cooper 1, Harley, Roberts 1; *F#m*, Cooper 1; *Em*, Roberts 1.

Sawny is a bonny lad, *Anthony Motteux*, G [d'-g''](f), Harley, Laurie 4, Roberts 2; *Eb*, Roberts 2.

She loves and she confesses too, *Abraham Cowley*, C [c'-a''](m), Laurie 1.

She that would gain, *Lady E—M—*, Bb [d'-a''b](f), Laurie 4, Roberts 2; *G*, Roberts 2.

She who my poor heart possesses, *Anon*, Gm [d'-g''](m), Laurie 1.

Since from my dear Astraea's sight, *The E— of M—*, Dm [d'-f''], Cooper 2, Kagen 2, Wishart 1; *Cm*, Cooper 2; *Bm*, Kagen 2.

Since one poor view has drawn my heart, *Anon*, C [c'-g''](f), Laurie 1.

Sound the trumpet, *N Tate*, C [e-b'b]; *Bb*, Cooper 1, Kagen 3; *G*, Cooper 1; *F*, Kagen 3.

Spite of the god-head, pow'rful love, *Anne Wharton*, Em [d'-g''](f), Laurie 3.

Strike the viol, *Anon*, Dm [a-b'b]; *Gm* Kagen 3; *Em*, Kagen 3.

Sweet, be no longer sad, *William Webbe*, Am [g'#-g''], Kagen 4; *Fm*, Kagen 4.

Sweeter than roses, *Thomas Norton*, Cm [d'-a''], Britten 6 Songs, Cooper 1, Kagen 1, Roberts 2; *Bm*, Tippett 1; *Am*, Cooper 1, Britten 6 Songs, Kagen 1, Wishart 1, S&B *Recitalist 2*; *Gm*, Tippett 4, Roberts 2.

Sylvia, now your scorn give over, *Anon*, C [g'-g''](m), Harley, Kagen 3, Laurie 3; *G*, Kagen 3.

Take not a woman's anger ill, *Robert Gould*, Bb [d'-f''](m), Britten 5 Songs, Cooper 2; *Ab*, Cooper 2.

Tell me, some pitying angel, *see* The blessed Virgin's expostulation.

The blessed Virgin's expostulation, *Nahum Tate*, Cm [e'b-a''b](f), Britten, Roberts 1; *Bbm*, Kagen 2, 4 Sacred,Tippett 1; *Am*, Roberts 1; *Gm*, Kagen 2, 4 Sacred.

The cares of lovers, *Anthony Motteux*, Gm [d'-g''], Roberts 2; *Em*, Roberts 2.

The earth trembled, *Francis Quarles*, A [c'#-f''#], Harley.

The fatal hour comes on apace, *Anon*, Em [d'#-g''], Kagen 3, Laurie 4, Roberts 1, Tippett 2; *Dm*, Roberts 1, Wishart 2, S&B *Recitalist 4*; *Cm*, Kagen 3; *Bm*, Tippett 4.

The knotting song, *Charles Sedley*, F [f'-g''](m), Britten Miscellany, B&H (Northcote) *Imperial 4*, Kagen 2, Laurie 4, Roberts 1; *D*, Roberts 1, *Db*, Kagen 2.

The plaint, *Elkanah Settle?*, Dm [d'-g''], Cooper 1; *Bm*, Cooper 1.

The Queen's Epicedium, *Herbert*, Cm [d'-a''b], Britten, Kagen 4, Laurie 4; *Am*, Kagen 4.

There's not a swain on the plain, *N Henley*, Em [b-g''], Britten 6 Songs, Kagen 4; *Cm*, Britten 6 Songs, Kagen 4.

They say you're angry, *Abraham Cowley*, Bb [d'-g''](m), Laurie 2.

They tell us that you mighty powers above, *Robert Howard*, Am [e'-g''](f) Thames (Bevan) *8 Restoration*.

This poet sings the Trojan wars, *see* Anacreon's defeat.

Thou wakeful shepherd. *see* A morning hymn.

Thus to a ripe consenting maid, *William Congreve*, Am [d'-g''], Cooper 1, Roberts 2; *Gm*, Roberts 2; *F#m*, Cooper 1.

Thy genius, lo, *Nathaniel Lee*, C [c-f'](m), Thames (Bevan) *6 Restoration*.

Thy hand, Belinda, *see* Dido's lament.

Tis nature's voice, *Nicholas Brady*, F [f-g']; *Eb*, Cooper 1, Kagen 3; *C*, Cooper 1; *Bb*, Kagen 3.

Thrice happy lovers, *see* An Epithalamium.

Through mournful shades, *Richard Duke*, Cm [e'*b*-g''], Laurie 1.

Turn then thine eyes *Elkanah Settle?*, Am [e'-a''], Britten 7 Songs; *Em*, Britten 7 Songs.

Twas within a furlong of Edinboro' town, *Thomas D'Urfey*, Gm [d'-g''], Roberts 2, Tippett 1; *Em*, Roberts 2, Tippett 4.

Urge me no more, *Francis Quarles*, Cm [c'-a''*b*], Laurie 1.

We sing to him, *Nathaniel Ingelo*, Cm [d'-a''*b*], Britten 3, B&H (Patrick) *Sacred Songs 1*; *Bm*, Kagen 1, 4 Sacred; *Gm*, Kagen 1, 4 Sacred.

Welcome, more welcome does he come, *Thomas Flatman*, Em [e'-g''], Cooper 1; *Cm*, Cooper 2.

What a sad fate is mine (1), *Anon*, Cm [g'-a''*b*](m), Laurie 4.

What a sad fate is mine (2), *Anon*, Am [e'-f''](m), Laurie 4.

What can we poor females do? *Anon*, Am [e'-g''](f), Kagen 1; *Fm*, Kagen 1.

What shall I do to show how much I love her? *Thomas Betterton?*, Dm [f'-a''], Tippet 2; *Cm*, Kagen 2, Wishart 1, S&B *Recitalist 3*; *Bm*, Cooper 2 *Am*, Cooper 2, Kagen 2; *Gm*, Tippett 5.

When first Amintas sued for a kiss, *Thomas D'Urfey*, A [e'-a''](f); *G*, Tippett 3; *E*, Tippett 5.

When first my shepherdess and I, *Anon*, Am [d'-g''](m), Laurie 2.

When her languishing eyes said 'Love', *Anon*, Em [e'-g''](m), Laurie 1.

When I am laid in earth, *see* Dido's lament.

When I have often heard young maids complaining, *Elkanah Settle?*, C [g'-a''](f), Roberts 1; *Bb*, Cooper 1; *G*, Cooper 1, Roberts 1.

When my Aemilia smiles, *Anon*, Bm [f'#-a''](m), Laurie 4.

When Strephon found his passion vain, *Anon*, G [g'-e''], Laurie 1.

While Thyrsis, wrapped in downy sleep, *Anon*, F [d'-f''], Laurie 2.

Whilst Cynthia sung, *Anon*, Dm [d'-g''], Laurie 2.

Who but a slave, *Anon*, Gm [d'-g''], Laurie 1.

Who can behold Fiorella's charms, *Anon*, F [d'-g''], Laurie 4.

With sick and famish'd eyes, *George Herbert*, Gm [c'-g''], Roberts 1; *Em*, Roberts 1.

Wondrous machine, *Brady*, Em, [B-e'](m), Kagen 6 for Bass.

Ye happy swains, whose nymphs are kind, *Anon*, Dm [d'-a''](m), Laurie 2.

You twice ten hundred deities, *Robert Howard*, Gm [G-e'*b*](m), B&H (Northcote) *Imperial 6*, Kagen 6 for Bass.

Attributed to Purcell in error:

Alleluia, *see* John Weldon.

Arise, ye subterranean winds, *see* John Weldon.

Fair and serene, *see* John Weldon.

My dear, my Amphitrite, *see* John Weldon.

The owl is abroad, *see* J C Smith.

Your awful voice I hear, *see* John Weldon.

Q

Roger Quilter. 1877 - 1953.
Collections: *Three Shakespeare Songs, Op 6* (high, medium & (low) keys), B&H 1905; *To Julia, Op 8* ((high) & low keys), B&H 1906; (*Songs of Sorrow, Op 10* (high & medium keys), *Seven Elizabethan Lyrics, Op 12* (high & low keys), B&H 1908; (*Four Songs, Op 14* (high & low keys), B&H 1910); (*Four Songs of Mirza Schaffy Op 2* (revised, high & low keys), Elkin 1911; (*Four Child Songs* (high & low keys), Chappell 1914); (*Two September Songs,* Elkin 1916); (*Three Songs of William Blake Op 20* (high & low keys), B&H 1917); *Five Shakespeare Songs, Op 23* (high & low keys), B&H 1921; (*Three Pastoral Songs* (high & low keys), Elkin 1921); (*Five Jacobean Lyrics Op 28* (high, medium & low keys), B&H 1926); (*Four Shakespeare Songs, Op 30* (high & low keys), B&H 1933); *Twelve Songs* (Introduction by Trevor Hold), Thames 1996.

A coronal, *Ernest Dowson*, B♭[b♭-f''], Thames 12 Songs; (*D♭*, B&H Op 10).
A land of silence, *Ernest Dowson*, D♭[b♭-g''♭], Thames 12 Songs; (*E*, B&H Op 10).
A last year's rose, *W E Henley*, D♭[e'-b-f''], Thames 12 Songs; (*E♭*, B&H Op 14).
(A song at parting, *Christina Rossetti*, Elkin.)
Amaryllis at the fountain, *Anon*, G [d'-a''], (B&H); *E*, Thames 12 Songs.
An old carol, *Anon*, D [c'-d''], Thames *Century 4*; (*G♭*, B&H).
(April, *William Watson*, A♭[d'-f''], B&H Op 14; *B♭*, Op 14).
Arab love song, *P B Shelley*, Cm [f'-f''], Thames 12 Songs; (*Dm, Bm*, B&H).
(At close of day, *Laurence Binyon*, Am [c'-f''#], B&H; Cm, B&H.)
Autumn evening, *Arthur Maquarie*, Gm [c'-e''], Thames 12 Songs; (*B♭m*, Op 14).
(Blossom time, *Nora Hopper*, G [g'-a''], B&H; *E*, B&H.)
Blow, blow, thou winter wind, *Shakespeare*, Cm [c'-e''], B&H Op 6, *Shakespeare; Em*, Op 6 (*E♭m*, Op 6).
Brown is my love, *Anon*, B♭[f'-g''](m), B&H Op 12; *G*, Op 12.
By a fountainside, *Ben Jonson*, C#m [c'#-g''#], B&H Op 12; *B♭m*, Op 12.
Cherry ripe, *Robert Herrick*, D [c'#-f''#](m), B&H Op 8 (F, B&H Op 8).
(Cherry valley, *Joseph Campbell*, E [b-e''], Elkin 3 Pastoral; *G*, 3 Pastoral.)
Come away, death, *Shakespeare*, Cm [c'-e''♭], B&H Op 6; *Em*, Op 6 (*E♭m*, Op 6). ·
(Come back, *Roger Quilter?* Elkin.)
(Cuckoo song, *Alfred Williams*, D [f'-a''], B&H; *B*, B&H).
Damask roses, *Anon*, E♭[f'-a''(g'')](m), B&H Op 12; *C*, Op 12.
(Daybreak, *William Blake*, E♭m [d'-b-e''♭], B&H Op 20; *F#m*, Op 20).
Dream valley, *William Blake*, D [b-d''], B&H, (Op 20); *G♭, New Imperial 2*, (Op 20); *F*, Thames 12 Songs.
(Drooping wings, *Edith Sterling-Levis*, Bm [d'-f'#], Chappell *English Recital 2.)*
Fair house of joy, *Anon*, D♭[f'-a''♭], B&H Op 12, *Heritage 4*, B&H; *B♭*, Op 12, B&H.
Fear no more the heat of the sun, *Shakespeare*, Fm [c'-e''♭], B&H Op 23; *G#m*, Op 23.
(Fill a glass with golden wine, *Henley*, C [c'-e''], B&H; *E, E♭, D♭*, B&H.)
(Go, lovely rose, *Edmund Waller*, E♭ [d'-e''♭](m), Chappell *English Recital 1.)*
Hey, ho, the wind and the rain, *Shakespeare*, C [d'-f''(d'')](m), B&H Op 23; *E♭*, Op 23.
How should I your true love know? *Shakespeare*, (B♭m [f'-f''], Thames 12 Songs, *Century 1*, (B&H Op 30; *B♭m*, Op 30).

(I arise from dreams of thee, *P B Shelley, Eb*m [g'-g''], B&H; *Cm*, B&H.)
(I dare not ask a kiss, *Robert Herrick, Db* [e'-e''b], B&H Op 28; *F, D*, Op 28.)
(I love the jocund dance, *William Blake*, G [e'-e'', Elkin; *Bb*, Elkin.)
I sing of a maiden *see* An old carol.
(I will go with my father a-ploughing, *Joseph Campbell, Ab* [c'-f''], Elkin 3 Pastoral; *Bb*, 3 Pastoral.)
(I wish and I wish, *Joseph Campbell*, Cm [c'-g''(e''b)], Elkin 3 Pastoral; *Dm*, 3 Pastoral.)
In spring, *Ernest Dowson*, E [b-e''], Thames 12 Songs; (*G*, B&H Op 10).
(In the bud of the morning-O, *James Stephens*, D [d'-e''], B&H; *F*, B&H.)
(In the highlands, *R L Stevenson*, Eb [bb-e''b], Elkin; *Gb, Elkin.*)
It was a lover and his lass, *Shakespeare*, E [c'#-e''], B&H Op 23; *Ab*, Op 23.
Julia's hair, *Robert Herrick*, Dm [c'-f''](m), B&H Op 8 (F, Op 8).
June, *Nora Hopper*, E [c'#-e''], B&H; F, B&H; (D, B&H).
Love's philosophy, *P B Shelley*, F [d'-a''], B&H *Heritage 4*, B&H; *C, D*, B&H.
(Morning song, *Thomas Heywood*, C [d'-f''], Chappell *English Recital 2.)*
(Music, *P B Shelley*, D [f'#-f''#], Curwen.)
Music and moonlight, *P B Shelley*, Eb [c'-e''b], Thames 12 Songs.
Music, when soft voices die, *P B Shelley*, Ab [f'-f''], Thames 12 Songs; (*Bb, Gb*, B&H).
My heart adorned with thee, *Mirza Schaffy (Friedrich Bodenstedt* tr. *Roger Quilter*, [high voice], Elkin.
My life's delight, *Thomas Campion*, G [g'-a''], B&H Op 12; *E*, B&H Op 12.
Now sleeps the crimson petal, *Alfred Lord Tennyson*, Eb [c'-e''b], B&H; *Gb, Imperial 4*, B&H; (*F, D*, B&H).
O mistress mine, *Shakespeare*, Eb [bb-e''b](m), B&H Op 6, *Imperial 5, Love and Affection*; *Gb* Op 6, *Heritage 3*, B&H; (*G*, Op 6).
(One word is too often profaned, *P B Shelley*, Gb [f'-g''b], Curwen.)
(Orpheus with his lute, *Shakespeare*, C [b-e''], B&H; *Eb*, B&H.)
(Over the land is April, *R L Stevenson*, C [d'-e''], Elkin; *D, Bb*, Elkin.)
Passing dreams, *Ernest Dowson*, Eb*m* [bb-f''], Thames 12 Songs; (*F#m*, B&H Op 10.)
(Sigh no more, ladies, *Shakespeare*, C [c'-d''], B&H Op 30; *Eb*, B&H Op 30.)
(Slumber song, *Clifford Mills*, Elkin.)
Song of the blackbird, *W E Henley*, Bb [d'-f''], B&H *Heritage 3*; (*C*, B&H Op 14).
(Song of the stream, *Alfred Williams*, E [c'#(d'#)-f'#], B&H; *D*, B&H.)
Spring is at the door, *Nora Hopper*, F [c(e')-a''(f')], Elkin; (D, Elkin).
Take, O take those lips away, *Shakespeare*, Db [e'b-D''b], B&H Op 23; *E*, Op 23.
(The bracelet, *Robert Herrick*, Bm, [c'#-f'#](m), B&H Op 8 (D, Op 8.)
(The constant lover, *John Suckling*, D [d'-f'#](m), B&H Op 28; *E, C*, Op 28.)
(The cradle in Bethlehem, *Rodney Bennett*, D [c'#-d''], Curwen.)
The faithless shepherdess, *Anon*, Bb*m* [f'-a''b], B&H Op 12; *Gm*, Op 12.
(The fuchsia tree, *Charles Dalmon?*, D [c'-d''], B&H; *Gb*, B&H.)
(The jealous lover, *Earl ofRochester*, D [d'-f'#](m), B&H Op 28; *F, C*, B&H 28.)
(The magic of thy presence, *Friedrich Bodenstedt* tr *R H Elkin*, Db [c'-f''(d''b)], Elkin; *F*, Elkin.)
The maiden blush, *Robert Herrick*, D [d'-e''](m), B&H Op 8 (F, Op 8.)
The night piece, *Robert Herrick*, Am [a'-e''](m), B&H Op 8 (C#m, Op 8).
(The secret, *Roger Quilter?* Elkin.)
(The valley and the hill, *Mary Coleridge*, Dm [c'-e''], Novello September; *Em*, September.)
(The wild flower's song, *William Blake*, G [b-d''], B&H Op 20; *Bb*, Op 20.)
(Through the sunny garden, *Mary Coleridge*, E [b-e''], Novello September; *G*, September.)

(To Althea from prison, *Richard Lovelace*, E♭[d'♭e''♭](m), B&H,Op 28; *F, D,* Op 28.)
To daisies, *Robert Herrick*, B♭[c'-f''](m), B&H Op 8; B&H; D♭, *Heritage 4*, (Op 8).
(To wine and beauty, *John Wilmot*, E♭[b♭(c')-f''(e''♭)], Elkin; *F*, Elkin.)
Under the greenwood tree, *Shakespeare*, D [d'-d''], B&H Op 23; *F*, Op 23.
Weep you no more, *Anon*, Fm [e'♭-g''], B&H Op 12, *Heritage 3*; *Dm*, Op 12.
When daffodils begin to peer, *Shakespeare*, A♭[e'♭e''♭](m), B&H *Shakespeare*, (Op 30; *C*, Op 30.)
When icicles hang by the wall, *Shakespeare*, E♭[a'♭-a''♭(g')], B&H *Shakespeare*; (C, B&H.)
(Where be you going? *John Keats*, D [c'♯-d''], Elkin; *F*, Elkin.)
(Who is Sylvia? *Shakespeare*, D [f'♯-d''], B&H Op 30; F, Op 30.)
(Why so pale and wan? *John Suckling*, C♯m [e'-e''], B&H Op 28; *Dm, Bm*, Op 28.)
(Wind from the South, *John Irvine*, F [d'-f''], Chappell *English Recital 1*.)
  Arrangements: *The Arnold Book of Songs*, B&H 1947.
Barbara Allen, *Anon*, D [d'-d''], B&H Arnold.
Believe me, if all those endearing young charms, *Thomas Moore*, E♭[e'♭e''♭], B&H Arnold.
Ca' the yowes to the knowes, *Robert Burns*, Am [c'-e''], B&H Arnold.
Charlie is my darling, *Anon*, Cm [c'-e''♭], B&H Arnold.
Drink to me only, *Ben Jonson*, E♭[e'♭e''♭], B&H Arnold, B&H.
My Lady Greensleeves, *John Irvine*, Fm [c'-e''♭](m), B&H Arnold.
My lady's garden, *Rodney Bennett*, D♭[d'♭e''♭], B&H Arnold.
Oh! 'tis sweet to think, *Thomas Moore*, G [d'-d''], B&H Arnold.
Over the mountains, *Anon*, G [d'-d''], B&H Arnold, B&H; *A*, B&H.
Pretty month of May, *Anon* tr. *Anon*, E♭[e'♭e''♭], B&H Arnold.
Since first I saw your face, *Anon*, E [e'-e''](m), B&H Arnold.
The ash grove, *Rodney Bennett*, A♭[d'♭e''♭], B&H Arnold.
The jolly miller, *Anon*, Gm [d'-d''], B&H Arnold.
The man behind the plough, *Rodney Bennett*, G [d'-e''], B&H Arnold.
Three poor mariners, *Anon*, E♭[b♭e''♭](m), B&H Arnold.
Ye banks and braes, *Robert Burns*, G♭[d'♭e''♭], B&H Arnold.

R

Priaulx Rainier. 1903 - 1986.
Collections: *Three Greek Epigrams*, Schott 1951.
    A bird, *Anyte of Tegea* tr. *Aldington*, [d'-e''*b*](f), Schott 3 Greek.
    A dolphin, *Anyte of Tegea* tr. *Aldington*, [f'-a''](f), Schott 3 Greek.
    For a fountain, *Anyte of Tegea* tr. *Aldington*, F# [d'-g''#](f), Schott 3 Greek.

Bernard Rands. 1935 -
    Ballad 2, *Gilbert Sorrentino*, [c'#-b''*b*](f), Universal.

Mark Raphael. 1900 - ?
Collections: *Three Blake Songs*, Roberton 1976; *Three D H Lawrence Poems*, Roberton 1973, *Two Thomas Moore Songs*, Roberton.
    At the mid hour of night, *Thomas Moore*, Cm [f'#-g''*b*], Roberton 2 Thomas Moore.
    Cherry robbers, *D H Lawrence*, E [c'#-e''], Roberton 3 D H Lawrence.
    Dog-tired, *D H Lawrence*, A [e'-g''#], Roberton 3 D H Lawrence.
    Flapper, *D H Lawrence*, G#m [e'-g''#], Roberton 3 D H Lawrence.
    Oh! breathe not his name, *Thomas Moore*, Cm [c'-e''*b*], Roberton.
    Row gently here, *Thomas Moore*, G [d'-f'#](m), Roberton.
    The fly, *William Blake*, E [c'#-e''], Roberton 3 Blake.
    The lamb, *William Blake*, F#m [d'-e''], Roberton 3 Blake.
    The shepherd, *William Blake*, Fm [d'-f''], Roberton 3 Blake.
    Weep no more, *John Fletcher*, Dm [c'-f''], Roberton.
    When through the piazzetta, *Thomas Moore*, G [d'-f'#], Roberton 2 Thomas Moore.

Alan Rawsthorne. 1905 - 1971.
Collections: (*Three French Nursery Songs*, B&H 1938); (*Two Songs*, OUP 1943).
    (Away, delights, *John Fletcher*, [c'#-g''*b*], OUP 2 Songs.)
    (Carol, *W R Rodgers*, B*b*m [d'-*b*-f''], OUP.)
    (Go bye-bye, Peterkin, *Anon* tr. *Alex Cohen*, Bm [f'#-f'#], B&H 3 French.)
    (God Lyaeus, *John Fletcher*, [e'-a''], OUP 2 Songs.)
    (I'm a darling little baby, *Anon*, tr. *Alex Cohen*, C [f'#-f''], B&H 3 French.)
    (Oh shepherdess, the rain's here, *Anon* tr. *Alex Cohen*, Em [e'-f''], B&H 3 French.)
    (Two fish, *Guillaume du Barthas* tr. *Joshua Sylvester*, [d'-a''*b*], OUP.)
    (We three merry maidens, *Anon* tr. *M D Calvocoressi*, [e'-a''](f), OUP.)

John Raynor. 1909 - 1970.
Collection: (*Eleven Songs* (introduction by Olwen Picton-Jones), S&B 1971.) (see also BMIC.)
    (An old lullaby, *Eugene Field*, E*b* [e'-*b*-g''], OUP.)
    (Bredon hill, *A E Housman*, G [d'-g''](m), S&B 11 Songs.)
    (Come, rock his cradle, *G R Woodward*, Gm [f'-d''], S&B 11 Songs.)
    (Down by the river, *Anon*, E*b* [d'-f''], S&B 11 Songs.)
    (Go, songs, *Francis Thompson*, G*b* [e'-*b*-a''*b*], S&B 11 Songs.)

(In Leinster, *Louise Imogen Guiney*, Em [d'-g''](f), S&B 11 Songs.)
(Lelant, *E K Chambers*, Bbm [d'*b*-e''*b*], S&B 11 Songs.)
(Love is a sickness, *Samuel Daniel*, Fm [f'-f''], S&B 11 Songs.)
(Love me again, *Anon*, Db [d'*b*-f''], S&B 11 Songs.)
(Loveliest of trees, *A E Housman*, E [e'-e''], S&B 11 Songs.)
(My own country, *Hilaire Belloc*, A [e'-f'#], OUP.)
(Spring, *Thomas Nashe*, B [d'#-b''(g''#)], OUP.)
(The Californy song, *Hilaire Belloc*, Eb [b*b*-e'*b*](m), OUP.)
(The loyal lover, *Anon*, Eb [e'*b*-g''](f), OUP.)
(The wakening, *Anon*, Gb [d'*b*-g''*b*], S&B 11 Songs.)
(West Sussex drinking song, *Hilaire Belloc*, D [c'#-f'#](m), S&B 11 Songs.)

Reginald Redman. 1892 - 1972.
Collections: (*Five Settings of Poems from the Chinese*, Curwen 1950); (*Five Chinese Miniatures*, Elkin 1951).
(A song of courtship, *Li Po* tr. *Arthur Waley*, [e'-g''], Elkin 5 Miniatures.)
(At the Kuang-Li Pavilion, *Su Tung-P'o* tr. *L Cranmer-Byng*, [d'-g''], Elkin 5 Miniatures.)
(Clearing at dawn, *Li Po* tr. *Arthur Waley*, [d'-f'#], Elkin 5 Miniatures.)
(In the mountains, *Li Po* tr. *Shigeyoshi Obata*, [c'-f'#], Curwen 5 Poems.)
(Immeasurable pain, *Li Hou-Chu* tr. *Arthur Waley*, [c'-f''], Elkin 5 Miniatures.)
(Nocturne, *Li Po* tr. *Shigeyoshi Obata*, [d'-g''], Curwen 5 Poems.)
(Silver, *Walter de la Mare*, Am [e'-g''], Curwen.)
(The dancing girl, *Li Po* tr. *Shigeyoshi Obata*, [d'*b*-g''], Curwen 5 Poems.)
(The last revel, *Ch'én Tzú-ang* tr. *L Cranmer-Bing*, [d'-f''], Curwen 5 Poems.)
(The night of sorrow, *Li Po* tr. *Shigeyoshi Obata*, [f'-f''], Curwen 5 Poems.)
(The Pavilion of Abounding Joy, *Ou-Yang Hsui* tr. *L Cranmer-Byng*, [f'#-a''], Elkin 5 Miniatures.)

Franz Reizenstein. 1911 - 1968. (see also BMIC.)
Collection: *Five Sonnets*, Bardic.
I love thee, *E B Browning*, [c'-b''], Bardic 5 Sonnets.
I think of thee, *E B Browning*, [c'-a''], Bardic 5 Sonnets.
Our two souls, *E B Browning*, [d'-a''], Bardic 3 Sonnets.
Perplexèd music, *E B Browning*, [c'#-b''*b*], Bardic 5 Sonnets.
The soul's expression, *E B Browning*, [d'-b''*b*], Bardic 5 Sonnets.

Mr Ridley.
A hunting song, *C L Esq*, D [d'-a''](m), Thames *Gentleman's Magazine*.

Alan Ridout. 1934 - 1996
When first mine eyes, *Thomas Wyatt*, [c'-b'], Thames *Countertenors 1*.

Hugh S Roberton. 1874 - 1952. (see also SMIC.)
All in the April evening, *Katherine Tynan*, E [e'-e''], Roberton.
As down by Banna's banks I strayed, *George Ogle*, C [c'-e''], Roberton.
Blake's cradle song, *William Blake*, Ab [e'*b*-g''], Roberton.
Maureen, *Hugh S Roberton*, C [c'-d''], Roberton.
The old woman, *Joseph Campbell*, F [c'-b'], Roberton; Eb, F, Roberton.

Arrangements: *Songs of the Isles*, Roberton.
  The fidgety bairn, *Hugh S Roberton*, E♭ [e'*b-e*''*b*](f), Roberton.
  Health and joy be with you, *Professor Blackie*, E♭ [c'-e''*b*], Roberton.
  Hebridean shanty, *Hugh S Roberton*, E♭ [b♭-e''*b*](m), Roberton.
  Highland cradle song, *Sir Walter Scott*, C [c'-e''](f), Roberton.
  Island spinning song, *Hugh S Roberton*, F#m [e'-c''#](f), Roberton.
  Joy of my heart, *Hugh S Roberton*, A [c'#-e''], Roberton.
  Lewis bridal song (Mairi's wedding), *Hugh S Roberton*, G [c'-e''], Roberton.
  Mingulay boat song, *Hugh S Roberton*, E [b-e''](m), Roberton.
  None so sweet, *Hugh S Roberton*, A♭ [e'*b-e*''*b*](m), Roberton.
  Rise and follow, love, *Anon*, G [a-e''], Roberton.
  Shuttle and loom, *Hugh S Roberton*, F#m [c'#-e''](f), Roberton.
  Sing at the wheel, *Hugh S Roberton*, Fm [c'-f''](m), Roberton.
  The wee toun clerk, *Anon*, B♭ [d'-e''*b*], Roberton.
  The windjammer, *Anon*, F#m [c'#-e''], Roberton.
  Uist tramping song, *Hugh S Roberton*, G [d'-e''], Roberton.
  Westering home, *Hugh S Roberton*, A [c'#-e''], Roberton.

Mervyn Roberts. 1906 - 1990. (See also BMIC).
  (Christmas Day, *Andrew Young*, G [d'-e''], Novello.)
  (Elsewhere, *G O Warren*, D [b'-f'#], Novello.)
  (Put a rosebud on her lips, *Francis H King*, F [c'-f''], Novello.)
  (St Govan, *A G Prys-Jones*, Fm [c'-f''], Novello.)
  (The sentry, *G O Warren*, D♭ [d'*b-f*''], Novello.)
Arrangements: *Six Welsh Folksongs*, Gwynn.

T Osborne Roberts. 1879 - 1948.
  A widow bird, *P B Shelley*, [mezzo], Snell.
  Sea wrack, *Moira O'Neill*, [mezzo/baritone], Gwynn.
  The black spring, *Cynan* tr. *Wil Ifan*, C [c'-e''], Gwynn.

Trevor Roberts. 1940 -
  Stopping by woods on a snowy evening, *Robert Frost*, [C#-d'](m), Welsh Music *Songs from Wales 2*.
Arrangements: *Five Welsh Folksongs*, Banks.

Betty Roe. 1930 -
Collections: *Noble Numbers*, Thames 1972; *Three Eccentrics*, Thames 1977; *These growing years*, Thames 1986; *Compliments of the Season*, Thames 1990; *Nine Songs, Seven Songs*, Thames 1993.
  As the holly groweth green, *King Henry VIII*, A [a-e''](m), Thames *Century 2*.
  After supper, *John Mole*, [a-e''], Thames Compliments.
  Beeches, *Diana Carroll*, [d'-f'#], Thames These growing Years.
  Distances, *Edward Storey*, [d'-g''], Thames 9 Songs.
  Gertrude's prayer, *Rudyard Kipling*, [f'-f'#], Thames 7 Songs.
  Harp song of the Dane women, *Rudyard Kipling*, [e'-a''](f), Thames 7 Songs.
  Hot sun, cool fire, *George Peel*, [e'-f'#], Thames 9 Songs.
  In the fall, *Diana Carroll*, [c'#-g''], Thames These growing Years.
  Infant song, *Charles Causley*, [e'*b-g*''*b*](f), Thames 7 Songs.

Legend of Rosemary, *Reginald Arkell*, [c'-g''], Thames 7 Songs.
Lullaby, *Anon* tr. *H E Kennedy & S Uminska*, [e'-d''#], Thames 9 Songs.
Lullaby for a baby toad, *Stella Gibbons*, [d'-g''#], Thames 9 Songs.
Morning and afternoon, *Leonard Clark*, [c'#-d''], Thames 9 Songs.
Mr Kartoffel, *James Reeves*, B [a-e''], Thames 3 Eccentrics.
Mr Tom Narrow, *James Reeves*, E [b-e''*b*], Thames 3 Eccentrics.
Musical chairs, *John Mole*, [a-e''], Thames Compliments.
My boy Jack, *Rudyard Kipling*, E [d'-e''], Thames 7 Songs.
My garden, *T E Brown*, D [b-d''], Thames 9 Songs,*Countertenors 1*.
Nursery Rhymes of Innocence and Experience, *C Causley*, E [d'#-e''], Thames 9 Songs, Thames..
Stop all the clocks, *W H Auden*, [a-g''](f), Thames 7 Songs.
The bakery, *Anon* tr. *Peter Hyun*, [d'-a''](f), Thames 7 Songs.
The walk, *John Mole*, B*b* [e'*b*(d')-f'#(e'')], Thames Compliments.
This enders night, *Anon*, [d'-g''#], Thames 9 Songs.
To God (My God, I'm wounded), *Robert Herrick*, [b-d''], Thames Noble Numbers.
To God (God gives not onely corne), *Robert Herrick*, [c'-d''], Thames Noble Numbers.
To his angrie God, *Robert Herrick*, [b-e''*b*], Thames Noble Numbers.
To His Saviour, a child, *Robert Herrick*, D [a-d''], Thames Noble Numbers.
To his sweet saviour, *Robert Herrick*, [c'-d''], Thames Noble Numbers.
Triolet, *Diana Carroll*, [d'-a''(g'#)], Thames These growing Years.
Two gardens, *Walter de la Mare*, D [b-e''], Thames 9 Songs.
Zackery Zed, *James Reeves*, [a-e''], Thames 3 Eccentrics.
Arrangements: *A Garland of Folksongs*, Thames 1984.
All things are quite silent, *Traditional*, [f'-f''](f), Thames Garland.
Cocky robin, *Anon*, [c'-e''], Thames Garland.
Johnny has gone for a soldier, *Anon*, [e'-f''](f), Thames Garland.
The lass from the low countree, *Traditional*, [d'-f''], Thames Garland.
The wee Cooper o' Fife, *Anon*, [c'#-e''], Thames Garland.
To people who have gardens, *Agnes Muir Mackenzie*, [f'-c''], Thames Garland.

Landon Ronald. 1873 - 1938.
Collection: *Twelve Songs*, Thames 1990.
A pair well matched, *John Dryden*, E [e'-b''(g''#)](m), Thames 12 Songs.
Had I the heavens' embroidered cloths, *W B Yeats*, E [c'#-f''#], Thames 12 Songs.
June rhapsody, *Edward Lockton*, F [c'-f''], Thames 12 Songs.
Love I have won you, *Harold Simpson*, A*b* [g'-a''*b*], Thames 12 Songs.
Love's philosophy, *P B Shelley*, E [c'#-g''#], Thames 12 Songs.
Oh lovely night, *Edward Teschemacher*, E*b* [e'*b*-g''], Thames 12 Songs.
Prelude, *Harold Simpson*, A*b* [d-b''*b*(g'')], Thames 12 Songs.
Remember, *Christina Rossetti*, Bm [b-e''], Thames 12 Songs.
Second thoughts, *Arthur Symons*, E*b* [c'-e''*b*], Mayhew *Collection 2*.
Strew on her roses. roses, *Matthew Arnold*, Fm [e'*b*-a''*b*], Thames 12 Songs.
The dove, *John Keats*, Fm [c'-g''], Thames 12 Songs.
The white sea mist, *Harold Simpson*, B*b* [d'-f''], Thames 12 Songs.
Were I the flower, *Edward Teschemacher*, C [c'-e''], Mayhew *Collection 1*.
Your waking eyes, *Helen Taylor*, E*b* [e'*b*-a''*b*], Thames 12 Songs.

Jasper Rooper. (BMIC.)

Cyril Rootham. 1875 - 1938.
Collections: *Six Songs*, S&B 1986; *Siegfried Sassoon Songs*, S&B 1990.
A boy's song, *James Hogg*, [d'-f''](m), S&B 6 Songs.
A child's prayer, *Siegfried Sassoon*, Db [d'b-e''b], S&B Siegfried Sassoon.
A poplar and the moon, *Siegfried Sassoon*, A [e'-f'#], S&B Siegfried Sassoon.
A supplication, *Thomas Wyatt*, F [d'b-e''], S&B 6 Songs.
Beyond the sea, *Thomas Love Peacock*, C [d'-g''], S&B 6 Songs.
Butterflies, *Siegfried Sassoon*, D [f'#-g''(a'')], S&B Siegfried Sassoon.
Everyone sang, *Siegfried Sassoon*, C [f'#-a''b], S&B Siegfried Sassoon, Thames *Century 3*.
Helen of Kirkconnell, *Traditional*, F [e'-g''](m), S&B 6 Songs.
I sorrowed, *Anon*, A [e'b-e''], S&B 6 Songs.
Idyll, *Siegfried Sassoon*, Am [e'-f'#], S&B Siegfried Sassoon.
Morning glory, *Siegfried Sassoon*, F [d'-e''b], S&B Siegfried Sassoon.
South wind, *Siegfried Sassoon*, D [d'-e''], S&B Siegfried Sassoon.
The spring-time of life, *Thomas Love Peacock*, D [a-d''], S&B 6 Songs.

Philip Rosseter. 1568 - 1623.
Collection: (edited Thurston Dart) *A Booke of Ayres*, S&B 1970. Only songs available in anthologies are listed individually here. Note that in the following: Pilkington = *English Lute Songs Book 1*, S&B; Keel 1/2 = *Elizabethan Lovesongs Books 1 & 2*, B&H, in high and low keys.
If I hope I pine, *Thomas Campion?* G [f'#-d''], Pilkington.
If I urge my kind desires, *Thomas Campion?* G [f'#-e''](m), Keel 1; *A*, Keel 1.
If she forsake me, *Thomas Campion?* G [d'-e''](m); *A*, Keel 1; *Eb*, Pilkington; *F*, Keel 1.
Kind in unkindness, *Thomas Campion?* Gm [f'-d''](m), Pilkington.
Shall I come if I swim, *Thomas Campion?* Dm [d'-d''](m), Pilkington,
Sweet, come again, *Thomas Campion?* G [g'-g''], Pilkington.
Though far from joy, *Thomas Campion?* Gm [f'-f''], Pilkington.
What then is love but mourning? *Thomas Campion?* Gm [g'-f''], Pilkington, Chester (Shavitz) *Celebrated 1*.
When Laura smiles, *Thomas Campion?* G [d'-e''], Keel 1; *A*, Keel 1; *F*, Pilkington, S&B.

Francis Routh. 1927 - (BMIC.)

Alec Rowley. 1892 - 1958. 30 more songs in B&H archive.
Song of the wind, *Edward Shenton*, Dm [d'-f''], Gwynn.
The fairy pedlar, Eb, B&H; G, Cramer.
The lorry driver, [mezzo/baritone], Gwynn.
When rooks fly homeward, Weinberger.

Edmund Rubbra. 1901 - 1986.
Collections: *Two Songs, Op 17*, Lengnick 1928; *Two Songs, Op 22*, Lengnick 1929; *Amoretti (2nd Series) Op 43*, S&B 1942; *Three Psalms, Op 61*, Lengnick 1947; *Ave Maria Gratia Plena, Two Songs for Voice and Harp or Piano*, Lengnick 1953; *Four Short Songs*, Lengnick 1976.
A Duan of Barra, *Murdoch Maclean*, C [d'-g''], Lengnick.
A hymn to the Virgin, *Anon*, Am [d'-g''], Lengnick Harp or Piano.

A prayer, *Ben Jonson*, Fm [b♭-g''], Lengnick Op 17.
A widow bird sate mourning, *P B Shelley*, [e'-g''], Lengnick.
Cradle Song, *Padraic Colum*, Am [d'-e''♭], Lengnick 4 Short.
Fly envious time, *John Milton*, [d'#-g''], Lengnick.
Fresh Spring, the herald of love's mighty king, *Edmund Spenser*, [c'-g''](m), S&B Op 43.
In dark weather, *Mary Webb*, [b-g''(b')], Lengnick.
Invocation to Spring, *James Thomson*, Dm [f'-g''], Lengnick Op 17.
It was a lover, *Shakespeare*, [c'-g''], Lengnick.
Jesukin, *St Ita*, [e'-f'#](f), Lengnick Harp or Piano.
Lackyng my love, I go from place to place, *Edmund Spenser*, [d'b-f'#](m), S&B Op 43.
Lyke as the culver, on the bared bough, *Edmund Spenser*, [c'#-a''♭](m), S&B Op 43.
Mark when she smiles with amiable cheare, *Edmund Spenser*, [c'-g''](m), S&B Op 43.
No swan so fine, *Marianne Moore*, B♭ [d'-f''], Lengnick.
Nocturne, *Alcman* tr. *H T Wade-Grey*, G♭ [c'-f''], Lengnick.
O Lord, rebuke me not, *Psalm 6*, [f#-e''], Lengnick Op 61.
Orpheus with his lute, *Shakespeare*, Dm [d'-e''], Lengnick 4 Short.
Out in the dark, *Edward Thomas*, [g'-a''♭], Thames *Century 1*, Lengnick.
Praise ye the Lord, *Psalm 150*, [b♭-f''], Lengnick op 61, Thames *Century 4*.
Rosa Mundi, *Rachel Annand Taylor*, [d'-e''♭], Lengnick 4 Short.
Rune of hospitality, *Kenneth Macleod*, Gm [f'-d''], Lengnick.
Take O take those lips away, *Shakespeare*, [e'-f'#], Lengnick Op 22.
The Lord is my shepherd, *Psalm 23*, [a-d''], Lengnick Op 61.
The night, *Hilaire Belloc*, [b-e''], Lengnick.
What guyle is this, that those her golden tresses? *Edmund Spenser*, [e'-a''♭](m), S&B Op 43.
Why so pale and wan? *John Suckling*, Cm [c'-a''♭], Lengnick Op 22.

Davidson Russel. *fl* 1735.
The modest question, *John Gay?*, F [c'-f''](m), S&B (Pilkington) *Georgian 1*.

Kennedy Russell.
Vale (Farewell), *de Burgh d'Arcy*, B♭ [f'-g''(b''♭], Cramer *Drawing Room Songs*.

John Rutter. 1945 -
Shepherd's pipe carol, *John Rutter*, F [c'-g''], OUP *Solo Christmas*; E♭, *Solo Christmas*.

S

Johann Peter Salomon. 1745 - 1815.
Go, lovely rose, *Edmund Waller*, E♭[c'♭-f''](m), OUP (Roberts) *O Tuneful Voice.*
O tuneful voice, *Anne Hunter*, E♭[d'-g''](f), OUP (Roberts) *O Tuneful Voice.*
Say not that minutes swiftly move, *Mary Robinson*, D [d'-f#''], OUP (Roberts) *O Tuneful Voice.*
Why still before those streaming eyes? *Anne Hunter*, Gm [c'#-g''], OUP (Roberts) *O Tuneful Voice.*

Lionel Salter. 1914 -
Counsel, *Robert Gould*, [g'-a''], Lengnick.
The high song, [high voice], Lengnick.
(The shepherdess, *Alice Meynell*, Dm [d'-g''], OUP.)

Timothy Salter. 1942 - (BMIC.)

Leonard Salzedo. 1921 - (BMIC.)

Harold Samuel. 1879 - 1937.
Diaphenia, *Henry Constable* or *Chettle*, D [c'#-e''(f'#)](m), B&H *Heritage 1.*
Nanny, *Thomas Percy*, F [c'-e''♭](m), B&H *Heritage 2.*
Oh! my sweeting, *Anon*, D♭[d'♭-f''](m), B&H *Heritage 1.*
The fairy boat, *Annette Horey*, G [d'-g''], B&H *Heritage 2.*
(Toy band, G, B&H.)

Wilfrid Sanderson. 1878 - 1935. A further 132 songs in B&H archive!
Captain Mac, *P J O'Reilly*, D [a(e)-f''#(e'')] B&H *Ballad Album 2.*
Friend o' mine, *Fred. E Weatherly*, C [d'(f')-g''] B&H *Ballad Album 1*; A♭, *Souvenirs*; (G, B♭, B&H.).
Shipmates o' mine, *Edward Teschemacher*, G [a-d''](m) B&H *Ballad Album 1*; (F, A, B&H.).

Anthony Scott. 1911 -
Collection: (*Four Songs from 'The Princess'*, B&H 1977.)
(As thro' the land at eve we went, *Alfred Lord Tennyson*, [d'-g''], B&H 4 Songs.)
(Lullaby, *Alfred Lord Tennyson*, [e'-d''](f), B&H.)
(O swallow, swallow, flying, flying South, *Alfred Lord Tennyson*, [c'-a''], B&H 4 Songs.)
(Sweet and low, *Alfred Lord Tennyson*, [d'♭-g''♭], B&H 4 Songs.)
(Tears, idle tears, *Alfred Lord Tennyson*, [c'-a''♭], B&H 4 Songs.)

Cyril Scott. 1879 - 1970.
Collection: (*Album of Songs (Soprano)*, *Album of Songs (Contralto)*, *Album of Songs (Tenor)*, (*Album of Songs (Baritone)*, Elkin 1912 .)
(A birthday, *Christina Rossetti*, Elkin.)
(A gift of silence, *Ernest Dowson*, F [c'-f''(e'')](m), Elkin Contralto, Baritone, Elkin.)
(A last word, *Ernest Dowson*, Elkin.)
(A little song of Picardie, *Rosamund Marriott Watson*, E [e'-f'#], Elkin Soprano; D, Elkin.)
(A lost love, *Anon* tr. *Herbert Giles*, A♭[g'-a''♭], Elkin Soprano; E♭, Contralto; F, Elkin.)

(A March requiem, *Norah Richardson*, Elkin.)
(A picnic, *Anon* tr. *Herbert Giles*, Elkin.)
(A prayer, *Charles Kingsley*, A, C, Elkin.)
(A reflection, *Anon* tr. *W R Paton*, F, Elkin Tenor; D, Elkin.)
(A roundel of rest, *Arthur Symons*, C [a-e''], Elkin; E*b*, Elkin.)
(A serenade, *Duffield Bendall*, D [d'-f'#](m), Elkin Baritone; F, Elkin Tenor.)
(A song of Arcady, *Ernest Dowson*, D, Elkin; F, Elkin.)
(A song of London, *Rosamund Mariott Watson*, Em [b*b*-e''(g')], Elkin Contralto, Elkin Baritone, Elkin.)
(A song of wine, *Anon* tr. *Herbert Giles*, Elkin.)
(A spring ditty, *Anon* tr. *John Addington Symons*, Elkin.)
(A valediction, *Ernest Dowson*, G, Elkin; B*b*, Elkin.)
(A vision, *Anon* tr. *Herbert Giles*, Elkin.)
(Afterday, *Cyril Scott*, G [d'-d''], Elkin Baritone; B*b*, C, Elkin.)
(Alone, *Anon* tr. *Herbert Giles*, Elkin.)
(An eastern lament, *Anon* tr. *Herbert Giles*, Cm, Elkin; Em, Elkin.)
(An old song ended, *D G Rossetti*, F [d'-f''], Elkin; E*b*, Elkin.)
(And so I made a villanelle, *Ernest Dowson*, B*b* [f'-d''], Elkin; G, Elkin.)
(Arietta, *Duffield Bendall*, C [a-e''], Elkin Baritone; E*b* Elkin Tenor.)
(Aspiration, *Irene McLeod*, Elkin.)
(Atwain, *F Leslie*, Elkin.)
(Autumn song, *Rosamund Marriott Watson*, B*b* [b*b*-e''*b*], Elkin; D, Elkin.)
(Autumn's lute, *Rosamund Mariott Watson*, [low], Elkin; [high], Elkin.)
(Autumnal, *Ernest Dowson*, B*b*, B&H.)
(Blackbird's song, *Rosamund Marriott Watson*,D [b-e''], Elkin; E*b*, F, Elkin.)
(Daffodils, *Ella Erskine*, C [g'-a''](f), Elkin Soprano; A, Elkin; B*b*, Elkin.)
(Don't come in sir, please, *Anon*, tr. *Herbert A Giles*, E [e'-g''#(f'#)](f), Elkin Soprano; D, Elkin.)
(Evening, *Ernest Dowson*, C, Elkin Contralto, Elkin; E*b*, Elkin.)
(Evening melody, *Cyril Scott*, [low], Elkin; [high], Elkin.)
(Exultation, *No text*, Elkin.)
(For a dream's sake, *Christina Rossetti*, A*b*, Elkin; C, Elkin.)
(From afar, *Rosamund Mariott Watson*, C, Elkin; E, Elkin.)
(Have ye seen him pass by? *Anon* tr. *Geoffrey Whitworth*, Elkin.)
(Immortality, *Bulwer-Lytton*, E*b*, Elkin; F, G, Elkin.)
(In a fairy boat, *Bernard Weller*, C, Elkin; E*b*, Elkin.)
(In absence, *Anon* tr. *Herbert Giles*, Elkin.)
(In the silver moonbeams, *Anon* tr. *Cyril Scott*, A [f'#-e'], Elkin; G, Elkin.)
(In the valley, *Rosamund Mariott Watson*, [medium], Elkin; [high], Elkin.)
(Insouciance, *Anon* tr. *Herbert Giles*, [low], Elkin; [high], Elkin.)
(Invocation, *Margaret Maitland Radford*, D, Elkin; F, Elkin.)
(Lady June, *Elizabeth Haddon*, Elkin.)
(Lilac-time, *Walt Whitman*, Elkin.)
(Looking back, *Christina Rossetti*, D*b*, Elkin; E*b*, F, Elkin.)
(Lovely kind and kindly loving, *Nicholas Breton*, Elkin Tenor, Elkin.)
(Love's aftermath, *Ernest Dowson*, B*b*, Elkin Contralto, Elkin; D*b*, Elkin.)
(Love's quarrel, *Bulwer-Lytton*, C [g'-a''], Elkin Tenor; B*b*, C, Elkin.)

(Lullaby, *Christina Rossetti*, F [d'-g''#(f')](f), Elkin; D♭, E♭, Elkin.)
(Meditation, *Ernest Dowson*, B♭, Elkin; C, Elkin.)
(Mermaid's song, *Tamar Faed*, Elkin.)
(Mirage, *Rosamund Marriott Watson*, A♭ [d'-f''], Elkin Soprano; Elkin.)
(My captain, *Walt Whitman*, F, Elkin; G, Elkin.)
(My lady sleeps, *Duffield Bendall*, D, Elkin Tenor, Elkin.)
(Night Song, *Rosamund Marriott Watson*, E♭ [c'-e''♭], Elkin; D♭, Elkin.)
(Night wind, *Teresa Hooley*, Elkin.)
(Nocturne, *Rosamund Mariott Watson*, A♭, Elkin; B, Elkin.)
(Old loves, *Cyril Scott*, G, Elkin; A, Elkin.)
(Osme's song, *George Darley*, D, Elkin; F, Elkin.)
(Oracle, *Cyril Scott*, E♭, Elkin; F, Elkin.)
(Our Lady of Violets, *Teresa Hooley*, C, Elkin; D, Elkin.)
(Pastorale, *No text*, [e'♭-a''(c''')], Elkin.)
(Pierrot and the moon maiden, *Ernest Dowson*, Elkin.)
(Rain, *Margaret Maitland Radford*, [low], Elkin; [high],Elkin.)
(Reconciliation, *Naomi Carvalho*, B♭, Elkin.)
(Requiem, *R L Stevenson*, C, Elkin; E♭, Elkin.)
(Retrospect, *Ernest Dowson*, C, Elkin; D, Elkin.)
(Rima's call to the birds (scena), *W H Hudson*, [soprano], Elkin.)
(Scotch lullabye, *Scott*, D, Elkin; F, Elkin.)
(Sea-fret, *Teresa Hooley*, C, Elkin; E♭, Elkin.)
(Sea-song of Gafran, *Felicia Hemans*, Elkin.)
(She's but a lassie yet, *James Hogg*, E♭, Elkin; F, Elkin.)
(Sleep song, *William Rands*, Elkin.)
(Sorrow, *Ernest Dowson*, E♭, Elkin Contralto, Elkin; F, Elkin.)
(Spring song, *Cyril Scott*, [low], Elkin; [high], Elkin.)
(Sundown, *Dorothy Grenside*, D [d'-d''], Elkin; F, Elkin.)
(Sunshine and dusk, *Margaret Maitland Radford*, [low], Elkin; [medium], Elkin.)
(The ballad of fair Helen, *Anon*, [d'-f''](m), Elkin.)
(The huckster, *Edward Thomas*, Elkin.)
(The little bells of Sevilla, *Dora Sigerson Shorter*, [medium], Elkin; [high], Elkin.)
(The little foreigner, *Cyril Scott*, Elkin.)
(The new moon, *Rosamund Marriott Watson*, G [d'-g''], Elkin Soprano; E, Elkin.)
(The pilgrim cranes, *Lord de Tabley*, Elkin.)
(The sands of Dee, *Charles Kingsley*, C, Elkin; E♭, Elkin.)
(The trysting tree, *Charles Sayle*, C, Elkin; D, Elkin.)
(The unforseen, *Rosamund Mariott Watson*, C [c'-g''], Elkin, B♭, Elkin.)
(The valley of silence, *Ernest Dowson*, C, Elkin; E♭, Elkin.)
(The watchman, *Jean Hildyard*, B♭, Elkin; C, D, Elkin.)
(The white knight, *Anon* tr. *Rosamund Mariott Watson*, D, Elkin; E, Elkin.)
(Time o' day, *O MacNaghten*, Elkin.)
(Tomorrow, *Christina Rossetti*, Elkin.)
Trafalgar, *Thomas Hardy*, C [c'-e''](m), Thames *Hardy Songbook*.
(Tranquillity, *No text*, [d'-b''], Elkin.)
(Tyrolese evensong, *Felicia Hemans*, C, Elkin; D, Elkin.)

Villanelle, *Ernest Dowson*, [d'-e''], B&H *Heritage 1*.
(Villanelle of firelight, *Naomi Carvalho*, B♭, Elkin; C, Elkin.)
(Villanelle of the Poet's Road, *Ernest Dowson*, C [d'-e''](m), Elkin Baritone, Elkin; E♭, Elkin.)
(Voices of vision, *Cyril Scott*, Elkin.)
(Waiting, *Anon* tr. *Herbert Giles*, Elkin.)
(Waterlilies, *P J O'Reilly*, C, Elkin; D♭, E♭, Elkin.)
(Why so pale and wan, *John Suckling*, Elkin.)
(Willows, *Cyril Scott*, Elkin.)

Francis George Scott. 1880 - 1958.
Collections: (*Scottish Lyrics Book I: 8 Songs for Female Voice, Book II: 9 Songs for Male Voice*; Bayley & Ferguson 1922); (*Scottish Lyrics Book III*, Bayley & Ferguson 1934); (*Scottish Lyrics Book IV - 13 Songs for Baritone Voice*, Bayley & Ferguson 1936); (*Scottish Lyrics Book V: 13 Songs for Medium Voice*, Bayley & Ferguson 1939); (*Seven Songs for Baritone Voice*, Bayley & Ferguson 1946); (*Thirty-five Scottish Lyrics and other poems*, Bayley & Ferguson 1949); *Songs*, Roberton 1979, (Preface Neil Mackay).
An apprentice angel, *Hugh MacDiarmid*, c'-e''♭], Roberton Songs.
Ane sang of the birth of Christ, *Luther* tr. *Wedderburn*, [d'♭-f''], Roberton Songs.
Ay waukin, O, *Robert Burns*, [b♭-f''](f), Roberton Songs.
Country life, *Hugh MacDiarmid*, [d'-g''], Roberton Songs.
Crowdieknowe, *Hugh MacDiarmid*, [c'#-e''♭], Roberton Songs.
Cupid and Venus, *Mark Alexander Boyd*, [e'♭-g''♭], Roberton Songs.
Empty vessel, *Hugh MacDiarmid*, [b-e''], Roberton Songs.
First love, *Hugh MacDiarmid*, [d'-f''♭](m), Roberton Songs.
Florine, *Thomas Campbell*, [b♭-e''♭](m), Roberton Songs.
Lourd on my hert, *Hugh MacDiarmid*, [c'-e''], Roberton Songs.
Mary Morison, *Robert Burns*, [b-e''](m), Roberton Songs.
Milkwort and bog-cotton, *Hugh MacDiarmid*, [c'-d''], Roberton Songs.
Moonstruck, *Hugh MacDiarmid*, [e'♭-g''#], Roberton Songs.
My luve is like a red, red rose, *Robert Burns*, [b♭-e''♭](m), Roberton Songs.
O were my love yon lilac fair, *Robert Burns*, [f'-f''](m), Roberton Songs.
Of ane blackamoor, *William Dunbar*, [d'♭-e''♭](m), Roberton Songs.
Phillis, *William Drummond*, [d'-e''](m), Roberton Songs.
Rattlin' roarin' Willie, *Robert Burns*, [c'-f''], Roberton Songs.
Reid-E'en, *Hugh MacDiarmid*, [b-d''#](m), Roberton Songs.
Rorate caeli desuper, *William Dunbar*, [c'-f''], Roberton Songs.
Scots, wha hae, *Robert Burns*, [b-e''](m), Roberton Songs.
Scroggam, *Robert Burns*, [g-e''](m), Roberton Songs.
Since all thy vows, false maid, *Anon*, [d'♭-f''](m), Roberton Songs.
St Brendan's graveyard, *Jean Lang*, [f'-f''], Roberton Songs.
The Deil o' Bogie, tr. *Alexander Gray*, [a-d''](m), Roberton Songs.
The discreet hint, *Robert Burns*, [b♭-d''], Roberton Songs.
The eemis stane, *Hugh MacDiarmid*, [d'-c''#], Roberton Songs.
The Kerry Shore - Loch Fyne, *George Campbell Hay*, [d'♭-f''](m), Roberton Songs.
The love-sick lass, *Hugh MacDiarmid*, [d'♭-e''♭], Roberton Songs.
The old fisherman, *George Campbell Hay*, [c'-c''](m), Roberton Songs.
The sauchs in the Reuch Heuch Hauch, *Hugh MacDiarmid*, [d'-g''], Roberton Songs.

The tryst, *William Soutar*, [d'*b*-g''*b*](m), Roberton Songs.
The twa corbies, *Anon*, [b*b*-e''], Roberton Songs.
The twa kimmers, *William Dunbar*, [c'-e''](m), Roberton Songs.
The Watergaw, *Hugh MacDiarmid*, [c'-e''], Roberton Songs.
The wee man, tr. *Willa Muir*, [c'-f''](f), Roberton Songs.
To a Lady, *William Dunbar*, [b-d''](m), Roberton Songs.
To a Loch Fyne fisherman, *George Campbell Hay*, [b*b*-d''*b*](m), Roberton Songs.
Wee Willie Gray, *Robert Burns*, [c'#-d''], Roberton Songs.
Wha is that at my bower-door, *Robert Burns*, [b*b*-e''*b*], Roberton Songs.
Wheesht, wheesht, *Hugh MacDiarmid*, [c'-d''], Roberton Songs.

Barry Seaman. 1946 - (see also BMIC).
Gabriel's greeting, *Anon*, [d'-e''], OUP *Solo Christmas;* [b*b*-c''], *Solo Christmas*.

Humphrey Searle. 1915 - 1982. (see also BMIC).
Collections: (*Two Songs of A E Housman*, S&B 1948); (*Three Songs of Jocelyn Brooke*, Faber 1969.)
(Counting the beats, *Robert Graves*, [c'-b''], Faberprint.)
(Epitaph, *Jocelyn Brooke*, [a#-b''*b*], Faber 3 Songs.)
(March past, *A E Housman*, [d'-g''](m), S&B 2 Songs.)
(Song for Christmas, *Jocelyn Brooke*, [c'-b''*b*], Faber 3 Songs.)
(The stinging nettle, *A E Housman*, [C'#-F''#], S&B 2 Songs.)
(The white helleborine, *Jocelyn Brooke*, [b-b''*b*], Faber 3 Songs.)

Matyas Seiber. 1905 - 1960.
Collections: *Four Greek Folksongs*, B&H 1947.
Each time, my love, you say farewell, *Anon*, tr. *Peter Carroll*, [a'*b*-f''#](f), B&H 4 Greek.
Have pity on me, *Anon*, tr. *Peter Carroll*, G [d'-e''], B&H 4 Greek.
(My peace is gone, *Goethe* tr. *Louis MacNeice*, Am [d'-e''](f), S&B.)
O my love, how long, *Anon*, tr. *Peter Carroll*, Am [g'-e''], B&H 4 Greek.
O your eyes are dark and beautiful, *Anon*, tr. *Peter Carroll*, Em [e'-d''], B&H 4 Greek.
(There was a king in Thule, *Goethe* tr. *Louis MacNeice*, Fm [c'-f''], S&B.)
(To Poetry (cycle), *Goethe, Shakespeare, Dunbar*, [d'*b*-g''], Schott.)

Bertram Luard Selby. 1853 - 1918.
A widow bird sat mourning, *P B Shelley*, Gm [d'-d''], B&H *Heritage 1*.
(La Marguerite, *William Morris*, D, B&H.)

Ronald Senator. 1926 -
A poet to his beloved, *W B Yeats*, [high], Lengnick.

Alys F Serrell. ? - 1941.
The bullfinches, *Thomas Hardy*, E*b* [e'-b-f''], Thames *Hardy Songbook*.

Martin Shaw. 1875 - 1958. 15 more songs, Cramer archive.
Collections: (*Two Songs from Shakespeare*, Cramer 1929) (*Six Songs of War, Two Songs of Spring*, B&H);
Seven Songs (Introduction Michael Pilkington), S&B 1989.
Annabel Lee, *Edgar Allan Poe*, F [e'-b-a''](m), S&B 7 Songs, Cramer; C, Cramer.
(At Columbine's grave, *Bliss Carman*, Am [c'-e''], Cramer.)

Cargoes, *John Masefield*, D [c'#-e''], S&B 7 Songs, Cramer.
(Child of the flowing tide, *Geoffrey Dearmer*, A♭ [c'-e''♭], Chappell *English Recital 1*.)
(Come away, death, *Shakespeare*, Gm [d'-e''♭], Cramer 2 Songs.)
Cuckoo, *Anon*, G [d'-d''], S&B 7 Songs.
Down by the salley gardens, *W B Yeats*, [b-e''], S&B 7 Songs.
(Easter carol, *Christina Rossetti*, C [c'-e''], Curwen.)
(England, my England, *W E Henley*, C, B&H.)
(Heffle cuckoo fair, *Rudyard Kipling*, A [e'-e''(a'')], Curwen.)
I know a bank, *Shakespeare*, F [c'-d''], Cramer; B♭, Cramer; (G, Cramer).
Merry Christmas, *Walter Scott*, D [d'-a''(f''#)], OUP *Solo Christmas*; F, *Sing Christmas*.
No, *Thomas Hood*, Em [b-e''], S&B 7 Songs.
(O, Falmouth is a fine town, *W E Henley*, [c'-e''](m), Curwen.)
(Old clothes and fine clothes, *John Pride*, B♭ [b♭-d''], Cramer; C, Cramer.)
(Old Mother Laidinwool, *Rudyard Kipling*, E♭ [c'-e''], Curwen.)
(Refrain, *Arthur Shearly Cripps*, B♭ [c'-e''♭], Curwen.)
(Ships of Yule, *Eugene Field*, G [d'-e''], Cramer; F, A, Cramer.)
Song of the palanquin bearers, *Sarojini Naidu*, E [e'-f''], S&B 7 Songs.
(The accursèd wood, *Harold Boulton*, [c'-e''♭], Cramer.)
(The bells of Christmas, *Eugene Field*, Bm [e'-d''], Cramer; Am, Dm, Cramer.)
(The caravan, *W B Rands*, F [d'-e''], Cramer; A, Cramer.)
(The conjuration, *Hung-So-Fan* tr. *Anon*, B♭ [d'-f'#](m), Cramer; A♭, Cramer.)
(The herald, *Geoffrey Dearmer*, E♭, B&H 2 Spring.)
(The land of heart's desire, *W B Yeats*, Am [c'-e''(g'')], Curwen.)
(The little waves of Breffny, *Eva Gore-Booth*, C [e'-a''], Cramer.)
(The melodies you sing, *Clifford Bax*, F [c'#-d''], Cramer.)
(The merry wanderer, *Shakespeare*, E [e'-a''♭(a'')], Cramer.)
(The rivulet, *L Larcom*, G [d'-f''], Cramer; A, Cramer.)
(Through softly falling rain, *Sybil L Ruegg*, A, B&H 2 Spring.)
(To Sea! *Thomas Lovell Beddoes*, G [b♭-f''], Cramer.)
When daisies pied, *Shakespeare*, C [e'-a''], S&B 7 Songs.
(Tides, *John Pride*, C [a'-e''], Cramer.)
(When that I was and a little tiny boy, *Shakespeare*, E♭ [b♭-e''♭](m), Cramer 2 Songs.)
(Wood magic, *John Buchan*, C#m [b-f''], Cramer; *Em*, Cramer.)
Arrangement:
(The banks of Allan Water, *M G Lewis*, B♭ [d'-f''], Cramer; A♭, C, Cramer.)
(Ye banks and braes, *Robert Burns*, A [e'-f''#](f), Cramer; G, A, Cramer.)

Johann Georg Christoph Schetky. 1737 - 1824.
The echo, *William?* Woods, B♭ [f'-a''], OUP (Roberts) *O Tuneful Voice*.

William Shield. 1748 - 1829.
Ere bright Rosina met my eyes, *Frances Brooke*, C [e'-g''](m), Novello (Bush) *Ballad Operas*.
Hope and love, *William Pearce*, G [e'-g''], OUP (Roberts) *O Tuneful Voice*.
Tis only no harm to know it, you know, *John O'Keefe*, B♭ [f'-g''](f), OUP (Roberts) *O Tuneful Voice*.
Ye balmy breezes gently blow, *John Rannie*, C [e'-g''](m), OUP (Roberts) *O Tuneful Voice*.

Pwyll ap Siôn. 1968 -
My lady, *Rhydwen Williams* tr. *John Stoddart*, [A#-e'](m), Welsh Music *Songs from Wales* 2.

Thomas George Smart. 1776 - 1867.
The forsaken maid, *Anon*, F [e'-g''(a'')], B&H (Lane Wilson) *Old English Melodies*.

John Christopher Smith. 1712 - 1795.
The owl is abroad, *Ben Jonson*, G [g-d''](m), B&H *Imperial 6*.

Robert Smith. 1922 -
Angharad, *Eifion Wyn* tr. *Brinley Rees*, Bm [f'#-g''], Gwynn.
Ease me, *John Donne*, [b-d''],Welsh Music *Songs from Wales* 2.
Love, *Eifion Wyn* tr. *John Stoddart*, [A-c'](m), Welsh Music.

Theodore Smith. *c.*1740 - *c.*1810.
Content, *Anon*, D [d'-f''#], OUP (Roberts) *O Tuneful Voice*.

M van Someren-Godfery.
Collections: (*Five Breton Songs*, B&H); (*Six Blake Songs*, S&B 1952); (*Four Songs, Three Songs*, S&B 1957.)
    (A cradle song, *William Blake*, Dm [c'#-e''], S&B 6 Blake.)
    (A little Fête, *Li-Tai-Po* tr. *Ian Colvin*, Ebm [c'-e''b], S&B.)
    (A night piece, *E N da C Andrade*, [d'-c''], S&B 3 Songs.)
    (A poison apple, *William Blake*, A [c'#-e''(g''#)], S&B 6 Blake.)
    (Ad domnulum suam, *Ernest Dowson*, Elkin.)
    (Anacreon, *Antipater* tr. *Humbert Wolfe*, Cm [b-e''], S&B.)
    (Ballad of Semmerwater, *William Watson*, Elkin.)
    (Birthright, Elkin.)
    (Biton to his Gods, *Humbert Wolfe*, Eb [bb-e''](m), S&B.)
    (Death, thy servant, *Rabindranath Tagore*, G [c'-f''], S&B.)
    (Go, teach the swan to swim, *E N da C Andrade*, F [c'-f''], S&B.)
    (Green candles, *Humbert Wolfe*, Ab [e'b-f''], S&B 4 Songs.)
    (Joy is my name, *William Blake*, Eb [e'b-f''#], S&B 6 Blake.)
    (Journey's end, *Humbert Wolfe*, [d(b)-d''#], S&B 4 Songs.)
·   (La Belle Dame sans merci, *John Keats*, Cm [c'-g''], S&B.)
    (Lamon to Priapus, *Humbert Wolfe*, F [c'-e''], S&B 4 Songs.)
    (Love and Peter, *Humbert Wolfe*, C [c'(b)-e''], S&B 4 Songs.)
    (Love's secret, *William Blake*, [c'-e''], S&B 6 Blake.)
    (Ozymandias, *P B Shelley*, Fm [bb-e''(f')], S&B.)
    (Piping down the valleys, *William Blake*, F [c'-f''(d'')], S&B 6 Blake.)
    (Shadow and smoke, *E N da C Andrade*, Em [c-g''], S&B 3 Songs.)
    (The day is no more, *Rabindranath Tagore*, Eb [b-e''], S&B.)
    (The house on fire, *E N da C Andrade*, Dm [c'#-f''#], S&B 3 Songs.)
    (The King of China's daughter, *Edith Sitwell*, Eb [d'-g''](m), S&B.)
    (The old nurse's song, *Edith Sitwell*, [bb-e''b](f), S&B.)
    (The parting, *Ma Huang Tschung* tr. *Ian Colvin*, F [c'-d''], S&B.)
    (The shepherd, *William Blake*, D [d'-e''], S&B 6 Blake.)

(The tears of St Joseph, *Ruth Rogers*, [b-e''], S&B.)
(The twa Corbies, *Anon*, [c'(a)-e''(f')], S&B.)
(The white dress, *Humbert Wolfe*, G [d'-f'#], S&B.)
(Thou art not fair, *Thomas Campion*, Am [c'#-e''](m), S&B.)

John Somers-Cocks. 1907 - (see also BMIC.)

Eager Spring, *Gordon Bottomley*, [d'-e''], Bardic.
Echo, *Christina Rossetti*, [c'-e''], Bardic.
Everyone sang, *Siegfried Sassoon*, e'-f'#], Bardic.
New Year's eve, 1913, *Gordon Bottomley*, [c'#-f'#], Bardic.
Song: When I am dead, my dearest, *Christina Rossetti*, [f'-g''], Bardic.

Arthur Somervell. 1863 - 1937.

Collections: *Maud*, B&H 1898; (*Love in Springtime*, B&H 1901); *A Shropshire Lad*, B&H 1904; (*James Lee's Wife*, B&H 1907.); (*Twelve Tennyson Poems*, B&H 1922); (*A Broken Arc*, B&H 1923).
(A kingdom by the sea, *Edgar Allan Poe*, E [e'-g''](m), B&H.)
A voice by the cedar tree, *Alfred Lord Tennyson*, F [a-e''](m), B&H Maud.
(Among the rocks, *Robert Browning*, Ab [bb-f''](f), B&H James Lee.)
(As through the land (1), *Alfred Lord Tennyson*, D [d'-f'#](m), B&H.)
(As through the land (2), *Alfred Lord Tennyson*, Eb [bb'-e''b](m), B&H 12 Tennyson)
Birds in the high hall-garden, *Alfred Lord Tennyson*, Eb [bb-d''b](m), B&H Maud, *New Imperial 5*, B&H.
Come into the garden, Maud, *Alfred Lord Tennyson*, G [g-e''b](m), B&H Maud, *Heritage 1*.
(Come to me in my dreams, *Matthew Arnold*, Em [b-e''], B&H.)
(Crossing the bar, *Alfred Lord Tennyson*, Eb [c'-e''b], B&H 12 Tennyson; F, B&H.)
(Dainty little maiden, *Alfred Lord Tennyson*, F [c'-f''], B&H Springtime.)
Dead, long dead, *Alfred Lord Tennyson*, Gm [a-e''b](m), B&H Maud.
(Dreamland, *Ethel Speare*, Eb [e'b-f''](m), B&H.)
(Evening shadows (Sleep, my baby), *Anon*, D [d'-e''](f), B&H; E, B&H.)
(Fain would I change that note, *Anon*, G [d'-g''], B&H.)
Go not, happy day, *Alfred Lord Tennyson*, F [bb-e''b](m), B&H Maud.
(Home they brought her warrior dead, *Alfred Lord Tennyson*, Am [c'(a)-e''], B&H 12 Tennyson.)
(I cannot tell what you say, *Charles Kingsley*, A e'-a''], B&H Springtime.)
I hate the dreadful hollow, *Alfred Lord Tennyson*, Dm [a-e''](m), B&H Maud.
I have led her home, *Alfred Lord Tennyson*, C [c'-d''](m), B&H Maud.
In summertime on Bredon, *A E Housman*, C [bb-e''](m), B&H A Shropshire Lad, *Heritage 1*.
(In the early dawning, *Ethel Speare*, Em [e'-e''](f), B&H.)
Into my heart an air that kills, *A E Housman*, Eb [bb-d''](m), B&H A Shropshire Lad.
(Love unto love, *Katherine Margeson*, Eb [bb-e''b], B&H.)
Loveliest of trees, *A E Housman*, E [b-d''#](m), B&H A Shropshire Lad.
Maud has a garden of roses, *Alfred Lord Tennyson*, Bb [bb-d''](m), B&H Maud.
(Mine own country, *Katherine Tynan*, G [d'-g''], B&H; E, F, B&H.)
My life has crept so long, *Alfred Lord Tennyson*, Bbm [a-e''b](m), B&H Maud.
O let the solid ground, *Alfred Lord Tennyson*, C [c'-e''](m), B&H Maud.
(O mistress mine, *Shakespeare*, Eb [e'b-f''](m), B&H.)
(O swallow, swallow, *Alfred Lord Tennyson*, G [d'-f''(g')], B&H 12 Tennyson.)

O that 'twere possible, *Alfred Lord Tennyson*, B [c'#-d''](m), B&H Maud.
(O what comes over the sea, *Christina Rossetti*, B [f'#-f'#], B&H Springtime)
(On a summer morning, *Ethel Speare*, C [c'-g''(e')](f), B&H; B♭, D, B&H.)
On the idle hill of summer, *A E Housman*, B [c'#-e''](m), B&H A Shropshire Lad, *Heritage 1.*
(Orpheus with his lute, *Shakespeare*, A♭ [e'b-e''b], B&H.)
She came to the village church, *Alfred Lord Tennyson*, Dm [a-d''](m), B&H Maud.
(Spring is here, *E S*, C [e'-a''], B&H; *G, B♭*, B&H.)
(Sweet and low, *Alfred Lord Tennyson*, E♭ [b♭-e''♭], B&H 12 Tennyson, B&H; *F, D*, B&H.)
(Take, O take those lips away, *Shakespeare*, D [d'-d''], Forsyth.)
(Tears, idle tears, *Alfred Lord Tennyson*, Dm [d'-e''], B&H 12 Tennyson; Fm, B&H.)
The bargain, *Philip Sidney*, C [a-e''], Thames *Century 2*; (E♭, B&H).
The fault was mine, *Alfred Lord Tennyson*, E♭m [b♭-d''♭](m), B&H Maud.
The lads in their hundreds, *A E Housman*, A♭ [d'-f''](m), B&H A Shropshire Lad, *Heritage 2.*
(The night-bird, *Charles Kingsley*, G [f'#-g''#], B&H Springtime.)
(The silent voice, *Laurence Alma Tadema*, Dm [e'-g''], B&H.)
The street sounds to the soldiers' tread, *A E Housman*, E♭ [b♭-e''♭](m), B&H A Shropshire Lad.
There pass the careless people, *A E Housman*, Em [b-e''](m), B&H A Shropshire Lad.
Think no more, lad; laugh, be jolly, *A E Housman*, G [g(d')-e''](m), B&H A Shropshire Lad.
(To Lucasta, on going to the wars, *Richard Lovelace*, Fm [e'-b-f''](m), B&H.)
(Underneath the growing grass, *Christina Rossetti*, B♭m [b♭-a''♭], B&H Springtime.)
When I was one-and-twenty, *A E Housman*, B [b-d''#](m), B&H A Shropshire Lad.
(When spring returns, *Arthur Somervell*, D♭ [e'b-a''b], B&H; C, B&H.)
White in the moon the long road lies, *A E Housman*, Bm [c'#-e''](m), B&H A Shropshire Lad, *Heritage 2.*
(Will you come back home? *Gilbert Parker*, C [c'-e''], B&H.)
Young love lies sleeping, *Christina Rossetti*, B♭ [f'-g''], B&H Springtime, *Heritage 2*, B&H.
Arrangements:
All through the night, *Anon*, Cramer.
Gathering daffodils, *Anon*, A♭, Cramer.
The gentle maiden, *Harold Boulton*, E♭ [b♭-e''♭](m), Cramer; *F*, Cramer.
The snowy breasted pearl, *Anon*, E, Cramer.
(The twa sisters of Binnorie, *Anon*, C [g-e''], B&H.)

Wallace Southam.
(Have you seen but a white lily grow?, *Ben Jonson*, E♭ [e'b-e''b], OUP.)
(Lesbos, *Lawrence Durrell*, [g-b'b], OUP.)

William Henry Squire. 1871 - 1963. A further 31 songs in B&H archives.
If I might come to you, *Fred. E Weatherly*, C [g'-g''] B&H *Ballad Album 2*; (A♭, B♭, B&H).
In an old-fashioned town, *Ada Leonora Harris*, F [d'-g''] B&H *Ballad Album 2*; (D, B&H).

Patric Standford. 1939 - (BMIC.)

Charles Villiers Stanford. 1852 - 1924.
Collections: (*Twelve Songs by Heine, S&B 1893*); (*An Irish Idyll Op 77* (high & low keys), B&H 1901;
(*Five Sonnets from 'The Triumph of Love' Op 82*, B&H 1903); *Songs of the Sea Op 91*, B&H 1904; (*Songs of Faith Op 97*, B&H 1908); (*Cushendall, A Fire of Turf*, S&B 1910); (*A Sheaf of Songs from Leinster*, S&B

1914); *(Six Songs from 'The Glens of Antrim'* Op. *174*, B&H 1920); *Six Songs*, S&B 1979 (Introduction Geoffrey Bush), *Musica Britannica 52*, S&B (Geoffrey Bush).
A broken song, *Moira O'Neill*, Fm [b♭-d"♭], Thames *Century 2*.
(A Corsican dirge, *Anon*, tr. *Alma Strettell*, Dm [c'-g"](f), S&B.)
(A hymn in praise of Neptune, *Thomas Campion*, C [e'-g"], B&H.)
A Japanese lullaby, *Eugene Field*, D♭ [d♭-f"](f), Banks; (B♭, E♭, Cramer).
(A message to Phillis, *Thomas Heywood*, A♭ [c'-f'(a"♭)](m), S&B.)
A fire of turf, *Winifred Letts*, D [a-d"](m), S&B MB 52, (A Fire of Turf).
A lullaby, *Thomas Dekker*, A♭ [e'♭-f"](f), S&B MB 52, B&H *Heritage 1*.
A soft day, *Winifred Letts*, D♭ [d'♭-d"♭], S&B MB 52, S&B, (Leinster), Banks; *F*, S&B.
(A song of the bow, *Reginald Heber*, G [d'-g"],(m), Cramer; E♭, Cramer.)
(Almansor dying, *Heinrich Heine*, tr. *Anon*, E♭m [b♭-g"], S&B 12 Songs.)
(As the moon's pale likeness quivers, *Heinrich Heine* tr. *Anon*, E♭ [d'-f"], S&B 12 Songs.)
(At sea, *Moira O'Neill*, B♭ [b♭-e"♭], B&H Songs of Antrim.)
Blackberry time, *Winifred Letts*, E [b-d"#], S&B MB 52, (A Fire of Turf).
(Boat song, *Walter Pollock*, F [e'-f"], B&H; *D*, B&H.)
Come away, death, *Shakespeare*, Fm [b♭-e"♭](m), S&B MB 52.
(Come to me when the earth is fair, *Walter Pollock*, G [e'-g"], B&H.)
Cowslip time, *Winifred Letts*, E♭ [c'-e"♭], S&B MB 52, (A Fire of Turf).
Crossing the bar, *Lord Tennyson*, B♭ [f'-g"], S&B MB 52.
(Cushendall, *John Stevenson*, B♭m [b♭-d"], S&B Cushendall.)
Cuttin' rushes, *Moira O'Neill*, F [b-d"], B&H *Heritage 2*, (B&H Op 77, B&H; *Ab, Op 77*, B&H.)
(Daddy-long-legs, *John Stevenson*, C [b-d"], S&B Cushendall.)
Dainty Davie, *Robert Burns*, F [d'-f'(a')](f), S&B MB 52.
(Denny's daughter, *Moira O'Neill*, Dm [c'-e"], B&H Songs of Antrim.)
Devon, O Devon, in wind and rain, *Henry Newbolt*, Gm [e'♭-e"](m), B&H Songs of the Sea.
(Did you ever see the sun? *John Stevenson*, B♭ [b♭-d"♭], S&B Cushendall.)
Drake's drum, *Henry Newbolt*, Dm [c'-e"](m), B&H Songs of the Sea, *Heritage 1*; (Cm, B&H).
Drop me a flower, *Lord Tennyson*, A♭ [e'♭-g"(a"♭)](m), S&B MB 52.
(Fairy lures, *Rose Fyleman*, E♭ [d'-g"], Cramer.)
From the red rose to the apple-blossom, *A P Graves*, A [c'-f"], S&B MB 52.
(Grandeur, *Winifred Letts*, Cm [b♭-c"], S&B Leinster.)
Homeward bound, *Henry Newbolt*, D♭ [d'♭-d"♭], B&H Songs of the Sea.
(How does the wind blow, *John Stevenson*, D [a-e"♭], S&B Cushendall.)
(I mind the day, *Moira O'Neill*, Dm [c'-e"♭], B&H Songs of Antrim.)
I praise the tender flower, *Robert Bridges*, F [g'-f"](m), S&B MB 52.
(I seal thy lips with kisses three, *Heinrich Heine*, tr. *Anon*, B [c'#-f'#], S&B 12 Songs.)
(Ireland, *John Stevenson*, F [c'-d"], S&B Cushendall.)
(Irish skies, *Winifred Letts*, Cm [b♭-d"], S&B Leinster.)
(Johneen, *Moira O'Neill*, D♭ [d'-d"♭], B&H Op 77; *F, Op 77*, B&H.)
Joy, shipmate, joy, *Walt Whitman*, D [c'-d"], S&B MB 52.
La Belle Dame sans merci, *John Keats*, Fm [b♭-f"], S&B MB 52, S&B.
Like as the thrush in winter, *Edmund Holmes*, G [d'-g"], S&B MB 52.
(Little Peter Morrisey, *Winifred Letts*, Dm [c'-d"], S&B Leinster.)
(Lookin' back, *Moira O'Neill*, C [a♭-e"♭], B&H Songs of Antrim.)
Luck comes in sleeping, *A Song of Lorraine* tr. *Anon*, E♭ [e'♭-g"], S&B MB 52.

(Lullaby, *George Leveson Gower*, F [c'-f''], Cramer.)
(Mopsa, *Philodemus*, tr. *Thomas Moore*, D [a-d''](m), Elkin.)
(My love is a flower, *Heinrich Heine* tr. *Anon*, Db [c'-f''], S&B 12 Songs.)
(Night, *John Stevenson*, F [c'-c''], S&B Cushendall.)
(Nonsense Rhymes, *Edward Lear*, set to music by 'Karel Drofnatski', 14 songs for various voices, S&B 1960).
O flames of passion, *Edmund Holmes*, Gm [g'-f''], S&B MB 52.
O mistress mine, *Shakespeare*, F [b-d''](m), B&H *Shakespeare*, S&B MB 52.
O one deep sacred outlet of my soul, *Edmund Holmes*, Cm [d'-b-g''], S&B MB 52.
(On the deep-blue-girdled heaven, *Heinrich Heine* tr. *Anon*, Eb [c'-g''], S&B 12 Songs.)
(On thy blue eyes, *Heinrich Heine* tr. *Anon*, G [f'-g''], S&B 12 Songs.)
Out upon it, *John Suckling*, Em [e'-f'#](m), S&B MB 52.
Outward bound, *Henry Newbolt*, Ab [e'-b-e''b](m), B&H Songs of the Sea, *Heritage*.
(Parted, *G H Jessop*, Eb [e'-b-g''](m), B&H.)
Phoebe, *Thomas Lodge*, Bb [c'-e''b(f')](m), S&B MB 52.
(Prince Madoc's farewell, *Felicia Hemans*, Dm [d'-e''b](m), B&H.)
Prospice, *Robert Browning*, G [c'-f''](m), S&B MB 52, 6 Songs.
(Queen and huntress, *Ben Jonson*, A [c'#-g''], B&H.)
(Requiescat, *Matthew Arnold*, Ab [e'-b-g''], B&H.)
(Sad is the spring-time, *Heinrich Heine*, tr. *R H Benson*, Em [d'#-f''], S&B 12 Songs.)
Say, O say! saith the music, *Robert Bridges*, F [e'-b-f''](m), S&B MB 52.
Scared, *Winifred Letts*, Cm [bb-e''b], S&B MB 52, (A Fire of Turf).
Since thou, O fondest and truest, *Robert Bridges*, D [d'-g''], S&B MB 52.
(Slumber-song, *Heinrich Heine*, tr. *Anon*, D [d'-e''], S&B 12 Songs.)
(Song of the bow, *Reginald Heber*, Eb [bb-e''b](m), Cramer; *G*, Cramer.)
(Song written at sea, *Charles Sackville*, F [c'-f''](m), B&H; *Ab*, B&H.)
(Spring, *Heinrich Heine* tr. *R H Benson*, Ab [d'-f'#(a''b)], S&B 12 Songs.)
Spring, *Alfred Lord Tennyson*, Eb [e'-b-a''b](m), S&B MB 52.
(Stars above me, golden footed, *Heinrich Heine* tr. *Andrew Lang*, D [c'#-f'#], S&B 12 Songs.)
(Sweeter than the violet, *Meleager*, tr. *Andrew Lang*, Eb [d'-a''b], B&H.)
Tears, *Walt Whitman*, Bm [b-e''(f')], S&B MB 52.
The battle of Pelusium, *Beaumont & Fletcher*, Cm [c'-e''b](m), S&B MB 52.
The bold unbiddable child, *Winifred Letts*, Dm [c'-e''b(g)], S&B MB 52, 6 Songs (Leinster); (*Cm*, S&B).
(The boy from Ballytearim, *Moira O'Neill*, Dm [c'-e''b], B&H Songs of Antrim.)
(The butterfly's love, *Heinrich Heine* tr. *H W Hoare*, D [d'-f'#], S&B 12 Songs.)
(The calico dress, *George H Jessop*, Fm [e'-b-f''(a''b)](f), B&H.)
The chapel on the hill, *Winifred Letts*, Dm [a'd''], S&B MB 52, 6 Songs, (A Fire of Turf).
(The crow, *John Stevenson*, Dm [a-d''], S&B Cushendall.)
The fair, *Winifred Letts*, D [d'-d''], S&B MB 52, (A Fire of Turf).
The fairy loch, *Moira O'Neill*, D [a-e''b], S&B MB 52, B&H *Heritage* 2, (B&H Op 77, B&H; *F*, Op 77).
(The lute song, *Alfred Lord Tennyson*, Dm [c'#-d''](f), S&B.)
(The merry month of May, *Thomas Dekker*, F [d'-f''], Cramer.)
(The rose of Killarney, *Alfred Percival Graves*, F [d'-g''(a')], Cramer; *Eb*, Cramer.)

The monkey's carol, *Winifred Letts*, Dm [d'-g''], Cramer, OUP *Solo Christmas*; Bm, *Solo Christmas*, Cramer.

(The old navy, *Captain Marryat*, C [b♭-e''](m), B&H; D, B&H.)

The old Superb, *Henry Newbolt*, B♭ [b♭-e''♭](m), B&H Songs of the Sea, *Heritage 2*; A♭, C, B&H).

The pibroch, *Murdoch Maclean*, Bm [a'-d''(m)], S&B MB 52, 6 Songs.

(The pilgramage to Kevlaar, *Heinrich Heine*, tr. *Anon*, D♭ [c'-a''♭], B&H.)

The rain it raineth every day, *Shakespeare*, D [c'-d''], S&B MB 52, B&H *Heritage 2, Shakespeare*.

(The Rhine wine, *Walter Pollock*, G [f'♯-g''](m), B&H.)

The sailor man, *Moira O'Neill*, A♭ [b♭-e''♭](m), S&B MB 52, *Recitalist 4*, (B&H Songs of Antrim).

(The sower's song, *Thomas Carlyle*, E♭ [e'-b♭-f''], Cramer.)

(The tragedy of life, *Heinrich Heine* tr. *Anon*, C [c'-f''], B&H.)

(The unknown sea, *Mary Kitson Clark*, F [d'-g''](f), Cramer.)

The west wind, *Winifred Letts*, F [c'-e''♭], S&B MB 52, (A Fire of Turf).

The winds of Bethlehem, *Winifred Letts*, Gm [d'-g''], B&H *Cramer Song Folio 1*.

There be none of beauty's daughters, *Lord Byron*, E♭ [e'-b♭-f''](m), S&B MB 52.

(Thief of the world, *Winifred Letts*, F [d'-f''], S&B Leinster.)

(Thou art my love, *Heinrich Heine* tr. *R H Benson*, E♭ [e'-b♭-g''], S&B 12 Songs.)

To carnations, *Robert Herrick*, G [e'-e''], S&B MB 52.

(To the rose, *Robert Herrick*, F [f'-f''](m), B&H.)

(To the skylark, *James Hogg*, G [d'(f'♯)-a''], B&H.)

To the soul, *Walt Whitman*, B♭ [b♭-e''♭], S&B MB 52.

Why so pale, *John Suckling*, Cm [e'-b♭-g''](m), S&B MB 52, *Recitalist 3*.

Windy nights, *R L Stevenson*, Dm [d'-f''], S&B MB 52.

(Witches charms, *Ben Jonson*, Fm [c'-f''], Cramer.)

Arrangements: 20 more songs in B&H archive.

Trottin' to the fair, *Anon* D, B&H.

My love's an arbutus, *A P Graves*, [A♭ [e'-b♭-f''](m), B&H *McCormack*.

John Stanley. 1713 - 1786.

(Be pleasant, be airy, *Sir John Hawkins*, G [d'-g''], Elkin (Bevan).)

Fie, Damon, fie, *a young lady*, Em [d'♯-f''](f), Thames *Gentleman's Magazine*.

Sweet pretty bird, *Mr McClennan*, A♭ [e'-b♭-a''♭](f), Braydeston (Bevan).

(Would's thou hope the nymph to gain, *Sir John Hawkins*, G [d'-g''], Elkin (Bevan).)

Christopher Steel. 1939 -

Collection: *Our Joyful'st Feast*, Banks 1978. (See also BMIC.)

So now is come our joyful'st feast, *George Wither*, [high], Banks Feast.

There was a time for shepherds, *Anthea Steel*, [high], Banks Feast.

What sweeter music can we bring? *Robert Herrick*, [high], Banks Feast.

Roger Steptoe. 1953 -

Collections: (*Three Sonnets to Delia*, S&B); *Chinese Lyrics Set One*, S&B 1986; *Chinese Lyrics Set Two*, S&B 1986, *Two Songs for Baritone and Piano*, Lengnick.

A gathering of the clans, *Anon*, tr. *Helen Waddell*, [c'-f''](f), S&B Chinese 1.

(A lament, *P B Shelley*, [baritone], Lengnick 2 Songs.)

A little music (cycle), *Humbert Wolfe*, [G♯-e'](m), Lengnick.

(Aspects (cycle), *Ursula Vaughan Williams*, [c'-a''], S&B.)

At the riverside village, *Anon* tr. *Kotewall* and *Smith*, [c'#-d''], S&B Chinese 2.
(Beautie sweet love, *Samuel Daniel*, [b♭-f''], S&B 3 Sonnets.)
Blue iris, *Anon*, tr. *Helen Waddell*, [e'♭-e''♭](f), S&B Chinese 1.
(Care-charmer sleep, *Samuel Daniel*, [d'-e''], S&B 3 Sonnets.)
Crossing the Han river, *Anon* tr. *Kotewall* and *Smith*, [c'#-c''#], S&B Chinese 2.
Green, green the riverside grass, *Anon* tr. *Kotewall* and *Smith*, [c'#-e''], S&B Chinese 2.
He protests his loyalty, *Anon*, tr. *Helen Waddell*, [f'#-f''#](f), S&B Chinese 1.
Inscribed on a small garden wall, *Anon* tr. *Kotewall* and *Smith*, [c'-c''#], S&B Chinese 2.
Let others sing of knights and palladines, *Samuel Daniel*, [d'-e''], S&B 3 Sonnets.)
(Music when soft voices die, *P B Shelley*, [baritone], Lengnick 2 Songs.)
Night, *Anon* tr. *Kotewall* and *Smith*, [c'-e''], S&B Chinese 2.
On early morning, *Anon*, tr. *Helen Waddell*, [c'-g''](f), S&B Chinese 1.
The morning glory, *Anon*, tr. *Helen Waddell*, [c'#-f''#](f), S&B Chinese 1.
White clouds are in the sky, *Anon* tr. *Helen Waddell*, [c'-c''#], S&B Chinese 2.

T C Sterndale-Bennett. ? - 1942. 18 more songs in B&H archive.
The carol singers, *Charles Hayes*, G [d'-e''(d'')](m), B&H *Cramer Song Folio 1.*

Bernard Stevens. 1916 - 1983.
Collections: *The Palatine Coast*, Lengnick 1953; *Two Songs*, Bardic; *Four John Donne Songs*, S&B 1984.
Death, be not proud, *John Donne*, [b-g''#], S&B 4 Donne.
Dream pedlary, *Thomas Lovell Beddoes*, [d'-g''], Bardic 2 Songs.
Go and catch a falling star, *John Donne*, [f'#-a''](m), S&B 4 Donne.
If we die, *Ethel Rosenberg*, [c'-a''♭], Bardic.
Lunar attraction, *Montague Slater*, [c'-g''], Lengnick Palatine Coast.
May Day carol, *Montague Slater*, [g'-g''], Lengnick Palatine Coast.
Mother Shipton's wooing, *Montague Slater*, [d'-g''], Lengnick Palatine Coast.
Song of the ship, *Thomas Lovell Beddoes*, [d'♭-b''♭], Bardic 2 Songs.
Sweetest love, I do not go, *John Donne*, [e'♭-f''#], S&B 4 Donne.
The good-morrow, *John Donne*, [c'-a''], S&B 4 Donne.
The true dark (cycle), *Randall Swingler*, [A-g'](m), Roberton.

James Stevens. (BMIC.)

Ronald Stevenson. 1928 - (BMIC.)

Robert Still. 1910 - 1971.
Beauty bathing, *Anthony Munday*, E [b-e''](m), Lengnick.
Upon Julia's clothes, *Robert Herrick*, G [d'-e''], Lengnick.

Richard Stoker. 1938 - (BMIC.)

Stephen Storace. 1762 - 1796.
Collection: *Seven Songs for High Voice* (edited Michael Pilkington), S&B 1979.
A sailor loved a lass, *Anon*, E♭ [c'-f''(e''♭)], B&H (Lane Wilson) *Old English Melodies.*
Be mine, tender passion, *Anon*, E♭ [b♭-b''♭](f), S&B 7 Songs.
Captivity, *Joshua Jeans*, E♭ [e'♭-a''♭](f), OUP (Roberts) *O Tuneful Voice.*
How mistaken is the lover, *Anon*, G [d'-g''](f), S&B 7 Songs, (Johnston) *Recitalist 1.*

How sweet the calm of this sequester'd shore, *Anon*, A [e'-f'#], OUP (Roberts) *O Tuneful Voice.*
My rising spirits thronging, *Anon*, Bb [f'-a''](f), S&B 7 Songs.
No more his fears alarming, *Anon*, A [e'-a''](f), S&B 7 Songs
Peaceful slumbering on the ocean, *Anon*, C [c'-g''](f), S&B 7 Songs.
The curfew, *Thomas Gray*, Dm [d'-f''], S&B 7 Songs, OUP (Roberts) *O Tuneful Voice.*
The pretty creature, *Anon*, F [c'-f'(d')](m), B&H (Lane Wilson) *Old English Melodies.*
The summer heats bestowing, *Anon*, A [e'-a''](f), S&B 7 Songs, (S&B (Ivimey)).

Arthur Sullivan. 1842 - 1900. 18 more songs in B&H archive.
Collections: *Songs Book 1*, S&B 1986; *Songs Book 2*, S&B 1987; *Songs Book 3*, S&B 1988.
Arabian love song, *P B Shelley*, Am [e'-g''(a')](f), S&B Book 2.
County Guy, *Walter Scott*, Em [b-e''(f'#)], S&B Book 3.
Edward Gray, *Alfred Lord Tennyson*, G [d'-g''](m), S&B Book 3.
Golden days, *Lionel Lewin*, Eb [bb-g''], Banks.
If doughty deeds, *Graham of Gartmore*, Eb [bb-e''b](m)), S&B Book 2.
Let me dream again, *B C Stephenson*, D [c'#(b)-f'#(a)](f), S&B Book 1; (C, B&H).
Mary Morison, *Robert Burns*, G [d'-e''](m), S&B Book 3; (Bb, B&H).
O fair dove! O fond dove, *Jean Ingelow*, D [b-f''](f), S&B Book 1.
Orpheus with his lute, *Shakespeare*, Bb [d'-g''(b''b)], S&B Book 1; A, B&H *Cramer Song Folio 1.*
Sigh no more, ladies, *Shakespeare*, D [e'-g''(a')], S&B Book 3.
Sometimes, *Lady Lindsay*, C [d'-g''], S&B Book 2.
Sweethearts, *W S Gilbert*, Ab [c'-g''], S&B Book 2.
Tears, idle tears, *Lord Tennyson*, Eb [bb-f''b], S&B Book 2.
The chorister, *Fred E Weatherly*, F [c'-f''], B&H *Cramer Song Folio 1.*
The distant shore, *W S Gilbert*, Eb [bb-e''b], S&B Book 3; (G, Chappell *English Recital 2*.)
The lost chord, *Adelaide Ann Proctor*, F [c'-f''], S&B Book 1, B&H; G, *Ballad Album 2*, Cramer
    Drawing Room Songs; Eb, B&H.
The willow song, *Shakespeare*, E [b-e''(c''#)], S&B Book 1, *Recitalist 2*, B&H *Shakespeare.*
Where the bee sucks, *Shakespeare*, Bb [c'-g''], S&B Book 1, *Recitalist 1*; (Db, B&H).

Freda Swain. (See also BMIC.)
(Blessing, *Austin Clarke*, F [c'-e''], Curwen.)
(Experience, *Anon* tr. *Arthur Waley*, [b-e''], S&B.)
(The green lad from Donegal, *Freda Swain*, Fm [e'b-f''], S&B.)
(The lark on Portsdown Hill, *Freda Swain*, [c'-f''], S&B.)
(Winter field, *A E Coppard*, Em [c'-e''], S&B.)

Donald Swann. 1923 - 1994.
Collections: *Songs to Poems by William Blake, Five Colourisations of Emily Dickinson's Poems, Two Songs by Edna St Vincent Millay*, Lengnick 1993.
Ah!, sun-flower, *William Blake*, [high], Lengnick Blake.
I must I then indeed, pain, live with you? *Edna St Vincent Millay*, [high], Lengnick Millay.
He who binds to himself a joy, *William Blake*, [high], Lengnick Blake.
I died for beauty, *Emily Dickinson*, [high], Lengnick Dickinson.
I felt a funeral in my brain, *Emily Dickinson*, [high], Lengnick Dickinson.
I had no time to hate, *Emily Dickinson*, [high], Lengnick Dickinson.
I heard a fly buzz when I died, *Emily Dickinson*, [high], Lengnick Dickinson.

The angel, *William Blake*, [high], Lengnick Blake.
The fly, *William Blake*, [high], Lengnick Blake.
The garden of love, *William Blake*, [high], Lengnick Blake.
The sick rose, *William Blake*, [high], Lengnick Blake.
Thou famished grave, *Edna St Vincent Millay*, [high], Lengnick Millay.
Tie the strings to my life, O Lord, *Emily Dickinson*, [high], Lengnick Dickinson.

John Sykes. 1909 - 1962. (*Songs of Innocence*, Blake; *Songs of Experience*, Blake; MSS held by BMIC.)

T

Phyllis Tate. 1911 - 1987.
Collections: (*Two Songs*, OUP 1948); *Scenes from Tyneside*, Emerson 1980 (*see* Appendix 2).
   (Cradle song, *William Blake*, Am [f'-e''](f), OUP.)
   (Epitaph, *Sir Walter Raleigh*, Am [b-f''], OUP.)
   (I sing of a maiden, *Anon*, [d'-g''], OUP.)
   (My love could walk, *W H Davies*, C [e'-b-a''b], OUP.)
   Of all the youths, *Anon*, Bb [d'-f''](f), Emerson Scenes.
   (The cock, *Anon*, G [c'#-g''], OUP 2 Songs.)
   (The falcon, *Anon*, [c'#-g''], OUP 2 Songs.)
   (The quiet mind, *Sir Edward Dyer*, G [a#-f''], OUP.)
Arrangements:
   Brother James's Air, [e'-f''], OUP.
   Long ago in Bethlehem, *C K Offer*, Eb [d'-e''b], OUP *Solo Christmas*; G, *Solo Christmas*.
   (O, the bonny fisher lad, *Anon*, Gm [bb-d''], OUP.)
   The lark in the clear air, *Samuel Ferguson*, Bb [bb-d''](m), OUP *Solo Baritone*, Ab OUP.
   (The snowy-breasted pearl, *Anon* tr. *Petrie*, D [d'-f''], OUP.)
   The water of Tyne, *Anon*, [b-d''], OUP.

John Taverner. 1944 -
Collection: (*Three Sections from the Four Quartets*, Chester 1969.)
   (A Mini Songcycle for Gina, *W B Yeats*, [d'-a''b], Chester.)
   (Lady, whose shrine stands on the promontory, *T S Eliot*, [e'-f''#](m), Chester 3 Sections.)
   (Lamentation, Last Prayer and Exaltation, [soprano], Chester.)
   (Prayer, for Szymanowski, [bass], Chester.)
   (The dove descending breaks the air, *T S Eliot*, [d'-a''](m), Chester 3 Sections.)
   (Time and the bell have buried the day, *T S Eliot*, [d'-b-g''b](m), Chester 3 Sections.)

Roy Teed. 1928 -
Collections: *Two Songs*, Chester 1955.
   April morning, *Bill Adams*, C [c'-e''], Chester 2 Songs.
   Holy Thursday, *William Blake*, C c'-g''(e')], Roberton.
   Song for sunrise, *James Kirkup*, C [e'-b-f''], Chester 2 Songs.
   Three jolly gentlemen, [medium], Chester.

Eric Thiman. 1900 - 1975.
Collection: *Thirteen Songs*, S&B 1987.
   An Easter prayer, *Irene Gass*, Am [e'-e''], B&H *Cramer Song Folio 1*.
   As Joseph was a-walking, *Anon*, E [c'-e''], S&B 13 Songs; (G, S&B.)
   Carol of the birds, Eb, B&H
   Dainty fine bird, *Anon*, Gm [d'-f''](m), S&B 13 Songs.
   Evening in lilac time, *T H Dipnall*, G [d'-d''], S&B 13 Songs.
   (Flower of heaven, Eb, Elkin; Gb, Elkin.)

(Happy is the man, Novello.)
I love all graceful things, *Kathleen Boland*, Ab[e'b-g''], Curwen.
I saw three ships, *Anon*, G[d'-d''], S&B 13 Songs.
I wandered lonely as a cloud, *William Wordsworth*, Db[c'-g''b], S&B 13 Songs, *Recitalist 2*.
(In the bleak midwinter, *Christina Rossetti*, D, Novello.)
(Jesus, the very thought of thee, *Bernard of Clairvaux*, tr. *Caswell*, Bb[bb-d''], Novello.)
Madonna and child, *Gerald Bullett*, F[e'-f''], S&B 13 Songs.
(My master hath a garden, F, Novello.)
Now sleeps the crimson petal, *Alfred Lord Tennyson*, Eb[c'-f''], S&B 13 Songs, *Recitalist 4*.
Sleeping, *Anon*, E[b-g''](m), S&B 13 Songs.
(Song in solitude, *Walter Savage Landor*, Ab[e'b-f'#], Elkin.)
Sweet Afton, *Robert Burns*, Db[e'b-a''b](m), S&B 13 Songs.
(The birds, *Hilaire Belloc*, C, Novello; D, Novello.)
(The God of love my shepherd is, Novello.)
(The maid of Dundee, *Sydney Bell*, Cm[c-e''b], Curwen.)
(The piper pipes a merry tune, *Anon*, G[d'-g''], Chappell *English Recital 2.)*
The rainbow, *Christina Rossetti*, E[b-e''], S&B 13 Songs.
The shepherd, *William Blake*, G[d'-f''], S&B 13 Songs.
(The silver birch, *E Nisbet*, C[b-d''(e'')], Curwen; F, Curwen.)
(The silver swan, *Anon*, Bbm[d'b-f''], S&B 13 Songs.
(The song-thrush, *Ann Phillips*, D[d'-g''], Curwen.)
(The wee road from Cushendall, *Sydney Bell*, F[c'-f''], Curwen.)
Where go the boats? *R L Stevenson*, F[c'-d''], S&B 13 Songs.

D Afan Thomas. 1881 - 1925.
Land of the silver trumpets, E [mezzo/contralto/baritone], Snell.

David Vaughan Thomas. 1873 - 1934.
Enter those enchanted woods, *George Meredith*, D [f'-a''] Welsh Music, *Songs from Wales 1*.
The seagull fair, *Dafydd ap Gwilym* tr. *H Idris Bell*, Dm [f'-f''], Gwynn.

J R Thomas.
Eileen Alannah, F, Weinberger; G, Ab, Weinberger.

Mansel Thomas. 1909 - 1986.
Collections: *Twelve Songs for Children*, Gwynn; *Four Prayers from the Gaelic*, Gwynn; *Three Songs for Joanna*, Gwynn.
Bless to me, God, *Anon* tr. *Alexander Carmichael*, Bb[d'-a''b], Gwynn 4 Prayers.
Blessing for a house, *Anon* tr. *Alexander Carmichael*, C [c'-g''], Gwynn 4 Prayers.
Gwynn ap Nudd, *Elfed* tr. *Grace Williams*, Dm [d'-a''b], Gwynn.
Life, *T Gwynn Jones*, Ab[e'b-a''b], Gwynn.
Little Tommy Twinkletoes, [soprano/mezzo/tenor/baritone], Gwynn Joanna.
Rob Robin, [soprano/mezzo/tenor/baritone], Gwynn Joanna.
Thanks to thee, O God, *Anon* tr. *Alexander Carmichael*, G [d'-g''], Gwynn 4 Prayers.
The bard, *R Williams Parry* tr. *T Gwynn Jones*, Am [e'-f''], Gwynn.
The crystal rill, *Eifion Wyn* tr. *Robert Davies*, G [d'-e''], Gwynn.
The goldfish, [soprano/mezzo/tenor/baritone], Gwynn Joanna.

Antonín Tucapský

The secret people, *A G Prys-Jones*, [d'-g''], Welsh Music, *Songs from Wales 1.*
Thou being of marvels, *Anon* tr. *Alexander Carmichael*, G [g'-g''], Gwynn 4 Prayers.

Muriel Thomas. 1898 - ?
(Buds in spring, *Rupert Brooke*, D*b* [d'*b*-a''*b*], B&H.)
Faithless as the winds, [mezzo], Snell.
Let my voice ring out over the earth, *James Thomson*, F [c'#-a''], Snell.
Music when soft voices die, *P B Shelley*, [soprano/tenor], Snell.
(My true love hath my heart, *Philip Sidney*, E [c'#-g''#](f), B&H.)
She walks in beauty, *P B Shelley*, [mezzo/contralto/baritone], Snell.

Vincent Thomas. 1873 - 1940.
April days, *Chester Dod*, Fm [e'-f''], Gwynn *Three Spring Songs.*

Cedric Thorpe Davie. 1913 - 1983. (SMIC).

Penelope Thwaites. 1944 - (see also BMIC.)
All the days of Christmas, *Phyllis McGinley*, [a-f''], Bardic.
Forestry, *Michael Thwaites*, [b-f''], Bardic.
Look at the children, *Penelope Thwaites*, [d'-d''], Bardic.
Reverie, *Carolyn James*, [c'-d''], Bardic.

Michael Tippett. 1905 -
Collections: *The Heart's Assurance*, Schott, 1951; *Songs for Ariel*, Schott, 1964.
Boyhood's end, (cantata), *W H Hudson*, [c'-b''*b*](m), Schott.
Come unto these yellow sands, *Shakespeare*, [d'-e''*b*], Schott Songs for Ariel.
Compassion, *Alun Lewis*, [c'-b''(a')], Schott The Heart's Assurance.
Full fathom five, *Shakespeare*, [c'-d''], Schott Songs for Ariel.
Remember your lovers, *Sidney Keyes*, [d'*b*-a''*b*], Schott The Heart's Assurance.
Song, *Alun Lewis*, [d'-a''], Schott The Heart's Assurance.
The dancer, *Alun Lewis*, [d'-a''], Schott The Heart's Assurance.
The heart's assurance, *Sidney Keyes*, [c'-a''*b*], Schott The Heart's Assurance.
Where the bee sucks, *Shakespeare*, [d'-e''*b*], Schott Songs for Ariel.

Pamela Torphichen.
Not yet, *Anon*, [d'-f''], Bardic.
Song of freedom, *Irina Ratushinskaya*, [c'-e''], Bardic.
The awakening, *Joseph Stansbury*, [e'-e''], Bardic.
The isle, *P B Shelley*, [e'*b*-a''*b*], Bardic.
To Electra, *Robert Herrick*, [e'-a''], Bardic.

Bryceson Treharne. 1879 - 1948.
Olwen, [soprano/tenor], Snell.
The Mixon bell, [baritone], Snell.
The thorn, [baritone/bass], Gwynn.
The wind, [soprano/mezzo/tenor], Gwynn.

Antonín Tucapský. (BMIC.) 1928 -

Percy Turnbull. 1902 - 1976.
Collections: *Songs, Volume 1, Songs Volume 2*, Thames 1988.
A boy's song, *James Hogg*, F [c'-f''](m), Thames Songs 1.
Cavalier, *John Masefield*, Em [b-e''], Thames Songs 1.
Chloris in the snow, *William Strode*, E [b-e''], Thames Songs 1.
Ejaculation to God, *Robert Herrick*, Cm [d'-e''♭], Thames Songs 1.
Guess, guess, *Thomas Moore*, Am [e'-g''](m), Thames Songs 2.
If doughty deeds, *Walter Scott?* E [c'#-f''#](m), Thames Songs 2.
In Fountain Court, *Arthur Symons*, Dm [a-f''], Thames Songs 1.
My bed is a boat, *R L Stevenson*, F [c'-f''], Thames Songs 1.
My Mopsa is little, *Thomas Moore*, Em [e'-g''](m), Thames Songs 2.
Piping down the valleys wild, *William Blake*, C#m [c'#-e''], Thames Songs 1.
The moon (1st version), *R L Stevenson*, A [e'-e''], Thames Songs 2.
The moon (2nd version), *R L Stevenson*, A [e'-e''], Thames Songs 2.
The rainy day, *Henry Wadsworth Longfellow*, Am [g'-a''], Thames Songs 2.
The reminder (1st version), *Thomas Hardy*, C [g-e''], Thames Songs 1.
The reminder (2nd version), *Thomas Hardy*, [b♭-f''], Thames Songs 1.
To blossoms, *Robert Herrick*, F [e'♭-f''], Thames Songs 2.
To God, *Robert Herrick*, C#m [g#-e''], Thames Songs 1.
To Julia, *Robert Herrick*, F [e'-a''(f)](m),Thames Songs 2.
When daffodils begin to peer, *Shakespeare*, F#m [c'#-f''#](m), Thames Songs 2.

V

Charles Vale. 1912 - 1984.

Litany to the Holy Spirit, *Robert Herrick*, Fm [a*b*-f''], Banks.

Ralph Vaughan Williams. 1872 - 1958.

Collections: *The House of Life*, Ashdown 1904; *On Wenlock Edge*, B&H 1911; *Five Mystical Songs*, S&B 1911; *Merciless Beauty*, Faber 1922; (*Two Poems by Seumas O'Sullivan*, OUP 1925); *Songs of Travel* (high & low keys), B&H 1960; *Song Album Volume 1*, B&H 1985; *Song Album Volume 2*, B&H 1990; *Collected Songs Volume 1, Collected Songs Volume 2, Collected Songs Volume 3*, OUP 1993.

A clear midnight, *Walt Whitman*, G [e'-f''](m), OUP Collected 1.

A piper, *Seumas O'Sullivan*, [c'-e''], OUP 2 Poems.

Antiphon, *George Herbert*, D [e'*b*-f'(g'')], S&B 5 Mystical.

Blackmwore by the Stour, *William Barnes*, E [b-d''#], B&H Album 1; G, B&H.

Boy Johnny, *Christina Rossetti*, Em [b-e''], B&H Album 1.

Bredon Hill, *A E Housman*, [e'*b*-a''](m), B&H Wenlock Edge.

Bright is the ring of words, *R L Stevenson*, C [a*b*-d''*b*](m), B&H Travel; *F*, Travel; (*D*, B&H).

Buonaparty, *Thomas Hardy*, Dm [d'-e''](m), B&H Album 2, Thames *Hardy Songbook*..

Claribel, *Lord Tennyson*, Fm [c'-f''], B&H Album 1.

Clun, *A E Housman*, [d'-g''](m), B&H Wenlock Edge.

Cradle song, *S T Coleridge*, E*b* [c'-e''*b*], B&H Album 2.

Death in love, *D G Rossetti*, C [c'-e''], Ashdown House of Life.

Dream-land, *Christina Rossetti*, D*b* [d'*b*-f''], B&H Album 1.

Easter, *George Herbert*, E*b* [e'*b*-f''](m), S&B 5 Mystical.

Four nights, *Fredegond Shove*, [a*b*-e''*b*], OUP Collected 2.

From far, from eve and morning, *A E Housman*, [g'-e''](m), B&H Wenlock Edge.

Hands, eyes, and heart, *Ursula Vaughan Williams*, E*b* [c'-e''*b*], OUP Collected 1.

Heart's haven, *D G Rossetti*, E [c'#-e''](m), Ashdown House of Life; *D, F*, Ashdown.

How can the tree but wither? *Lord Vaux*, Cm [a-e''*b*], OUP Collected 2.

Hugh's Song of the Road, *Harold Child*, Fm [e'*b*-a''](m), Faber.

I got me flowers, *George Herbert*, G*b* [d'*b*-e''*b*], S&B 5 Mystical.

I have trod the upward and the downward slope, *R L Stevenson*, Dm [c'-d''](m), B&H Travel; *Gm* Travel.

If I were a queen, *Christina Rossetti*, E [b-e''], B&H Album 2.

In dreams, *R L Stevenson*, Cm [d'*b*-f''](m), B&H Songs of Travel; *Ebm*, Travel.

In the spring, *William Barnes*, D [c'#-e''](m), OUP Collected 2.

Is my team ploughing? *A E Housman*, [d'-a''](m), B&H Wenlock Edge.

Joy, shipmate, joy, *Walt Whitman*, G [e'-f''](m), OUP Collected 1.

Let beauty awake, *R L Stevenson*, [e'-e''](m), B&H Songs of Travel; *[g'-g'']*, Travel.

Let us now praise famous men, *Ecclesiasticus*, E [e'-g''#], Curwen.

Linden Lea, *William Barnes*, G [d'-e''], B&H Album 1; F, A, B&H.

Love bade me welcome, *George Herbert*, Em [d'-f''], S&B 5 Mystical.

Love-sight, *D G Rossetti*, A [b-e''], Ashdown House of Life.

Love's last gift, *D G Rossetti*, F [c'-f''], Ashdown House of Life.

Love's minstrels, *D G Rossetti*, D [a-e''](m), Ashdown House of Life.

Menelaus, *Ursula Vaughan Williams*, Cm [c'-e''], OUP Collected 1.
Motion and stillness, *Fredegond Shove*, [c'-d''], OUP Collected 2.
Nocturne, *Walt Whitman*, [b-f'](m), OUP Collected 1.
Oh, when I was in love with you, *A E Housman*, [g'-f'#](m), B&H Wenlock Edge.
On Wenlock Edge, *A E Housman*, [d'-g''](m), B&H Wenlock Edge.
(Orpheus with his lute (1), *Shakespeare*, G [d'-g''], Keith Prowse; *F*, Keith Prowse.)
Orpheus with his lute (2), *Shakespeare*, G [d'-f'#], OUP Collected 1.
Procris, *Ursula Vaughan Williams*, Em [c'-e''], OUP Collected 1.
See the chariot at hand, *Ben Jonson*, C [c'-f'#](m), OUP Collected 2.
Silent noon, *D G Rossetti*, E♭ [c'-e''♭], Ashdown House of Life; *D♭, F, G*, Ashdown.
Since I from Love escapéd am so fat, *Geoffrey Chaucer*, [a'-a''](m), Faber Merciless.
So hath your beauty from your hertë, *Geoffrey Chaucer*, Dm [e'-f''](m), Faber Merciless.
Take, O take, *Shakespeare*, Em [b-f''], OUP Collected 1.
Tears, idle tears, *Lord Tennyson*, Cm [b-f''], B&H Album 2.
The bird's song, *Psalm 23*, E♭ [d'♭-f''], Collected 3, OUP.
The call, *George Herbert*, E♭ [e'♭-f''], S&B 5 Mystical.
The infinite shining heavens, *R L Stevenson*, Dm [c'-e''](m), B&H Travel; *Fm*, Travel.
The new ghost, *Fredegond Shove*, [d'-f''], OUP Collected 2, Thames *Century 1*.
The oxen, *Thomas Hardy*, F#m [e'-f'#], OUP *Solo Christmas*, Dm, *Solo Christmas*.
The pilgrim's psalm, *St Paul & Psalms*, [d'-f''], OUP Collected 3.
The roadside fire, *R L Stevenson*, D♭ [b-e''](m), B&H Travel; *F*, Travel; *C*, *Heritage 1*.
The sky above the roof, *Paul Verlaine*, tr. *Mabel Dearmer*, Am [c'-e''], B&H Album 1, B&H.
The song of the leaves of life and the water of life, *Revelations*, [d'-e''], Collected 3.
The song of the pilgrims, *John Bunyan*, D [d'-e''], OUP Collected 3.
The song of Vanity Fair, *Ursula Wood*, E♭ [c'-f'♭], Collected 3.
The splendour falls, *Alfred Lord Tennyson*, C [e'-f''], B&H Album 1, B&H; (A♭, B♭, B&H).
The twilight people, *Seumas O'Sullivan*, [b♭-e''♭], OUP Collected 2; ([c'-f''], OUP 2 Poems.)
The vagabond, *R L Stevenson*, Cm [a-e''♭](m), B&H Travel, *Heritage 2*, B&H; *Em*, Travel, (B&H).
The water mill, *Fredegond Shove*, C [c'-d''], OUP Collected 2, *Solo Contralto*; E♭, OUP.
The winter's willow, *William Barnes*, A♭ [e'♭-g''](m), B&H Album 1; (F, B&H).
The woodcutter's song, *John Bunyan*, G [d'-e''], Collected 3.
Tired, *Ursula Vaughan Williams*, D♭ [b♭-d''♭], OUP Collected 1.
Watchful's song, *Psalms & Isaiah*, [c'#-e''], OUP Collected 3.
(When I am dead, my dearest, *Christina Rossetti*, Gm [g'-g''], Keith Prowse; Dm, Keith Prowse.)
When icicles hang by the wall, *Shakespeare*, Fm [e'♭-f''], OUP Collected 1.
Whither must I wander? *R L Stevenson*, E♭ [b♭-e''♭](m), B&H Travel, *Heritage 2*, B&H; *G*, Travel; (D, B&H).
Wither's rocking hymn, *George Wither*, Gm [f'-g''], OUP *Solo Christmas*, Em, *Solo Christmas*.
Your eyën two will slay me suddenly, *Geoffrey Chaucer*, Gm [c'-a''](m), Faber Merciless.
Youth and love, *R L Stevenson*, G [c'-e''](m), B&H Travel, *Heritage 2*; *B♭*, Travel.
Arrangements:
Greensleeves, *Anon*, Fm [c'-e''♭](m), OUP Collected 1.
L'amour de moy, *Anon*, tr. *Paul England*, C [c'-d''], B&H Album 1.
Reveillez-vous Piccarz, *Anon*, tr. *Paul England*, Em [d'-e''](m), B&H Album 2.
She's like the swallow, *Anon*, Dm [d'-f''](m), OUP *Solo Tenor*.
The Spanish Ladies, *Anon*, A [e'-e''](m), B&H Album 1.

W

Ernest Walker. 1870 - 1949.
Corinna's going a-maying, *Robert Herrick*, E♭[a-e"♭](m), B&H *Heritage 2*; (F, B&H).
(Sleep song, *Sydney Dobell*, Dm[d'-g"], OUP.)
(Summer rain, *Sydney Dobell*, D[c'-f'#], OUP.)

William Vincent Wallace. 1812 - 1865.
Cradle song, *Lord Tennyson*, A[a-c"#](f), S&B (Bush & Temperley) *MB 43*.

Newell Wallbank.
A great time, *W H Davies*, B♭[d'-g"], Lengnick.
I gave her cakes and I gave her ale, *Anon*, A[e'-a"], Lengnick.
It was a lover and his lass, *Shakespeare*, G[d'-g"], Lengnick.
Rhyme in the tropics, *Dorothy Una Radcliffe*, E♭[f'-f'#], Lengnick.

Leslie Walters. 1902 - (BMIC.)
Daffa-down-dilly, *W Graham Robertson*, D[d'-d"], Gwynn *Three Spring Songs*.
(Plesant Grounde, *Anon*, E♭[c'-g"], Chappell.)
(Spring, the travelling man, *Winifred Letts*, F[e'-a"(g")], Cramer.)
(The singer and the song, *A J Redpath*, D[d'-f'#], Chappell.)
(When I set out for Lyonesse, *Thomas Hardy*, Em[b(d')-e"(g")](m), Cramer.)

Richard Walthew. 1872 - 1951. Another 30 songs in B&H archive.
Mistress mine, *Shakespeare*, B♭[c'-f"](m), B&H *Heritage 1*.
The splendour falls, *Lord Tennyson*, E♭[b♭-e"♭], B&H *Heritage 2*.

William Walton. 1902 - 1983.
Collection: (*Three Songs*, OUP 1932); (*A Song for the Lord Mayor's Table*, OUP 1962); *A Song Album*, OUP 1991.
Beatriz's song, *Louis MacNeice*, Dm[f'-d"](f), OUP Album.
Daphne, *Edith Sitwell*, [c'-a"](f), OUP Album, (3 Songs).
Fain would I change that note, *Anon*, [c'#-a"](m), OUP Album.
Glide gently, *William Wordsworth*, [a-g"](f), OUP Album, (Lord Mayor).
Holy Thursday, *William Blake*, [b-g"](f), OUP Album, (Lord Mayor).
I gave her cakes and I gave her ale, *Anon*, [d'-b"♭](m), OUP Album.
Lady, when I behold the roses, *Anon*, [c'-a"](m), OUP Album.
My love in her attire, *Anon*, [c'-a"](m), OUP Album.
O stay, sweet love, *Anon*, [c'-g"♭](m), OUP Album.
Old Sir Faulk, *Edith Sitwell*, [c'#-g"], OUP Album, (3 Songs).
Rhyme, *Anon*, [c'-g"](f), OUP Album, (Lord Mayor).
The contrast, *Charles Morris*, C[b♭-g"](f), OUP Album, (Lord Mayor).
The Lord Mayor's table, *Thomas Jordan*, A♭[b♭-a"♭](f), OUP Album, (Lord Mayor).
The winds, *A C Swinburne*, Em[e'♭-a"](f), OUP Album.
Through gilded trellises, *Edith Sitwell*, c'#-a"](f), OUP Album, (3 Songs).

To couple is a custom, *Anon*, [c'-a''](m), OUP Album.
Tritons, *William Drummond*, [e'-a''], OUP Album.
Under the greenwood tree, *Shakespeare*, Gm [d'-g''], OUP Album.
Wapping Old Stairs, *Anon*, Gm [c'-f'#](f), OUP Album, (Lord Mayor).

Peter Warlock. 1894 - 1930.
Collections: (*Saudades*, Chester 1923); *Peterisms, 1st Set*, Chester 1923; (*Lilligay*, Chester 1923); (*Candlelight*, S&B 1924); *A Book of Songs*, OUP 1931; *A Second Book of Songs*, OUP 1967; *Song Album*, B&H 1967; *13 Songs for High Voice*, S&B 1970; *Eight Songs*, Thames 1972; *Songs Volumes 1-8*, Thames 1982-93.
A lake and a fairy boat, *Thomas Hood*, [d'-g''b](m), Thames 8 Songs, Songs 1.
A prayer to St Anthony of Padua, *Arthur Symons*, Eb [e'-b-e''b], OUP 2nd Book; Db, Thames Songs 6.
A sad song, *John Fletcher*, Bm [e'#-f''], ; Chester Peterisms 1; Am, Thames Songs 4.
Adam lay ybounden, *Anon*, Cm [c'-f''], Thames Songs 3.
After two years, *Richard Aldington*, Db [d'-b-f''](m), Thames Songs 8.
Along the stream, *Li Po*, tr. *L Cranmer Byng*, [e'-f''#], Thames Songs 1, (Chester Saudades).
And wilt thou leave me thus? *Thomas Wyatt*, Bbm [c'#-f''], OUP Book of Songs, Thames Songs 8.
As ever I saw, *Anon*, Db [d'-b-g''b](m), B&H Songs, Thames Songs 2; Eb, Mayhew *Collection 1*.
Arthur O'Bower, *Anon*, Gb [b'-bb-g''b], Thames Songs 5; (Ab, S&B Candlelight).
Autumn twilight, *Arthur Symons*, Cm [c'-e''b], Thames Songs 4.
Away to Twiver, *Anon*, Bm [d'-f'#], OUP 2nd Book, Thames Songs 6.
Balulalow, *Martin Luther*, tr. *Wedderburn*, Eb [e'-b-f''], Thames Songs 2, OUP *Solo Christmas*; C, *Solo Christmas*.
Bethlehem Down, *Bruce Blunt*, Dm [c'#-e''b], Thames Songs 8, B&H.
Burd Ellen and young Tamlane, *Anon*, Gm [d'-f'#], Thames Songs 4; (Am, Chester Lilligay) .
Captain Stratton's fancy, *John Masefield*, F [c'-f''](m), S&B 13 Songs, S&B, Thames Songs 3, Mayhew *Singer's Collection 2*; D, S&B; (G, S&B).
Carillon, carilla, *Hilaire Belloc*, G [c'-e''], Thames Songs 8.
Chanson du jour de noël, *Clément Marot*, tr. *David Cox*, A [e'-f'#], Thames Songs 6; (C, B&H).
Chopcherry, *George Peele*, A [e'-e''](m) Chester Peterisms 1, *Celebrated 2*, Thames Songs 4.
Consider, *Ford Madox Ford*, Eb [bb-f''], Thames Songs 4; (F, OUP).
Cradle song, *John Philip*, Dm [d'-f''](f), OUP Book of Songs, Thames Songs 7.
Dedication, *Philip Sidney*, Bb [bb-f''](m), Thames Songs 2; (Db, B&H).
Eloré lo, *Anon*, F [c'-f''](m), S&B 13 Songs, *Recitalist 4*, Thames Songs 8.
Fair and true, *Nicholas Breton*, Eb [e'-b-e''b],OUP Book of Songs, Thames Songs 6.
Fill the cup, Philip, *Anon*, Eb [bb-e''b](m), Thames 8 Songs, Songs 8.
Good ale, *Anon*, F [c'-f''](m), Thames Songs 3; (Ab, S&B).
Ha'nacker mill, *Hilaire Belloc*, Dm [c'-f''], OUP 2nd Book, Thames Songs 7.
Heraclitus, *Callimachus*, tr. *W J Cory*, [c'-f''], Thames Songs 1, (Chester Saudades).
Hey, troly loly lo, *Anon*, [c'-f''], S&B 13 Songs, Thames Songs 3.
How many miles to Babylon, *Anon*, Fm [f'-f''], Thames Songs 5, (S&B Candlelight).
I asked a thief to steal me a peach, *William Blake*, Eb [c'-f''](m), Thames 8 Songs, Songs 1.
I had a little pony, *Anon*, Cm [c'-e''], Thames Songs 5, (S&B Candlelight).
I have a garden, *Thomas Moore*, Dm [d'-e''], Thames Songs 5.
I held love's head, *Robert Herrick*, Fm [c'-f''], Thames Songs 5.

I won't be my father's Jack, *Anon*, Eb [d'-c''], Thames Songs 5, (S&B Candlelight).

In an arbour green, *Robert Wever*, F [c'-f''](m), Thames Songs 4; (G, Paterson).

Jennie Gray, *Anon*, Em [d'-e''], Thames Songs 5.

Jillian of Berry, *Beaumont & Fletcher?*, Bb [d'-f''](m) OUP Book of Songs, Thames Songs 6.

Johnnie wi' the tye, *Anon*, *[c'-f'']*(m), Thames Songs 4; ([d'-g''], Chester Lilligay).

Late summer, *Edward Shanks*, E [b-f'#], S&B 13 Songs, Thames Songs 3.

Little Jack Jingle, *Anon*, F [c'-f''], Thames Songs 5, (S&B Candlelight).

Little Tommy Tucker, *Anon*, G [d'-e''], Thames Songs 5, (S&B Candlelight).

Little trotty wagtail, *John Clare*, Dm [c'-f''], Thames Songs 3.

Love for love, *Anon*, E [b-e''](m); G, Mayhew *Collection 2*.

Lullaby, *Thomas Dekker*, Dm [a(b)-d''], B&H Songs, Thames Songs 2; (F, B&H).

Lusty Juventus, *Robert Wever*, C [d'-a''(g'')](m), OUP 2nd Book; A, Thames Songs 4.

Maltworms, *Bishop Still?*, F [c'-f''](m), OUP 2nd Book, Thames Songs 6.

Milkmaids, *Anon*, F [d'-g''], Thames Songs 4; (G, Enoch; E, Enoch).

Mockery, *Shakespeare*, [e'-g''], OUP 2nd Book; *[d'-f']*, Thames Songs 7.

Mourn no more, *John Fletcher*, C [c'-f''], Thames Songs 2; (Eb, B&H).

Mr Belloc's fancy, *John Squire*, G [d'-g''](m), S&B 13 Songs; Eb, Thames Songs 3.

Music, when soft voices die, *P B Shelley*, F [d'-f''], Thames 8 Songs, Songs 1.

My gostly fader, *Charles D'Orleans?* G [e'-b-f'#], B&H Songs, Thames Songs 2; (E, B&H).

My little sweet darling, *Anon*, G [b-g''](f), B&H *Heritage 3*; F, Thames Songs 2; (E, B&H).

My own country, *Hilaire Belloc*, F [c'-e''], OUP 2nd Book, Thames Songs 7, Ab, OUP.

O my kitten, *Anon*, C [c'-e''], Thames Songs 5; (D, S&B Candlelight).

One more river, *Anon*, F [c'-d''], Thames Songs 6.

Passing by, *Anon*, G [d'-g''](m), OUP Book of Songs, Thames Songs 7.

Peter Warlock's fancy, *Anon*, Eb [bb-e''b](m), Thames Songs 5; (F, Paterson).

Piggesnie, *Anon*, G [d'-g''](m), S&B 13 Songs, Mayhew *Collection 2*; F, Thames Songs 3; (E, S&B).

Play-acting, *Anon*, Em [b-g''](m), Thames 8 Songs, Songs 3.

Pretty ring-time, *Shakespeare*, Eb [d'-g''(f'), OUP Book of Songs, Thames Songs 6.

Queen Anne, *Anon*, C [e'-e''](f), Thames Songs 7.

Rantum-tantum, *Victor Neuburg*, C [c'-f''], Thames Songs 4; (Db, Chester Lilligay).

Rest, sweet nymphs, *Anon*, F [f'-f''], OUP Book of Songs, *Solo Tenor*, Thames Songs 3.

Robin and Richard, *Anon*, A [d'#-e''], Thames Songs 5, (S&B Candlelight).

Robin Goodfellow, *Anon*, A [e'-f'#], OUP Book of Songs, Thames Songs 6.

Roister Doister, *Nicholas Udall*, F [f'-d''](m), OUP 2nd Book, Thames Songs 4, Mayhew *Collection 1*.

Romance, *R L Stevenson*, Bb [bb-f''](m), Thames Songs 2.

Rutterkin, *John Skelton?*, Ab [e'-b-a''], Chester Peterisms 1; F, Thames Songs 4.

Sigh no more, ladies, *Shakespeare*, Eb [e'-b-f''], OUP Book of Songs, Thames Songs 7.

Sleep, *John Fletcher*, Gm [d'-e''b], OUP Book of Songs, *Solo Baritone*, OUP, Thames Songs 3.

Spring the sweet spring, *Thomas Nashe*, Ab [c'-g''b], OUP 2nd Book; G, Thames Songs 4.

Suky, you shall be my wife, *Anon*, Eb [e'-b-f''], Thames Songs 5, (S&B Candlelight).

Sweet-and-twenty, *Shakespeare*, Ab [e'-f''](m), OUP 2nd Book; G, Thames Songs 5.

Sweet content, *Thomas Dekker*, G [d'-g''], B&H Songs, *Heritage 4*; F, Thames Songs 2.

Take, O take those lips away (1), *Shakespeare*, Fm [c'-f''], Thames Songs 1, (Chester Saudades).

Take, O take those lips away (2), *Shakespeare*, Em [b-f'#], B&H Songs, *Heritage 4*; F#, Thames Songs 2, (B&H).

The bachelor, *Anon*, F#m [c'#-f''#](m), S&B 13 Songs; *E*, Thames Songs 3.

The baily berith the bell away, *Anon*, E♭ [g-e''♭], B&H Songs; *F*, Thames Songs 2; (*G*, B&H).

The birds, *Hilaire Belloc*, E♭ [d'-e''♭], Thames Songs 6, Mayhew *Collection 1*.

The cloths of heaven, *W B Yeats*, [c'-g''], Thames Songs 1.

The contented lover, *James Mabbe*, A♭ [e'♭-a''♭](m), S&B 13 Songs, *Recitalist 3*; *F*, Thames Songs 8.

The countryman, *John Chalkhill*, F [c'-f''], B&H Songs, Thames Songs 6; (A♭, B&H).

The cricketers of Hambledon, *Bruce Blunt*, E♭ [b♭-f''](m), S&B 13 Songs, Thames Songs 8.

The distracted maid, *Anon*, B♭m [d'♭-f''], Thames Songs 4, (Chester Lilligay).

The droll lover, *Anon*, F [b-e''♭](m), S&B 13 Songs, Thames Songs 8.

The everlasting voices, *W B Yeats*, B♭m [e'♭-a''♭(g''♭)], Thames Songs 1.

The first mercy, *Bruce Blunt*, [f'-f''], B&H Songs, B&H, Thames Songs 7.

The fox, *Bruce Blunt*, Dm [d'-f''#], Thames Songs 8.

The frostbound wood, *Bruce Blunt*, [d'-e''], Thames Songs 8.

The jolly shepherd, *Anon*, G [c'-e''(g'')], Thames Songs 7; *A* B&H Songs.

The lover mourns for the loss of love, *W B Yeats*, [d'-e''♭](m), Thames Songs 1.

The lover's maze, *Thomas Campion?*, Fm [e'♭-f''], OUP Book of Songs, Thames Songs 7.

The magpie, *Harry Hunter*, E [b-e''], Thames Songs 5.

The night, *Hilaire Belloc*, Em [d'-e''], OUP 2nd Book, Thames Songs 7.

The passionate shepherd, *Christopher Marlowe*, F [c'-f''](m), Thames Songs 8; (*G*, Elkin).

The shoemaker, *Anon*, B♭m [f'-f''], Thames Songs 4, (Chester Lilligay).

The sick heart, *Arthur Symons*, [c'-g''], OUP 2nd Book; *[b♭-f'']*, Thames Songs 6.

The singer, *Edward Shanks*, F [c'-f''], Thames Songs 3; (*G*, S&B).

The sweet o' the year, *Shakespeare*, F [c'-f''](m), Thames Songs 8.

The toper's song, *Anon*, Em [b-e''](m), Thames Songs 5.

The water lily, *Robert Nichols*, [d'-g''], Thames 8 Songs, Songs 1.

The wind from the west, *Ella Young*, E♭ [d'-f''], Thames 8 Songs, Songs 1.

There is a lady sweet and kind, *Anon*, B♭ [b♭-f''](m), B&H Songs, Thames Songs 2; (*D♭*, B&H).

There was a man of Thessaly, *Anon*, F#m [b-d''], Thames Songs 5, (S&B Candlelight).

There was an old man, *Anon*, B♭m [f'-f''], Thames Songs 5, (S&B Candlelight).

There was an old woman, *Anon*, Fm [c'-f''], Thames Songs 5, (S&B Candlelight).

Thou gav'st me leave to kiss, *Robert Herrick*, G [d'-f''], Thames Songs 5.

To the memory of a great singer, *R L Stevenson*, A♭ [d'♭-g''], S&B 13 Songs; *G♭*, Thames Songs 1.

Tom Tyler, *Anon*, G [d'-f''#(g'')](m), S&B 13 Songs, Thames Songs 8.

Twelve oxen, *Anon*, E [b-e''], OUP Book of Songs, Thames Songs 5.

Tyrley tyrlow, *Anon*, Am [e'-f''], Thames Songs 3.

Walking the woods, *Anon*, F [c'-f''](m), B&H Songs, Thames Songs 7.

What cheer? good cheer, *Anon*, E♭ [b-e''♭], Thames Songs 7.

Whenas the rye reach to the chin, *George Peele*, G [c'(d')-f''](m), B&H Songs, *Heritage 4*; *F*, Thames Songs 2, (B&H).

Where riches is everlastingly, *Anon*, Dm [d'-f''], Thames Songs 7.

Yarmouth Fair, *Hal Collins*, F [c'-f''](m), Thames Songs 5; *E*, *D*, OUP (*G*, OUP).

Youth, *Robert Wever*, F [c'-f''](m), Thames Songs 8.

Raymond Warren. 1928 -

Songs of old age (cycle), *W B Yeats*, [a'-g''], Novello.

William Webb. *c.*1620 - 1656.
As life what is so sweet, *Anon,* Cm [c'-e''*b*], S&B (Spink), *Recitalist 2.*
Of thee, kind boy, Dm [d'-f'](m), *Dolmetsch 1.*
Since 'tis my fate to be thy slave, *Anon,* G [e'-e''](m), S&B (Spink) *Cavalier Songs.*

Judith Weir. 1954 -
Collections: *Songs from the Exotic,* Chester 1991; *Scotch Minstrelsy,* Novello.
Bessie Bell and Mary Gray, [high], Novello Scotch Minstrelsy.
Bonnie James Campbell, [high], Novello Scotch Minstrelsy.
In the lovely village of Nevesinje, *Anon,* [b-e''], Chester Exotic.
Lady Isobel and the elf-knight, [high], Novello Scotch Minstrelsy.
(On buying a horse, *Anon,* [d'-f''](f), Chester.)
Sevdalino, my little one, *Anon,* [c'#-c''], Chester Exotic.
The braes of Yarrow, [high], Novello Scotch Minstrelsy.
The gypsy laddie, [high], Novello Scotch Minstrelsy.
The romance of Count Arnaldos, *Anon,* [a-e''], Chester Exotic.
The song of a girl ravished away by the fairies in South Uist, *Anon,* [b-f'#], Chester Exotic.

John Weldon. 1676 - 1736.
Alleluia, Gm [f'-g''], B&H (Britten) Two Divine Hymns and Alleluia (attributed to Purcell in error).
Arise, ye subterranean winds, *Thomas Shadwell,* C [E-d'], International (Kagen) 6 Songs for Bass, B&H (Northcote) *New Imperial 6* (attributed to Purcell in error).
Fair and serene, *Thomas Shadwell,* Cm [g-e'*b*], Thames (Bevan) *6 Restoration.*
From grave lessons, *Anon,* D [d'-g''] S&B (Pilkington) *Georgian 2.*
Halcyon days, *Thomas Shadwell,* C [d'-g''], Novello (Dent) 15 Songs 1; *A,* 15 Songs 1 (attributed to Purcell in error).
He will not suffer thy foot to be moved, *Psalm 121, v. 3,* A [c'#-e''], B&H (Patrick) *Sacred Songs.*
My dear, my Amphitrite, *see* Fair and serene.
The Lord shall preserve thee from all evil, *Psalm 121, v. 7,* A [e'-f'#], B&H (Patrick) *Sacred Songs.*
The wakeful nightingale, *Anon,* Gm [d'-f''], S&B (Pilkington) *Georgian 1, Recitalist 2; (Am,* B&H (Keel) *12 18th Century).*
Your awful voice, *Thomas Shadwell, Bb [d'-g''],* International (Kagen) 40 Songs 2, Novello (Dent) 15 Songs 2; *G,* 40 Songs 2, 15 Songs 2 (attributed to Purcell in error).

Egon Wellesz. 1885 - 1974.
Collection: (*On Time,* Lengnick 1950).
(Ah! fading joy, *John Dryden,* Cm [c-e'](m), Lengnick On Time.)
(On time, *John Milton,* C [c'-e''](m), Lengnick On Time.)
(The poet and the day, *Elizabeth Mackenzie, Eb* [B*b*b-e'](m), Lengnick On Time.)

Samuel Wesley. 1766 - 1837.
Might I in thy sight appear, *Charles Wesley,* F [c'-f''], S&B (Bush & Temperley) *MB 43.*
What shaft of fate's relentless power, *Anon,* Gm [a-a''], S&B (Bush & Temperley) *MB 43.*

Samuel Sebastian Wesley. 1810 - 1876.
Collect for the Third Sunday in Advent, *Cranmer,* F [b*b*(G)-f'](m), S&B (Bush & Temperley) *MB 43.*

By the rivers of Babylon, *Lord Byron*, Em [d'#-f'#], S&B (Bush and Temperley) *MB 43.*

J A Westrup. 1904 - 1975.
(Come away, death, *Shakespeare*, [f'#-a''], S&B.)
(Orpheus with his lute, *Shakespeare*, [f'-a'*b*], S&B.)
(Take, O take those lips away, *Shakespeare*, [d'*b*-a''], S&B.)

H Burgess Weston.
Row, burnie, row, *Walter D Smith*, E*b* [b*b*-e''*b*](f), B&H *Heritage 2*; (D, F, G, B&H).
(Song of the North, *Walter C Smith*, D, B&H.)

Eric Wetherell. 1925 -
Collection: *Three Shakespeare Sonnets*, Thames 1996.
How like a winter, *Shakespeare*, B*b* [b*b*-d''], Thames 3 Shakespeare.
Let me not, *Shakespeare*, F [c'-d''], Thames 3 Shakespeare.
Shall I compare thee? *Shakespeare*, Dm [b*b*-e''], Thames 3 Shakespeare.

Maude Valérie White. 1855 - 1937. 15 more songs in B&H archive.
Collection: *Two Love Songs*, Banks 1993; *Three Little Songs*, Banks 1995.
A memory, *Anon*, [medium], Banks 3 Little Songs.
A youth once loved a maiden, *Heine*, tr. *M V White*, Am [d'#-f''], Banks 2 Love Songs.
Crabbed age and youth, *Shakespeare?*, F [a(g)-d''], B&H *Heritage 1.*
Let us forget, *Goethe* tr. *M Darmesteter*, [medium], Banks 3 Little Songs.
Ophelia's song, *Shakespeare*, Em [d'-f''], B&H *Heritage 2.*
(So we'll go no more a-roving, *Lord Byron*, C [b-e''], *Chappell* English Recital 1; D*b*, E, Chappell).
When I think on the happy days, *Robert Burns*, Am [e'-f''], Banks 2 Love Songs.
When the swallows homeward fly, *German Volkslied* tr. *Anon*, [medium], Banks 3 Little Songs.

Robin le Rougetel White. See also BMIC.
Where shall we adventure? (cycle), *R L Stevenson*, [d'-g''#], Banks.

William Giles Whittaker. 1876 - 1944. (SMIC.)

Ian Whyte. 1901 - 1960. (see also SMIC.)
(I love you my dear, *Don Whyte*, F [c'-f''], Curwen.)

David Willcocks. 1919 -
Arrangements:
Sussex Carol, *Anon*, G [d'-e''], OUP *Solo Christmas.*
The infant king, *S Baring-Gould*, F [c'-f'], OUP *Solo Christmas*, D, *Solo Christmas.*

Grace Williams. 1906 - 1977.
Thou art the one truth, *Dhan Gopal Mukerji*, [G-f'#](m), Welsh Music.
To death, *Caroline Southey*, Am [c'#-a''], Welsh Music *Songs from Wales 1.*
Arrangements:
Jim Crow, *Anon*, Gwynn.
The loom, *Grace Williams*, Gm [b*b*-e''*b*](f), OUP *Solo Soprano*, OUP.
(Watching the wheat, *Wil Hopkin* tr. *Grace Williams*, E [d'#-f'#](m), OUP.)

Meiron Williams. 1901 - 1976.
Ora pro nobis, [mezzo/baritone/bass], Gwynn.
The blossoms by my door, *John Evans* tr. *Caerwyn*, Fm [c'-a''], Gwynn.

W Albert Williams. 1909 - 1946.
By the sea, *Huw Emrys Griffith* tr. *Caerwyn*, Dm [d'-e''], Gwynn.
The wind's lament, *John Morris-Jones* tr. *H Idris Bell*, Dm [bb-f''], Gwynn.

W Matthews Williams. 1885-1972.
Bronwen, Bb [soprano/tenor], Snell.
John of the glen, *Lewis Glyn Cothi* tr. *H Idris Bell*, Cm [c'-f''], Gwynn.
Llanfihangel Bachellaeth, *Cynan* tr. *H Idris Bell*, Fm [c'-e''b(f')], Gwynn.
My land, *Dewi Havnesp* tr. *T Gwynn Jones*, F [c'-f''], Gwynn.

W S Gwynn Williams. 1896 - 1978.
Collection: *Three Welsh Lyrics*, Gwynn.
A prayer, *John Newton*, Eb [e'b-e''b], Gwynn *Three Spring Songs*.
Fairies, *T Gwynn Jones* tr. *Anon*, Fm [e'b-f''], Gwynn 3 Lyrics, Gwynn.
Glyndwr's dream, *Emyr* tr. *H Idris Bell*, Gm [d'-e''b], Gwynn 3 Lyrics, Gwynn.
God's mercy, [mezzo/baritone], Gwynn; [soprano/tenor], Gwynn.
The apple tree, *I D Hooson* tr. *H Idris Bell*, Gm [d'-f''], Gwynn 3 Lyrics, Gwynn.
The skylark, *James Hogg*, Eb [d'-g''], Gwynn.

Malcolm Williamson. 1931 -
Collections: *Six English Lyrics*, Weinberger 1967; *From a Child's Garden*, Weinberger 1968; *A Vision of Beasts and Gods*, B&H 1969; *Three Shakespeare Songs*, Weinberger 1973.
A birthday, *Christina Rossetti*, G [b-d''], Weinberger 6 Lyrics.
A Christmas carol, *G K Chesterton*, D [c'#-d''], Weinberger.
A good boy, *R L Stevenson*, F [e'-f''], Weinberger Child's Garden.
Celebration of Divine Love (cycle), *James McAuley*, [d'b-c'''], Novello.
Come away, death, *Shakespeare*, Em [e'-f'#], Weinberger 3 Shakespeare.
Crossing the bar, *Alfred Lord Tennyson*, C [b-d''], Weinberger 6 Lyrics.
Dedication, *George Barker*, [f'-f'#], B&H A Vision.
Epitaph for many young men, *George Barker*, [d'#-g''], B&H A Vision.
Fear no more the heat of the sun, *Shakespeare*, [c'-a''b], Weinberger 3 Shakespeare.
From a railway carriage, *R L Stevenson*, [e'b-a''b], Weinberger Child's Garden.
Full fathom five, *Shakespeare*, (unaccompanied), [db-f'#], Weinberger 3 Shakespeare.
Go, lovely rose, *Edmund Waller*, F [c'-c''](m), Weinberger 6 Lyrics.
Happy thought, *R L Stevenson*, Gm [a'-a''], Weinberger Child's Garden.
Jenny kiss'd me, *Leigh Hunt*, [c'-d''], Weinberger 6 Lyrics.
Looking forward, *R L Stevenson*, Ebm [e'b-a''b], Weinberger Child's Garden.
Love letter, *George Barker*, [e'-a''b], B&H A Vision.
Marching song, *R L Stevenson*, [e'b-f''], Weinberger Child's Garden.
My bed is a boat, *R L Stevenson*, Gb [f'-g''b], Weinberger Child's Garden.
On the death of Manolette, *George Barker*, [d'-a''], B&H A Vision.
Rain, *R L Stevenson*, D [g'-g''], Weinberger Child's Garden.
Sweet and low, *Alfred Lord Tennyson*, Eb [d'b-d''](f), Weinberger 6 Lyrics.

H Lane Wilson

The ballad of wild children, *George Barker*, [e'-a''], B&H A Vision.
The flowers, *R L Stevenson*, F [f'-f''#], Weinberger Child's Garden.
The lamplighter, *R L Stevenson*, A [e'-f''#], Weinberger Child's Garden.
Time to rise, *R L Stevenson*, [d'-g''b], Weinberger Child's Garden.
To a child, *George Barker*, [f'-g''], B&H A Vision.
When I am dead, *Christina Rossetti*, F#m, [a-e''b], Weinberger 6 Lyrics.
Where go the boats? *R L Stevenson*, A [e'-e''], Weinberger Child's Garden.
Whole duty of children, *R L Stevenson*, Eb [f'-a''b], Weinberger Child's Garden.
Arrangements: *North Country Songs*, Weinberger 1966.
Adam Buckham O! *Anon*, [a-b'b], Weinberger North Country.
Bonny at morn, *Anon*, [bb-c''], Weinberger North Country.
Captain Bover, *Anon*, F [c'-e''b], Weinberger North Country.
Derwentwater's farewell, *Anon*, [bb-c''], Weinberger North Country.

H Lane Wilson. 1871 - 1915. These songs are unattributed, and they may be original compositions.
Collection: *Old English Melodies*, B&H 1899.
Ah! willow, *Anon*, Gm [b-c''], B&H *Old English.*
Come let's be merry, *Anon*, Bb [b-e''(f')], B&H *Old English.*
False Phillis, *Anon*, A [a-d''](m), B&H *Old English.*
Ralph's ramble to London, *Anon*, F [c'-e''](m), B&H *Old English.*
The happy lover, *Anon*, Eb [bb-e''b](m), B&H *Old English.*
The sailor's life, *Anon*, E [b-e''](m), B&H *Old English.*
The slighted swain, *Anon*, C [c'-d''](m), B&H *Old English.*

John Wilson. 1595 - 1674.
In a season all oppressed, *Anon*, Am [g'#-e''], S&B (Spink) *Cavalier Songs.*
Since love hath in thine and mine eye, *Anon*, Eb [d'-f''], S&B (Spink) *Cavalier Songs.*
Take, O take those lips away, *Shakespeare*, Gm [g'-g''], S&B (Spink) *Cavalier Songs.*
Wherefore peep'st thou, envious day? *John Donne?* G [g'-a''], S&B (Spink) *Cavalier Songs.*

Arthur Wills. 1926 - (BMIC.)

James Wilson. 1922 - (BMIC.)

Thomas Wilson. 1927 - (BMIC.)

Geoffrey Winters. 1928 - (BMIC.)

Peter Wishart. 1921 - 1984.
Collection: (*Two Songs*, OUP 1953); *Two Shakespeare Songs*, Banks 1989; *Twelve Songs* (introduction by Brian Trowell), S&B 1993; (See also BMIC).
Bird of paradise, *Robert Graves*, [medium], Banks.
Cat goddesses, *Robert Graves*, [c'#-f''], S&B 12 Songs.
(Dirge, *Shakespeare*, Fm [e'b-f''], OUP 2 Songs.)
Fidele, *Shakespeare*, Fm [e'b-f''], Banks.
Henry and Mary, *Robert Graves*, C [c'-e''], S&B 12 Songs.
Lament, *Anon*, D [b-f''](f), S&B 12 Songs.
My God, why hast thou forsaken me?, *St Augustine*, G [bb-c''], S&B 12 Songs.

O mistress mine, *Shakespeare*, [medium], Banks 2 Shakespeare.
Orpheus with his lute, *Shakespeare*, [medium], Banks 2 Shakespeare.
Spring sadness, *Anon*, tr. *Helen Waddell*, B [c'#-f'#], S&B 12 Songs.
The bedpost, *Robert Graves*, G [d'-f'#], S&B 12 Songs.
The jackdaw, *William Cooper*, Em [c'-e''], S&B 12 Songs.
The magpie, *James McAuley*, A [a'-f'#], S&B 12 Songs.
(The mountebank's song, *Anon*, F [e'-a''](m), OUP 2 Songs.)
The pessimist, *Benjamin King*, D [d'-d''], S&B 12 Songs.
Tune for swans, *James McAuley*, [e'-f''], S&B 12 Songs.
You are a refuge, *St Augustine*, Cm [c'-c''], S&B 12 Songs.

Charles Wood. 1866 - 1926.
Collection: (*Five Songs for High Voice*, B&H 1927); (*Ten Songs for Low Voice*, B&H 1927).
  (Ask me no more, *Alfred Lord Tennyson*, Eb, B&H 5 Songs High, B&H.)
  (At sea, *Moira O'Neill*, B&H 10 Songs Low.)
  (At the mid hour of night, *Thomas Moore*, F, B&H 5 Songs High, B&H.)
  (Birds, *Moira O'Neill*, B&H 10 Songs Low.)
  (Darest thou now, O soul, *Walt Whitman*, B&H 10 Songs Low.)
  (Denny's daughter, *Moira O'Neill*, B&H 10 Songs Low.)
  (Echo, *Christina Rossetti*, Db, B&H 5 Songs High, B&H.)
  Ethiopia saluting the colours, *Walt Whitman*, A [a-d''], Thames *Century 2*; (Ab, Bb B&H)
  (Fortune and her wheel, *Alfred Lord Tennyson*, B&H 5 Songs High.)
  (Goldthred's song, *Walter Scott*, Dm, B&H 10 Songs Low, B&H.)
  (Holy Thursday, *William Blake*, Am, B&H.)
  (O Captain! my captain, *Walt Whitman*, Bb, B&H.)
  (One morning in May, *Alfred Percival Graves*, Eb, B&H.)
  (Shall I forget? *Christina Rossetti*, B&H 10 Songs Low.)
  (Song of the Cyclops, *Thomas Dekker*, Cm, B&H 10 Songs Low, B&H.)
  (The dead at Clonmacnois, *Enoch O'Gillan* tr. *T W Rolleston*, Eb, B&H 10 Songs Low, B&H.)
  (The outlaw of Loch Lene, *Anon* tr. *J J Callanan*, B&H.)
  (The potato song, *Alfred Percival Graves*, B&H.)
  (The rover, *Walter Scott*, B&H 10 Songs Low.)
  (The sailorman, *Moira O'Neill*, B&H 10 Songs Low.)
  (The splendour falls, *Alfred Lord Tennyson*, B&H 5 Songs High.)
Arrangements: (*Irish Folk Songs — Twentyfive Old Irish melodies*, B&H 1897); *Seven Irish Folksongs*, Thames 1982.
  Curly locks, *P J M'Call*, Eb [bb-f''](m), Thames 7 Irish.
  His home and his own country, *Emily H Hickey*, Fm [e'b-a''b](f), Thames 7 Irish.
  Oh, the marriage, *Thomas Davis*, Dm [c'-f''](f), Thames 7 Irish.
  Oliver's advice, *William Blacker*, Dm [d'-f''](m), Thames 7 Irish.
  Sho-ho (or Lullaby), *Alfred Percival Graves*, Eb [e'b-f''](f), Thames 7 Irish.
  The battle-eve of the brigade, *Thomas Davis*, Eb [bb-e''b](m), Thames 7 Irish.
  The drinaun dhun, *Robert Dwyer Joyce*, Bb [bb-d''](m), Thames 7 Irish.

Haydn Wood. 1882 - 1959.
  (Memories of yesterday, *Lilian Glanville*, G d'-g''], Chappell *English Recital 2.)*

Hugh Wood. 1932 -
Collections: *(The Horses, Op 10,* Chester 1968); *Robert Graves Songs Set 1, Op 18,* Chester 1987; *(Graves Songs Set 2, Op 22,* Chester 1986; *Songs, Op 23,* Chester 1984; *Graves Songs Set 3, Op 25,* Chester 1986).
A last poem, *Robert Graves,* [c'-b''*b*](m), Chester Graves 1.
Always, *Robert Graves,* [d'*b*-a''], Chester Graves 1.
(Amor, *Pablo Neruda* tr. *Alastair Reid,* [d'*b*-b''*b*], Chester Op 23.)
(Bird of Paradise, *Robert Graves,* [d'*b*-b''*b*](m), Chester Graves 3.)
(Dog-tired, *D H Lawrence,* [c'-b''*b*](m), Chester Op 23.)
(Fragment, *Robert Graves,* [d'-a''*b*], Chester Graves 2.)
(Gloire de Dijon, *D H Lawrence,* [c'#-b''*b*](m), Chester Op 23.)
(Home from abroad, *Laurie Lee,* [d'*b*-b''*b*], Chester Op 23.)
(Ice, *Stephen Spender,* [d'-a''], Chester Op 23.)
(Lines to Mr Hodgson, *Lord Byron,* [a-c''](f), Chester.)
(Ouzo unclouded, *Robert Graves,* [d'-a''], Chester Graves 2.)
(Penines in April, *Ted Hughes,* [a-b''], Chester The Horses.)
Records, *Robert Graves,* [b-b''*b*](m), Chester Graves 1.
(Seldom yet now, *Robert Graves,* [c'-a''*b*], Chester Graves 2.
(September, *Ted Hughes,* [c'#-a''], Chester The Horses.)
(Symptoms of love, *Robert Graves,* [c'-a''], Chester Graves 2.
(The blue coat, *Yevgeny Yevtushenko* tr. *Anon,* [c'#-a''], Chester Op 23.)
(The door, *Robert Graves,* [c'#-g''](m), Chester Graves 3.)
The foreboding, *Robert Graves,* [e'*b*-a''](m), Chester Graves 1.
The green castle, *Robert Graves,* [c'-e''*b*](m), Chester Graves 1.
(The hazel grove, *Robert Graves,* [d'*b*-b''*b*](m), Chester Graves 3.)
(The horses, *Ted Hughes,* [a-a''*b*], Chester The Horses.)
The rose, *Robert Graves,* [d'-a''](m), Chester Graves 1.
(The visitation, *Robert Graves,* [c'-a''*b*](m), Chester Graves 2.)
(To tell and be told, *Robert Graves,* [c'#-g''], Chester Graves 3.)

Amy Woodforde-Finden. 1860 -1919. 30 more songs in B&H archives.
Collections: *Four Indian Love Lyrics* (introduction Andrew Lamb 1950), B&H (low key B&H 1903);
(Aziza, B&H); *(A Dream of Egypt* (high & low keys), B&H); *(Golden Hours* (high & low keys), B&H);
(A Lover in Damascus (medium voice), B&H); *(Myrtles of Damascus* high & low keys), B&H); *(On Jhelum River* (high & low keys), B&H); *(Stars of the Desert* (high, medium & low keys), B&H); *(To the Hills,* B&H).
Kashmiri song, *Laurence Hope,* D [d'-f'#], B&H 4 Indian, *Ballad Album 1;* (B*b,* C, B&H).
Less than the dust, *Laurence Hope,* Cm [c'-f''(a''*b*)], B&H 4 Indian; (A, B&H).
The temple bells, *Laurence Hope,* Em [d'-g''], B&H 4 Indian; (Dm, B&H).
Till I wake, *Laurence Hope,* Dm [d'-f''], B&H 4 Indian; (Cm, B&H).

Leonard Woodson. *c.* 1565 - 1619.
The marigold of golden hue, *Anon,* G [g'-g''](m), S&B (Greer) *Manuscript 2.*

John Woolrich. 1954 -
Collection: *Three Cautionary Tales,* Faber 1996.
(Here is my country (cycle), *de Quincey, de Nerval, Schumann, Anderson,* [c'#-g''](f), Faber hire.)

(La Cantarina, *Jo Shapcott*, [high soprano] Faberprint.)
Poor Mr Snail, *Macedonian* tr. *Harvey & Pennigton*, [d'-d'''*b*(b'')], Faber 3 Cautionary.
The North Wind, *Anon*, [b-c'''(a'')](f), Faber 3 Cautionary.
The Turkish Mouse, *Turkish* tr. *John Woolrich*, [d'-f'#](f), Faber 3 Cautionary.

William Wordsworth. 1908 - 1988. (SMIC).

David Wynne. 1900 - 1983.
Go. lovely rose, *Edmund Waller*, [soprano/tenor], Snell.
Irish lullaby, *Francis A-Fahy*, [b*b*-f''](f), Welsh Music.
The sleeping sea, *John Freeman*, [d'*b*-f''#], Welsh Music *Songs from Wales 2.*

Y

Anthony Young. 1685 - ? Note: these are three different versions of the same song!
Phillis, *Michael Diack*, Gm [a-g''](m), Paterson 100 Best 4.
Phillis has such charming graces, *Anon*, D [e'-g''](m), B&H (Lane Wilson) *Old English.*
The shy shepherdess, Cm [d'-g''](f), S&B (Pilkington) *Georgian 2.*

Douglas Young. 1947 -
Collection: *Four Nature Songs*, Faber 1980.
Full fathom five, *Shakespeare*, [a'-d''], Faber 4 Nature.
The cat and the moon, *W B Yeats*, [b-a''#], Faber 4 Nature.
The wild swans at Coole, *W B Yeats*, [b*b*-b''(a'')], Faber 4 Nature.
To blossoms, *Robert Herrick*, [b-e''], Faber 4 Nature.

Appendix 1. Settings of foreign texts.

This section includes settings of Welsh originals, but not translations into Welsh.

Arnold Bax. 1883 - 1953.
Collection: (*Traditional Songs of France*, Chappell 1921); (*Trois Enfantines*, Chester).
(Femmes, battez vos marys, *Anon*, E [e'-f''#],Chappell France.)
Frülingsregen, *Friedrich Ruckert*, G#m [d'#-g''#], Thames Six Songs.
(La targo, *Anon*, E [e'-b'], Chappell France.)
(Languedo d'amours, ma douce fillette, *Anon*, F [d'-f''], Chappell France.)
(Me soui mesocu danso, *Anon*, F [f'-f''], Chappell France.)
(Sarabande, *Anon*, Bm [e'-f''#], Chappell France.)

Adrian Beaumont. 1937 -
Arrangements: *Dwy Gân Werin (Two Welsh Folk Songs)*, Gwynn.
Clychau Aberdyfi, *Anon*, G [d'-g''], Gwynn 2 Welsh.
Wrth fynd hefo Deio i Dywyn, *Anon*, F#m [c'#-f''#], Gwynn.

Lennox Berkeley. 1903 - 1989.
Collection: *Complete French Songs*, Chester.
Automne, *Guillaume Apollinaire*, [e'b-f''], Chester French.
Ce caillou chaud de soleil, *Charles Vildrac*, F#m [c'#-f''#], Chester French.
Cet enfant de jadis, *Charles Vildrac*, [c'-g''], Chester French.
D'un vanneur de blé aux vents, *Joachim du Bellay*, G [d'-g''], OUP, Chester French.
Ode du premier jour du Mai, *Jean Passerat*, F [c'#-a''], Chester French.
Pastourelle, *Anon*, [d'-e''], Chester French.
Rondeau, *Charles D'Orleans*, F [A-a'](m), Chester French.
Sonnet, *Louise Labé*, [c'#-g''], Chester French.
Sur quel arbre du ciel, *Charles Vildrac*, Em [d'-d''], Chester French.
Tant que mes yeux, *Louise Labé*, [c'#-g''], OUP, Chester French.
Tombeau (cycle), *Jean Cocteau*, [c'-a''], Chester French.

Lord Berners. 1883 - 1950.
Collection: *The Collected Vocal Music*, Chester 1982.
Du bist wie eine Blume, *Heine*, [e'-f''], Chester Collected.
Konig Wiswamitra, *Heinrich Heine*, [e'b-f''], Chester Collected.
L'Etoile filante, *G Jean-Aubry*, [c'-e''], Chester Collected.
La fiancee du timbaliér, *G Jean-Aubry*, [c'-a''b], Chester Collected.
Romance, *G Jean-Aubry*, [c'-e''], Chester Collected.
Weinachstlied, *Heinrich Heine*, [b-d''], Chester Collected.

Carey Blyton. 1932 - (BMIC; French.)

Benjamin Britten. 1913 - 1976.
Collections: *Seven Sonnets of Michelangelo*, B&H 1943; *Sechs Hölderlin-Fragmente*, B&H 1963; *The Poet's Echo*, Faber 1967.

A che più debb' io mai l'intensa voglia, *Michelangelo*, [e'-a''](m), B&H 7 Sonnets.
Angel, *Pushkin*, [c'-g''], Faber Poet's Echo.
Die Heimat, *Friedrich Hölderlin*, A [e'-b-g''], B&H Hölderlin.
Die Jugend, *Friedrich Hölderlin*, G [c'#-a''], B&H Hölderlin.
Die Linien des lebens, *Friedrich Hölderlin*, Ebm [e'-b-g''b], B&H Hölderlin.
Echo, *Pushkin*, [c'-a''b], Faber Poet's Echo.
Epigram, *Pushkin*, [e'-g''], Faber Poet's Echo.
Hälfte des lebens, *Friedrich Hölderlin*, Bb [e'-a''b], B&H Hölderlin.
Lines written during a sleepless night, *Pushkin*, [c'-a''b], Faber Poet's Echo.
Menschenbeifall, *Friedrich Hölderlin*, F [e'-b-g''], B&H Hölderlin.
My heart... *Pushkin*, [d'-b-f''#], Faber Poet's Echo
Rendete a gli occhi miei, o fonte o fiume, *Michelangelo*, [f'-a''b](m), B&H 7 Sonnets.
Sì come nella penna e nell' inchiostro, *Michelangelo*, [c'-a''](m), B&H 7 Sonnets.
S'un casto amor, s'una pietà superna, *Michelangelo*, [f'-f''#](m), B&H 7 Sonnets.
Socrates und Alcibiades, *Friedrich Hölderlin*, D [c'#-a''b], B&H Hölderlin.
Spirto ben nato, in cui si specchia e vede, *Michelangelo*, [c'-a''](m), B&H 7 Sonnets.
The nightingale and the rose, *Pushkin*, [d'#-a''], Faber Poet's Echo.
Tu sa' ch'io so, signior mie, che tu sai, *Michelangelo*, [d'-a''](m), B&H 7 Sonnets.
Veggio co' bei vostri occhi un dolce lume, *Michelangelo*, [d'-b''](m), B&H 7 Sonnets.
Arrangements: *Folksongs Volume 2* (high & medium keys), B&H.
La Noël passée, *Anon*, Bbm [f'-g''], B&H Folksongs 2; Gm, Folksongs 2;
Eho! Eho!, *Anon*, Am [a'-g''], B&H Folksongs 2; F#m, Folksongs 2;
Fileuse, *Anon*, G [d'-d''](f), B&H Folksongs 2.
Il est quelqu'un sur terre, *Anon*, Bbm [f'-f''](f), B&H Folksongs 2; Gm, Folksongs 2;
La belle est au jardin d'amour, *Anon*, Bb [f'-d''], B&H Folksongs 2.
Le roi s'en va-t'en chasse, *Anon*, Ab [e'-b-e''b], B&H Folksongs 2.
Quand j'étais chez mon père, *Anon*, A [a'-e''](m), B&H Folksongs 2; G, Folksongs 2;
Voici le Printemps, *Anon*, Gm [f'#-d''], B&H Folksongs 2.

Robert Bryan. 1858 - 1920.
Mon a Menai, [soprano/tenor], Snell.

Dafydd Bullock.
Collection: Canueon o Hanes Cymru, Op 65, Gwynn.
Cawr Mawr Bychan, [baritone/bass], Gwynn Caneuon.
Minnau, Fardd Rhian Feinir, [baritone/bass], Gwynn Caneuon.
Na ad Arglwydd swydd i Sais, [baritone/bass], Gwynn Caneuon.
Oni welwch chwi? [baritone/bass], Gwynn Caneuon.
Stafell Cynddylan, [baritone/bass], Gwynn Caneuon.
Yr Addwynau, [baritone/bass], Gwynn Caneuon.

Gordon Crosse. 1937 -
Collection: *Three Songs to Medieval French Texts*, OUP 1970.
Aube, *Anon*, [b-e''](f), OUP 3 Songs.
Motet One, *Anon*, [c'#-f''#](f), OUP 3 Songs.
Motet Two, *Anon*, [bb-f''#](f), OUP 3 Songs.

Walford Davies. 1869 - 1941.
Arrangements:
Aderyn Du 'n rhodio'r Gwyledydd, Gwynn.
Bedd fy Nghariad, Gwynn.

William Davies. 1859 - 1907.
Llwybr Yr Wyddfa, [ten], Snell.

Frederick Delius. 1862 - 1934.
Collections: *Twenty-two Songs*, S&B 1987; *Sixteen Songs*, B&H 1987; *Nineteen Songs*, OUP 1987.
Aus deinen Augen fliessen meine Lieder, *Heinrich Heine?*, Db [e'-b-g''b], S&B 22 Songs.
Avant que tu t'en ailles, *Paul Verlaine*, [d'#-a''], B&H 16 Songs.
Chanson d'Automne, *Paul Verlaine*, [b#-f''], OUP 19 Songs.
Chanson de Fortunio, *Alfred de Musset*, G [bb-f''#], S&B 22 Songs.
Der Einsame, *Friedrich Nietzsche*, [d'-g''], B&H 16 Songs.
Der Fichtenbaum, *Heinrich Heine*, F [e'-f''], S&B 22 Songs.
Der Wandrer, *Friedrich Nietzsche*, Gm [b-g''], B&H 16 Songs.
Der Wandrer und sein Schatten, *Friedrich Nietzsche*, C#m [c'-e''], B&H 16 Songs.
Ein schöner Stern geht auf in meiner Nacht, *Heinrich Heine*, B [e'#-g''#], S&B 22 Songs.
Hör ich das Liedchen klingen, *Heinrich Heine*, Ab [e'bb-a''b], S&B 22 Songs.
Il pleure dans mon coeur, *Paul Verlaine*, Bbm [c'#-f''#], OUP 19 Songs.
La lune blanche, *Paul Verlaine*, [c'-f''], OUP 19 Songs.
Le ciel est, par-dessus le toit, *Paul Verlaine*, [d'-b-g''b], OUP 19 Songs.
Mit deinen blauen Augen, *Heinrich Heine*, F [e'-b-a''], S&B 22 Songs.
Nach neuen Meeren, *Friedrich Nietzsche*, C#m [d'-f''#], B&H 16 Songs.
Noch ein Mal, *Friedrich Nietzsche*, B [B-d'#](m), B&H 16 Songs.
Nuages, *Jean Richepin*, Db [e-g''b], S&B 22 Songs.
O schneller mein Ross, *Emanuel Geibel*, D [d'-b''b(g')], S&B 22 Songs.
Traum Rosen, *Marie Heinitz*, Eb [bb-e''b], S&B 22 Songs.

Bernard van Dieren. 1884 - 1936.
(Chanson, *Nicolas Boileau Despréaux*, [d'-b-f''], OUP.)
(Der Asra, *Heinrich Heine*, [b-f''#], OUP.)
(Epiphanias, *Goethe*, [c'-a''b], OUP.)
(Mädchenlied, *Otto Julius Bierbaum*, [b-f''], OUP.)
(Mon bras pressait ta taille frêle, *Victor Hugo*, [d'-f''#], OUP.)
(Oh! quand je dors, *Victor Hugo*, c'#-f''#], OUP.)
(Rondel, *Charles d'Orleans*, [d'-a''], OUP.)
(Schöne Rohtraut, *E Mörike*, [b-a''], OUP.)
(Spleen, *Paul Verlaine*, [d'-g''], OUP.)
Arrangement:
(Mon coeur se recommande à vous, *Orlando di Lasso*, [d'-g''], OUP.)

Oliver Edwards. 1902 - 1979.
Aeth Gaeaf yn ei dro, [mezzo/baritone], Gwynn.
Hwiangerdd, [soprano/mezzo], Snell.
Y Crythor o Ben Dein, [mezzo/baritone], Gwynn.

T D Edwards. 1859 - 1907.
   Bugeiles Y Glyn, [soprano/tenor], Snell.
   Hen Iaith Fy Mam, [soprano/tenor], Snell

Brian Elias. 1948 -
Collection: (*Two Songs*, Chester 1969.)
   (Chanson d'automne, *Paul Verlaine*, [b♭-b''](f), Chester 2 Songs.)
   (Le ciel est, par dessus le toit, *Paul Verlaine*, [c'-a''](f), Chester 2 Songs.)

Dilys Elwyn-Edwards. 1918 -
Collection: *Bro a Mynydd*, Welsh Music 1993; *Caneuon Natur*, Gwynn; *Caneuon y Tri Aderyn* ,
Gwynn; *Che Chân i Blant* (text I D Hooson, [d'♭-f''] , Gwynn.
   Berwyn, *Robert Ellis*, C [c'-g''(e')], Welsh Music Bro a Mynydd.
   Deilen, *Gwyn Thomas*, C [e'-a''], Gwynn Natur.
   Eifionydd, *R Williams Parry*, Dm [a-e''], Welsh Music Bro a Mynydd, *Songs from Wales 2.*
   Mae Hiraeth yn y Mô, *R Williams Parry*, A♭ [f'-a''♭], Gwynn Aderyn.
   Nos o Haf, *Alafon*, E [e'-a''], Gwynn Natur.
   Tylluanod, *R Williams Parry*, Gm [d'-a''], Gwynn Aderyn.
   Y Gylfinir, *R Williams Parry*, F [e'♭-g''], Gwynn Aderyn.
   Y Mynydd, *R Williams Parry*, Am [e'-a''], Gwynn Natur.

Colin Evans.
Arrangements: *Tair Cân Werin* , Gwynn.
   Ble'r wyt ti yn myned? Gwynn Tair.
   Cân Serch, Gwynn Tair.
   Canu Cwnsela, Gwynn Tair.

David Evans. 1874 - 1948.
   Dychwelwch Y Delyn, [contralto/baritone], Snell.

D Pughe Evans. 1866 - 1897.
   Cartrof Fy Nghalon, [soprano/tenor], Snell.
   Dan Yr Ywen, [soprano/tenor], Snell.
   Y Ddwy Delyn, E♭ [contralto/baritone], Snell.

T Hopkin Evans. 1879 - 1940.
   Adgofion, E♭ [soprano/tenor], Snell
   Ger Y Don, [tenor], Snell.

Michael Finnissy. 1946 - (see also BMIC.)
   Fairest noonday, *Friedrich Holderlin*, [A#-d''#](m), Universal.

Roberto Gerhard. 1896 - 1970.
Arrangements: (*Six Catalan Folksongs*, B&H 1933, *see* main catalogue); (*Cancionero*, Keith Prowse 1957).

Alexander Goehr. 1932 -
   Das Gesetz der Quadrille (cycle), *Franz Kafka*, [a♭-e''], Schott.

Eugene Goossens. 1893 - 1962.
Collection: (*Two proses lyriques*, (text Edwin Evans), Chester.)

Julian Grant.
Collection: (BMIC; Italian.)

Michael Head. 1900 - 1976.
Ave Maria, Am [a-e''], B&H; Cm, B&H.
(O gloriosa Domina, G [d'-g''], B&H.)
(Sancta et Immaculata Virginitas, *St Augustine*, Em [e'-g''#], B&H.)

John Henry. 1859 - 1914.
Cenwch Im Yr Hen Ganiadau, [soprano/tenor], Snell.
Gwlad Y Canu, [soprano/tenor], Snell; [contralto/baritone], Snell.
Marchogion Arthur, [soprano/tenor], Snell; [contralto/baritone], Snell.

Leigh Henry.
Ceisiaid, Gwynn.

Alun Hoddinott. 1929 -
Arrangements: *Six Welsh Folksongs*, OUP 1984; *see* main catalogue for details.

Antony Hopkins. 1921 -
(Recueillement, *Charles Beaudelaire*, [cb(d')-g''], Chester.)
Arrangements: *Five French Folk Songs*, Chester 1973.
Gai lon la, *Quebec-Canada*, Eb [e'-e''b](f), Chester 5 French.
Hollaïka, *Bretagne*, Gb [g'b-e''b](f), Chester 5 French.
(La bergère aux champs, *Anon*, A [e'-e''(a'')](f), Chester.)
(Le Roi Renaud, *Anon*, Dm [a-d''], Chester.)
Les trois rubans *Bretagne*, Gb [d'b-d''b](f), Chester 5 French.
Me suis mise en danse, *Bas Quercy*, E [e'-e''](f), Chester 5 French.
Quand mon mari se fâchera, *Bretagne*, G [d'-d''](f), Chester 5 French.

Arwel Hughes. 1909 - 1988.
Romani, *Crwys*, G [d'-a''], Gwynn.
Y Groglith, *Rhiannon Bowen Thomas*, Am e'-a''], Gwynn.

R S Hughes. 1855 - 1893.
Bedd Y Bugail, [soprano/tenor], Snell.
Cymru, [baritoen], Snell.
Hen Groesffordd Y Llan, [soprano/tenor], Snell.
Llam Y Cariadau, [soprano], Snell.
Merch Y Cadben, [baritone], Snell.
Profiad Plentyn Y Meddwyn, [contralto/baritone], Snell.
Rwyn Mynd I'r Nef, [soprano/tenor], Snell.
Y Bachgen Ffarweliodd A'r Wlad, [baritone], Snell.
Y Mynydd I Mi, [baritone/bass], Snell.
Y Tair Mordiath, [baritone], Snell.

Y Wlad Well, [soprano/tenor], Snell.

Llifon Hughes-Jones. 1918 - 1996.
Melin Trefin, *Crwys*, Cm [a-e''*b*], Welsh Music *Songs from Wales 2.*

John Hywel. 1941 -
Ffarwel i Eryri, [mezzo/baritone], Gwynn.

George Jeffreys. *c.* 1610 - 1685.
Collection: Two Devotional Songs, (Introduction and Notes Peter Aston) Novello1988.
O quam suave, *Phillippians 2. vv. 9-10*, Dm [D-d'](m), Novello 2 Devotional.
Speciosus forma, *Psalm 45. v. 2*, Am [D(E)-d'](m), Novello 2 Devotional.

David Jenkins. 1848 - 1915.
Castiau Gwraig, [baritone], Snell.
Concwest Y Groes, G [soprano/tenor], Snell.
Crist Yn Achub, C [any voice], Snell.
Cymru Fad, G [any voice], Snell.
Dagrau'r Iesu, B*b* [contralto/baritone], Snell.
Deio Bach, [contralto/baritone], Snell.
Gwna Bobpeth A Wnei Fel Cymro Pur, [tenor/baritone], Snell.
Hen Fwthyn Fy Nhad, E*b* [any voice], Snell.
Hiraeth, Cm [soprano/tenor], Snell; Am, [contralto/baritone], Snell.
Y Nyth A'r Aderyn, [soprano/contralto], Snell.
Peidiwch Gofyn Imi Ganu, [soprano/tenor], Snell.
Plentyn Duw, [mezzo/contralto], Snell.

W Bradwen Jones. 1892 - 1970.
Collection: *Two Songs for Tenor*, Snell.
Can Osain, [tenor], Snell 2 Songs.
Canmolwn yn awr y Gwŷr Enwog, *Ecclesiasticus 44*, Em [A*b*-c'](m), Gwynn.
Casglu A Rhannu, [any voice], Snell.
Gardd F'Anwylyd, *Eifion Wyn*, E [c'#-e''(g''#)], Gwynn.
Iar Fach Yr Haf, [any voice], Snell.
Llanarmon, *Cynan*, Dm [d'-a''], Gwynn.
Mab Y Mor, [baritone], Snell.
Mab Y Ystorm, [baritone], Snell.
Mawredd Duw, [mezzo/contralto], Snell.
Mor Ber Yw Hi, [tenor], Snell 2 Songs.
Paradws Y Bardd, [soprano/tenor], Snell.
Yr Ehedydd, [soprano/tenor], Snell.

Richard Roderick Jones. 1947 -
Y Dderwen, *William Thomas "Islwyn"*, [G(A)-d'](m), Welsh Music *Songs from Wales 2.*

Antoinette Kirkwood.
Der Schiffbrüchige, *Heinrich Heine*, [a-a''], Bardic.
Krönung, *Heinrich Heine*, [b*b*-b''*b*], Bardic.

Liza Lehmann. 1862 - 1918.
Die Nachtigall, als ich sie fragte, *Friedrich Bodenstedt*, Dm [d'-f"], S&B (Bush) *MB* 56.
Im Rosenbusch, *Hoffmann von Fallersleben*, Db [d'b-g"b(b"b)], S&B (Bush) *MB* 56.

Idris Lewis. 1889 - 1952.
Bugail Aberdyfi, [soprano/tenor], Snell.
Clychau Cantre'r Gwaelod, [soprano/tenor], Snell.
Geneth Y Fro, G [baritone/bass], Snell.
Mab Y Mynydd, [mezzo/baritone], Snell.
Y Wennol Gyntaf, [soprano/tenor], Snell; [contralto/baritone], Snell.

David de Lloyd. 1883 - 1948.
Arrangements:
Ceinion Conwy, [mezzo/baritone], Gwynn.
Y Dryw Bach, [soprano], Snell.
Y Gog Lwydlas, [mezzo/baritone], Gwynn.

John Morgan Lloyd. 1880 - 1960.
Dilys, *Rhosyr*, Bbm [d'b-g"b], Gwynn.
Yr Awr Aur, *Crwys*, Em [d'#-g"#], Gwynn.

Collin Matthews. 1946 -
Un Colloque Sentimental (cycle), *Verlaine, Baudelaire, de Nerval*, [a-g"#(f"#)], Faber.

Islwyn Morgan.
Ebrill, [soprano/mezzo/tenor/baritone], Gwynn.

Haydn Morris. 1891 - 1965.
Cartre'r Gan, [baritone], Snell.
Doli, [tenor], Snell.
Gwenfron A Mi, [soprano/tenor], Snell.
Hei Ho, [soprano], Snell.
Meibion Gwalia, [soprano/tenor], Snell.
Y Clochydd, [baritone], Snell.
Y Peilot, [baritone/bass], Snell.
Yr Hen Wladgarwr, [soprano/tenor], Snell.

Dominic Muldowney. 1952 -
Five Theatre Poems (cycle), *Bertolt Brecht*, [G-f'], Universal.

J Morgan Nicholas. 1895 - 1963.
Y Crud Gwag, [soprano/tenor], Gwynn
Y Dieithryn, [tenor], Gwynn.

Michael Nyman. 1944 -
Anne de Lucy Songs (cycle), *Fray Luis de Léon*, [g-b"](f), Chester .

Robin Orr. 1909 - (BMIC; German.)

Joseph Parry. 1841 - 1903.
Baner Ein Gwlad, [baritone], Snell; [tenor], Snell.
Cymru Fydd, C[contralto/baritone], Snell; E [soprano/tenor], Snell.
Fy Mam, [soprano/tenor], Snell.
Merch Y Cadben, [soprano/tenor], Snell.
Myfanwy, G, Snell; B*b*, Snell.
Pleserfad Y Niagara, [baritone], Snell.
Y Dewr Milwr, [tenor/baritone/bass], Snell.
Y Marchog, [baritone], Snell.
Yr Ehedydd, [soprano/tenor], Snell.

D E Parry-Williams. 1900 -
Ar Gynywair, [soprano/tenor], Gwynn.

Anthony Powers. 1953 - (BMIC; French.)
Souvenirs du Voyage (cycle), *Baudelaire*, [soprano], OUP.

Daniel Protheroe. 1866 - 1934.
Bendithiaist Goed y Meusydd, [contralto/baritone], Snell.
Bob Nos.Oleu Leuad, [soprano/tenor], Snell.
Y Gan Orchfygol, [tenor/baritone], Snell.
Y Seren-Ddydd, [contralto/baritone], Snell.
Yr Heliwr, [baritone], Snell.

Alan Rawsthorne. 1905 - 1971.
Collection: (*Trois Chansons de Nourrice*, B&H 1938.)
(Fais do-do, Pierrot, *Anon*, Bm [f'#-f'#], B&H 3 Chansons.)
(Il pleut, il pleut, bergère, *Anon*, Em [e'-f'#], B&H 3 Chansons.)
(Je suis un petit poupon, *Anon*, C [f'#-f''], B&H 3 Chansons.)
(Nous étions trois filles, *Anon*, [e'-a''], OUP.)

Mervyn Roberts. 1906 - 1990.
Arrangements: *Chwe Chân Werin Gymreig* , Gwynn.

T Osborne Roberts. 1879 - 1948.
Cymru Annwyl, [mezzo/soprano/tenor], Snell.
Dafydd Y Garreg Wen, G [contralto/baritone], Snell.
Min Y Mor, [mezzo/contralto/baritone], Snell.
Pistyll Y Llan, F [soprano/mezzo], Snell.
Y gwanwyn du, *Cynan*, C [c'-e''], Gwynn.
Y Mab Afardion, [soprano/tenor], Snell; [contralto/bass], Snell.
Y Nefoedd, F [mezzo/contralto/baritone], Snell.

Edmund Rubbra. 1901 - 1986.
Salve, Regina, *Hermann?* [f-c''#], Lengnick.

Leonard Salzedo. 1921 - (BMIC; Spanish.)

Humphrey Searle. 1915 - 1982. (BMIC; French.)

Pwyll ap Siôn. 1968 -
Merch, *Rhydwen Williams*, [A#-e'](m), Welsh Music *Songs from Wales.*

Robert Smith. 1922 -
Angharad, *Eifion Wyn*, Bm [f'#-g''], Gwynn.
Serch, *Eifon Wyn*, [A-c'](m), Welsh Music.

Kaikhosru Sorabji. 1892 - 1988. (*Trois Fêtes Galants*, Curwen 1924); see also BMIC; French.)
(À la Promenade, *Paul Verlaine*, [c'-g''#], Curwen 3 Fêtes.)
(Dans la Grotte, *Paul Verlaine*, [a#-g''], Curwen 3 Fêtes.)
(L'allée, *Paul Verlaine*, [e'-g''], Curwen 3 Fêtes.)

Ethyl Smyth. 1858 - 1944.
Collection: (*Lieder*, Peters .)
(Mittagsruh, *J von Eichendorff*, Fm [c'-f''], Peters Lieder.)
(Nachtgedanken, *Paul Heyse*, C#m [c'#-g''], Peters Lieder.)
(Nachtreiter, *Klaus Groth*, E [c'#-f''#], Peters Lieder.)
(Schlummerlied, *E von Wildenbruch*, C [c'-e''], Peters Lieder.)
(Tauzlied, *G Büchner*, Gm [c'#-f''#], Peters Lieder.)

Charles Villiers Stanford. 1852 - 1924.
Collection: (*Twelve Songs by Heine*, S&B 1893.)
(An die blaue Himmelsdecke, *Heinrich Heine*, Eb [c'-g''], S&B 12 Songs.)
(Dass du mich liebst, *Heinrich Heine*, Eb [e'-g''], S&B 12 Songs.)
(Der Schmetterling ist in die Rose verliebt, *Heinrich Heine*, D [d'-f''#], S&B 12 Songs.)
(Der sterbende Almansor, *Heinrich Heine*, Ebm [b-g''], S&B 12 Songs.)
(Die Wallfahrt nach Kevlaar, *Heinrich Heine*, Db [c'-a''b], B&H.)
(Ernst ist der Frühling, *Heinrich Heine*, Em [d'#-f''#], S&B 12 Songs.)
(Frühling, *Heinrich Heine*, Ab [d'-f''#(a''b)], S&B 12 Songs.)
(Ich halte ihr die Augen zu, *Heinrich Heine*, B [c'#-f''#], S&B 12 Songs.)
(Ich lieb' eine Blume, *Heinrich Heine*, Db [c'-f''], S&B 12 Songs.)
Le bien vient en dormant, *Anon*, Eb [e'b-g''](m), S&B MB 52.
(Mit deinen blauen Augen, *Heinrich Heine*, G [f'-g''], S&B 12 Songs.)
(Schlummerlied, *Heinrich Heine*, D [d'-e''], S&B 12 Songs.)
Sterne mit den goldnen Füsschen, *Heinrich Heine*, D [c'-f''#], S&B MB 52, (12 Songs.)
(Tragödie, *Heinrich Heine*, Am [c'-f''], B&H.)
(Wie des Mondes Abbild zittert, *Heinrich Heine*, Eb [d'-f''], S&B 12 Songs.)

Arthur Goring Thomas. 1850 - 1892.
Les papillons, *Théophile Gautier*, Bb [e'b-g''](m), S&B (Bush) *MB 56.*
S'il est un charmant gazon, *Victor Hugo*, E [e'-g''#], S&B (Bush) *MB 56.*

D Afan Thomas. 1881 - 1928.
Paradws Y Bardd, [soprano/tenor], Snell.

David Vaughan Thomas. 1873 - 1934.

Collection: *Dwy Gan I Fariton*, Snell.
    Angladd Y Marchog, [baritone], Snell.
    Berwyn, [baritone], Snell Dwy Gan.
    Caledfwlch, [contralto/baritone], Snell.
    Can Hen Wr Y Cwm, [contralto/baritone], Snell.
    Einioes, [contralto/baritone], Snell.
    Nant Y Mynydd, [baritone], Snell.
    O Fair Wen, [baritone], Snell Dwy Gan.
    Y Bwthyn Bach To Gwelli, [contralto/baritone/bass], Snell.
    Ymadawiad Arthur, [contralto], Snell.
    Yr wylan deg, *Dafydd ap Gwilym*, Dm [f'-f''], Gwynn.
    Ysbryd Y Mynydd, [tenor], Snell.

Mansell Thomas. 1909 - 1986.
Collections: *Caneuon Grace a Siân* [c'-f''], Gwynn.
    Ffrwd Fach Loyw, *Eifion Wyn*, G [d'-e''], Gwynn.
    Gwyn ap Nudd, *Elfed*, Dm [d'-a''*b*], Gwynn.

Vincent Thomas. 1873 - 1940.
Collection: *Tair cân Wanwyn (Three Spring Songs)*, Gwynn.
    Dyddiau Ebrill, [soprano, mezzo, tenor, baritone], Gwynn 3 Spring.
    Gweddi, [soprano/mezzo/tenor/baritone], Gwynn 3 Spring.
    Lili'r Garawys, [soprano/mezzo/tenor/baritone], Gwynn 3 Spring.

Bryceson Treharne. 1879 - 1948.
    Y Draen, [baritone/bass], Gwynn.
    Y Gwynt, [soprano/mezzo/tenor], Gwynn

Ralph Vaughan Williams. 1872 - 1958.
Arrangements:
    L'Amour de moy, *Anon*, C [c'-d''], B&H Song Album 2.
    Reveillez-vous Piccarz, *Anon*, Em [d'-e''](m), B&H Song Album 1.

Judith Weir. 1954 -
    (A Spanish Liederbooklet (cycle), *Anon*, [e'*b*-a''](f), Chester.)

Egon Wellesz. 1885 - 1974.
    Ode an die Musik, *Pindar* tr. *Hölderlin*, [mezzo/baritone], Universal.

Maude Valérie White. 1855 - 1937.
    Anfangs wollt' ich fast verzagen, *Heinrich Heine*, A*b* [e'-d''*b*], S&B (Bush) *MB 56*.
    Aus meinen Thränen spriessen, *Heinrich Heine*, D [d'-e''], S&B (Bush) *MB 56*.
    Die Himmelsaugen, *Heinrich Heine*, B*b* [d'-d''], S&B (Bush) *MB 56*.
    Ein jüngling liebt ein Mädchen, *Heinrich Heine*, Fm [b-d''*b*], S&B (Bush) *MB 56*.
    Im wunderschönen Monat Mai, *Heinrich Heine*, E [b-e''], S&B (Bush) *MB 56*.
    Liebe, *Heinrich Heine*, C#m [g#-c''#], S&B (Bush) *MB 56*.
    Parle moi, *Alphonse de Lamartine*, D*b* [d'*b*-d''*b*], S&B (Bush) *MB 56*.
    Ton nom, *Sully Prudhomme*, E*b* [f'-f''], S&B (Bush) *MB 56*.

Philip Wilby. 1949 -
Collection: *Ten Songs of Paul Verlaine*, Chester.

Meiron Williams. 1901 - 1976.
  Adlewych (cycle), [c'-d''], Gwynn.
  Cloch Y Llan, [baritone], Snell.
  Flarwel Iti, Gymru Fad, [soprano/tenor], Snell.
  Y Blodau ger y Drws, *John Evans*, Fm [c'-a''], Gwynn.

W Albert Williams. 1909 - 1946.
  Cwyn y Gwynt, *John Morros-Jones*, Dm [b♭-f''], Gwynn.
  Min y Môr, *Huw Emrys Griffith*, Dm [d'-e''], Gwynn.

W Matthews Williams. 1885 - 1972.
  Fy Ngwlad, *Dewi Havnesp*, F [c'-f''], Gwynn.
  Gardd Y Rhosynnau, [soprano/tenor], Snell.
  Llanfihangel Bachellaeth, *Cynan*, Fm [c'-e''*b*(f')], Gwynn.
  Siôn y Glyn, *Lewis Glyn Cothi*, Cm [c'-f''], Gwynn.

W S Gwynn Williams. 1896 - 1978.
Collection: *Tair Telyneg Gymraeg*, Gwynn.
  Breuddwyd Glyndwr, *Emyr*, Gm [d'-e''*b*], Gwynn Tair, Gwynn.
  Tosturi Duw, [mezzo/baritone], Gwynn; [soprano/tenor], Gwynn.
  Tylnyth teg, *T Gwynn Jones*, Fm [e''*b*-f''], Gwynn Tair, Gwynn.
  Y Pren Afalau, *I D Hooson*, Gm [d'-f''], Gwynn Tair, Gwynn.

Peter Wishart. 1921 - 1984.
Collection: *Twelve Songs*, S&B 1993.
  Quatre petits nègres blancs, *Anon*, E [b-e''], S&B 12 Songs.

John Woolrich. 1954 -
Collection: (*Five Italian Songs.*, Faber hire.1984.)

Appendix 2 — Other accompaniments.

English and foreign texts are included together in this section.

Stephen Adams. 1844 - 1913.
The star of Bethlehem, *Fred. F Weatherley*, G [d'-g''], Mayhew *Holy Night* [organ].

Thomas Adès. 1971 -
(Aubade, *Philip Larkin*, [c#-d''''](f) Faber hire [unaccompanied].)
(Life story, *Tennessee Williams*, [soprano], Faber hire [2 bass clarinets and double bass].)

Julian Anderson. 1967 -
(I'm nobody who are you, *Emily Dickinson*, [tenor/high baritone], Faber hire [violin and piano].)
(Seadrift, *Walt Whitman*, [soprano], Faber hire [flute, clarinet and piano].)

Denis ApIvor. 1916 -
Collection: (*Seis Canciones*, Bèrben [guitar].)
(Canción de jinete, *Frederico García Lorca*, [b-a''b], Bèrben Canciones.)
(La guitarra, *Frederico García Lorca*, [e'-g''], Bèrben Canciones.)
(La niña del bello rostro, *Frederico García Lorca*, [c'-g''], Bèrben Canciones.)
(Pueblo, *Frederico García Lorca*, [f'-g''], Bèrben Canciones.)
(Raíz amarga, *Frederico García Lorca*, [c'#-g''], Bèrben Canciones.)
(Virgen con miriñaque, *Frederico García Lorca*, [e'-g''#], Bèrben Canciones.)

Malcolm Archer. 1952 -
Arrangement:
Child in the manger, *Mary MacDonald* tr. *Lachlan Macbean*, D [d'-e''], Mayhew *Holy Night* [organ].

Thomas Arne, 1710 - 1778, arr. Henry Lazarus. 1815 - 1885.
When daisies pied, Eb [bb-e''b](f), Emerson [clarinet and piano].

Peter Aston. 1938 -
Collection: *Five Songs of Crazy Jane*, Novello 1964 [unaccompanied].
Crazy Jane grown old looks at the dancers, *W B Yeats*, [d'#-g''](f), Novello 5 Songs.
Crazy Jane talks with the bishop, *W B Yeats*, [d'-a''b](f), Novello 5 Songs.
I am of Ireland, *W B Yeats*, Gm [d'-a''b](f), Novello 5 Songs.
Those dancing days are gone, *W B Yeats*, [e'-a''](f), Novello 5 Songs.
Three things, *W B Yeats*, [e'-a''](f), Novello 5 Songs.

David Barlow. 1927 - 1975. (BMIC [Unaccompanied].)

Bernard Barrell. 1919 - (BMIC [Guitar; Unaccompanied].)

Joyce Barrell. 1917 - 1989. (BMIC [Unaccompanied].)

Gerald Barry. 1952 -
(Things that gain by being painted, *The Pillow Book of Sei Shonagon*, [voice], OUP hire [speaker, cello and piano].)

Alison Bauld. 1944 -
　Dear Emily, *Alison Bauld*, [soprano], Novello [harp/harpsichord/piano].

Sally Beamish. (BMIC [violin].) 1956 -

David Bedford. 1937 -
　(Come in here, child, *Kenneth Patchen*, [d'-b''](f) Universal [amplified piano].)
　(O now the drenched land awakes, *Kenneth Patchen*, [baritone], Universal [piano duet].)

Richard Rodney Bennett. 1936 -
　Nightpiece, *Charles Baudelaire*, [f'-c'''#](f), Universal, [tape].
　(Tom O'Bedlams Song, *Anon*, [c'-a''*b*](m), Novello hire [cello].)

Lennox Berkeley. 1902 - 1989.
Collection: *Songs of the Half-light*, Chester 1966 [guitar]; (*Herrick Songs Op 89*, Chester 1974 [harp]).
　All that's past, *Walter de la Mare*, Am [e'-a''], Chester Half-light.
　(Dearest of thousands, *Robert Herrick*, [f'*b*-g''*b*], Chester Herrick.)
　Full moon, *Walter de la Mare*, D [d'-g''], Chester Half-light.
　(If nine times you your bridegroom kiss, *Robert Herrick*, [f'-g''], Chester Herrick.)
　(My God, look on me, *Robert Herrick*, [e'-g''], Chester Herrick.)
　(Now is your turne, *Robert Herrick*, [d'-g''], Chester Herrick.)
　Rachel, *Walter de la Mare*, Em [g'-g''], Chester Half-light.
　The fleeting, *Walter de la Mare*, [f'-g''#], Chester Half-light.
　The moth, *Walter de la Mare*, [e'-a''], Chester Half-light.
　(These springs were maidens once, *Robert Herrick*, [f'-g''*b*], Chester Herrick.)
　Una and the Lion, Op 98, *Edmund Spenser*, [soprano], Chester [recorder, viola da gamba and
　　harpsichord].

Michael Berkeley, 1948 -
Collection: *Wessex Graves*, OUP 1985 [harp]. Medium key version available on hire.
　Ah, are you digging my grave? *Thomas Hardy*, [c'-a''], OUP Wessex Graves.
　Drummer Hodge, *Thomas Hardy*, [e'-g''], OUP Wessex Graves.
　Her secret, *Thomas Hardy*, [e'*b*-b''*b*], OUP Wessex Graves.
　In the moonlight, *Thomas Hardy*, [c'#-g''#], OUP Wessex Graves.
　She at his funeral, *Thomas Hardy*, [b'-b''*b*], OUP Wessex Graves.
　Rain, *Edward Thomas*, [tenor], OUP hire [violin and cello].

Harrison Birtwistle. 1934 -
　Four Songs of Autumn (cycle), *Anon*, [soprano], Universal [string quartet].
　Deowa, [soprano], Universal [clarinet].
　La plage, *Alain Robbe-Grillet*, Universal [3 clarinets, piano and marimba].
　Monody for Corpus Christe, *Anon, Martin Luther* tr. *Wedderburn*, [soprano], Universal [flute, vio-
　　lin and horn].
　Ring a dumb carillon, *Christopher Logues*, [soprano], Universal [clarinet and percussion].

Howard Blake. 1938 -
　(Shakespeare Songs, [tenor], Faberprint [string quartet].)
　(A Toccata of Galuppi's, Robert Browning, [baritone], Faberprint 1978 [harpsichord].)

Arthur Bliss. 1891 - 1975.
Collections: *Two Nursery Rhymes*, Chester 1921 [clarinet and piano]; *Four Songs for Voice, Violin and Piano*, Novello 1984.
A Christmas carol, *Arthur S Cripps*, Bb [e'-b-g''], Novello 4 Songs [violin and piano].
Sea love, *Charlotte Mew*, [c'-f'#](f), Novello 4 Songs, [violin].
The mad woman of Punnet's Town, *L A G Strong*, [d'-a''], Novello 4 Songs [violin and piano].
The dandelion, *Frances Cornford*, Em [e#-g''](f), Chester 2 Nursery [clarinet].
The ragwort, *Frances Cornford*, E [f'#-g''#](f), Chester 2 Nursery [clarinet and piano].
Vocalise, D [f'#-a''], Novello 4 Songs [violin].

Carey Blyton. 1932 -
Collection: *Moresques*, Fentone 1993 [flute, harp and piano]; *What then is Love?*, Roberton 1960 [clarinet and Piano], (see also BMIC [string quartet]).
A yellow flower, *David Munro*, A [c'#-g''#](f), Fentone Moresques.
Love is a sickness full of woes, *John Daniel*, [d'-f''](f), Roberton What is Love.
Love-song of the lady of Granada, *David Munro*, F [c'-a''b](f), Fentone Moresques'
Simoom, *David Munro*, Eb [c'-a''b](f), Fentone Moresques.
Stay, O sweet, and do not rise, *John Donne*, Dm [e'-e''](f), Roberton What is Love.
(Symphony in yellow, *Oscar Wilde*, [c'#-g], B&H [harp].)
Tell me where is fancy bred? *Shakespeare*, [d'-g''](f), Roberton What is Love.
Western wind, when will thou blow, *Anon*, G [f'-g''](f), Roberton What is Love.

Anne Boyd.
(Cycle of Love, *Koreen Sijo* tr. *Don'o Kim*, [counter-tenor], Faberprint [alto flute, cello and piano].)
(My name is Tian, *Don'o Kim*, [soprano], Faberprint [flute/alto flute/piccolo, percussion, harp and viola].)

Frank Bridge. 1879 - 1941.
Collection: *Three Songs*, Thames 1982 [viola and piano].
Far, far from each other, *Matthew Arnold*, F#m [d'#-e''], Thames 3 Songs.
Music when soft voices die, *P B Shelley*, Cm [c'-e''], Thames 3 Songs.
Where is it that our soul doth go? *Heine*, tr. *Kate Kroeker*, Em [e'-e''], Thames 3 Songs.

Benjamin Britten. 1913 - 1976.
Collection: *Songs from the Chinese*, B&H 1959 [guitar]; *Evening, Morning, Night*, B&H 1988 [harp].
A Birthday Hansel (cycle), [c'-b''b], Faber [harp].
Canticle III, Still falls the rain, *Edith Sitwell*, [c'-a''](m), B&H [horn and piano].
Canticle V, The Death of Saint Narcissus, *T S Eliot*, [b-g''#](m), Faber [harp].
Dance Song, *Anon* tr. *Arthur Waley*, E [d'-a''], B&H Chinese.
Depression, *Po Chü-i* tr. *Arthur Waley*, [e'-b-g''b], B&H Chinese.
Evening, *Ronald Duncan*, B [f'#-e''b], B&H Evening.
Morning, *Ronald Duncan*, G [e'-d''], B&H Evening.
Night, *Ronald Duncan*, Bm [c'-f''], B&H Evening.
The Autumn wind, *Wu-ti*, tr. *Arthur Waley*, E [e'-f'#], B&H Chinese.
The big chariot, *Anon* tr. *Arthur Waley*, F [e'-g''], B&H Chinese.
The herd-boy, *Lu Yu* tr. *Arthur Waley*, Gm [d'-g''], B&H Chinese.
The old lute, *Po Chü-i* tr. *Arthur Waley*, [e'-g''], B&H Chinese.

Three Songs from 'The Heart of the Matter' (cycle) *Edith Sitwell*, [d'-g''](m), B&H [horn and piano].

Arrangements: *Folksongs Volume 6*, B&H [guitar]; *Eight Folksong Arrangements*, Faber [harp].
Bird scarer's song, *Anon*, Bb [f'-g''](m), Faber 8 Folksong.
Bonny at morn, *Anon*, Gm [f'-g''], B&H Folksongs 6.
Bonny at morn, *Anon*, Fm [e'b-f'], Faber 8 Folksong.
David of the white rock, *Anon* tr. *Thomas Oliphant*, Fm [c'-a''b](m), Faber 8 Folksong.
I was lonely and forlorn, *Anon* tr. *Ossian Ellis*, F [e'-g''](m), Faber 8 Folksong.
I will give my love an apple, *Anon*, Am [c'-e''](m), B&H Folksongs 6.
Lemady, *Anon*, [b-f'#]m, Faber 8 Folksong.
Lord! I married me a wife, *Anon*, Em [e'-e''](m), Faber 8 Folksong.
Master Kilby, *Anon*, A [e'-f'#], B&H Folksongs 6.
Sailor-boy, *Anon*, Bm [f'#-f'#](m), B&H Folksongs 6.
She's like the swallow, *Anon*, [e'-g''](m), Faber 8 Folksong.
The false knight upon the road, *Anon*, F [c'-f''], Faber 8 Folksong.
The shooting of his dear, *Anon*, F#m [e'-f'#], B&H Folksongs 6.
The soldier and the sailor, *Anon*, G [d'-g''], B&H Folksongs 6.

Christopher Brown. 1943 -
Collection: (*All year round* Op 46, Chester 1976 [guitar].)
(A fine day, *Adrian Bell*, [d-a'](m), Chester All Year.)
(Suffolk harvest song, *Alice Cochrane*, [d-a'](m), Chester All Year.)
(Suffolk mist, *Cloudesley Brereton*, [c-a'b](m), Chester All Year.)
(Winter: East Anglia, *Edmund Blunden*, [c-a'#](m), Chester All Year.)

Gavin Bryars. 1943 -
The black river, Schott [organ].

Alan Bullard. 1947 - (BMIC [violin; clarinet; oboe].)

John Buller.
(Two Night Pieces from Finnegans Wake, *James Joyce*, [soprano], OUP [flute, clarinet, cello and piano].)

Geoffrey Burgon. 1941 -
At the round earth's imagined corners, *John Donne*, [soprano], Chester [trumpet and organ].
(Cantata on medieval Latin Texts, [counter-tenor], Chester [flute, oboe and bassoon].)
(Dira Vi Amores Terror, [counter-tenor], Chester [unaccompanied].)
Lunar beauty, [counter-tenor], Chester [lute/guitar].
Nunc Dimittis, [voice], Chester [organ, optional trumpet].
(Songs of Mary, [mezzo], Chester [viola and piano].)
(The night is come, [high], Chester [cello].)
(Three Folksongs, [high] Chester [guitar].)
(Threnody, [tenor], Chester [piano and harpsichord (amplified)].)
(Two love songs, [tenor], Chester [guitar].)
Worlde's bliss, [counter-tenor/contralto], Chester [oboe].

Martin Butler. 1960 -
Collection: (*Three Emily Dickinson Songs*, [soprano], OUP 1987, [clarinet and piano].)

James Butt. 1929 - (BMIC [harp; organ].)

Arthur Butterworth. 1923 -
(The night wind, [soprano], Chester [clarinet in A and piano].)

Cornelius Cardew. 1936 - 1981. (BMIC [unaccompanied].)

Rebecca Clarke. 1886 - 1979.
Arrangements: *Three Old English Songs*, B&H 1995 (Introduction, Calum MacDonald) [violin].
　　It was a lover and his lass, *Morley*, E♭ [e'*b*-e''*b*], B&H 3 Old English Songs.
　　Phillis on the new made hay, *Anon*, D [c'#-e''], B&H 3 Old English Songs.
　　The tailor and his mouse, *Anon*, Gm [d'-d''], B&H 3 Old English Songs.

Arnold Cooke. 1906 -
Collections: *Three Songs of Innocence*, OUP 1960 [clarinet and piano]; *Nocturnes*, OUP 1963 [horn and piano].
　　Boat song, *John Davidson*, E♭ [d'-g''*b*](f), OUP Nocturnes.
　　Piping down the valleys wild, *William Blake*, A [e'-a''*b*](f), OUP 3 Songs.
　　Returning, we hear the larks, *Isaac Rosenberg*, B♭m [c'-g''](f), OUP Nocturnes.
　　River roses, *D H Lawrence*, F#m [c'#-f''](f), OUP Nocturnes.
　　The echoing green, *William Blake*, Am [e'-a''](f), OUP 3 Songs.
　　The moon, *P B Shelley*, Am [c'#-g''](f), OUP Nocturnes.
　　The owl, *Alfred Lord Tennyson*, F [c'-g''](f), OUP Nocturnes.
　　The shepherd, *William Blake*, F [f'-f''](f), OUP 3 Songs.

Peter Crossley-Holland. 1916 -
Collection: *Songs*, Forsyth 1997.
　　Fairy workers, *Patrick MacGill*, E♭ [b♭-g''], Forsyth Songs [sopranino recorder and piano].
　　Song for a Chinese play, *Lian-Shin Yang*, A♭ [e'*b*-f''](f), Forsyth Songs [flute].
　　The secret, *Kevin Crossley-Holland*, [b♭-g''], Forsyth Songs [descant recorder and piano].
　　This is the fountain of life, *from an ancient liturgy*, Bm [d'-d''], Forsyth Songs [unaccompanied].
　　You have put on Christ, *adapted from St Paul*, D [d'-d''] Forsyth Songs [unaccompanied].

Gordon Crosse. 1937 -
　　(Verses in memoriam David Munrow, [counter-tenor], OUP hire [recorder, cello and harpsichord].)

Benjamin Dale. 1885 - 1943.
　　Come away, death, *Shakespeare*, G♭ [d'*b*-e''*b*](m), Novello [viola and piano].

Peter Dickinson. 1934 - (BMIC [harpsichord and cello].)
　　(Reminiscences, *Lord Byron*, [mezzo], Novello, [saxophone and piano].)
　　(Surrealist Landscape, *Lord Berners*, [any voice], Novello [piano and tape].)

James Dillon. 1950 -
　　A roaring flame, *Anon/Clara d'Anduza*, [g'-b''*b*](f), Peters [double bass].

Time Lag Zero, *The Song of Songs (in Hebrew)*, [g#-d'''](f), Peters [viola].

Brian Elias. 1948 -
(Peroration, [soprano], Chester [unaccompanied].)
(Personal stereo, [soprano], Chester [backing tape].)
(Song, [soprano], Chester [hurdy-gurdy].)

Michael Finnissy. 1946 -
Collection: *Beuk O'Newcassel Sangs*, OUP 1990 [clarinet and piano]; *Unknown Ground*, OUP 1991 [violin, cello and piano].
A' the neet ower an' ower, [soprano], OUP Beuk.
A patch of blackened earth, [baritone], OUP Unknown.
As me an' me marra was gannin' ta wark, [soprano], OUP Beuk.
Buy broom buzzems, [soprano], OUP Beuk.
I am nearly blind, [baritone], OUP Unknown.
I come from London, [baritone], OUP Unknown.
I don't think of death, [baritone], OUP Unknown.
I thought to marry a parson, [soprano], OUP Beuk.
I was afraid, [baritone], OUP Unknown.
It's O but aw ken weel, [soprano], OUP Beuk.
Moon's goin' down, *No text*, [b♭-e'''](m), Universal [Unaccompanied].
Mountainfall, *No text*, [d-a''](f), Universal [Unaccompanied].
Ohi! ohi! ohi!, *No text*, [e♭-a''], Universal [Unaccompanied].
Our lives, [baritone], OUP Unknown.
Song 1, *Torquato Tasso*, [g-c'''](f), Universal.
Song 14, *Walt Whitman*, [b♭-c'''#](f), BMIC [Unaccompanied].
Song 15, *No text*, [g-d'''♭](f), BMIC [Unaccompanied].
Song 16, *Francesco Petrarca*, [g-b''](f), Universal [Unaccompanied].
There's Quayside fer sailors, [soprano], OUP Beuk.
Trapped in crystal, [baritone], OUP Unknown.
Up the Raw, maw bonny, [soprano], OUP Beuk.

Gerald Finzi. 1901 - 1956.
Collection: *By Footpath and Stile*, B&H 1984 [string quartet].
Christmas Eve, and twelve of the clock, *Thomas Hardy*, [b-e''](m), B&H Footpath.
Everybody else, then, going, *Thomas Hardy*, [c'-g''(e''♭)](m), B&H Footpath.
I went by footpath and by stile, *Thomas Hardy*, [c'-d''](m), B&H Footpath.
These flowers are I, *Thomas Hardy*, [b-e''(f'#)](m), B&H Footpath.
We are budding, master, budding, *Thomas Hardy*, [a(b)-f'#](m), B&H Footpath.
Where we made the fire, *Thomas Hardy*, [c'-d''](m), B&H Footpath.

Peter Racine Fricker. 1920 - 1990.
(O mistress mine, *Shakespeare*, [c'-g''](m), Schott [guitar].)

Roberto Gerhard, 1896 - 1970.
(The Akond of Swat, *Edward Lear*, [a-a''♭](f), OUP hire [percussion].)

Armstrong Gibbs. 1889 - 1960.
The oxen, *Thomas Hardy*, Fm [d'-f''], Mayhew *Holy Night* [organ].

Alexander Goehr. 1932 -
The mouse metamorphosed into a maid, *Marianne Moore*, [b♭-c'''] Schott [unaccompanied]

Adam Gorb. 1958 -
Wedding breakfast: a Tribute to Stravinsky, *Anon*, [a-a''](f), Lengnick [tambourine, played by singer].

David Gow. 1924 - 1993. (BMIC [guitar].)

Percy Grainger. 1882 - 1961.
Arrangement:
Foweles in the frith, *Anon*, [f'-b''♭], Bardic [viola].

Terence Greaves. 1933 -
Collection: *A Garden of Weeds*, Thames 1971 [clarinet and piano]; *Three Rustic Poems of John Clare*, Emerson 1978 [clarinet].
Bella donna, *Jacqueline Froom*, [e'-f''#], Thames Garden.
Buttercup, *Jacqueline Froom*, E♭ [e'♭-e''], Thames Garden.
Little trotty wagtail, *John Clare*, E [c'-a''](f), Emerson 3 Rustic Poems.
Nettle, *Jacqueline Froom*, Cm [a'♭-g''♭(b''♭)], Thames Garden.
November, *John Clare*, [b-g''](f), Emerson 3 Rustic Poems.
Poppy, *Jacqueline Froom*, Cm [c'-e''♭], Thames Garden.
Quail's nest, *John Clare*, E [c'-f''#](f), Emerson 3 Rustic Poems.
Thistle, *Jacqueline Froom*, F [e'♭-f''], Thames Garden.

Ivor Gurney. 1890 - 1937.
Collections: (*Ludlow and Teme*, S&B 1923 [string quartet and piano]); (*The Western Playland*, S&B 1926 [string quartet and piano].) See main catalogue for details.

Jonathan Harvey. 1939 -
(Nachtlied, *Goethe* , *Rudolf Steiner*, [soprano], Faber hire [piano and tape].)
(You, [soprano], Faberprint [clarinet, viola, cello and double bass].)

Michael Head. 1900 - 1976.
(A piper, *Seumas O'Sullivan*, Dm, B&H [flute & piano].)
Be merciful unto me, O God, *Psalm 57*, C [a-g''(f')], Roberton [organ].
Bird-song, *Marjorie Rayment*, Fm [c'#-c'''(b'')(f'')], (f), B&H [flute and piano].
Child on the Shore, *Nancy Bush*, D [b♭-e''], Roberton [violin and piano].
(Foxgloves, *Mary Webb*, A♭, B&H [string quartet]; C, B&H [string quartet].)
(Green rain, *Mary Webb*, Gm, B&H [string quartet and harp].)
(I arise from dreams of thee, *P B Shelley*, G, B&H [cello and piano].)
I will lift up mine eyes, *Psalm 121*, C [b-e''], Roberton [organ].
Make a joyful noise unto the Lord, *Psalm 100*, G [d'b''(g'')], Roberton [organ].
(O gloriosa Domina, E, [b-e''], B&H [string quartet and piano.].)
(Sancta et immaculata Virginitas, *St Augustine*, Cm [c'-e''], B&H [string quartet and piano].)

The little road to Bethlehem, *Margaret Rose*, A*b* [e'*b*-a''*b*], Mayhew *Holy Night* [organ].
The singer, *Bronnie Taylor*, Fm [c'-a''*b*], B&H [unaccompanied].
The world is mad, *Louis MacNeice*, [a-f''](f), Emerson [clarinet and piano].

John Henry. 1859 - 1914.
Pluck not the tender flowers, [soprano], Snell [violin].

Trevor Hold. (BMIC [guitar].) 1939 -

Robin Holloway. 1943 -
Collection: (*Tender only to one Op 12*, B&H 1978 [unaccompanied]); (*The Noon's Repose Op 39*, B&H 1979 [harp].)
(Another weeping woman, *Wallace Stevens*, [c'#-a''](m), B&H Noon's Repose.)
(Conundrums Op 33b, *Anon*, [soprano], B&H [wind quintet].)
(Five little songs about death (cycle) Op 21, *Stevie Smith* [g'-g''](f) B&H [unaccompanied].)
(Four Housman Fragments Op 7, *A E Housman*, [soprano], B&H [violin, cello, percussion and piano].)
(Killing Time (cycle), *Auden, Stevie Smith, Raleigh*, [a*b*-b''*b*](f), B&H [unaccompanied].)
(La figlia che piange, *T S Eliot*, [e'*b*-g''](m), B&H Noon's Repose.)
(Love will find out the way, *Anon*, [soprano], B&H [2 clarinets, viola, cello and double bass].)
(Nor we to her of him, *Stevie Smith*, [c'-d''](f), B&H Tender.)
(Nursery Rhymes Op 33, *Anon*, [soprano], B&H [wind quintet].)
Nursery Rhymes Op 33a, *Anon*, [soprano], B&H [wind quintet].)
(On a drop of dew, *Andrew Marvell*, [d'-g''b](m), B&H Noon's Repose.)
(So to fatness come, *Stevie Smith*, [c'-a''](f), B&H Tender.)
(Tender only to one, *Stevie Smith*, [e'*b*-b''*b*](f), B&H Tender.)
(The abominable lake, *Stevie Smith*, [c'-a''*b*](f), B&H Tender.)
(The blue doom of summer (cantata) Op 35/1, *Ronald Firbank*, [c'#-b''*b*], B&H [harp].)
(Willow Cycle Op 35/2, *Shakespeare, Raleigh, Anon*, [c'-g''#(g'')](m), B&H [harp].)

Gustav Holst. 1874 - 1934.
Collection: *Four Songs for Voice and Violin*, Chester 1920 [violin].
I sing of a maiden, *Anon*, [e'-g''], Chester 4 Songs.
Jesu sweet, now will I sing, *Anon*, [d'-e''], Chester 4 Songs.
My leman is so true, *Anon*, [d'-e''], Chester 4 Songs.
My soul has nought but fire and ice, *Anon*, [c'-d''], Chester 4 Songs.
Personent hodie, *Piae Cantiones* tr. *Jane Joseph*, Fm [e'*b*-f''], Mayhew *Holy Night* [organ].

Herbert Howells. 1892 - 1983.
Balulalow, *Martin Luther* tr. *Wedderburn*, [c'#-f''#], Mayhew *Holy Night* [organ].

Eric Hudes. 1920 - (BMIC [cello].)

Elaine Hugh-Jones. 1927 - see also BMIC [clarinet and piano].
Collection: *Seven Songs of Walter de la Mare*, Thames 1988 [clarinet and piano].
Echo, *Walter de la Mare*, Fm [b*b*-f''], Thames 7 Songs.
Ghosts, *Walter de la Mare*, Am [e'-f''], Thames 7 Songs.
Silver, *Walter de la Mare*, B*b*m [e'*b*-f''], Thames 7 Songs.

Solitude, *Walter de la Mare*, F#m [c'#-f''#], Thames 7 Songs.
The hare, *Walter de la Mare*, Fm [c'-g''], Thames 7 Songs.
The ride-by-nights, *Walter de la Mare*, C#m [c'#-a''], Thames 7 Songs.
Winter, *Walter de la Mare*, E♭ [d'♭-g''♭], Thames 7 Songs.

Pelham Humfrey. 1647 - 1674.

Collection: *Complete Solo Devotional Songs* (edited by Peter Dennison), Novello 1974 [organ].
Lord, I have sinned, *Jeremiah Taylor*,[f'#-b''♭], Novello Devotional.
O the sad day, *Thomas Flatman*, Gm [d'-g''](m), Novello Devotional.
Sleep downy sleep come close mine eyes, *Anon*, Dm [e'-a''], Novello Devotional.
Wilt thou forgive that sin, *John Donne*, Gm [c'-f''], Novello Devotional.

William Yeates Hurlstone. 1876 - 1906.

Cradle song, *Anon*, G [d'-f''], Mayhew *Holy Night* [organ].

John Ireland. 1879 - 1962.

Lowly, laid in a manger, *Herbert S Brown*, Fm [c'-g''], Mayhew *Holy Night* [organ].
(When I am dead, my dearest, *Christina Rossetti*, F [d'-d''], OUP hire [string quartet].)

Gordon Jacob. 1895 - 1984.

Collection: (*Three Songs*, OUP [clarinet].)
(Flow my tears, *John Dowland?* Dm [c#-b♭(g)](f), OUP 3 Songs.)
(Ho, who comes here? *Thomas Morley?* G d'-a''](f), OUP 3 Songs.)
(Of all the birds that I do know, *Anon*, A [e'-f'#](f), OUP 3 Songs.)

John Jeffreys. 1927 -

Collection: *With Words of Love*, Roberton 1987 [bassoon].
And would you fain the reason know? *Thomas Campion?*, F [d'-d''](m), Roberton Words of Love.
My little pretty one, *Anon*, E [e'-e''](m), Roberton Words of Love.
My mistress frowns, *Anon*, G [d'-f''](m), Roberton Words of Love.
That ever I saw, *Anon*, D [d'-e''(d')](m), Roberton Words of Love.

Robert Sherlaw Johnson. 1932 -

The praises of heaven and earth, [soprano], OUP [piano and tape].

Wilfred Josephs. 1927 -

Collection: *Four Japanese Lyrics*, Novello 1975 [clarinet and piano]. Note: the clarinet part can alternatively be played by oboe, cor anglais, violin, viola or cello.
If I had known, *Anon*, tr. *Bownas & Thwaite*, [e'-e''], Novello 4 Japanese, [piano].
Lullaby, *Anon*, tr. *Bownas & Thwaite*, [b'-a''](f), Novello 4 Japanese [clarinet and piano].
Silent, but.... *Tsuboi Shigeji*, tr. *Bownas & Thwaite*, f'#-f''(f), Novello 4 Japanese [clarinet].
Tourist Japan, *Takenaka Iku*, tr. *Bownas & Thwaite*,[b'-a''], Novello 4 Japanese [clarinet and piano].

Frederick Keel. 1871 - 1954.

When the herds were watching, *W Canton*, F#m [c'#-e''], Mayhew *Holy Night* [organ].

Oliver Knussen. 1952 -

Four Late Poems and an Epigram of *Rainer Maria Rilke* (cycle) tr. *Mitchell*, [g(b♭)-b''](f), Faber [unaccompanied].

Rosary Songs, *Georg Trakl*, [soprano], Faber [clarinet, viola and piano].
Trumpets, *Georg Trakl*, [soprano], Faber [3 clarinets].

Philip Lane. 1950 - (BMIC [unaccompanied].)

Gordon Lawson. 1931 -
Sestette to fish, *Walter Elliott*, A*b* [b-f''], Thames *Century 4* [unaccompanied].

Nicola LeFanu. 1947 -
But stars remaining, *C Day Lewis*, [a*b*-b''*b*](f), Novello [unaccompanied].
Il Cantico dei Cantici II, *Song of Songs 2*, [a*b*-a''](f), Novello [unaccompanied].
Rondeaux, *French Medieval Love Poems*, [c'-a''](m), Novello [horn].

Samuel Liddle. 1868 - 1951.
Whence is that goodly fragrance, *Anon* tr. *Allen Beville Ramsey*, F [f'-f''], Mayhew *Holy Night*
[organ].

David Lumsdaine. (BMIC [recorder].) 1931 -

Elizabeth Lutyens. 1906 - 1983. (BMIC [flute, viola, piano/accordion; guitar; lute; unaccompanied].)

Margaret Lyall.
Sweet pastorale, *Nicholas Breton*, [b*b*-f''], Bardic [flute and piano].

Elizabeth Maconchy. 1907 - 1994.
Collection: (*Three Songs*, Chester 1974 [harp].)
(A widow bird sat mourning, *P B Shelley*, [c'-g''#](m), Chester 3 Songs.)
(Butterflies, [voice], Chester [harp].)
(L'Horloge, [soprano], Chester [clarinet and piano].)
(So we'll go no more a-roving, *Lord Byron*, [d'-g''](m), Chester 3 Songs.)
(The knot there's no untying, *Thomas Campbell*, [d'#-g''#](m), Chester 3 Songs.)

Cecilia McDowell. 1951 - (BMIC.)

George Alexander MacFarren. 1813 - 1887.
The widow bird, *P B Shelley*, Gm [d'-g''], S&B *MB 43* [clarinet and piano].

Alexander Mackenzie. 1847 - 1945.
Dormi, Jesu, *Anon*, E [e'-e''], S&B (Bush) *MB 56* [violin and piano].

Roger Marsh. 1949 -
Another silly love song, *St Bernard of Clairvaux/Roger Marsh*, [soprano], Novello [clarinet and
piano].
Dum (cycle), *Various*, [male], Novello, [percussion].

Colin Matthews. 1946 -
(Cantata on the death of Antony, *Dion Cassius*,[soprano], Faberprint [E*b* clarinet, bass clarinet,
viola, cello and double bass].)
(Five Sonnets: To Orpheus (cycle), *Rainer Maria Rilke*, tr. *J B Leishman*, [a'#(c'#)-a''*b*(g'')), (m), Faberprint [harp].)

(Pli de Lin, *Tom Paulin*, [soprano], Faberprint [2 violins, viola, cello and piano].)

David Matthews. 1943 -
(A congress of passions, *Sappho*, [counter-tenor], Faberprint [oboe and piano].)
(Loveliest of trees, *A E Housman*, [soprano], Faber hire [string quartet].)
(Marina, *T S Eliot*, [baritone], Faberprint [basset horn, viola and piano].)
(Skies are now skies (String Quartet No 7), [tenor], Faber hire [string quartet].)
(Spell of Sleep, *Kathleen Raine*, [baritone], Faberprint [clarinet and piano].)
(Spell of Sleep, *Kathleen Raine*, [soprano], Faberprint [2 clarinets, viola , cello and double bass].)

John McCabe. 1939 -
Collection: *Three Folk Songs*, Novello 1967 [clarinet and piano].
Hush-a-ba, Birdie, croon, croon, *Anon* F#m [e'-f''#], Novello 3 Folk Songs.
John Peel, *Anon*, F [e'-g''], Novello 3 Folk Songs.
Johnny has gone for a soldier, *Anon*, [e'-e''], Novello 3 Folk Songs.

Nicholas Maw. 1935 -
Collection: *Six Interiors*, B&H 1977 [guitar].
At tea, *Thomas Hardy*, [d'-f''#], B&H 6 Interiors.
I look into my glass, *Thomas Hardy*, [c'#-f''], B&H 6 Interiors.
In tenebris, *Thomas Hardy*, [g-g''], B&H 6 Interiors.
Inscriptions for a Peal of Eight Bells, *Thomas Hardy*, [b-a''*b*], B&H 6 Interiors.
Neutral tones, *Thomas Hardy*, [b-g''], B&H 6 Interiors.
Roman Canticle, *Robert Browning*, [mezzo soprano], Faber [flute, viola and harp].
(The head of Orpheus, *Robert Kelly*, [soprano], Faberprint [2 clarinets].)
To life, *Thomas Hardy*, [d'*b*-g''], B&H 6 Interiors.

Michael Maxwell. 1958 -
Arrangement:
(The water of Tyne, *Anon*, E*b* [e*b*-g''](f), Schott [clarinet and piano].)

Peter Maxwell Davies. 1934 -
Dark angels (cycle), *George Mackay Brown*, [e'*b*-b''*b*](f), B&H [guitar].
The Medium (monodrama), *Maxwell Davies*, [d(e)-c'''](f), B&H [unaccompanied].

P Napier Miles.
Collection: (*Four Songs*, OUP 1933 [oboe].)
(The cliff top, *Robert Bridges*, [A-e'](m), OUP 4 Songs.)
(The poppy, *Robert Bridges*, [d'-f''](m), OUP 4 Songs.)
(Thou art alone, fond lover, *Robert Bridges*, [B-f#](m), OUP 4 Songs.)
(When June is come, *Robert Bridges*, [c-f''](m), OUP 4 Songs.)

Dominic Muldowny. 1952 -
(On suicide, *Berthold Brecht*, [soprano], Faber hire [2 clarinets, viola, cello and double bass].)
(Out of danger, *James Fenton*, [soprano], Faber hire [2 clarinets, viola, cello and double bass].)

Thea Musgrave. 1928 -
Collection: *Five Love Songs*, Chester [soprano and guitar].

Primavera, *Amalia Elguera*, [a(b*b*)-c'''](f), Chester [flute].
Sir Patrick Spens, *Anon*, [b*b*-a''](m), Chester [guitar].

Bayan Northcott. 1940 -
Collections: *(Three English Lyrics*, S&B [clarinet, viola and double bass]); *(Six Japanese Lyrics*, S&B [clarinet and violin].)
    (Across the snow, *Mishudo* tr. *Bayan Northcott*, [b*b*-c'''](f), S&B 6 Japanese.)
    (Blaze of sultry noon, *Seiji Tanaka* tr. *Bayan Northcott*, [d'-a''](f), S&B 6 Japanese.)
    (Experimenting, *Hokushi* tr. *Bayan Northcott*, [b-b''](f), S&B 6 Japanese.)
    (In the village, *Ryōkan* tr. *Bayan Northcott*, [c'#-b''](f), S&B 6 Japanese.)
    (Like a child's kite, *Lady Onitsumi* tr. *Bayan Northcott*, [d'-c'''](f), S&B 6 Japanese.)
    (O westron winde, *Anon*, [c'#-f'#](f), S&B 3 English.)
    (Pleasure it is, *Cornyshe*, [c'-f'#](f), S&B 3 English.)
    (Poet nightingale, *Anon* tr. *Bayan Northcott*, [c'-b''](f), S&B 6 Japanese.)
    (The maidens came, *Anon*, [d'-b''*b*](f), S&B 3 English.)

Michael Nyman. 1944 -
    (Tomorrow, *No text*, [a*b*-c'''#](f), Chester [organ].)

Buxton Orr. 1924 - (BMIC [unaccompanied].)

Nigel Osborne. 1948 -
Collection: *Two Spanish Songs*, Universal [unaccompanied].
    (Como las flores, *Anon*, [soprano], Universal 2 Spanish.)
    (Four loom weaver, *Anon*, [soprano], Universal [tape].
    (Madeleine de la Ste-Baume, *Latin, Greek, Aramaic*, [soprano], Universal [double bass].
    (Oyó sus gritos, *Anon*, [a*b*-a''*b*], Universal 2 Spanish.)

Priti Paintāl. (BMIC [clarinet; cello].)

Krinió Papastavrou.
Collection: *Seven Songs for a Child*, Bardic [harp]. (For details see main catalogue).

John Paynter. 1931 -
    (Shine out, fair sun, *Anon*, [d'*b*-b''*b*], OUP [organ].)

John C Philips.
Collection: *Young Jesus Sweit*, Banks [unaccompanied].
    O my dear heart, young Jesus sweit, *Martin Luther* tr. *Wedderburn*, [d'-g''], Banks Young Jesus.
    There is no rose of such virtue, *Anon*, [c'-a''], Banks Young Jesus.
    When Christ was born of Mary free, *Anon*, [c'#-a''], Banks Young Jesus.

Thomas Pitfield. 1903 -
Collection: Selected Songs, Forsyth1989.
    Alone, *Walter de la Mare*, B [f'#-g''#](f), Forsyth Selected [violin].
    Desdemona's song, *Shakespeare*, Em [c'-g''], Forsyth Selected [guitar].
    The fiddler, *Walter de la Mare*, F [f'-a''](f), Forsyth Selected [violin].
    The horseman, *Walter de la Mare*, Gm [e'*b*-b''*b*](f), Forsyth Selected [violin].

The willow, *Thomas Pitfield*, Dm [b♭-f''], Forsyth Selected [treble recorder/flute/clarinet and harpsichord/piano].

Winter song, *Katherine Mansfield*, [d'-e''], Forsyth Selected [sopranino recorder/flute/ oboe and piano].

Roger Quilter. 1877 - 1953.
Collection: (*Three Pastoral Songs*, Elkin 1921 [violin, cello and piano].)

(Cherry valley, *Joseph Campbell*, E [b-e''], Elkin 3 Pastoral.)

I sing of a maiden, *Anon*, G [f'-g''], Mayhew *Holy Night* [organ].

(I will go with my father a-ploughing, *Joseph Campbell*, A♭ [c'-f''(e''♭)], Elkin 3 Pastoral.)

(I wish and I wish, *Joseph Campbell*, Cm [c'-g''(e''♭)], Elkin 3 Pastoral.)

Priaulx Rainier. 1903 - 1986.
Collection: *Cycle for Declamation*, Schott 1954 [unaccompanied]. 'Soprano, Alto or Baritone should transpose to suit the tessitura of the voice'.

Dance of the rain, *Eugene Marais* tr. *Uys Krige*, [d'-g''](m), Schott [guitar].

In the wombe of the earth, *John Donne*, [f'-g''], Schott Cycle.

Nunc, lento sonitu, *John Donne*, [d'-a''], Schott Cycle.

Ubunzima, *Zulu poem*, [e'♭-b''♭(a''♭)], Schott [guitar].

Wee cannot hide the fruits, *John Donne*, [e'♭-a''], Schott Cycle.

Bernard Rands. 1935 -
Ballad 3, *Gilbert Sorrentino*, [a-a''](f), Universal [tape].

Alan Rawsthorne. 1905 - 1971.
(Tankas of the Four Seasons, *Charles Riba* tr. *J L Gili*, [tenor], OUP hire [oboe, clarinet, bassoon, violin and cello].)

(Scena Rustica, *John Skelton*, [e'-b''♭](f), OUP [harp].)

Betty Roe. 1930 -
Collection: *Jazz Songs* Yorke 1972 [double bass]; *Noble Numbers*, Thames 1972 [harpsichord], *Verities*, Thames 1972 [clarinet]; *Cat and Mouse*, Yorke 1987 [double bass]; *Four Shakespeare Songs*, Thames 1974 [flute and piano]; *London Fantasies*, Thames 1992 [double bass]; *Madam Songs*, Thames 1992 [double bass]; *Madam's Three Callers*, Thames [cello].

An appeal to cats in the business of love, *Thomas Flatman*, [d'-a''](f), Yorke Cat and Mouse.

Carol of the beasts, *James Reeves*, E♭ [c'-e''♭], Thames [flute and piano].

Come away, death, *Shakespeare*, [e'-e''], Thames 4 Shakespeare.

Euphonium Dance, *Jacqueline Froom*, D [a'-f''#](f), Yorke Jazz.

Grave by the sea, *Charles Causley*, [e'-a''♭](f), Thames Verities.

I am the great sun, *Charles Causley*, [e'-g''](f), Thames Verities.

Legato Leicester Square, *Jacqueline Froom*, [d'-e''♭], Thames London.

Madam and the fortune teller, *Langston Hughes*, [c'#-e''](f), Thames Madam Songs.

Madam and her might-have-been, *Langston Hughes*, [d'#-g''](f), Thames Madam Songs.

Madam and the census man, *Langston Hughes*, Cm [g-e''♭](f), Thames Three Callers.

Madam and the Minister, *Langston Hughes*, C [g-e''](f), Yorke Jazz.

Madam and the Minister, *Langston Hughes*, E [b-e''](f) Thames Three Callers.

Madam and the wrong visitor, *Langston Hughes*, C [g-e''♭](f) Thames Three Callers.

Madam's calling cards, *Langston Hughes*, [e'-g''](f) Thames Madam Songs.
Mouse, *Clifford Dyment*, [c'-e''](f), Yorke Cat and Mouse.
Now, *Charles Causley*, [f#-g''#](f), Thames Verities..
Nursery Rhyme, *Anon*, [c'-d''](f), Yorke Cat and Mouse.
Nursery Rhyme, *Anon*, [b-b'](f), Yorke Cat and Mouse.
Orpheus with his lute, *Shakespeare*, D [d'-d''], Thames 4 Shakespeare.
Pizzicato Piccadilly, *Jacqueline Froom*, [e'-g''(f'#)], Thames London.
Sigh no more, *Shakespeare*, G [d'-d''], Thames 4 Shakespeare.
Thames a tempo, *Jacqueline Froom*, [c'#-e''], Thames London.
The silver hound (cycle), *Ursula Vaughan Williams*, [b-b''*b*](m), Thames [horn and piano].
The two mice, *James Reeves*, [c'-f''](f), Yorke Cat and Mouse.
The willow song, *Shakespeare*, [d'-d''], Thames 4 Shakespeare.
To God, an anthem, *Robert Herrick*, [b-d''], Thames Noble Numbers.
To God, *Robert Herrick*, [c'-d''], Thames Noble Numbers.
To his angrie God, *Robert Herrick*, [b-e''*b*], Thames Noble Numbers.
To his Saviour, a child; A Present, by a child, *Robert Herrick*, [a-d''], Thames Noble Numbers.
To his sweet saviour, *Robert Herrick*, [c'-d''], Thames Noble Numbers.

Edmund Rubbra. 1901 - 1986.
Collection: *Amoretti (2nd Series)*, S&B 1942 [string quartet] *see* main catalogue for details; *Ave Maria Gratia Plena*, Lengnick 1953 [string quartet]; *Two Songs*, Lengnick 1953 [harp]; *Two Sonnets*, Lengnick 1955, [viola and piano]; *The Jade Mountain*, Lengnick 1963 [harp],
    A hymn to the virgin, *Anon*, Am [d'-g''], Lengnick 2 Songs.
    A night thought on terrace tower, *Wêi Chuang*, tr. *Witter Bynner*, [f'#-b''], Lengnick Jade.
    A song of the southern river, *Li Yi*, tr. *Wittner Bynner*, [a'-a''], Lengnick Jade.
    An autumn night message, *Wêi Ying-Wu*, tr. *Wittner Bynner*, [a'-a''*b*], Lengnick Jade.
    Cantata Pastorale (cycle), *Plato* tr. *Leaf*, *St Augustine* tr. *Waddell*, [d'-a''*b*], Lengnick [Treble Recorder/Flute, Harpsichord/Piano and Cello].
    Farewell to a Japanist Buddhist priest bound homeward, *Ch'ien Ch'i*, tr. *Wittner Bynner*, [e'-a''], Lengnick Jade.
    Jesukin, *St Ita*, [e'-f'#], Lengnick 2 Songs.
    O excellent Virgin Princess, *François Villon*, tr. *D G Rossetti*, [d'-g''], Lengnick Ave.
    O my deir hert, young Jesus sweit, *Martin Luther*, tr. *Wedderburn*, [d'-g''], Lengnick Ave.
    On hearing her play the harp, *Li Tüan*. tr. *Wittner Bynner*, [g'-g''], Lengnick Jade.
    On the reed of our Lord's passion, *William Alabaster*, [a'-e''], Lengnick 2 Sonnets.
    Rosa mundi, *Rachel Annand Taylor*, Gm [d'-e''*b*] Lengnick 4 Short [2 violins].
    The mystery, *Ralph Hodgson*, [f'-e''], Lengnick 4 Short [unaccompanied].
    Upon the crucifix, *William Albaster*, D [c'#-e''], Lengnick 2 Sonnets.

Reginald Smith Brindle. 1917 -
Collection: *Two Poems of Manley Hopkins*, [low voice], Schott [guitar].

Daryl Runswick. 1946 -
    Lady Lazarus, *Sylvia Plath*, amplified female voice, Faber [unaccompanied].

Leonard Salzedo. 1921 - (BMIC [harp].)

Rhian Samuel. (BMIC [guitar].)

Peter Sander. (BMIC [guitar].)

Robert Saxton. 1953 -
(Brise Marine, *Stéphane Mallarmé*, [c'-b''*b*](f), Chester [piano and tape].)
(Cantata No 2, [tenor] Chester [oboe and piano].)

Colin Seamarks.
Six mehitabel magpies (cycle), *Don Marquis*, [b-b''](f), Yorke [double bass].

Cyril Scott. 1879 - 1970.
(Idyll, *Cyril Scott*, [d'*b*-c'''](f), Elkin [flute].)
(Idyllic fantasy, *Cyril Scott*, Elkin [oboe and cello].)

Matyas Seiber. 1905 - 1960.
Collection: (*Four Hungarian Folksongs*, S&B 1956 [violin].); (*Drei Morgenstern Lieder*, Universal 1956 [clarinet].); *Four French Folk Songs*, Schott 1959 [guitar].
(Das Knee, *Morgenstern*, [b*b*-f''](f), Universal 3 Morgenstern.)
(Das Nasobëm, *Morgenstern*, [d'-a''](f), Universl 3 Morgenstern.)
(Die Trichter, *Morgenstern*, [b*b*-a''](f), Universal 3 Morgenstern.)
(Farewell, *Anon* tr. *A L Lloyd*, [c'-d''], S&B 4 Hungarian.)
J'ai descendu, *Anon*, [e'-e''], Schott 4 French.
(Lament, *Anon* tr. *A L Lloyd*, d'-e''], S&B 4 Hungarian.)
Le Rossignol, *Anon*, [e'-d''], Schott 4 French.
Marguerite, elle est malade, *Anon*, [e'-e''], Schott 4 French.
(Quarrel, *Anon* tr. *A L Lloyd*, [c'-e''], S&B 4 Hungarian.)
Réveillez-vous, *Anon*, [a'-e''], Schott 4 French.
(Soldier's song, *Anon* tr. *A L Lloyd*, [d'-f''], S&B 4 Hungarian.)

Michael Short. 1937 - (see also BIMC [Guitar].)
Collection: *Six Mediaeval Lyrics*, Thames 1996 [clarinet].
Bird on briar, *Anon*, [f'-g''](f), Thames Lyrics.
Go, heart, *Anon*, [f'-f''](f), Thames Lyrics.
Ivy, chief of trees, *Anon*, [f'-f''], Thames Lyrics.
Now welcome, summer, *Anon*, [e'-g''], Thames Lyrics.
Of ev'ry kind of tree, *Anon*, [e'-e''](f), Thames Lyrics.
There is none so wise a man, *Anon*, [g'-e''], Thames Lyrics.

Naresh Sohal. 1939 -
Kavita II, *John Donne*, [soprano], Novello [flute and piano].

Tim Souster. 1943 - 1994. (BMIC [Viola].)

Charles Villiers Stanford. 1852 - 1924.
(A song of battle, *Psalm 124*, Gm [d'-e''], S&B; *Bbm*, S&B [organ].)
(A song of freedom, *Psalm 126*, C [e'*b*-f''], S&B; *Eb*, S&B [organ].)
(A song of hope, *Psalm 130*, Dm [b*b*-d''], S&B; *Fm*, S&B [organ].)

(A song of peace, *Isaiah 9*, A [a'-f''], S&B; C, S&B [organ].)
(A song of trust, *Psalm 121*, D♭[c'-e''♭], S&B; F, S&B [organ].)
(A song of wisdom, *Ecclesiasticus 24*, C [c'-e''(g')], S&B; E♭, S&B [organ].)
Fling out your windows wide, *Arthur Quiller-Couch*, E♭[e'♭-f''], Mayhew *Holy Night* [organ].
The winds of Bethlehem, *Winifred Letts*, Gm [d'-g''], Mayhew *Holy Night* [organ].

Roger Steptoe. 1953 -
Collection, Arrangemenst: *Two Folk Song Arrangements for baritone and violin*, S&B 1987 [violin];
(*Chinese Lyrics Set 1*, S&B; [string quintet] see main catalogue for details).
  Brigg Fair, *Anon*, [E(G)-e'](m), S&B 2 Folk Songs.
  Early one spring, *Anon*, [c-d'](m), S&B 2 Folk Song.
  From the Spanish Descent, *David Defoe*, Lengnick [violin, cello and piano].

Phyllis Tate. 1911 - 1987.
Collections: (*Two Ballads*, OUP 1974 [guitar]); *Scenes from Tyneside*, Emerson 1980 [clarinet and piano].
  Died of love, *Anon*, [b-g''](f), Emerson Scenes.
  Elsie Marley, *Anon*, [b♭-f''](f), Emerson Scenes, [tambourine].
  Gan to the kye wi' me, *Anon*, [d'-g''](f), Emerson Scenes.
  (Mary, Mary Magdelen, *Charles Causley*, [b♭-f'#](f), OUP 2 Ballads.)
  Of all the youths, *Anon*, B♭ [d'-f'](f), Emerson Scenes, [unaccompanied].
  Songs of Sundrie Kindes (cycle), *Raleigh, Herrick, Wither, Anon*, [c'-b''♭](m), OUP [lute/ guitar].
  (The ballad of the red-headed man, *Patricia Beer*, [g-f'#](f), OUP 2 Ballads.)
  The quayside shaver, *Anon*, [b♭-g], Emerson Scenes.
  The Sandgate lass's lament, *Anon*, F [b♭-g''](f), Emerson Scenes.
Arrangements: (*Trois Chansons Tristes*, OUP [guitar].)
  (La dernière écuelle, *Anon*, [g'e''♭], OUP Trois Chansons.)
  (Le vieux blaise, *Anon*, [e'-f'#], OUP Trois Chansons.)
  (Les fillettes de mon âge, *Anon*, [f'#-b''♭], OUP Trois Chansons.)

John Taverner. 1944 -
Collection: *Akhmatova Songs* [high], Chester [cello].
  (Lamentation, Last Prayer and Exaltation, [soprano], Chester [handbells].)
  (Meditation on the light, [counter-tenor], Chester [guitar and handbells].)
  Three Surrealist Songs, [e-b''♭](f), Chester [tape and piano doubling bongos].
  · (To a child dancing in the wind, [soprano], Chester [alto flute, viola and harp].)

Michael Tippett. 1905 -
Collection: *Songs for Achilles*, Schott 1964 [guitar].
  Across the plain, *Michael Tippett*, [e'-b''♭](m), Schott Achilles.
  By the sea, *Michael Tippett*, [c'#-b''♭](m), Schott Achilles.
  In the tent, *Michael Tippett*, [d'-a''](m), Schott Achilles.

Ralph Vaughan Williams. 1872 - 1958.
Collection: *On Wenlock Edge*, B&H 1911 [string quartet and piano]; *Four Hymns*, B&H 1920 [viola and piano]; *Merciless Beauty*, Faber 1922 [string trio]; *Along the Field*, OUP 1954 [violin]; *Ten Blake Songs*, OUP 1958 [oboe]; *Three Vocalises*, OUP 1960 [clarinet].
  A poison tree, *William Blake*, Dm [d'-f''](m), OUP 10 Blake.
  Ah! sun-flower, *William Blake*, Dm [d'-f''](m), OUP 10 Blake.

Along the field, *A E Housman*, [c'-f''](m), OUP Along the Field
Bredon Hill, *A E Housman*, e'*b*-a''](m), B&H Wenlock Edge.
Clun, *A E Housman*, [d'-g''](m), B&H Wenlock Edge.
Come Love, come Lord, *Richard Crashaw*, Gm [g'-g''](m), B&H 4 Hymns.
Cruelty has a human heart, *William Blake*, [c'-g''], OUP 10 Blake.
Eternity, *William Blake*, A*b* [e'*b*-f''], OUP 10 Blake.
Evening Hymn, *Robert Bridges*, E [e'-a''](m), B&H 4 Hymns.
Fancy's knell, *A E Housman*, [b-g''], OUP Along the Field.
From far, from eve and morning, *A E Housman*, [g'-e''](m), B&H Wenlock Edge.
Good-bye, *A E Housman*, [d'-a''], OUP Along the Field.
In the morning, *A E Housman*, [d'-f'#], OUP Along the Field.
Infant joy, *William Blake*, G*b* [e'*b*-e''*b*], OUP 10 Blake.
Is my team ploughing? *A E Housman*, [d'-a''](m), B&H Wenlock Edge.
London, *William Blake*, Dm [d'-f''](m), OUP 10 Blake, [unaccompanied].
Lord, come away, *Jeremy Taylor*, Dm [d'-b''*b*](m), B&H 4 Hymns.
Prelude, *no text*, [c'-c'''](f), OUP 3 Vocalises.
Oh, when I was in love with you, *A E Housman*, [g'-f'#](m), B&H Wenlock Edge.
On Wenlock Edge, *A E Housman*, [d'-g''](m), B&H Wenlock Edge.
Quasi minuetto, *no text*, [c'-c'''](f), OUP 3 Vocalises.
Scherzo, *no text*, [d'-b''*b*](f), OUP 3 Vocalises.
Since I from Love escapëd am so fat, *Geoffrey Chaucer*, [a'-a''](m), Faber Merciless.
So hath your beauty from your hertë, *Geoffrey Chaucer*, Dm [e'-f''](m), Faber Merciless.
The divine image, Fm [d'*b*-f''], OUP 10 Blake, [Unaccompanied].
The half-moon westers low, *A E Housman*, [e'-f'#], OUP Along the Field.
The lamb, *William Blake*, Fm [e'*b*-f''](m), OUP 10 Blake.
The piper, *William Blake*, [e'*b*-f'#], OUP 10 Blake.
The shepherd, *William Blake*, F [d'-g''], OUP 10 Blake, [Unaccompanied].
The sigh that heaves the grasses, *A E Housman*, [c'-f''], OUP Along the Field.
We'll to the woods no more, *A E Housman*, [d'-g''], OUP Along the Field.
Who is this fair one? *Isaac Watts*, Fm [e'*b*-a''](m), B&H 4 Hymns.
Your eyën two will slay me suddenly, *Geoffrey Chaucer*, Gm [c'-a''](m), Faber Merciless.
Arrangements: *Two English Folk-songs*, OUP 1935 [viola and piano].
Searching for lambs, *Anon*, Am [e'-e''], OUP 2 Folk-songs.
The lawyer, *Anon*, Am [c'-e''], OUP 2 Folk-songs.

Robert Walker. 1946 -

Collection: *Six Songs of Mervyn Peake*, Banks [2 clarinets and piano].
If I could see, no surfaces, *Mervyn Peake*, [high], Banks 6 Songs.
Rather a little pain, *Mervyn Peake*, [high], Banks 6 Songs.
The colt, *Mervyn Peake*, [high], Banks 6 Songs.
The two fraternities, *Mervyn Peake*, [high], Banks 6 Songs.
Two seasons, *Mervyn Peake*, [high], Banks 6 Songs.
What is it muffles the ascending moment? *Mervyn Peake*, [high], Banks 6 Songs.

William Walton. 1902 - 1983.

Collection: (*Anon. in love*, OUP 1960 [guitar].)

Other accompaniments — Peter Warlock

Beatriz's Song, *Louis MacNeice*, Dm [f'-d''](f), OUP [guitar].
(Fain would I change that note, *Anon*, [c'#-a''](m), OUP Anon. in love.)
(I gave her cakes and I gave her ale, *Anon*, [d'-b''*b*](m), OUP Anon. in love.)
(Lady, when I behold the roses, *Anon*, [c'-a''](m), OUP Anon. in love.)
(My love in her attire, *Anon*, [c'-a''](m), OUP Anon. in love.)
(O stay, sweet love, *Anon*, [c'-f'#](m), OUP Anon. in love.)
(To couple is a custom, *Anon*, [c'-a''](m), OUP Anon. in love.)

Peter Warlock. 1894 - 1930.
Collection: *Songs of Peter Warlock Volume 9*, Thames 1997 [string quartet].
A sad song, *John Fletcher*, Cm [f'#-g''], Thames Songs.
Adam lay ybounden, *Anon*, Cm [c'-f''], Mayhew *Holy Night* [organ].
Balulalow, *Martin Luther* tr. *Wedderburn*, E*b* [e'*b*-f''], Mayhew *Holy Night* [organ].
Bethlehem Down, *Bruce Blunt*, Dm [c'#-e''*b*], Mayhew *Holy Night* [organ].
Chopcherry, *George Peele*, A [e'-e''], Thames Songs.
Mourn no moe, *John Fletcher*, C [c'-f''], Thames Songs.
My gostly fader, *Charles D'Orleans*, G [e'*b*-f'#], Thames Songs.
My lady is a pretty one, *Anon*, [c'-g''](m), Thames Songs.
My little sweet darling, *Anon*, G [b-g''], Thames Songs.
Sleep, *John Fletcher*, [d'-e''*b*], Thames Songs.
The Curlew (cycle), *W B Yeats*, [c'-a''](m) S&B, Thames, [flute, cor anglais and string quartet].
Take, O take those lips away, *Shakespeare*, Em [b-f'#], Thames Songs.
The fairest may, *Anon*, C [c'-f''], Thames Songs.
The first mercy, *Bruce Blunt*, Gm [f'-f''], Mayhew *Holy Night* [organ].
Where riches is everlastingly, *Anon*, Dm [d'-f''], Mayhew *Holy Night* [organ].

David Watkins.
Arrangements: *Folk Songs*, S&B 1984 [harp].
Barbara Allen, *Anon*, D*b* [d'*b*-d''*b*], S&B Folk Songs.
Now is the month of maying (Morley), *Anon*, G [d'-d''] S&B Folk Songs.
Scarborough Fair, *Anon*, Em [d'-e''](m), S&B Folk Songs.
Summer is a-coming in, *Anon*, E*b* [d'-e''*b*], S&B Folk Songs.

John Weeks. (BMIC [unaccompanied; clarinet; viola; organ].)

Judith Weir. 1954 -
(Don't let that horse, *Lawrence Ferlinghetti*, [c'-e''*b*](f), Chester [horn].)
(The romance of Count Arnaldos, [soprano], Chester [2 clarinets, viola, cello and double bass].)
King Harald's Saga, *Judith Weir*, [f#-b''](f), Novello [unaccompanied].

Egon Wellesz. 1885 - 1974.
The leaden echo and the golden echo, *Gerard Manley Hopkins*, [high], Schott [violin, clarinet, cello and piano].

Peter Wiegold. 1949 -
Saving the sun, *Nick Otty*, [c'-a''](m), Universal [tape].
Sing lullaby, *Peter Wiegold*, [g-c'''#](f), Universal [double bass].

Philip Wilby. 1949 -
(Easter wings, [voice] Chester [2 clarinets, viola, cello and double bass].)
(Winter portrait in grey and gold, [soprano], Chester [clarinet, piano and off-stage melody instrument].)

Grace Williams. 1906 - 1977.
Japanese fragments, [soprano], Chester [viola/guitar].

Malcolm Williamson. 1931 -
Collection: *Three Shakespeare Songs*, Weinberger 1973 [guitar].
Come away, death, *Shakespeare*, Em [e'f''#], Weinberger 3 Shakespeare.
Fear no more the heat of the sun, *Shakespeare*, [c'a''b], Weinberger 3 Shakespeare.
Full fathom five, *Shakespeare*, [db-g''], Weinberger 3 Shakespeare [unaccompanied].
(Pietà, [soprano], Weinberger, [oboe, bassoon and piano].)

Arthur Wills. 1926 -
Sonnet: When our two souls, *E B Browning*, [c'-c'''#](f), Nova [clarinet and piano].

Geoffrey Winters. 1928 - (BMIC [guitar; harp].)

Peter Wishart. 1921 - 1984.
(To the Holy Spirit, [soprano], S&B [flute, viola da gamba and harpsichord].)

Charles Wood. 1866 - 1926.
Mater ora filium, *Anon*, Eb [d'-e''b], Mayhew *Holy Night* [organ].

Hugh Wood. 1932 -
Collection: *Four Songs Op 2*, [contralto], Chester [clarinet, violin and cello].
Marina Op 31, *T S Eliot*, [soprano], Chester [viola, harp, horn and alto flute].

John Woolrich. 1954 -
(Ariadne laments, *Ottavino Rinuccini*, [soprano], Faber hire [2 violins, viola, cello and double bass].)
(Berceuse, *Anon*, [soprano], Faber hire [alto flute, oboe, clarinet/bass clarinet, viola and cello].)
(Four Songs after Hoffmann, *E T A Hoffman*, [soprano], Faberprint 1981 [clarinet and piano].)
(Harlequinade, *Anon*, [soprano], Faberprint [clarinet, violin, cello and piano].)
(Light and rock, *Anon*, tr. *Harvey & Pennington*, [soprano], Faberprint [basset clarinet in A and piano].)
(Serbian Songs, *Serbian folk poem*, [soprano], Faberprint [clarinet and percussion].)
(Songs and broken music, *Elvis Costello*, [soprano], Faber hire [violin, cello and piano].
Three Cautionary tales, *Anon*, [soprano], Faberprint [soprano saxophone/clarinet, bass clarinet/clarinet, viola, cello and double bass].

William Wordsworth. 1908 - 1988.
The solitary reaper, *William Wordsworth*, [e'-a''#(b)], Roberton [clarinet and piano].

David Wynne. 1900 - 1983.
Collection: *Chwe Chân i Denor a Thlyn*, Gwynn 1970.
Creulondeb Merch, *Anon*, [e'-a''b](m), Gwynn Chwe.

I Wahodd Dyddgu, *Dafydd ap Gwilym*, [f'-a''](m), Gwynn Chwe.
I wallt Llio, *Anon*, [f'-a''*b*](m), Gwynn Chwe.
Llys Ifor Hael, *Ieuan Fardd*, [c'-a''](m), Gwynn Chwe.
Marwnad Bun, *Dafydd Nanmor*, [f'-a''*b*](m), Gwynn Chwe.
Y Gwynt, *Maredydd ap Rhys*, [e'-a''](m), Gwynn Chwe.

Peter Young. 1969 -
Collection: *Three Songs of Ben*, Banks 1989 [clarinet and piano].
Drink to me only with thine eyes, *Ben Jonson*, [d'-g''](f), Banks 3 Ben.
Oh do not wanton with those eyes, *Ben Jonson*, [d'-f''](f), Banks 3 Ben.
Still to be neat, still to be dressed, *Ben Jonson*, [e'*b*-a''*b*](f), Banks 3 Ben.